DATE DUE

SINCE COLUMBUS

Poverty and Pluralism
in the History of the Americas

SINCE COLUMBUS

Poverty and Pluralism
in the History of the Americas

Peter d'A. Jones
Professor of History in the University of Illinois

HEINEMANN
LONDON

Heinemann Educational Books Ltd
LONDON EDINBURGH MELBOURNE AUCKLAND
TORONTO HONG KONG SINGAPORE KUALA LUMPUR
IBADAN NAIROBI JOHANNESBURG
LUSAKA NEW DELHI

ISBN 0 435 31525 0

Published by Heinemann Educational Books Ltd
48 Charles Street London W1X 8AH

Filmset in Lumitype Times
Printed by St Paul's Press Ltd., Malta

For
Kathryn and Barbara
I will love you always

Foreword

It is impossible to write a satisfactory history of the entire Western Hemisphere, let alone to accomplish the task in under 300 pages of typescript. What I offer is a modest attempt to introduce the subject to students, teachers and, if I am lucky, to the general reader. I have deliberately adopted certain interpretive devices and concepts on which to hang the story, such as 'dependency', 'containment', 'neo-colonialism', 'import-substitution', 'cultural pluralism' and 'mass society'. History without implicit or explicit theory does not exist. At least I have made these concepts explicit. The job will have been worthwhile if readers argue with and reject some of these ideas, after having used them to form an overview of the story of the continent. Naturally I welcome letters from readers.

My personal interest in the possibility of viewing the hemisphere as a whole was stimulated by my teaching work in the early 1960s at Smith College, where I helped my friend Professor Ramón E. Ruiz on a large freshman course known as 'History 13': the History of the Americas. I hope that he, and the Smith students of those years, will regard this little book with affection.

Since Columbus also reflects twenty years of friendship with Alan Hill of Heinemann, who took time out from the duties of directing an international publishing house to exercise a personal interest in the manuscript and see it through all its stages. In my hungry student days in London he sent editing jobs my way; but his love of books and his humane spirit sustained me more. I was lucky to have received both.

Historical Institute
University of Warsaw
Poland
1974

Contents

Foreword   vi

List of Maps   xiii

List of Illustrations   xiv

Acknowledgements   xvi

Part One
Differentiation and Revolution
(1492 to about 1830)   3

CHAPTER 1.   DEPENDENCY   6

Central and South America in 16th and 17th centuries
Columbus—ecological disaster
Indian depopulation
An empire of silver and forced labour
Spanish trade controls
Feudalism, American-style: haciendas and plantations
The political structure of Spanish America
Cabildo self-government
'Spiritual conquest': the Church Militant
Jesuit communes
Triumph of the Church

Settling North America
New Amsterdam and New Sweden
Creation of New France
Independence enterprise in British America
Capitalists found 'Virginia'
Africans in North America
Puritan Utopias
Pilgrims and Indians
Massachusetts: Puritan Commonwealth

The Puritan image
Differentiation and political change
The Restoration: proprietary colonies
New England comes down to earth
The Americas in about 1700

CHAPTER 2. EMERGENCE   44

Central and South America
The burden of race
Traffic in African slaves
Growing colonial separatism

North America in the 18th century
Political structure of British America
Styles of economic life
American society in the 18th century
The struggle for Canada
North America becomes British

CHAPTER 3. INDEPENDENCE: THE CREATION OF
            NEW SOCIETIES, 1776–1830   60

Revolution in North America
Violence and the Stamp Act Congress
Parliament tries again
First blood: the Boston 'Massacre'
Canada and the Quebec Act, 1774
Declaration of Independence
The American Revolution reviewed

Revolution in the Spanish and Portuguese colonies
Haiti: black republic
Revolutions in South America: origins
British role: invasion of Rio de la Plata
Formation of juntas
Revolution and independence in Mexico
Hidalgo's caste war
Indian nationalism: Morelos
The Mexican Revolution subverted: Iturbide
Revolution further south: Bolívar and San Martín
The idealism of San Martín
Bolívar as dictator
The Monroe Doctrine, 1823
Brazil, sleeping colony of Portugal
The bandeirantes
Revolution by consent

Brazilian society: slavery and race
Aftermath of revolutions: differentiation in the
Americas
The US Constitution and political cohesion
The American Dream

Part Two
Containment and Growth
(About 1830 to 1920)   89

CHAPTER 4. CAPITALISM   92

Capitalism in North America
Two visions of America: Hamilton v. Jefferson
Growth of 'party' organisation: Federalists and
Republicans
Expansion and material growth
Frontier nationalism and the War of 1812
Canadian nationalism
Victims of white expansion: Indians and Negroes
The political compromise of 1820 safeguards slavery
Economic Revolution
The coming of majoritarian politics
Cotton culture and black slaves
The American as reformer
Coming of the Civil War
Escalation I: the Mexican–American War
Escalation II: the miracle no longer works
Impact of the Civil War at home
Creation of modern Canada

CHAPTER 5. CAUDILLISMO   111

Creole containment: rise of caudillos
Lack of formal parties
Mexico: counter-revolution and tyranny
'La Reforma': Juárez and mestizo rule
Central America: federation and independence
The 'Spanish Main': Venezuela and Colombia
Argentina: gaucho versus city
Creation of the new Argentina
Sarmiento: the intellectual in office
'Facundo': civilization or barbarism
Paraguay and Uruguay: study in contrast
Chile: stability and oligarchy
The new 'Indian' nations of the Andes

Bolivia: cholos and caudillos
The Portuguese heritage: Brazil
Pedro II and the Republic of Brazil
Immigration and race in South America

CHAPTER 6. IMMIGRATION, REFORM AND
IMPERIALISM, 1880–1920   133

The US: immigrants and cities
The myth of the Melting Pot
Workers and radicalism
Moderate reform: the power of the middle-class
conscience
Populism: the farmers get angry
City reformers: Progressivism
Social-imperialism
The Spanish-American War, 1898
US imperialism: the Caribbean
Creation of Panama, 1903
US intervention in Mexico
Canada: survival and growth
*Neo-colonialism and domestic politics in Central
and South America*
Mexico: Porfirio Díaz
Argentina, boom and slump
Chile: the coming of parliamentary government
Brazil: *Os Sêrtões*

Part Three
The Building of Plural Societies
(From the 1920's)   155

CHAPTER 7. GROWTH AND DEPRESSION IN
NORTH AMERICA   158

North America and World War I
Black Americans in World War I
The dictated peace of 1919
The Twenties: Consumer Capitalism
Prohibition: legislating morality
The 'New Era': moral rhetoric and Big Business
The perils of uneven growth
Farmer radicals

Social class in the Jazz Age
The High Culture of the Twenties
Black nationalism: Marcus Garvey
The Twenties in Canada
The collapse of prosperity
What did the Depression mean?
Coming of the New Deal: pragmatism
New Deal: recovery and reform
The new ecology: conservation
Labour and the New Deal
Belated arrival of the Welfare State in the US
The New Deal and minorities
The Depression in Canada

CHAPTER 8.   REVOLUTION AND INTERVENTION   180

The Mexican Revolution
Civil War, 1913–14: Carranza emerges
José Vasconcelos and popular culture
'Christ the King': religious warfare, 1926–29
The Revolution is institutionalized: the PNR
Land reform: the ejido revived
The US and Mexico: the Good Neighbour policy
The ABC nations: Argentina
Justicialism: the rule of Perón
The failure of civilian government: Frondizi
Uruguay: democratic success story?
The ABC nations: Chile
Socialism in Chile
Chile's cultural achievements
Brazil and Vargas
Tenentismo: the Revolution of 1930
Brazil after Vargas
The Indian Andes: Ecuador
Peru: dictatorship and native radicalism
The Aprista compromise: Belaúnde
Bolivia: the Chaco War
The Bolivian National Revolution
Bolivia's legacy
Colombia: violence without revolution
Venezuela: from caudillismo to welfare state
Betancourt: the welfare state, 1959–64
Central America under the US shadow
Guatemala: the low-point in US relations

CHAPTER 9.   PLURAL SOCIETY AND ITS
             PROBLEMS   227

Social impact of World War II
Civil rights in World War II
Nuclear terror: the US uses the atom bomb
The anti-communist crusade
The military-industrial-complex
American aid and trade
Mexico: halfway to modernity
Argentina: Perón returns
The civil rights revolution in North America
The Canadian crisis
US economic penetration of Canada
National values
The continuing contrasts, North and South
Economic retardation—the tragedy of South America

A BOOKSHELF OF READINGS   261
INDEX   264

List of Maps

1. Columbus—ecological disaster. 8
2. Demographic catastrophe. 10
3. Extremes of economic control. 15
4. Dutch exploitation of the Portuguese colony of Brazil, 1623–54. 17
5. The government of Spanish America. 20
6. The Church in Spanish America. 23
7. The Dutch colony of New Netherlands, 1614–64. 25
8. New France: exploration and settlement in the 16th and 17th centuries. 27
9. The British move in. 32
10. Slavery in the New World during the 17th century. 35
11. North America 1756, before the outbreak of the French and indian War. 42
12. 1781: the world turned upside down. 66
13. Two liberators: Bolívar and San Martín. 77
14. The Americas: the aftermath of revolution. 83
15. Turbulent North America, 1814–61. 103
16. Confederation, 1867. 109
17. Rivalry and war in Central and Southern America. 128
18. U.S. imperialism. 142
19. Argentina. 149
20. North America: some racial and ethnic problems, 1901–41. 169
21. The fate of the Indians. 176
22. Brazil in the 20th century. 203
23. Territorial disputes since 1900. 214
24. The United States and its strategic priorities. 239
25. North and Central America since 1945. 253

List of Illustrations

1. 'Portuguese Carracks off a Rocky Coast'
   (early 16th century).   13
2. Morelia Cathedral, Mexico.   45
3. Slaves cutting sugar cane in the West Indies.
   From *Ten Views in the Island of Antigua* by William
   Clarke (London, 1823).   49
4. An auction bill for the sale of slaves, 1829.   50
5. Old houses at Point Lévis, Quebec.   58
6. 'The First Blow for Liberty'—the Battle of Lexington,
   Mass., 19 April 1775.   64
7. Toussaint L'Ouverture (1743–1803), engraved after
   F. Philippoteau.   71
8. 'The Trail of Tears' by Robert Lindneux.
   From the original oil painting of Cherokee Indians in
   Woolaroo Museum, Bartlesville, Oklahoma.   98
9. An accident on the Great Western Railway, near
   Hamilton, Ontario.   107
10. Marcus Garvey parading in New York.   167
11. A group of rebels after capturing Mazatlán in 1913
    during the Mexican Civil War.   183
12. President Allende's last day, 11 September 1973. Wearing
    glasses, he emerges from a building with a gun in
    his hand.   201
13. São Paulo, Brazil.   206
14. The Candango Monument, Brasilia.   207
15. A street scene in Peru, 1923.   211
16. Bolivian revolutionaries take shelter in a narrow street
    on the outskirts of La Paz during the National
    Revolution, 1952.   216
17. The scene in Bogotá after mob riots, 1948.   219

18. Typical primitive thatched huts in the Indian village of
Santiago on Lake Atitlan, Guatemala.   225
19. John, Robert and Edward Kennedy photographed
together at the former's home at Hyannis Port, Mass.,
when he was campaigning for the Presidency,
July 1960.   234
20. A Soviet ship carrying eight canvas-covered missiles and
transporters, which are visible on its decks, as it steams
away from Cuba, 7 November 1962.   238
21. Perón flanked by bodyguards outside his home in Buenos
Aires after his return from exile, November 1972.   244
22. An aerial view of the Lincoln Memorial, Washington,
during the massive demonstration for Civil Rights,
28 August 1963.   246
23. A police guard of honour carrying the coffin of Pierre
Laporte, Canadian Labour Minister, into the court-
house in Montreal.   251

Acknowledgements

The author and publishers wish to thank the following for permission to reproduce illustrations on the pages indicated:

Associated Press, 216, 219, 238, 246, 251
Brazilian Embassy, 206, 207
Camera Press, 225, 244
The Crown Agents, 49
Mary Evans Picture Library, 107
Keystone Press Agency, 201
Mansell Collection, 58, 71
Mexican National Tourist Council, 45
National Maritime Museum, 13
Popperfoto, 167, 234
Radio Times Hulton Picture Library, 50, 64, 183, 211
Western Americana Picture Library, 98

Maps researched and designed by Brian Catchpole.

Part One

Differentiation and Revolution

(1492 to about 1830)

What used to be called the New World is made up today of 24 independent nations and 21 dependent, colonial or 'associated' societies. Many of these 45 political units contain within them multiple ethnic, racial and religious groups. They share some common historical experiences. The independent states are all the ex-colonies of European powers. Most have been affected and shaped by immigration from abroad. In varying degrees they are conscious of their 'plural' character and are deeply concerned with their national identity. Such concerns are constantly voiced in Canada, with its French, English, Ukrainian and other ethnic groups, in the United States, which has over sixty different groups, and in Mexico, Brazil, and elsewhere.

Cultural pluralism is the most striking similarity among the nations of the Western Hemisphere. The most striking dissimilarity today is still the disparity in economic growth between the nations of the north and those of the centre and south. Linked with this difference is the higher degree of political stability seen in the USA and Canada. The northern continent is called by geographers 'Anglo-America'. One can see why: the contribution of British legal, political and economic traditions, especially capitalism and representative, party government, has been enormous. But 'Anglo-America' is a hopelessly inadequate title for these complex societies. The French, Catholic *Canadiens* as well as the many 'New' Canadians from other ethnic and national groups seem excluded from Canada's history by this title, while in the USA a varied population-mix of peoples of African, Asian, South American and continental European descent can hardly be lumped together as 'Anglo-Americans'. As early as the first US census of 1790 the *English* formed statistically under 50% of the population in the ex-colonies. And what of the contributions of the native Amerindians, and the smaller groups such as Aleuts and Eskimos, who have played a significant role in Alaska and the North?

The southern and central part of the Western Hemisphere often goes by the title 'Latin' America. Yet over vast stretches of its territory there is not much that is truly 'Latin'. The Indians are consistently undercounted in official censuses, and five major nations are predominantly Indian in character rather than 'Latin'—Ecuador, Bolivia, Peru, Paraguay and Guatemala. 'Latin' America has many non-European speaking peoples. Indian tongues persist: 70 or 80 are at present under study in Mexico City. In some areas such as the Caribbean, Costa Rica, Uruguay and Argentina few native Indians managed to survive the trauma of white European invasion. Sometimes the destruction of Indian cultures was deliberate; as

3

late as 1879 General Roca rounded up the remaining Indians of Argentina for planned assimilation, and today Indians are reportedly still being hunted like wild animals in Paraguay and Brazil. Yet the rural language of the Andes nations is not Spanish but Aymara or Quechua; the language of Paraguay is Guaraní and Spanish; that of the Yucatan is still Maya. Indians have resisted cultural assimilation into the dominant 'Latin' way of life in Guatemala, Brazil, Mexico and in remoter regions all over South America. In North America they still resist but are hampered by far smaller numbers and greater accessibility of their young people to mass media.

What should we call the southern continent? . . . 'Indo-Latin America'? What of the millions of people of African descent? The Negro presence and profound Negro cultural influence are felt in many parts of the region, particularly in the West Indies and Brazil. 'Indo-Afro-Latin America' is too unwieldy and takes no account of the newer immigration of other-than-Spanish Europeans, as well as Asians, in the 20th century. The British too, played a large economic role. For convenience and accuracy the simple geographical terms, North, Central and South America will suffice here.

It is obvious that in a few pages one cannot do full justice to the varied history of the many groups which make up the story of the Western Hemisphere. By the mid-1970s the hemisphere was the home of about 550,000,000 human individuals, about 300,000,000 of them in Mexico and the West Indies, Central and South America. In this book I hope to give an *impression* of the variety and subtlety of the social, cultural and political history of their societies. Their history, clearly, is no mere extension of the history of European culture, though this short account begins with the common trauma of European invasion, the result of the amazing expansion of Western Europe over the face of the globe that took place in the late 15th, 16th and 17th centuries. European armies, European technology and ideas, and European diseases disrupted and sometimes destroyed traditional cultures, almost annihilated native populations and imposed an attempted European way of life. After conquest came settlement. Once settlement was stabilized it was not always clear who had conquered whom, and cultures assimilated *to each other* in some parts of the hemisphere where the numerical advantage was not too heavily in favour of the invader. Out of this cauldron of change a variety of independent nations eventually emerged in the hemisphere as distinct from each other as Haiti is from Uruguay, the USA from Bolivia, or Canada from Brazil.

The individual national histories of New World societies have been moulded by particular geographic, climatic and locational differences; by whatever pre-existing native cultures were already there and by the particular type, source and timing of the European invasion. Spanish military conquerors, French trappers and traders, British settlers and farmers, all approached the New World in different ways. Thus the

Spanish sought to create almost separate, individual kingdoms in the hemisphere, each directly related to the Crown of Castile but not to each other—a circumstance which helped to shape the entire later history of the southern continent (in contrast with the federated United States or Canada). The French attempted to build in Canada a 'New France' which would be a direct feudal extension of the old, but they failed. The British for many decades left colonisation to private business adventurers and religious groups and the government took little interest. Meanwhile the *timing* of the invasions was crucial: the Spanish colonies were settled very early, in the late 15th and early 16th centuries, the time of Divine Right and absolutist monarchy in Europe and of inherited rule by noble families. This world was far removed from that of the individualistic, alienated English Puritans who settled Massachusetts in the 17th century, men who sprang from the intense revolutionary turmoil of those later decades. Common to all the societies the Europeans founded was the tragic and often bloody clash of cultures. Indian, African, European and even Asian cultures met head-on in the New World. The 'Americans' of the Western world, from Canada to Chile and Argentina, are more than merely 'transplanted Europeans' and are the product of this culture clash, a rich mingling of traditions in ideas, arts and music which has produced much of the distinguished writing (for example) of the 20th century—written by Americans from Brazil, Argentina, the USA, Mexico and elsewhere. Socially, racial and ethnic pluralism is forging new popular cultures in the West, in nations such as the US, Canada, Brazil and Mexico.

1
Dependency

The re-discovery, settlement and exploitation of the western world by several European powers, chiefly Spain, Portugal, France and Britain but to a lesser degree also the Netherlands, Sweden and Russia, represented a decisive relocation of the world's resources as a whole. The settlement of the West was nothing less than a global shift of investment and population. The full economic, political and cultural impact of this shift was delayed by about three hundred years of colonial dependency in the New World. After the great migrations to North America in the later 19th and early 20th century the full meaning of the shift was to be seen with the rise to world power of Canada and the USA and the overshadowing of Europe.

Meanwhile the central and southern half of the continent seemed left behind in many respects and economically retarded in growth by comparison with the richer north, although the living standards of some parts of South America are well above those of large areas of the globe today. The political achievements of the southern continent seemed meagre, since many nations there suffered one bogus 'revolution' after another, rarely signifying a true attack on the semi-feudal landholding and social systems but more a 'palace revolution' or military coup, a mere change of personnel at the top with no alteration of the power-structure or distribution of rewards. All but a few South American nations had failed to achieve that special political miracle which marks other western democracies, the peaceful and orderly transfer of power between succeeding regimes. In the most advanced and successful nations a large measure of economic and social progress was achieved with the coming of welfare states, often attempting to follow the Swedish model, in the 20th century. Such progress was hindered by the continuing economic dependency of South American nations on Europe and the USA; they remained exporters of raw materials and staple products. They were still semi-colonial, exporting economies. Political and economic conditions were of course closely interrelated and dependent on each other. The miracle of the peaceful transfer of political power was as essential to liberty and to equality as it was to political order, but was difficult to achieve in conditions of gross economic inequality and poverty. Similarly, orderly economic investment and growth were difficult under conditions of political instability. The whole situation was an invitation to external intervention.

This outcome of the processes of history, so familiar to modern observers, would have been unthinkable in the 17th and 18th centuries. Then the Spanish colonies were far in advance of either the English or French in every way, especially economically and culturally. In those years Spanish America was a magnificent civilisation with great universities, baroque cathedrals and flourishing urban centres. French Canada, or the English settlements in Virginia and New England were very poor indeed by comparison. What happened? The surprising outcome can be partly explained by examining the motives and the conditions of colonisation and the historical background of the respective colonising powers.

CENTRAL AND SOUTH AMERICA IN THE 16th–17th CENTURIES

The Spanish *Conquistadores* went to the Americas seeking gold. They organised military expeditions to loot the New World and this motive even overshadowed the Catholic Church's aims of Christian conversion and 'spiritual conquest'. Priests accompanied every adventure; the first buildings erected were usually churches; some priests fought hard to save the Indians from the rapacity of miners and soldiers. But finally even the Church succumbed and became conservative and rich on the pickings of the New World.

Later the English too sought gold. The Spanish found it; that was their long-term undoing. The silver and gold looted from the New World became the basis for the magnificence of Spanish America, and indeed of Spain's 'Golden Age' at home. The magnificence was relatively short-lived. Spain's still-feudal economic and social system proved unable to absorb so much wealth. It was never wisely used. It did not lead to the growth of home industries, or to what modern economists call 'social overhead' or 'infrastructure' (better public education for a skilled labour force and professional class; better transportation and roads; more efficient bureaucracy, and services). Instead American gold encouraged Spain to maintain its old feudal ways. The upper classes came to hold all labour and trade in disdain, in contrast with later English attitudes; they became idle and corrupt, as did the Church. Other nations benefited more from Spain's treasure, in spite of her attempt to keep a rigid national control over all trade with the colonies.

Columbus—ecological disaster

Many of the disasters that came with the Spanish conquest of the Caribbean and mainland shores (the 'Spanish Main') were due directly to Christopher Columbus. His ruthless and unquenchable gold-fever made

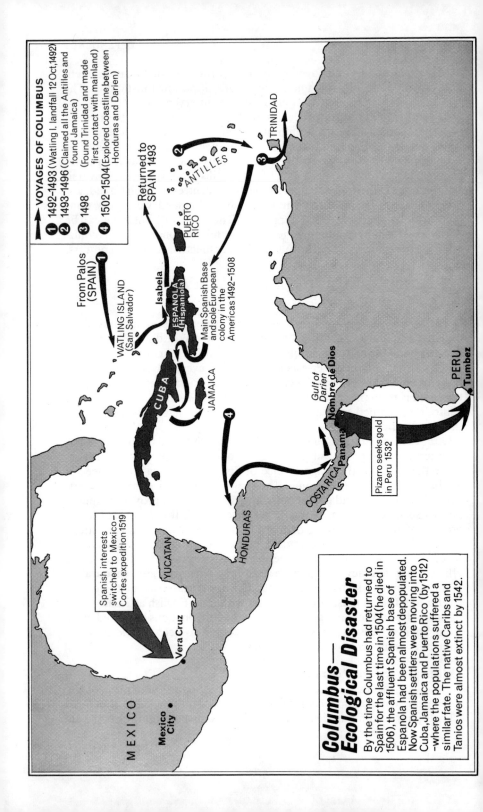

VOYAGES OF COLUMBUS

➊ 1492–1493 (Watling I. landfall 12 Oct,1492)
➋ 1493–1496 (Claimed all the Antilles and found Jamaica)
➌ 1498 (Found Trinidad and made first contact with mainland)
➍ 1502–1504 (Explored coastline between Honduras and Darien)

TRINIDAD

➋ ANTILLES ➌ TRINIDAD

Returned to SPAIN 1493

From Palos (SPAIN) ➊

WATLING ISLAND (San Salvador)

Isabela

PUERTO RICO

ESPANOLA (Hispaniola)

Main Spanish Base and sole European colony in the Americas 1492–1508

CUBA

JAMAICA

➍

Gulf of Darien

Nombre de Dios

PERU
Tumbez

Pizarro seeks gold in Peru 1532

COSTA RICA
Panama

HONDURAS

Spanish interests switched to Mexico – Cortes expedition 1519

YUCATAN

Vera Cruz

MEXICO

Mexico City

Columbus — Ecological Disaster

By the time Columbus had returned to Spain for the last time in 1504 (he died in 1506), the affluent Spanish base of Espanola had been almost depopulated. Now Spanish settlers were moving into Cuba, Jamaica and Puerto Rico (by 1512) – where the populations suffered a similar fate. The native Caribs and Tanios were almost extinct by 1542.

him insist he had already found the Far East. He called this territory the 'Indies' and its natives 'Indians', a name which has stuck over the centuries. Columbus wrested from the Spanish Crown an astonishing contract, an almost absolute dictatorship for himself and his heirs, in perpetuity, over all lands he 'discovered'. Armed with this he treated all who accompanied him as his personal creatures; he put down dissent by force. The man sent out by Spain to replace him in 1500 found Spaniards hanging in gibbets in the harbour and despatched Columbus and his two brothers home in chains.

Columbus set the tone for the conquest not only in his greed for gold but in his cruel Indian policies. He demanded a rigid gold levy—each Indian had to provide him with so much gold per head. The tribute was to be collected by local Indian leaders (*caciques*), who paid with their lives for any failure. This system was unworkable. There was not that much readily available placer-gold on the island of Española (present-day Dominican Republic and Haiti). The terrible shock of the levy system rapidly reduced the Indian population. Those the Spaniards did not kill were wiped out by new diseases introduced by the conquerors from Europe, especially smallpox.

Estimates of the ecological and demographic impact of Spanish intrusion in the Caribbean vary. Las Casas, the priest who was the Indians' chief defender and who lived on Española, claimed three million Indians died between the years 1494 and 1508. Another estimate of 1518 claims at least one million. Even Columbus himself was shocked when he returned, to find the island almost depopulated. These Indians were not especially fierce as others were; they had been friendly and timid. The islands, described by early Spanish visitors as a paradise, were by 1570 reduced to shabby poverty. Few Spaniards lived there (about 1,500 altogether), the Indians were virtually annihilated, and the bulk of the population was made up of African slaves, imported to make up the huge losses in the labour-force. Tropical vegetation was again reclaiming the former Spanish settlements.

A brief attempt to treat the Indians better and to save the situation was made in the years 1516–18 under the Spanish regency of the aged Cardinal Cisneros, but on his death the old policies returned, pushed by Juan Rodriguez de Fonseca, the power behind the throne both of Ferdinand and later of the Emperor Charles V. Spanish colonial interests had now moved to Mexico and Peru, which proved to be far more productive of silver and gold than the islands ever had been. The once-famed Spanish Main was abandoned. The coming of the sugar plantation later brought the area back to life under European control.

Indian depopulation

The tragedy of culture-contact in the islands of the subtropics was repeated to large degree in Mexico and Peru. Here however there were

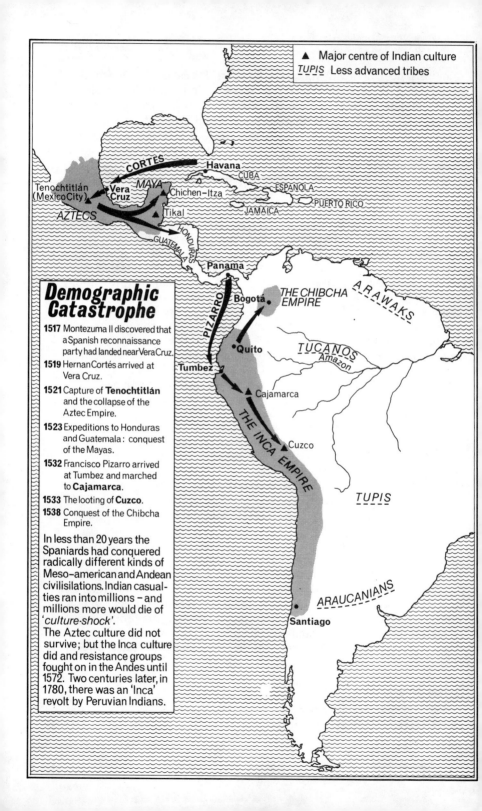

▲ Major centre of Indian culture
TUPIS Less advanced tribes

Havana
CUBA
ESPAÑOLA
PUERTO RICO
JAMAICA

CORTES
Tenochtitlán (Mexico City)
Vera Cruz
MAYA
Chichen-Itza
Tikal
AZTECS
HONDURAS
GUATEMALA

Panama

PIZARRO
Bogota
THE CHIBCHA EMPIRE
A R A W A K S

Quito

TUCANOS
Amazon

Tumbez
Cajamarca

THE INCA EMPIRE
Cuzco

TUPIS

ARAUCANIANS
Santiago

Demographic Catastrophe

1517 Montezuma II discovered that a Spanish reconnaissance party had landed near Vera Cruz.

1519 Hernan Cortés arrived at Vera Cruz.

1521 Capture of **Tenochtitlán** and the collapse of the Aztec Empire.

1523 Expeditions to Honduras and Guatemala: conquest of the Mayas.

1532 Francisco Pizarro arrived at Tumbez and marched to **Cajamarca**.

1533 The looting of **Cuzco**.

1538 Conquest of the Chibcha Empire.

In less than 20 years the Spaniards had conquered radically different kinds of Meso-american and Andean civilisilations. Indian casualties ran into millions – and millions more would die of *'culture-shock'*.
The Aztec culture did not survive; but the Inca culture did and resistance groups fought on in the Andes until 1572. Two centuries later, in 1780, there was an 'Inca' revolt by Peruvian Indians.

more Indians and they did survive. After about 1650 their numbers began to increase once more, along with those of the Spaniards, *mestizos* (Indian-Spanish), and others. By then the trauma was over. European invasion of the ancient centers of Indian civilisation—Aztec, Maya, Inca—had been a demographic catastrophe of immense proportions, which belittles even twentieth century holocausts such as the annihilation of the European Jews. About 25 million Indians of Mexico are said to have been reduced to one million in the years 1519–1605. A recent estimate of the depopulation ratio for the region as a whole is 20 to 1 (from pre-invasion to about 1650).

So the irrigation civilisations of the Indians, considerably older than those of the invaders, were destroyed, and their peoples drastically reduced by smallpox, measles, typhoid, and by brutality, war, forced labour and what anthropologists call 'culture-shock', or the apathy and low birth-rates of subjected people. Insofar as cultures like the Incas were already militarised, rigidly stratified, deferential and theocratic, they were well prepared for absorption into the Catholic, Spanish colonial system. Cleverly the Church built its cathedrals on former pagan temple sites; Catholic priests replaced pagan priests; Spaniards and creoles replaced the Indian upper classes and some of them married their daughters. The Indians were never totally defeated by the Spanish: in the late 20th century bands of Indians are still fighting rearguard actions against whites in places like Ecuador and Colombia, and Indian religious beliefs have endured, particularly where they have been allowed to keep control of their lands. Spanish culture and the Christian religion did not go very deep. Often the Indians became nations within nations.

An empire of silver and forced labour

Official Spanish records reveal that in the course of about 150 years down to 1660, 18,600 tons of silver and 200 tons of gold were shipped to Spain from the colonies. Smuggling would add 50% more to the total estimate. This rich mining boom, at its peak in the Andes and Mexico around 1545–1610, was the result of adding European technical organisation to an already existing forced labour system used by the Incas. This system, called the *mita* in Peru, was so bad as to contribute greatly towards the depopulation of the mining country and the eventual decline of mine output through labour shortage. Under the mita system the Indians worked by forced draft. They were kept in the mines on a 24-hour a day basis, and fed and slept there. They were released only when worn out, to be replaced with another draft of workers, rounded up by collaborating local Indian leaders, the caciques of Mexico and the *curacas* of Peru.

The Spanish state also profited from a monopoly of all mercury output (farmed out to contractors) and from demanding one-fifth of silver output. In addition the state levied indirect taxes on its exports of necessities and a few luxuries to the colonies. Mining profits paid the costs of Empire.

11

Yet by the early 1600s the system was failing; it could not last. The colonists were expected to achieve maximum silver output, were forced to sell it at the lowest price, and were allowed to import only a restricted supply of European goods at highly inflated prices. Everything was channelled through Spain, where large profits were raked off. That, indeed, was the simple theory of colonisation. Spanish America existed purely for the profit of the state and of several interlocking extended families of oligarchs and merchants who had relatives and friends managing the trade in the leading American centres and in Spain. A steady economic recession set in and mine output dropped after 1600. In the colonies the wealthy and the wise invested more in ranching and agriculture or went home to Spain with whatever profits they had made.

Spanish trade controls

Colonial trade was organised entirely in favour of Spain and of the *peninsulares*, the mainland Spanish who lived in America. The growing creole class (*criollos*—American-born Spanish) were largely excluded, and even more so were the mestizos and others of mixed races. Creole resentment was very bitter on occasions and built up over time; the later independence movements owed much to disgruntled creoles and mestizos.

The then-current theory of imperialism, *mercantilism*, was based on the idea that all world trade was limited, therefore one nation could only expand at the cost of another; all trade was a kind of cold war. Mercantile theory was a rationalisation for princely, dynastic power—the driving-force of the new nation-states emerging in Europe. Colonies existed for the mother country as a source of raw materials and as a market for her finished goods. No foreigners were to be allowed into this closed economic system. Colonials themselves were not supposed to profit from trade or to engage in manufacture to supply their fellows. Although practice was not as pure as theory and foreigners did infiltrate Spanish trade, the system was surprisingly efficient in keeping Spanish America in a relatively stunted condition and in isolating the colonies from the outside world. Unlike the English colonies to the north, which were deliberately neglected and which developed largely on their own at least until 1763, the Spanish dominions suffered extremes of economic control and bureaucracy.

In one notable case, Rio de la Plata (later Argentina), all legal trade had to go via Peru: an incredibly irrational routing. Necessities from Sevilla would travel over the Atlantic to Porto Bello, an unhealthy tropical port on the Isthmus of Panama, then by mule overland to Panama on the Pacific, then by sea down the Pacific coast to Callao, Peru, then by an incredible journey inland, crossing the Andes mountain chain and the vast prairies of Argentina (the *pampas*) by mule-train and oxcart, and down to the Atlantic coast again. Such a hindrance to trade retarded the economic development of the Argentine area immeasurably and was certainly unknown in the colonies of France or Britain. The best way to make a quick fortune on the Plata trade was to own a string of mules at the bottleneck over the Panama isthmus.

All Spanish colonial trade was controlled through one port alone: Sevilla until 1717, Cadiz thereafter. The American ports were Porto Bello and Vera Cruz (Mexico). Two institutions regulated the economy of the 'Indies'. First, the Board of Trade or *Casa de Contratación*, created in 1503 and long dominated by the minister Fonseca at Sevilla, issued licences for all colonial shipping, and collected customs and Crown profits on mining and trade. Second, the merchant gilds, or *consulados* in principal centres—Lima, Mexico City, Sevilla—actually organised the trade itself. The consulados were managed only by Castilians, for within Spain local separatism remained very strong and regions were divided by customs, status and language. Spain was not genuinely united by the famous marriage of Ferdinand and Isabella of 1469. The empire was virtually a Castilian affair. Consulado merchants in Lima and Mexico were often connected by marriage, extended kinship or godparents—and always by region—to their counterparts in Sevilla. Thus a few families and friends managed colonial economic affairs for their own, and incidentally the

1. *'Portuguese Carracks off a Rocky Coast', artist unknown; early 16th century.*

Crown's, profits. They kept exclusive control and rejected innovations or reforms, such as the joint-stock company idea which proved so creative for other nations. Above all, the consulados fronted for foreign merchants and siphoned off the wealth of the colonial connection to outside powers. Trade to the Americas was permitted only in regularly scheduled convoys of escorted vessels, *galeones*, down to 1740. These were the famous Spanish galleons so often attacked by pirates for their huge treasure and still being sought today by deep-sea divers. However, few of the merchant ships in such fleets were Spanish or carried Spanish-made goods. Usually the Castilian merchants of the consulados did not own ships or goods. They merely received fees from foreigners for expediting trade. Like Columbus the Spanish were so taken up by gold-fever and mining that supplying the products of New World trade was left by default to foreigners, to the Dutch, British, French and Italians. Yet ironically the real long-term 'wealth of the Indies' lay in the manufacture and supply of such goods. All that glitters is not gold. Of course, foreign goods had first to be sent to Sevilla and then re-exported at a fee, and one side-result of the lack of Spanish carriers was that the large and profitable African slave-trade was not a Spanish affair. The Spanish-American colonies were a large market for slaves, but the rich slavers were usually the Dutch, British, French and Portuguese.

Feudalism, American-style: haciendas and plantations

The relative decline of silver mining after 1600 brought an alteration in the pattern of colonial economic life. By 1700 farming and ranching, both originally begun for subsistence and to support the thriving mining communities, had become economically significant. The Crown could not successfully stifle the emergence of commercial farming for very long. A more serious obstacle was the shortage of labour. This was solved for the sugar plantations by use of African *slaves*. Elsewhere the growth of *latifundia*, large-scale farming or ranching units, proved viable using Indian labour tied to the land through a complex of unpayable debts.

Two forms evolved, the *hacienda* (called *estancia* in Argentina, *fazenda* in Brazil), and the plantation. The major historical difference between the two forms was that the hacienda was originally more of a self-sustaining system, the plantation more export-oriented and commercial. Both used *debt-peonage* to immobilize Indian labour. The landlord or *hacendado* was a patriarch—judge, jailer, provider and father-figure. His Big House dominated the community, which provided tools, seed, medical care, priest and defence for the peons in return for labour-services as in a medieval manor. The Indians were often forced off their communal lands to labour on the hacienda, and lived such self-sufficient and enclosed life-styles in these miniature communities that their legal rights were in-applicable and theoretical.

Native Indian communes however, as in the Andes, in Mexico and in

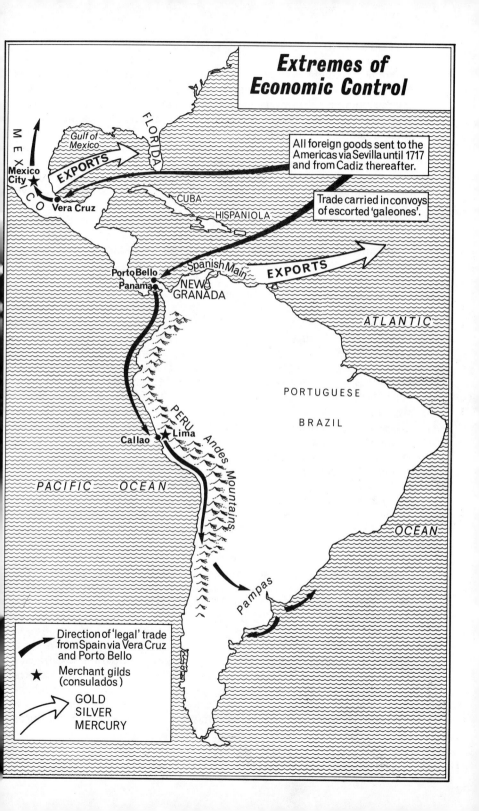

Extremes of Economic Control

All foreign goods sent to the Americas via Sevilla until 1717 and from Cadiz thereafter.

Trade carried in convoys of escorted 'galeones'.

MEXICO

Gulf of Mexico

FLORIDA

EXPORTS

Mexico City

Vera Cruz

CUBA

HISPANIOLA

Porto Bello

Panama

Spanish Main

EXPORTS

NEW GRANADA

ATLANTIC

PORTUGUESE

BRAZIL

PERU

Andes Mountains

Callao

Lima

PACIFIC OCEAN

Pampas

OCEAN

Direction of 'legal' trade from Spain via Vera Cruz and Porto Bello

★ Merchant gilds (consulados)

GOLD
SILVER
MERCURY

Guatemala, fought constantly against the encroachments of the land-hungry hacendados, who grabbed all the better lands of the valleys and lower slopes and took every opportunity to nibble away at Indian rights. During the wars of independence for example, Indian communal lands were stolen in the name of liberal individualism. The Indian communes were the antithesis of the large haciendas in structure: all members participated in the internal political process; the Indian community organised public works, schools, road-building, and police protection; each commune had its own personality and traditions. A few survive today.

The plantation evolved in 17th century Brazil chiefly to produce sugar. This form of organisation spread to tobacco production and other export crops and by the 18th century was also to be found in the Spanish-American regions, Rio de la Plata, Cuba, Venezuela. Large tropical estates used African slave-labour to specialise on one-crop commercial output usually for the European market. They were financed by European capital which controlled their marketing. The perfect 17th century example of a foreign-financed, one-crop plantation system was the Dutch investment in Brazilian sugar production. The Portuguese, who as world-explorers had their hands full, paid little attention to Brazil for some time after they acquired vague rights in the area. Sugar production migrated westwards across the ocean from the Mediterranean via the Atlantic islands. Dutch capital developed a strip of the Northeast coast of Brazil where rich soils and good rainfall made irrigation unnecessary. Labour was scarce and Portuguese *bandeirantes* roamed into the interior, seeking and enslaving Indians. When this proved inadequate, the African slave trade filled the labour gap, with perhaps half a million Negroes being forcibly imported in the 17th century mainly from Guinea and Angola.

The Dutch came to control the bulk of the trade between lax Portugal and her Brazilian colony. The sugar they owned was processed in Dutch refineries in Amsterdam. They traded the slaves that grew the crop and they marketed the refined sugar in Europe. Finally they took the political leap. After failing to hold Bahia in 1624, the Dutch West India Company invaded this area of Brazil in 1630 and held it under a Dutch governor, John Maurice, who tried to placate the local Portuguese and make the colony ('Pernambuco') an economic success. He also captured Angola in West Africa, thus safeguarding both ends of the rich slave trade—the source and the market. 'Pernambuco' was also the site of the Negro 'republic' of Palmares, made up of slaves who had escaped from the large sugar plantations after 1630. After being ousted from Brazil in 1654, Dutch sugar entrepreneurs developed plantations in Guiana and Curaçao.

The large semi-feudal estate system was a way of life, not merely a form of agricultural production. The constant call for 'land-reform' that echoes throughout the 19th and 20th centuries in South America is a protest against the dead hand of the latifundia, a massive conservative force

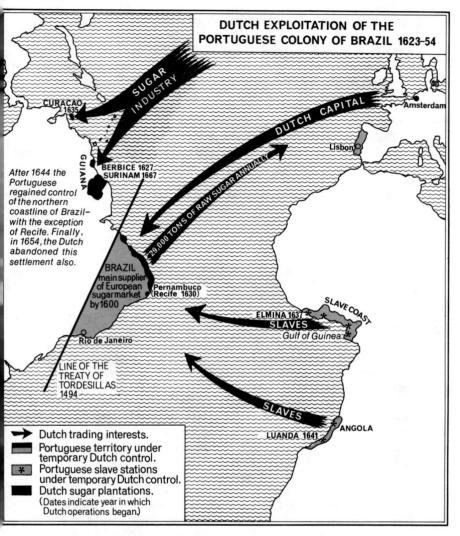

DUTCH EXPLOITATION OF THE PORTUGUESE COLONY OF BRAZIL 1623–54

SUGAR INDUSTRY

CURACAO 1635

Amsterdam

DUTCH CAPITAL

Lisbon

29,000 TONS OF RAW SUGAR ANNUALLY

After 1644 the Portuguese regained control of the northern coastline of Brazil– with the exception of Recife. Finally, in 1654, the Dutch abandoned this settlement also.

GUIANA

BERBICE 1627
SURINAM 1667

BRAZIL main supplier of European sugar market by 1600

Pernambuco (Recife 1630)

ELMINA 1637
SLAVES
Gulf of Guinea

SLAVE COAST

Rio de Janeiro

LINE OF THE TREATY OF TORDESILLAS 1494

SLAVES

LUANDA 1641
ANGOLA

➤ Dutch trading interests.
▨ Portuguese territory under temporary Dutch control.
✳ Portuguese slave stations under temporary Dutch control.
■ Dutch sugar plantations.
(Dates indicate year in which Dutch operations began.)

impeding many hopes of change. In Mexico and elsewhere the hacienda was also political, being linked up intimately with local political bosses (the *caciquismo* network). Haciendas intimidated the small towns, which failed to become autonomous. In Argentina the estancia similarly was linked with regional *caudillo* bosses. So the hacienda-plantation system, not unlike the plantation system of the southern states of the United States, was a retarding force: it discouraged the emergence of a sizeable commercial and industrial middle-class; it discouraged crop experimentation and diversification; it tied down the labour force, and prevented it from being upgraded in skills; it discouraged most internal 'social overhead' construction; it was anti-technological in spirit and feudal in style.

Finally, it retarded capital accumulation. Yet it is hard to see that the independent family farm, beloved more of North American theory than of practice, could really have sustained itself in the South American tropics, producing crops like sugar and tobacco.

The political structure of Spanish America

The feudal economic system had its counterpart in politics, though Spain's hold over her colonies remained shaky until the 18th century and she was constantly under attack from pirates and at war with Indians. The Viceroyalty of New Granada was not established until as late as 1717, that of Rio de la Plata not until 1776. This was very late in colonial history, when Spain herself was already declining as a world power and losing population. The bad long-term effects of her inability to absorb New World treasure and administer her over-extended empire were now much in evidence.

Reforms came in the 18th century and brought with them a burst of prosperity for the colonies–too late. Bullion from the colonies had made the Spanish monarch financially independent for too long. Unlike English kings he had never needed to truckle to elected assemblies, begging for tax revenues in an age of inflation and rising costs of government. But it was in that bitter struggle over control of the purse in 17th century Britain that parliamentary government was born. There, ideas and practices were learnt that were transmitted whole to the North American colonies and later put to good use. This helps to account for the greater political maturity and experience in self-government of the British Americans when they emerged from war in 1783 with their new-found independence. The Spanish colonial tradition offered very little in the way of training in self-government for its colonial subjects and its economic tradition offered little in the way of economic autonomy.

Over time a political structure was built up to govern Spanish America. At the top, representing the King's supreme authority, was the *Council of the Indies* created by Charles V in 1524 (1604 for Portugal). The Council was all-powerful in matters of legislation, justice, finance and trade (through the Casa de Contratación); it also supervised Church administration under a special Papal agreement. Governing in the colonies themselves were Viceroys (first-rank) and Captains-General (second-rank), with viceregal courts or *audiencias*. The early Viceroys, who were usually Spanish noblemen of first rank, were expected to govern vast territories. The Viceroy of New Spain allegedly controlled most of Central America, and after the conquest of the Philippines began in 1564, those Pacific islands too, from his capital in Mexico City. The Viceroy of Peru was responsible to the King for most of South America. Lima was his seat and he always travelled with tremendous pomp and splendour. The great show of authority to some extent helped to cover up a lack of power, for the Viceroys were less omnipotent than they appeared.

Apart from the impossibilities of geographical distance, Viceroys did not keep office long enough to do very much. The average tenure or *residencia* was three to five years. In practice office-holders had to depend on the more permanent administration, the bureaucrats who actually governed the colonies. The audiencia, made up of lawyers from the best Spanish colleges, wielded broad administrative and judicial powers, substituted for the Viceroy when needed, and enabled the King and Council to keep a check on viceregal powers. The *fiscales* (Crown attorneys) of these courts were much closer to the localities and understood local needs better than the distant and ceremonial Viceroy. In the later 17th century the men chosen for Viceroy came from the ranks of lesser nobility. With increasing sale of offices in Spain itself, the quality of colonial personnel declined. This gave still more power to the audiencias and the secretariats in Lima and Mexico.

As in colonial situations elsewhere in history, the officers of the establishment rapidly became instruments of interest-groups in the colonies. The most powerful Council of the Indies itself became a mouthpiece for the colonies rather than a supreme authority over them. Viceroys, like British colonial governors in North America, had to placate local groups in order to succeed and sometimes ended up in greater sympathy with the colonies. (In the British colonies the assemblies gained control over governors' salaries—a very potent device.) In fact the whole system, whatever its official hierarchy, was made to work by *patronage* and balancing-off conflicting interest-groups. The lands were vast, terrain very difficult and communications poor. Real government at the local level fell into the hands of local gentry—silver-mine owners, *hacendados*, and the lawyers who advised them.

The Crown of Castile treated Spanish America not as a direct extension of Spain (as France did 'New France' in Canada), but as a group of separate cities and power-centres. Temporary officials were sent out for a number of years to administer these centres and little attempt was made, despite the Council and Laws of the Indies, to govern them as a whole. Thus the Crown encouraged the separatism that later troubled the history of South America. The local strong men on whom colonial government really rested were prototypes of later *caudillos* (men on horseback) of the 19th and 20th centuries.

Cabildo self-government

The one institution where the local-born Spanish could exercise some leadership was the town council or *cabildo*, controlled normally by the creole elite. The audiencias were staffed only with peninsulares born in Spain, as were the lesser administrative offices, the governors, *corregidores* and *alcalde mayores*. But in the town councils creoles could wield limited power, dispense modest funds and flatter themselves with flashy uniforms and titles. Until the later 18th century they seemed content to do this; they

19

Saint Domingue, formerly Hispaniola, was the scene of Toussaint L'Overture's remarkable revolution in 1791.

VICE-ROYALTY OF NEW SPAIN

Mississippi

Ohio

U.S.A.

Rio Grande

Havana

Mexico City

CAPTAINCY-GENERAL OF CUBA

Guatemala

CAPTAINCY GENERAL OF GUATEMALA

VICE-ROYALTY OF NEW GRANADA

Caracas

C.G OF VENEZUELA

Dutch French GUIANA

Bogota

AUDENCIA OF SANTA FE

Quito

Amazonas

PORTUGUESE BRAZIL

The Government of Spanish America

By the beginning of the 18th century the aim was to improve the quality of administration in Spanish America. The Viceregal governments based on LIMA and MEXICO CITY were incapable of exercising control over Spain's vast possessions.

1714 MINISTRY OF THE INDIES co-ordinated the work of the Council of the Indies and the Casa de Contratacion.

1717 Viceroyalty of NEW GRANADA based on BOGOTA established to oversee Quito, Guatemala and Venezuela.

1776 Viceroyalty of LA PLATA based on BUENOS AIRES to oversee the wealth of the River Plate Provinces in general and the bullion mined from the 'mountain of silver' at Potosi in particular.

1759-1788 (Reign of Charles III) Spain employed an increasing number of creoles in her armed forces to maintain law and order.
Several future leaders of independence movements emerged from the creole officer class.

AUDENCIA OF LIMA

Lima

VICE-ROYALTY OF PERU

Potosi

C.G. OF CHILE

Santiago

VICE-ROYALTY OF LA PLATA

Buenos Aires

River Plate

Bullion exports to Spain

complained of peninsular snobbery and exclusiveness, but rarely questioned the system itself—*Viva el rey, y muera el mal gobierno*! was their usual cry (Long live the King and death to bad government). In any case some of the more frustrating regulations of the bureaucratic, mercantilist state were simply ignored at the local level, shrugged off with the traditional attitude: *Obedezco, pero no cumplo* (I obey but do not fulfil). Alcalde mayores and corregidores came to be called corregidores without distinction with the passage of time. In fact the *corregimiento* was originally a district created to govern remote and scattered Indians and to collect taxes from them. Corregidors were the most corrupt and tyrannical of all Spanish administrators. They had total control over the Indians. They sold their lands out from under them, farmed them out as labour, controlled their water rights, forced them to sell their products at low prices and to buy ridiculous and useless European goods at high prices (such as eye-glasses and silk stockings). The Indians were threatened with enslavement and even with excommunication for failure to accept the corregidor's decrees.

Corregidors were peninsular Spaniards with some sort of legal background. They sometimes borrowed money to take up their posts in the colonies. Salaries were nominal, for the office-holder was expected to enrich himself by bribes and corruption during his four or five years of tenure and then return home. This system was not reformed until the late 18th century. It corrupted the Spaniards, it made the creoles jealous, it corrupted the Indians (by use of the caciques), and it even corrupted the Church.

'Spiritual conquest': the Church Militant
The Catholic Church was the conscience of the conquest. This was a Church in abnormal times, the Spanish Church of the Counter-Reformation, of the reformist zeal and drive of the Council of Trent (1545–1563), of great Saints like Theresa of Avila and John of the Cross. It was the Church of the Jesuits (founded in 1534 to spread the faith as 'soldiers of Christ'), and of the Inquisition. Moors and Jews had been driven out of Spain; now the world was ready for the faith.

This Church is usually credited with two major colonial achievements, the transmission of Spanish culture, through schools, religious art and architecture and conversion of Indians, and the humanising or tempering of policy towards the Indians. Writers who claim to see a difference between North American and South American treatment of the Indians, or between United States slavery and Brazilian slavery, point to the influence of the Church as an institution, an influence that they find lacking in the North.

In the early years of conquest and colonisation certain Church fathers did play a large role in propagandising the treatment of the Indians, notably Bartolomé de *Las Casas*, 1474–1566. This Bishop, a Spanish

Dominican often called the 'Apostle of the Indies', was the first priest to be ordained and to preach in the New World (from 1510). He knew at first hand what happened to the Indians on Española. He crossed the ocean over a dozen times seeking aid for the Indians and had much to do with the enactment of the famous *Laws of the Indies* (1542). The new laws demanded the abolition of Indian slavery, the elimination of *encomiendas* (land grants to Spaniards that included the Indians on the land) with the death of present holders, and the printing of colonial laws in various Indian languages. Such reforms did not happen; white colonial opposition was much too fierce and South America was too far away.

Las Casas, in his propaganda writings on the 'tears of the Indians' did much to create the 'Black Legend' of the extreme cruelties of Spanish rule. The Legend was later used for political purposes against Catholic Spain by Protestants, especially the Dutch and English. But the humanitarian work of Las Casas himself stands as one example that the Black Legend was an exaggeration and that other colonising powers were little better in their conduct. Las Casas loved his Indians so much he was fully prepared to sacrifice the *Africans* to save them. He suggested the use of African slave labour to replace the overworked Indians.

Jesuit communes

As time passed the Church grew rich and lost many of its early ideals. Its dignitaries in the upper clergy were all white and Spanish though by 1700 some mestizos had entered at the parish level. It served the state and found all dissent to colonial power to be 'heretical'. By the time of independence the upper clergy supported Spain, the lower the revolution. Rich families controlled Church wealth in mines, agriculture, and trade and inherited their positions. The wealth of the colonial Church helped to support the Pope himself.

However, on the frontiers of Spanish America and in distant Franciscan and Jesuit missions, the old religious zeal was still alive. In the wilds of Paraguay the Jesuits established communes—*reducciones*—to convert and teach the Guaraní. From the late 16th to the mid-18th century, for about 150 years these reducciones existed, almost as a state within a state, scattered throughout what is now Paraguay, parts of Uruguay, N. Argentina and S. Brazil. By 1700 or so thirty such communes, with an average of 3,000 Indians in each, had worked wonders in the wilderness. They introduced cattle in large herds, taught crafts and trades ranging from boat-building to weaving and exported commercial products such as maté, hides, lumber, cotton and tobacco. Merchants and plantation owners in coastal regions became fearful and jealous of the communes, as they already were of the Jesuits themselves.

In the reducciones all land and property were communally held. Labor was held sacred and was the duty of everyone. The Indians marched to the common fields to the sound of Churchly music, led by priests. They

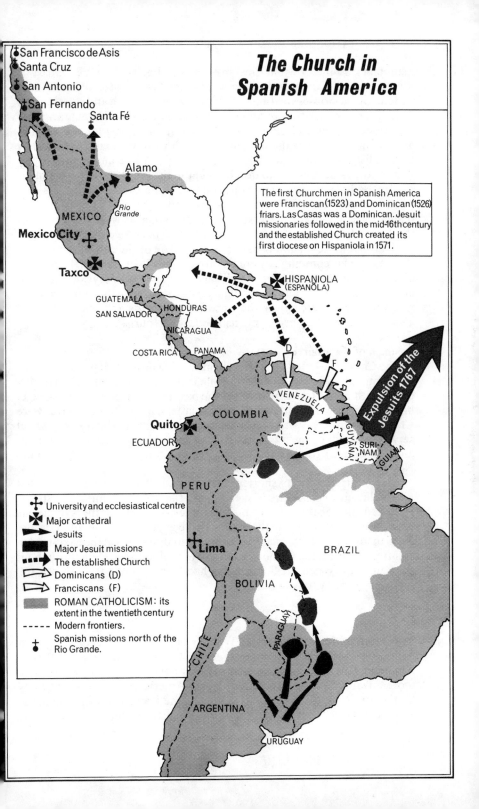

The Church in Spanish America

The first Churchmen in Spanish America were Franciscan (1523) and Dominican (1526) friars. Las Casas was a Dominican. Jesuit missionaries followed in the mid-16th century and the established Church created its first diocese on Hispaniola in 1571.

San Francisco de Asis
Santa Cruz
San Antonio
San Fernando
Santa Fé

Alamo

MEXICO

Rio Grande

Mexico City

Taxco

GUATEMALA
SAN SALVADOR
HONDURAS
NICARAGUA
COSTA RICA
PANAMA

HISPANIOLA (ESPAÑOLA)

Expulsion of the Jesuits 1767

VENEZUELA
COLOMBIA
GUYANA
SURINAM
GUIANA

Quito
ECUADOR

PERU

Lima

BOLIVIA

BRAZIL

PARAGUAY

CHILE

ARGENTINA

URUGUAY

Legend

✝ University and ecclesiastical centre
✠ Major cathedral
→ Jesuits
▬ Major Jesuit missions
▪▪▶ The established Church
▷ Dominicans (D)
▷ Franciscans (F)
ROMAN CATHOLICISM: its extent in the twentieth century
----- Modern frontiers.
✝ Spanish missions north of the Rio Grande.

manufactured their own musical instruments. Each commune centre was a village green for common grazing of sheep, surrounded on three sides by long block-houses for Indian families, with a Church and storehouses. This was the realization of an ancient ideal of religious communism.

Despite the cultural achievements of the Jesuits, the gorgeous illuminated manuscripts and the humane way of life, they remained essentially paternalistic towards the Indians, treating them like children in a way that is always destructive to development in the long run. The communes had to be heavily fortified against rapacious Portuguese intruders, the bandeirantes, seeking to enslave Indians to work on the coastal sugar plantations. When the slavers came, local Spaniards were too jealous of the Jesuits to come to defend them. Indians were carried off, workers and student-priests alike, and many of them died on the forced march back to the coast. The communes were destroyed. In 1767 Charles III saw fit to eject the Jesuits from all Spanish lands, and for some years the Pope abolished the Order altogether. The jungle undergrowth soon reclaimed its own, and covered over the once-ordered fields and village centers. Those re-exposed by archaeologists today are tourist sites.

Triumph of the Church

The Church, whatever its effect in mitigating harsh Indian policies, was the dominant influence in everyday life throughout the colonies. The day began with masses, and bells tolled the passage of time. Rites of passage, births, marriages, deaths, were Church matters. Most public services were Church organised—whatever education there was, medical and hospital service and aid for the poor. Religious architecture and art filled the cities and the Church transmitted the glories of Spain's 'Golden Age' to the New World.

Above all, despite its shortcomings, the Church spiritually embraced all conditions and colours of men. It gave the Indians identity and status. It linked all together in a spiritual enterprise. From the sumptuous churches of Quito, high in the Andes, to the great universities of Lima and Mexico or the squat, massive church buildings of earthquake-ridden Central America, the Catholic Church was visible and present throughout the centuries. When the Spanish flag had long gone the Church was still a power in the Americas.

SETTLING NORTH AMERICA

Up to the Mexican-American War of 1846–48 a large section of North America, in the Southwest and Far West, was in truth part of 'Latin' America. This vast Mexican territory was not developed however. The more advanced eastern section of North America was colonised briefly by the Swedes and Dutch, and mainly by the French and English in the 17th century. The struggle for control of North America fought out by

England and France was part of a global rivalry that involved a world war and a complex of European military alliances. It ended in 1763 with the decisive victory of Britain both in North America and in India. However, the moment Britain defeated France her new empire began to break up, and within twenty years the United States had split off as an independent nation. The Americans were aided by France, fear of whom had kept them within the British defensive Empire for so long.

New Amsterdam and New Sweden

The Dutch, whose remarkable activities in Brazil and the Caribbean we have noted, were virtually pushed into the adventure of empire-building by their struggle for political freedom from Spain. They won independence militarily in 1595, but it was not formally granted until 1648. Meanwhile, cut off from vital European markets by the long struggle, they had built the finest merchant fleet in the world and explored not

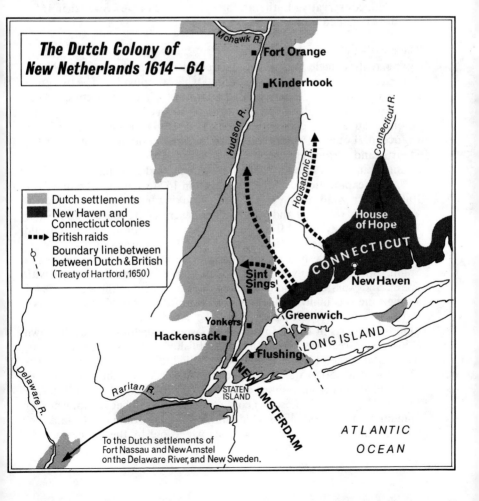

The Dutch Colony of New Netherlands 1614–64

Legend:
- Dutch settlements
- New Haven and Connecticut colonies
- ▪▪▪▶ British raids
- ᵒ Boundary line between between Dutch & British (Treaty of Hartford, 1650)

Mohawk R.
Fort Orange
Kinderhook
Hudson R.
Housatonic R.
Connecticut R.
House of Hope
CONNECTICUT
New Haven
Sint Sings
Greenwich
Yonkers
Hackensack
Flushing
LONG ISLAND
STATEN ISLAND
NEW AMSTERDAM
Raritan R.
Delaware R.
ATLANTIC OCEAN

To the Dutch settlements of Fort Nassau and New Amstel on the Delaware River, and New Sweden.

only South and Central America, but the Russian Arctic, the Far East and Southeast Asia, the Indian Ocean and South Africa. In North America they sent Hudson up the river that bears his name and started a colony at New Amsterdam (New York) fifteen years later in 1624. They bought Manhattan from the Indians for a famous sum of $26 in 1626. The Dutch did not do very well in New Amsterdam, though they built a fine small city with solid Dutch houses. A procession of unpopular governors were sent out, the last being Peter Stuyvesant, and the fur trade did not pay enough. Immigration of common folk was discouraged by the system of land tenure by which all the richest land went to large grantees, the *patroons*, some of whose names became famous later in US history: the important Dutch capitalists like the Van Cortlandts, Schuylers and Van Rensselaers. The British kept raiding from the Connecticut area and in 1664 a British fleet came, and the Dutch were assimilated altogether. Since the Dutch had themselves already swallowed up the small, conservative Lutheran fortress-colony of New Sweden in 1655, the British gained both colonies in one move.

The creation of New France
The real struggle was to be between Britain and France in North America, both powers using the Indians wherever possible. The two great rivals were about a century behind Spain in their colonial conquests in the New World, a distinct advantage of 100 years for building viable colonies on a firm economic basis. The 'Divine Right' monarchy in France of Louis XIV and still more, the revolutionary Britain of the Stuarts and Cromwell, were very different from the feudal, divided Spanish kingdoms ruled earlier by Ferdinand and Isabella.

French exploration of America began in 1524 when they financed the Italian, Verrazano, to sweep the coast, looking for the mythical 'Northwest Passage' to China and to the riches described by Marco Polo. Since Verrazano surveyed land from the Carolinas to Newfoundland, this would have been an immense 'New France'. But France was slow to colonize, though she was the first power to offer serious challenge in the area to Spain. Intensely involved in European politics, dynastic struggles with Spain, and wars of religion, the French engagement in the Americas for a long time was limited to piracy, trading and occasional explorations.

Ten years after Verrazano the famed Jacques Cartier claimed Newfoundland, parts of Labrador and the Gaspé region for the French crown (1534). Montreal was noticed as an established Indian site the next year, but a later attempt to settle at Quebec failed in 1542 and the region was abandoned for 50 years. The French fished for cod off the Grand Banks and traded furs from Indians along the coast. In Brazil in the 1550's a French Huguenot (Protestant) colony survived briefly near Rio. Another Huguenot group settled in Florida in 1564 not far from present Jacksonville, on the St. John's River, but was wiped out by the Spaniards who

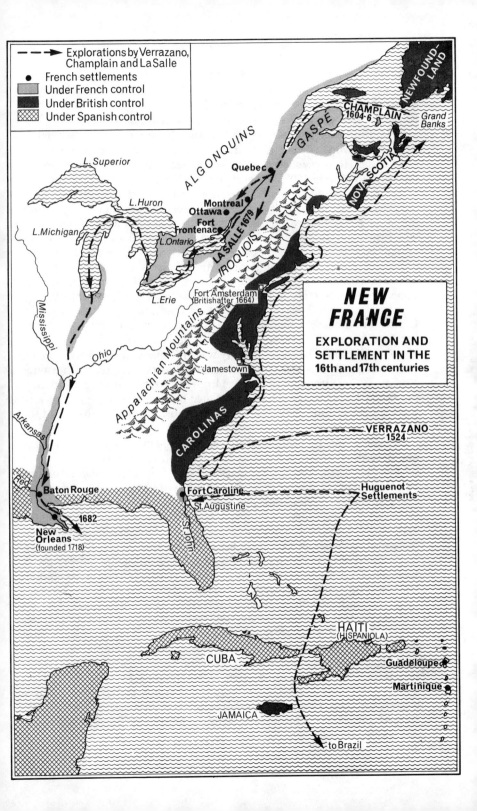

Explorations by Verrazano, Champlain and La Salle

● French settlements

▨ Under French control

■ Under British control

▩ Under Spanish control

L. Superior

L. Huron

L. Michigan

L. Ontario

L. Erie

ALGONQUINS

GASPÉ

CHAMPLAIN 1604-6

NEWFOUND-LAND

Grand Banks

NOVA SCOTIA

Quebec

Montreal

Ottawa

Fort Frontenac

LA SALLE 1679

IROQUOIS

Mississippi

Ohio

Appalachian Mountains

Fort Amsterdam
(British after 1664)

Jamestown

NEW FRANCE

EXPLORATION AND SETTLEMENT IN THE 16th and 17th centuries

CAROLINAS

VERRAZANO 1524

Arkansas

Red

Baton Rouge

1682

New Orleans
(founded 1718)

Fort Caroline

St.Augustine

St. John

Huguenot Settlements

HAITI (HISPANIOLA)

CUBA

Guadeloupe

Martinique

JAMAICA

to Brazil

established St. Augustine in 1565, the oldest existing city in the US today. The French *Fort Caroline* had been little more than a raiding-base from which to attack the galleons. Thus at the opening of the 17th century, France still had no real colonial foothold in America.

Colonisation began more earnestly with the great pioneer Samuel de Champlain, who had visions of a truly settled and developed 'New France' in Canada. He succeeded in putting Quebec, the future French capital, on a firm footing in 1608, and pushed French claims westwards to present Wisconsin. Champlain entangled himself in Indian affairs and supported the Algonquins in their war against the Iroquois—a poor choice, since the latter never forgave the French, much to the comfort of the Dutch and British in later battles. Champlain died in 1635 with his ambitions unrealised; he had come up against what was to be the perennial problem of French colonisation compared with the British, inability to attract adequate emigration from Europe. In fact British Canada inherited the same problem, in relation to the United States in the 19th century.

It was not that French policy-makers failed to grasp this problem. Cardinal Richelieu, real governor of France under Louis XIII, chartered the *Company of 100 Associates* in 1627 with the express purpose of sending out emigrants. But the company was only made to guarantee to send out a minimum of 4,000 emigrants over 15 years, to settle an enormous land grant that stretched (on paper) from the Arctic to Florida, and from the Great Lakes to the Atlantic. It failed miserably on its very first venture: a fleet of four ships was taken by British pirates in 1628, and the English captured the little settlement at Quebec in 1630.

Richelieu was preoccupied with many European and domestic matters, and in colonial affairs always gave more attention to the West Indies than to the cold North. The profitable slave-trade of Guadeloupe, Martinique, French Guiana and later of Haiti seemed more attractive to France. A sharp change of policy took place under Louis XIV with the coming to power of France's finance minister, Jean-Baptiste Colbert, who ran the economy for over twenty years (1661–1683). The leading exponent of mercantilist theory in European history (it is sometimes called 'Colbertism'), he tried to make the colonies an extension of mainland France. A Council of Commerce was to regulate the chartered trading companies from now on, and French *manufacturers* were represented on this board—in great contrast with Spanish mercantilism. Emigration was planned, colonial defences strengthened, and soldiers serving in the colonies expected to marry. The French merchant fleet and the navy were built up. This was what economists today would call a 'development plan'.

Colbert worked against himself in several crippling ways. For example, he allowed the *seigneurial* system of landholding to grow up in New France: this was a feudal structure, land grants being given to large owners who then required masses of peasants (called *habitants* in Canada) to work the estates. This was not so different from the Spanish-American system and certainly discouraged the large-scale popular emigration Colbert needed. His economic nationalism led France into tariff wars and wars of expansion, for instance against the Dutch, which ate away French resources. Finally, Louis XIV prohibited the Huguenots and they promptly left France to live elsewhere; talented Protestant business leaders, professional people and artisans, they helped build Berlin, gave a boost to the economy of England, and migrated to English colonies. French persecution of the Huguenots was a grave error. As a result, though the population of New France did grow, immigration had little to do with it. The native birth-rate was high and intermarriage with Indians quite common. The English colonies however rapidly outstripped New France.

Independent enterprise in British America

Though John Cabot sailed from Bristol in 1497 and 1498 to explore the coasts of New England, some years before the Dutch and French pioneers of North America, it was not until eighty years later that Drake circumnavigated the globe (1577–80), and that three Englishmen, Frobisher (1576), Gilbert (1583) and Davis (1585) probed the North American seaboard area looking for a way through to Asia, the 'Northwest Passage' that tantalized Verrazano. Sir Humphrey Gilbert claimed the Newfoundland area for Queen Elizabeth I, though Cartier had already claimed it for France. Vagueness and confusion characterised early American exploration.

In the 1580s the failure of Sir Walter Raleigh's famous 'Lost Colony' on Roanoke Island (present North Carolina coast) revealed the obvious lesson; successful colonisation took money and planning. In Britain at that time, while she was undergoing an early commercial and industrial revolution (the 'Industrial Revolution of the Sixteenth Century'), this meant *corporate organisation*. When successful English settlement did come, it was the product of private-enterprise, company investment in the New World. 'Women's liberationists' might note that the first English child born in America, at Roanoke in 1587, was a girl: Virginia Dare. But the entire colony had vanished by 1590, leaving only the Indian word 'Croatoan' carved on a tree.

Unlike the state-dominated city-colonies of Spanish-America and the Colbertist ventures of New France, British America was first settled by private joint-stock companies, organised to make a profit out of taking emigrants to the New World, supplying them, and selling their products in Europe. British America was founded as a business enterprise. This does not deny other motives: intense English nationalism and sense of destiny, seen in Shakespeare, in Raleigh, in Elizabeth herself; adventure, escapism, to say nothing of religious idealism and freedom from persecution—the Pilgrim 'Separatists' of Plymouth and the Puritans of Massachusetts Bay. The form of organisation however, and the rationality behind it, was essentially businesslike.

The British became a colonial power in the 17th century as did the French. The economic basis of this imperial expansion was the growth of industries, new and old, in the years 1540–1640, and the prosperity of the English wool and cloth trade. Britain broke her long economic dependence on Continental Europe and sought markets in the Spanish colonies, the Mediterranean and wherever they could be found. Her natural opponents were the Dutch and the French. Gradually Britain captured much of the carrying-trade formerly organised by the Dutch. She developed the New England area for her naval stores, the essential for building a military and merchant navy—lumber especially was becoming scarce in England as the iron industry consumed more charcoal and land was cleared through population growth. She entered the Caribbean, acquiring Jamaica in 1655 and taking over much of the lucrative slave-trade. In truth, the British exploited the Spanish colonial trade and made more profit out of the Spanish Empire in the long run than did Spain herself. With Portugal she had an ancient agreement (still the oldest existing alliance in the world today), and British merchants penetrated the Portuguese economy.

The local basis of British power and energy and the explanation of her burst of colonizing activity in the 17th century was her own political unity and the inheritance of the Tudor way of governing. The Tudor monarchy was not absolutist like that of France or Spain. The separation altogether of the Church of England from the Pope's governance, and a unique Tudor 'alliance' of Crown, local gentry and middling groups in the shires, tempered the English monarchy and prepared the way for further separation of Church and State, religious toleration, and some degree of representative government. What the Tudor system left out, the British revolutions of the mid-17th century made up for. The Puritan Civil War and the later peaceful Glorious Whig Revolution of 1688 lifted Britain out of the 17th century mode. This was not yet full constitutional monarchy with a democratic legislature; but politically, England was far in advance of the France of the Sun King, Louis XIV, who did not die until 1715 and who firmly believed that his personal power came directly from Heaven.

So what the British North Americans inherited, the cultural baggage they took with them to the New World, was different. In the holds of those first emigrants' ships came capitalism and some rudimentary 'rights of Englishmen'. British nationalism too, was less a matter of mere dynastic and military pride and more one of common Englishmen boasting of their superior freedoms.

Geography is always important in the early economic history of an area. The British colonies, called 'plantations' in the early years, though unlike those of Brazil, were small, scattered along the coast, and separated. It was easier to go to Europe than to travel between colonies. Capital—cash, tools and other supplies—and labour were very scarce. Yet they were vital. Colonization costs money: the Virginia Company was an investment of £100,000 on very long odds; Massachusetts Bay Colony, twice that amount. Usually London merchants would prefer the surer returns from trading with Russia and the East. By the 1600s a number of trading companies existed promising attractive returns to the investor in Europe.

The problem of labour-shortage was even more crucial than capital. Clearing the wilderness and building the first settlements, however primitive, is labour-intensive in the extreme. Europe was politically unpleasant enough and the religious and personal drives of the emigrants strong enough, to people the British colonies far more rapidly than those of France further north. Once established the British colonies developed an extraordinary high native birth-rate.

Geography and historical timing created thirteen separate colonies hemmed in behind the Appalachian mountain barrier. Geography, soils and climate determined the major economic activities of each colony. First to be settled, and for long the richest and most politically influential section of the colonies and nation, was Virginia.

Capitalists found 'Virginia'

Under a company charter of 1606 two groups were allowed to set out for North America. One sailed from Plymouth to the Maine coast and failed because it lacked adequate backing. The other, underwritten by a group of rich London business adventurers, landed at Jamestown in 1607, and after a couple of tragic years (the 'starving time'), managed to survive. This group was better funded and organised. The secret of successful colonisation in the New World was follow-through.

The climate and soils were more welcoming farther south. The myth of America as a Garden of Eden was boosted that beautiful morning in April 1607 when Captain Christopher Newport guided his ship into Chesapeake Bay and found 'fair meadows, goodly tall trees, . . . fresh waters.' Here were oysters, turkeys, strawberries four times the size of those in England, Indian maize, tobacco: the wealth of America. At first, men 'died like dogs' and suffered 'cruel diseases, such as swellings, fluxes, burning fevers'. And they starved too, in this land of plenty, until they came to terms with the environment and were taught valuable lessons by the Indians.

In 1616 and 1618 the economic organisation of the colony was revised. Private ownership of land was introduced through the 'headright' system, to create better incentive. Previously, land had been communally owned and jointly cultivated. The profits were to be split at some time in the future. After 1616 the colonists worked harder for their own individual profits. The headright system allowed fifty acres of land to each colonist

31

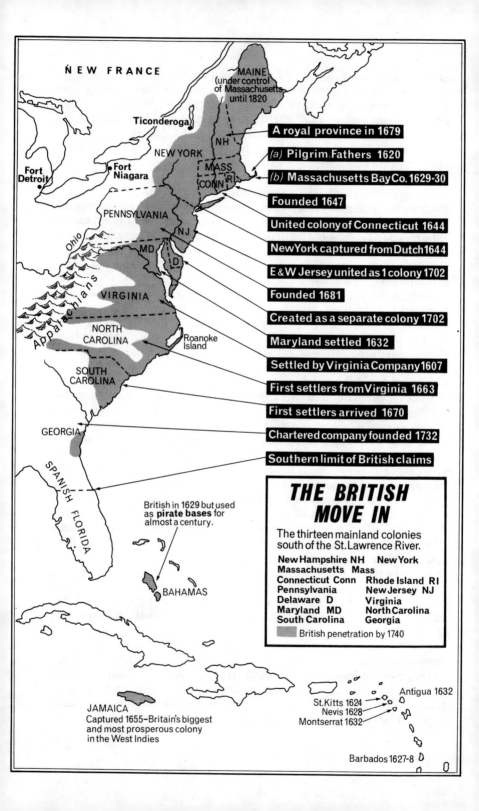

NEW FRANCE

MAINE (under control of Massachusetts until 1820)

Ticonderoga

Fort Detroit

Fort Niagara

NEW YORK

NH

MASS

CONN R

PENNSYLVANIA

Ohio

NJ

MD

D

Appalachians

VIRGINIA

NORTH CAROLINA

Roanoke Island

SOUTH CAROLINA

GEORGIA

SPANISH FLORIDA

A royal province in 1679

(a) Pilgrim Fathers 1620

(b) Massachusetts Bay Co. 1629-30

Founded 1647

United colony of Connecticut 1644

New York captured from Dutch 1644

E & W Jersey united as 1 colony 1702

Founded 1681

Created as a separate colony 1702

Maryland settled 1632

Settled by Virginia Company 1607

First settlers from Virginia 1663

First settlers arrived 1670

Chartered company founded 1732

Southern limit of British claims

British in 1629 but used as **pirate bases** for almost a century.

BAHAMAS

THE BRITISH MOVE IN

The thirteen mainland colonies south of the St. Lawrence River.

New Hampshire NH   New York
Massachusetts Mass
Connecticut Conn   Rhode Island RI
Pennsylvania   New Jersey NJ
Delaware D   Virginia
Maryland MD   North Carolina
South Carolina   Georgia

British penetration by 1740

JAMAICA
Captured 1655 – Britain's biggest and most prosperous colony in the West Indies

Antigua 1632
St. Kitts 1624
Nevis 1628
Montserrat 1632

Barbados 1627-8

who subscribed £12½ to the colony. Another fifty acres could be obtained for each actual settler in Virginia, and a further fifty to anyone who would pay the passage of a settler to the colony. Nevertheless in 1624 the colony failed financially, the company lost its charter and Virginia became England's first Crown colony. The private company made no real profits; there was no placer-gold or silver in Virginia as there was in the Carribbean and South America.

Economic self-government was buttressed by the beginnings of political self-government in 1619. The Virginia House of Burgesses was created. This was a one-chambered body, made up of elected representatives, two from each town and plantation, sitting with the governor and his nominated council. Formally and officially Virginia was supposed to be under company government, controlled by the company's directors who met occasionally thousands of miles away in London. Geographical distance and local needs made such a system ludicrous. From the start the Burgesses began to exercise two essential functions, rights that other nations have taken many decades and much bloodshed to attain: the right to initiate legislation, and the control of the purse. The Virginians enjoyed these prerogatives before they were achieved in England.

Equally remarkable is that the Burgesses were allowed to continue uninterrupted when Virginia became a Crown colony in 1624. Later in the century the assembly became bicameral:the elected section withdrew to meet in a separate chamber. In this cradle of representative government were trained many leaders of the future Revolution, and four of the first six Presidents of the United States (Washington, Jefferson, Madison, Monroe). The Spanish American cabildos of course, were elective in the 16th century; but by the 17th, councillors were purchasing office and the scope of these town governments was always restricted. Such an assembly as the Virginia Burgesses in *Spanish* America could have altered the history of the subcontinent; but there were no free-enterprise 'company governments' there to begin with.

Africans in North America

The year 1619 in Virginia produced not only the first meeting of an assembly, but the very beginnings of black history in North America. 'About the last of August came in a Dutch man of warre,' reported the pioneer John Rolfe (of tobacco fame), 'that sold us twenty Negars.' We do not know whether these first Africans were automatically treated as slaves for life or kept as servants. Thirty years later there were still only about 300 Africans in Virginia (total white population was 15,000), but by the 1640s evidence shows that some Negroes were perpetual slaves, along with their children, born into slavery in America. After 1660 slavery was written into the law codes of Virginia and Maryland and very soon it was buttressed by laws against racial mixing.

The first large-scale enslavement of blacks by the English took place in the sugar islands of the Caribbean: Barbados, the Leeward islands and later Jamaica. In the 1640s and 50s large numbers were shipped there, to be worked literally to death and rapidly replaced by others. The first Negro revolt happened as early as 1638 on Providence Island, a temporary British Puritan possession off Central America. The British, whatever their religion, seem to have had no qualms about slavery in the tropics. Further north in Virginia the only hope for white survival was to develop a cash crop for export—tobacco. That took lots of cheap, unskilled labour which was not forthcoming from England. The 'indentured' (temporarily bound) labour of English immigrants proved inadequate, and slaves profitable. Gradually, inhibitions against the idea dissolved, and as slaves grew in numbers and the tobacco dynasts prospered, the institution became entrenched in Maryland and Virginia.

In the Carolinas, Barbados planters deliberately introduced slaves to work rice plantations and in the 1690s South Carolina statutes were modelled on the harsh Barbados slave codes. Here the institution was more severe. Perhaps the example of successful use of black slave-labour by Spain and Portugal convinced the English colonists, and helped them to overcome the many restraints against it they must have inherited from their English past. The very words 'Negro' and 'mulatto' were taken by the English from Spanish. But above all, slavery grew because it seemed to work. In fact without the labour of many Africans the American colonies could never have grown so fast economically and outstripped their French rivals in the New World. Colonial economic growth depended on external trade. That was the first major contribution made by Negroes to American history.

Puritan Utopias

Negro slavery existed in 17th century New England. It was a very marginal addition to the labour-force. Puritan dogma allowed the enslavement of captives in a 'just war.' The Pequot Indian war of 1637 was so considered, and Indian captives from various wars were enslaved and often shipped out to the West Indies, where they were exchanged, ironically, for Africans. The New England area was also colonised like Virginia, by corporate enterprises. The main drive was different however: religious idealism. Whether those who escaped the upheavals of England were religious 'radicals' or religious 'conservatives' depends on one's theology. The New England dissidents emigrated to re-create the true church; they felt England was backsliding and would suffer torment for its aberrations. The political compromise that was the 'Church of England' created by Elizabeth I did not please them; its language, style and rituals were ambiguous and still too 'Roman'. It was however a *national* Church and most 'Puritans' did not wish to leave it entirely. They meant to 'purify' it from within by abolishing the hierarchy of bishops and by simplifying services and ritual. Consciousness of God dominated their

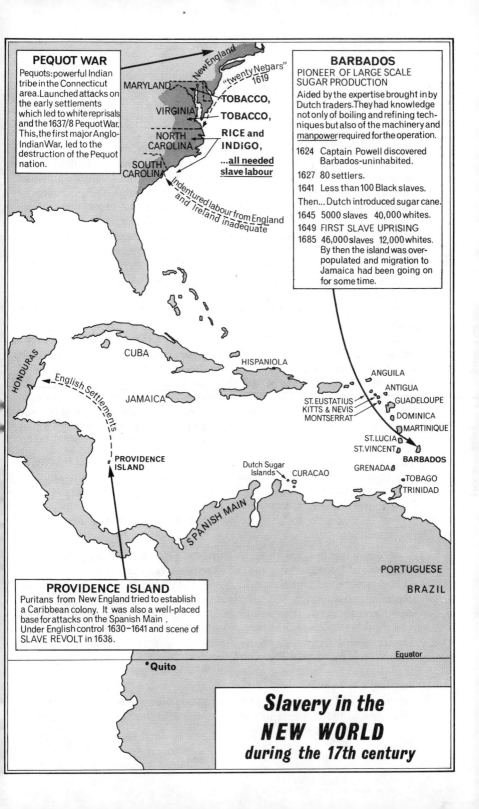

PEQUOT WAR

Pequots: powerful Indian tribe in the Connecticut area. Launched attacks on the early settlements which led to white reprisals and the 1637/8 Pequot War. This, the first major Anglo-Indian War, led to the destruction of the Pequot nation.

New England

"twenty Negars" 1619

MARYLAND

TOBACCO,

VIRGINIA

TOBACCO,

NORTH CAROLINA

RICE and INDiGO,

SOUTH CAROLINA

...all needed slave labour

Indentured labour from England and Ireland inadequate

BARBADOS

PIONEER OF LARGE SCALE SUGAR PRODUCTION

Aided by the expertise brought in by Dutch traders. They had knowledge not only of boiling and refining techniques but also of the machinery and manpower required for the operation.

1624 Captain Powell discovered Barbados-uninhabited.

1627 80 settlers.

1641 Less than 100 Black slaves.

Then... Dutch introduced sugar cane.

1645 5000 slaves 40,000 whites.

1649 FIRST SLAVE UPRISING

1685 46,000 slaves 12,000 whites. By then the island was over-populated and migration to Jamaica had been going on for some time.

HONDURAS

English Settlements

CUBA

HISPANIOLA

JAMAICA

ANGUILA

ANTIGUA

ST. EUSTATIUS
KITTS & NEVIS
MONTSERRAT

GUADELOUPE

DOMINICA

MARTINIQUE

ST. LUCIA
ST. VINCENT

BARBADOS

PROVIDENCE ISLAND

Dutch Sugar Islands

CURACAO

GRENADA

TOBAGO
TRINIDAD

SPANISH MAIN

PORTUGUESE

BRAZIL

PROVIDENCE ISLAND

Puritans from New England tried to establish a Caribbean colony. It was also a well-placed base for attacks on the Spanish Main.
Under English control 1630–1641 and scene of SLAVE REVOLT in 1638.

Equator

°Quito

Slavery in the
NEW WORLD
during the 17th century

everyday thinking and they wished to live according to God's law. This was no longer possible in England, so, reluctantly and sadly, they left it, to build a Utopia in the wilderness, a 'city upon a hill'. The main body of Puritans therefore, those who came with John Winthrop to Massachusetts Bay in 1630, were dissenting Anglicans.

The earlier Pilgrims who came in 1620 were not. Often confused with the greater number of Puritans, the Pilgrims were 'independents', tough separatists who abandoned the Anglican Church as hopeless and had already set up new churches of their own in England. From one of these persecuted churches, William Brewster's at Scrooby, came some of the Pilgrims. First they escaped to Leyden in Holland in 1609 and over ten years later set sail for America via England on a journey beset by mishaps and false starts. Under-financed, reduced to one vessel, the *Mayflower*, and a full degree off course, the Pilgrims finally agreed to settle in the Cape Cod area even though this made their colony extra-legal. They never held a royal charter, and since they settled outside the lands of the Virginia Company from whom they had scrounged their original patent, they were never a company colony.

Having no charter the Pilgrims were free to experiment and create a political society of their own. In this unprecedented situation, 41 adult males drew up the *Mayflower Compact* on board ship while resting at what is now Provincetown on the tip of Cape Cod. Their agreement enacted quite literally the 'social contract' theory of government which explicitly rests government on the consent of the governed and the will of the majority. Unrest in the group had produced a crisis, resolved by this agreement. On November 11th 1620 they pledged to:

> covenant and combine our selves together into a civill body politick ... and by vertue hearof to enacte, constitute, and frame shuch just and equall laws ... from time to time, as shall be thought most meete and convenient for the generall good of the Colonie, unto which we promise all due submission and obedience.

It was a remarkable idea, though it drew strength from the 'congregational' principles of Puritan-Independent church government already entrenched: a structure without hierarchy, governed by the church meeting itself. It was not easy, in the face of severe hardship and the death of half the expedition in the first few months, to maintain this democratic sort of rule. Further south in Virginia, Captain John Smith felt it necessary to impose virtual dictatorship to save the colony from breaking up entirely. This did not happen in Plymouth.

Pilgrims and Indians

Friendly Indians helped to save the little colony in its first year, but the bitterness of the struggle to survive in the wilderness and the difficulties of relationship with the Indians soon produced friction and warfare. Ultimately the Indians were the losers. Governor William Bradford, a man skilful and sympathetic enough to have held the colony together (he was elected in 1621 and for thirty years thereafter), could bring himself to relish the destruction of a Pequot Indian stockade in Biblical terms: 'It was a fearful sight to see them frying in the fire and the streams of blood quenching the same, and horrible was the stink and stench thereof. But the victory seemed a sweet sacrifice, and (we) gave praise thereof to God.'

Here again, as in South and Central America, two technically unequal civilisations met head-on in a tragic confrontation. There were however far fewer Indians in North America, only about 200,000 of all tribes, east of the Mississippi, in contrast with the millions faced by the Spanish, many of them of a more developed culture than in the North. The North eastern tribes were consequently almost entirely exterminated. There seemed to be little of that guilt-feeling felt by Las Casas and some fellow-Catholics, among the Pilgrims. The Indian wars simply were not viewed as 'genocide'.

'New Plymouth' grew strong enough to defend itself against marauding Indians, even to defeat them and build a stable colony which could attract immigrants from its bigger Puritan cousin. In 1691 however the Pilgrim experiment was absorbed into the Massachusetts Bay Colony; by that date most members were glad. They were not so Independent that they could not see the advantages of joining the larger community, which was at least 'Puritan'.

Massachusetts: Puritan Commonwealth

Massachusetts had already grown fast when it swallowed up New Plymouth. Good timing had helped: in the first ten years, 1630–40, Massachusetts received an inrush of Puritan refugees, the 'Great Migration' of about 20,000 people. This slowed after 1640 when a Parliament was called in England and it seemed that Puritans would gain some civil rights there; but it picked up again later.

The Massachusetts colony began with a company charter granted in 1629. Its members, though profoundly religious in motivation, hoped to make a profit out of the venture too. John Winthrop, leader for about twenty years, left England because he was deeply troubled in his conscience at the moral and religious state of English society and sought what he called 'a shelter and a hiding place' at which to begin anew. Yet he was a substantial gentleman, a prosperous attorney, affected by the decline of the cloth-trade in his native Suffolk and convinced he could be an economic success in America. A telling combination of motives drove Winthrop and his colleagues: men of property, they went to Massachusetts for religious freedom, but invested their personal capital there and made it work. They were neither conquistadors seeking gold nor traders, but true *settlers*, committed to give themselves to this New World and to build a new 'Commonwealth'.

Governor Winthrop was a dedicated moderate. He resisted purism, separatism, snobbery and self-righteousness. To this extent he was no 'radical'. The world was not to be made better by escaping from it, he thought; it had taken him a long time to become convinced he should leave Britain at all. Unlike more 'radical' types with whom he disagreed sometimes to the point of banishment from the community of Saints, Winthrop was not a perfectionist. This world could not be made perfect; the most one could do was strive to do the right thing.

So in 1638 Winthrop exiled the radically independent Anne Hutchinson after she defied the community consensus and held religious meetings in her own house, setting herself up against the church. Roger Williams, another extreme Protestant individualist, left in 1635 to begin his own religious settlement in Indian territory at Narragansett (later Rhode Island). Williams eventually relaxed and came round to the position of allowing to others the sort of individual freedom he had always demanded for himself. What hurt Winthrop in his split with Williams, was Williams' insistence on the pursuit of his own personal holiness: he threw off the English churches, then the churches of Massachusetts, and ended up, absurdly, 'communicating' (sharing worship) with no one but his own wife. To Winthrop this sort of philosophical position was a sin. The later Williams was closer in spirit to the moderation and reasonableness of Winthrop.

The Puritan image

Many people today still think of the Puritans in extreme terms as drab, narrow-minded, sexually repressed, witch-hunting bigots. This is inaccurate and reflects the arrogance partly of the 1920s which satirised Puritanism as 'the haunting fear that someone, somewhere, might be happy.' Puritan life was not especially drab. Everyday clothes were often gaily-coloured, though formal dress would be dark. Men like Winthrop, from the well-to-do country squirearchy of England, were used to drinking and eating well and enjoying God's gifts, without abusing them by excess. Puritans, with exceptions, were rarely bigots; they loved to talk, to argue and to listen. Winthrop was no democrat, but from his own inner battles he knew the value of talking things out. The charter did not make it necessary but at the outset he allowed broader political participation by classifying all churchmen as 'freemen'. Later he allowed them to elect representatives to an assembly and to create local governments responsive to local needs. The New England 'town meeting', which survives today in some small towns, was an enduring legacy.

The colonists were at a great political advantage from the start because Winthrop schemed with others to bring the company charter with him on board ship, and because by oversight the document did not state where the council was to meet. There was thus no myth of government from far-off London. The common distinction between underwriters and actual settlers was forever blurred in the case of Massachusetts.

Economically an inauspicious beginning was soon followed by success. Poor, stony soils in New England yielded up some corn for subsistence and allowed grazing of sheep and cattle. Luxury pelts could be traded with the Indians. After the first migration tailed off in the 1640s New England survived by developing cash products for export. New Englanders became fishermen, boat-builders, and merchants. They farmed the sea for cod, and they felled the northern forests of the soft white pine for ship's timbers and masts to meet the voracious demands of the Royal Navy and British merchant fleets. Boston, Salem and Gloucester grew up as fishing and coastal supply ports; New England merchants won global recognition. Like Virginia, and like all European colonies, whatever their religion and political natures, New England lived by foreign export trade.

Differentiation and political changes

Meanwhile in the more hospitable South, the first *proprietary* colony was established in 1632. Maryland began as a personal gift by Charles I to George Calvert, Lord Baltimore: a would-be feudal domain in the New World. In theory this Catholic aristocrat was absolute ruler of Maryland. In practice the conditions of frontier life made absolutism unworkable, in the same way as they pressured the Saintly oligarchy of Massachusetts and the tobacco aristocracy of Virginia to give way. The Calverts were forced to allow an elected assembly which took the right to initiate legislation, as did the Virginia Burgesses. This assembly granted a limited religious toleration in 1649. The colony was already mainly Protestant. As in Virginia its chief means of support was tobacco, grown as a cash export crop. Large feudal-type land grants were typical in Maryland, and Catholic gentry came over from England with their families and servants to establish a local elite. Most immigrants however were yeomen farmers; the rents they paid to landholders were nominal, if irritating. Tension was high and resistance to Calvert family rule never ceased.

The various upheavals of 17th century England, the Civil War and Puritan Commonwealth established in 1649, the Restoration of the Stuart monarchy in 1660, and the Glorious Revolution of 1688, all had impact on the colonies, on their politics, and on who settled there. New England expanded in the 1630s and 40s with the establishment of settlements in Connecticut, Rhode Island, the New Haven area, New Hampshire and Maine. Fear of the Indians and the Dutch produced a loose defensive alliance in 1643, the *New England Confederation*. Events in England brought a decline of emigration in the 1640s, while Massachusetts at the same time began to feel more independent. Nathaniel Ward's new code of law, the *Body of Liberties* of 1641, was an independent-minded step, and in 1646 even Winthrop, under criticism, declared that English law was not binding to those who did not live in England. In 1652 Massachusetts ignored Parliament and became an independent Commonwealth.

The new Puritan zeal in England under Cromwell after Charles was beheaded in 1649, caused Massachusetts to re-examine its own faith and adopt a less reasonable stance. Persecutions of dissidents followed. Quakers suffered badly for their individualistic, 'Inner Light' doctrine of personal roads to salvation. In Maryland, the English Civil War had direct repercussions; as a proprietary colony it was closely linked to changes in the power-structure at home. The Protestant majority seized the opportunity to overthrow the Calvert family government by force. The Act of Tolerance of 1649 was repealed in 1654 so that Catholics could be deprived of political rights. There was a local civil war, but the Stuart Restoration brought the Calverts back to power in the 1660s. They were again overthrown by violence led by the Protestant Association in 1689—encouraged by the Whig Revolution in England and abdication of the last of the Stuarts, James II. In contrast, the Virginians did not seem to react so violently to events in England; they did not care who governed there, provided the English at home continued to smoke tobacco.

The Restoration: proprietary colonies

Joint-stock corporations could not make money on colonies in the New World, though in India the East India Company hung on until 1858. After the Stuart Restoration in 1660 most new colonies created in America were of the proprietary sort, like Maryland. Charles II gave large land grants to Stuart sympathisers. In quick succession the Carolinas (1663), New York and New Jersey (1664) and Pennsylvania (1681), were granted. Much later, in 1732, Georgia was settled by James Oglethorpe as a philanthropic venture, a home for debtors and the unemployed.

The English nobles who were given the Carolinas succumbed as had the Calverts to the need to placate colonists with religious toleration, local assemblies and generous 'headrights' (land grants). The area would not have been settled otherwise. Feudalism could not survive in North America. Settlement of New York was delayed until its grantee, Charles II's brother, himself became James II in 1685. The Dutch in that region surrendered and the King gave a section (New Jersey) to a couple of his favourites. William Penn, a Quaker convert, inherited Pennsylvania in 1681 in payment for an old Stuart debt to his father. His colony, in many ways the most rationally planned and settled, openly advertised for religious refugees and dissidents, offered them liberal land policies, representation, and freedom of worship. Many immigrants came: Pennsylvania 'Dutch', German sectarians, Welshmen, Quakers. Rapid economic growth made Philadelphia a cultural center. Pennsylvania was soon a prototype of the future United States: a *pluralistic* society.

New England comes down to earth

During the Civil War and the Puritan dictatorship of Cromwell in England, the New England colonies enjoyed 'cosmic significance'. They were part, and some thought the most advanced part, of a great religious revolution. Once persecuted and despised, they now controlled England and its colonies. Cromwell punished Ireland, invaded Scotland, became Lord Protector of England and turned down the offer of the Crown itself. These triumphant years were short-lived. With the Stuart Restoration New England abruptly lost its sense of being at the very centre of world events. More than this, New England Puritanism began to 'come down to earth' in other ways: it could no longer afford to be so exclusive. This Puritan 'declension' (as it is known) was both erosion and corrosion, internal and external. The *sect* could not keep its original impetus as its first generation of leaders died, the 'Visible Saints' (John Cotton, Thomas Hooker and others). It evolved into the Congregational *Church*.

The Stuarts immediately tried to tighten royal grip on the New Englanders, though they failed. Charles II nullified the Massachusetts Bay charter in 1684; the next year James brought the whole of the area under one form, the *Dominion of New England* ruled by Governor Edmund Andros, without any local representative assemblies. This new arrangement did not outlive the Whig Revolution of 1688 any more than did James's own reign; the colonists themselves threw over the 'Dominion' and went back to things as before.

Things were not exactly the same as before however. Puritan government had never been a theocracy (government by priests); but the Bible was a constant source and guide, and Puritans, though they held to separation of Church and State, found it only natural to weigh the advice of ministers very heavily in affairs of state. Such consultations no longer seemed wise or natural in the later 17th and 18th century. Moreover, not only secularisation but new and rival faiths now threatened: the Baptists of Rhode Island (fruits of Roger Williams' gospel) and the Presbyterians waxed strong. Fewer faces were seen in congregations. The young had to be attracted to the church. So the *Half-Way Covenant* was agreed to in Massachusetts in 1662. The 'exclusiveness' of Puritan church membership had been based on religious experience. To be a full, voting member one had to claim to have had a *conversion*. This was easier for persecuted pioneers than for second-generation offspring. The new rules relaxed the requirement: second-generation Puritans could stay in the church, even baptise their own children; they were not to vote or take the Lord's Supper. The idea was to fill the halls while keeping control of the church in the hands of avowed Saints. But, like most such reforms, the Half-Way Covenant opened the flood-gate. Soon Rev. Solomon Stoddard was preaching full membership for all Godly folk in the Connecticut Valley, and in Boston the Brattle Street church (1699) put this into practice.

A body-blow to Puritan orthodoxy was the witch-hunting at Salem in

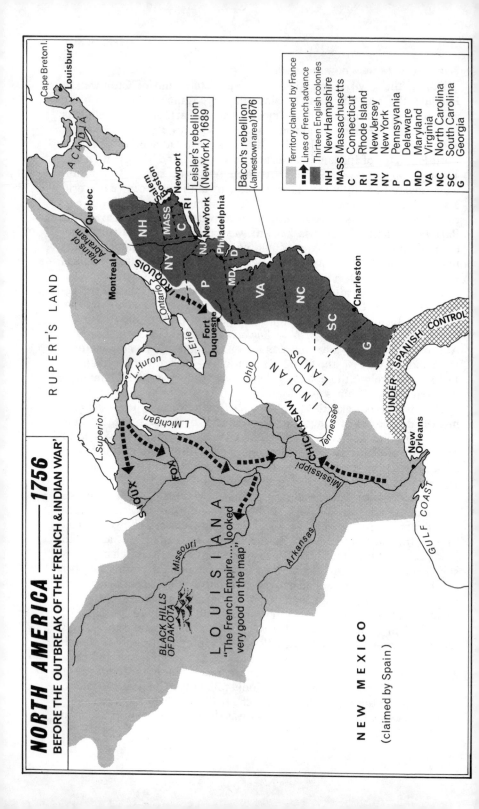

NORTH AMERICA — 1756
BEFORE THE OUTBREAK OF THE 'FRENCH & INDIAN WAR'

Territory claimed by France
Lines of French advance
Thirteen English colonies

NH New Hampshire
MASS Massachusetts
C Connecticut
RI Rhode Island
NJ New Jersey
NY New York
P Pennsylvania
D Delaware
MD Maryland
VA Virginia
NC North Carolina
SC South Carolina
G Georgia

Leisler's rebellion
(NewYork) 1689

Bacon's rebellion
(Jamestown area)1676

Cape Breton I.
Louisburg
ACADIA
Quebec
Plains of Abraham
Montreal
RUPERT'S LAND
L. Superior
L. Michigan
L. Huron
L. Erie
L. Ontario
IROQUOIS
Salem
Boston
Newport
NH
MASS
C
RI
NY
NJ
New York
Philadelphia
P
D
MD
VA
NC
SC
G
Charleston
Fort Duquesne
Ohio
INDIAN LANDS
Tennessee
CHICKASAW
Mississippi
New Orleans
UNDER SPANISH CONTROL
GULF COAST
Arkansas
Missouri
BLACK HILLS OF DAKOTA
SIOUX
FOX
LOUISIANA
"The French Empire.... looked very good on the map"

NEW MEXICO
(claimed by Spain)

1692. In truth there was nothing especially 'Puritan' about it. Mass-suggestion occurs throughout history in isolated episodes, not limited to religion. The tragedy at Salem was that Puritan elders failed to put a stop to it until too late. Several witches were hanged, not burnt, as in Europe. The effect on the church was bad. The humane William Penn, when asked to take action against witches in his own colony, said he could not, because 'there was no law in Pennsylvania against riding on broomsticks.' The contrast with Massachusetts was obvious.

The Americas in about 1700
By about 1700, then, the British had a string of settlements along the Atlantic coast of North America, founded in various ways, but all of them very independent-minded and resistant to royal control. In the tricky relationship among governors, councils and assemblies, and royal prerogatives, the British colonists had already built up a hundred years of political experience. Economically however they were still far behind Spanish America in development. Britain herself still regarded its West Indies islands as far more significant than the struggling, recalcitrant settlements of North America.

Meanwhile the French had barely begun to map out the geographical framework for an empire in North America. This outline for an empire they never did, in fact, manage to fill in. The Spanish had constructed a remarkable *baroque* edifice, but its foundations were already beginning to wash away. In Brazil the Portuguese had scarcely begun to realise the possibilities of the region.

All the colonies in the Americas were heavily dependent on Europe for supplies, for immigrants, for capital and for cultural and psychological sustenance. But various signs had appeared, especially in British America, that this would not always be so. Such signs of 'Americanisation' and the growth of an independent culture would become unmistakable in the next century.

2
Emergence

All the American revolutions for independence shared a common feature, though the revolution of the United States came two or three decades earlier than the Spanish wars of independence. In the 18th century for a variety of reasons the European governments attempted to reform their colonial administrations in the New World. These reforms, intended to strengthen colonial ties, ended up in stimulating independence movements. Meanwhile a growing 'American' self-consciousness was to be seen in many of the colonies in the 18th century. Its emergence is the chief theme of 18th century colonial history in the Western Hemisphere and it produced the independent United States in 1783 and a number of independent central and southern American republics in the early 19th century. In Canada the imperial ties were maintained.

CENTRAL AND SOUTH AMERICA

The civilisation of Spanish America was at its peak in the 18th century. By 1790 Mexico City was a major cultural centre of about 100,000 people and was greater than any city in Europe except London and Paris. In contrast the first US census of 1790 claimed only 42,000 people for Philadelphia, 33,000 for New York and 18,000 for Boston. The cultural life of Spanish American cities was derivative but it contained all the elements found in Spain together with Indian additions, and the Spanish colonies shared in the mainstream of European cultural trends, which was no mean achievement.

The most visible evidence today of that Spanish American civilisation is colonial architecture. Hundreds of churches, monasteries and palaces were built: massive classical and Renaissance structures characterising the 16th century, baroque the 17th century, and more ornate, *Churrigueresque* buildings the 18th. Copying the noted Salamanca architect,

2. Morelia Cathedral, Mexico. ▶

44

Churriguera, colonial sculptors and builders covered their buildings with elaborate fruit, cherubs, twisted pillars and other ornamentation of this Spanish version of the *rococo* style. Examples can be seen in Quito, Taxco and elsewhere. The current styles and influences of mainland Spain were transferred by church architects, sculptors and painters to the New World, sometimes subtly altered by the hands of Indian craftsmen: 11th century and 16th century Italian, 13th century French Gothic, Moslem, *plateresque* (with gorgeous detail, as in Morelia cathedral in Mexico). Colonial painters, like Miguel de Santiago (Ecuador), Juán Herrera (Mexico) and others, followed a great Spanish tradition of the Golden Age—major artists such as El Greco, Zurbarán, Vélasquez. Most colonies had organised schools of art.

Spanish American writers and poets deserve a volume to themselves. Among prose writers the historians and reporters of the conquest stand out and are still read: Diaz's *True History of the Conquest of New Spain* attacked Cortés, Las Casas defended the Indians, and an early mestizo writer, Garcilaso de la Vega reflected the ambiguities of mestizo identity in books idealizing both the Incas (his mother) and the Spanish conquest of Florida (his father). Much poetry was written—an old Spanish habit—some of it influenced by the Spaniard, Luis de Góngora. *Gongorismo* as the style was called, was baroque in poetry: exaggerated, sometimes precious and artificial. More authentic was Ercilla y Zuñiga's epic of the Indian wars in what is now Chile, *La Araucana* (1568), partly written on the battlefield and very sympathetic to the Araucanian Indians. This has been a source for the 'noble savage' ideal and for *Indianism*, both of which are constant themes in South American thought. A leading woman poet of Mexico, Juana Inés de la Cruz, a young prodigy, beautiful and talented at the age of fifteen, created secular and religious verse. She entered a convent at the age of eighteen and was ordered to give up all her books. The great dramatist Juan Ruiz de Alarcón was perhaps the most famous of all colonial writers, though he left Mexico when he was twenty and lived much of the time in Spain.

The patrons of these individuals were Church and State. In its universities, Spain went still further in encouraging learning and the arts. The education of Indians was neglected, except for the work of Franciscans, much of which had lapsed by the end of the 17th century. For upper-class whites, and occasional mestizos, 25 institutions of higher learning were created. Many were not much better than secondary schools, but several became great universities, modelled on the University of Salamanca, one of Europe's top institutions. Outstanding were Mexico and Lima. Among the scholars at Mexico was Sigüenza, mathematician, astronomer, poet, philosopher and historian, a great empiricist who held the Chair of Mathematics for twenty years. Mexico also added schools of medicine, botany and mines in the 18th century.

The flaw in this civilisation was that so much depended on the Church, whose intellectual and moral decline in later years would bring down much with it. The movements of the later 18th century, the Enlightenment, secularism and positivism, made great inroads in Spanish American thought, as they did in Puritan thought in New England and all over Europe. Anticlerical feelings weakened the credibility and prestige of the Church, the only true, continuous link between Indian and Spanish cultures. Exclusion of the Indian masses from cultural opportunities bred problems for the future stability and growth of South American civilisations. But in the later 18th century the Spanish colonial universities seemed to be flourishing.

The burden of race

The Spanish and Portuguese were not especially racist; no more so than any other nations or groups. World history teaches that no one has a monopoly on racism—white, black, brown or yellow. No one is entirely free from it. But the Spanish encountered so many more 'Indians' than did the British in North America: millions of them, with several different cultures and languages. This they had not expected. Checked, they began a long war of attrition against the Indians which continues even today. There were several good reasons why the Spanish and Portuguese might have respected Indian cultures, and African ones too for that matter. They had both been in close cultural contact with superior dark-skinned people of higher culture, the Moors: dark, Moslem conquerors of the Iberian peninsula, fine architects and agriculturists and men of learning. It was the dark Moors who lived in the castles, the lighter Spaniards and Portuguese who labored as their serfs. The Brazilian writer Gilberto Freyre points out that the ideal of beauty for the Portuguese was dark: the brown-skinned woman, or *moura encantada*. To be dark was to be powerful, beautiful, dominant, wealthy, cultured.

Certainly the Anglo-Americans had not experienced such a relationship with darker peoples. But it is hard to prove that the whites of South America, still less of Central America, modified their cruel and forceful policies towards the Indian and Negro because of it. One major difference between race-contact in North and in South America was race-*mixing*. This is partly explained by numbers. The first European emigrants to South America were men; they did not take their women and families with them as the British colonists did. A sizeable class of people of mixed blood emerged. This was noticeable by the 18th century, and in the 19th the mestizos (Indian-European) became a political force. *Mulattoes* (African-European) grew in number as did a great variety of *castas*—other mixtures, including *zambos* (Indian-African) and mulatto-mestizo mixes. With the addition of immigrant streams from Europe and Asia these now make up the distinctive racial complexity of what is superficially called 'Latin' America.

Racial mixing did not remove race-consciousness. A racial pyramid existed in the 18th century as it still does today: the apex is white and the color darkens as one moves down to the broader base at the bottom. *Castas* rank low, and in Brazil today Negroes fare so badly that they are dying out. Indians, by contrast, are increasing in population; they remain separated in the countryside.

By the late 18th century South America was already becoming a continent of white-dominated cities and Indian countryside. Among the socially in-between groups, the mestizos identified with the white ruling class, often abandoning all Indian connections. Even Juárez, a pure Indian who rose to power in Mexico, paid little attention to Indian needs. Mulattoes reacted differently: they led the abolitionist movement and sided with the Negroes. The children of zambos however, were happy to pass into Indian society and out of the less privileged Negro subculture. The racial complexities of South and Central America stand out in contrast to the two major cultures north of the Rio Grande, where comparatively little race-mixing has so far taken place.

The traffic in African slaves

When did the first Africans arrive in the Americas? Probably with Columbus in 1492. Long before that date the Portuguese had begun trading Africans in Europe (since at least 1441), and Portugal itself had many Negroes in its population. In 1510 the Casa de Contratación authorised slaveshipments to Española, later to Cuba and throughout the Caribbean. Negro slaves replaced the diminishing Indians, as Las Casas had suggested. From the 1530s the Portuguese began using African slaves in Brazil. The Spanish did not deal with the African end of this traffic: they left it to the English, Portuguese, French, Dutch and Danes. Of these the English carried the bulk, but also led the movement to abolish the trade altogether. With the persuasion of British pressure and of the Royal Navy, the slave-trade was abolished in the early 19th century, though France, despite its Revolution, hung on until 1818. Over the centuries from 1441 down to the abolition of the trade and then of slavery itself (USA, 1863; Brazil, 1888), millions of Africans were forcibly shipped and sold, and millions more were born into slavery.

Was slavery the product of racism? Slavery had existed in Europe since Roman times—the enslavement of captives was a normal procedure for which elaborate slave codes existed. Negro slavery followed on Jewish slavery, slavery of Moors, and of Spaniards, in the Iberian tradition. Yet captives were not considered *racially* inferior and doomed to slavery by blood. White slavery had died out in Europe, while the Negro slaves in the Spanish colonies inherited the ancient slave practices: slaves had a legal personality and certain rights; they could marry, testify in court, buy their freedom, train for the priesthood. They were not mere 'chattel slaves'— private property—as they became in North America and in the British West Indies, where no such ancient traditions existed. So it is said that

3. *Slaves cutting sugar cane in the West Indies.*
From Ten Views in the Island of Antigua *by William Clarke (London, 1823).*

the Iberians were cruel to the *slaves*, the English were cruel to the *Negroes*. Negro slaves in North America had fewer rights, though the available evidence does not reveal that Portuguese or Spaniards were less cruel; perhaps the opposite. *Free* Negroes were more readily accepted in South America, albeit at the bottom of the social scale. As for slavery, the British had to pressure the newly-independent nations of South America to abolish the trade and 'Latin' nations were the last to abolish the institution, Cuba not until 1890.

TO BE SOLD & LET

BY PUBLIC AUCTION,

On *MONDAY the* 18th *of MAY,* 1829,

UNDER THE TREES.

FOR SALE,

THE THREE FOLLOWING

SLAVES,

VIZ.

HANNIBAL, about 30 Years old, an excellent House Servant, of Good Character.
WILLIAM, about 35 Years old, a Labourer.
NANCY, an excellent House Servant and Nurse.

The MEN belonging to "LEECH'S" Estate, and the WOMAN to Mrs. D. SMIT

TO BE LET,

On the usual conditions of the Hirer finding them in Food, Clothing and Medical

THE FOLLOWING

MALE and FEMALE

SLAVES,

OF GOOD CHARACTERS,

ROBERT BAGLEY, about 20 Years old, a good House Servant.
WILLIAM BAGLEY, about 18 Years old, a Labourer.
JOHN ARMS, about 18 Years old.
JACK ANTONIA, about 40 Years old, a Labourer.
PHILIP, an Excellent Fisherman.
HARRY, about 27 Years old, a good House Servant.
LUCY, a Young Woman of good Character, used to House Work and the Nursery.
ELIZA, an Excellent Washerwoman.
CLARA, an Excellent Washerwoman.
FANNY, about 14 Years old, House Servant.
SARAH, about 14 Years old, House Servant.

Also for Sale, at Eleven o'Clock,

Fine Rice, Gram, Paddy, Books, Muslins, Needles, Pins, Ribbons, &c. &c.

AT ONE O'CLOCK, THAT CELEBRATED ENGLISH HORSE

BLUCHER,

4. An auction bill for the sale of slaves, 1829; three are to be sold outright to the highest bidder and eleven more are 'to be let', as if they were animals.

50

Whether white North Americans were more 'racist' or not towards the Negroes and Indians, one fact stands out. Negroes assimilated far more readily to the prevailing dominant culture, Latin or Anglo, than did the Indians. Indian resistance to assimilation almost amounted to what has been called 'collective suicide'. Negroes in the North became 'Americans' and rapidly lost their African heritage; Negroes in the South became 'Latin', though, as in Brazil, they managed to maintain more of their religious and musical traditions because newer additions were being made to their numbers from West Africa until later in the 19th century. The abolition of the slave-trade was more efficient in the United States, and consequently the growth of the Negro population was only due to natural increase: slaves born in captivity who had never known any culture but the United States.

While historians continue to wrestle with the concept of 'racism', let us remember that slavery was a *labour-system*. It was born of the classic problem of the frontier and colony—labour shortage and land availability. This was as true in the southern cotton states of the United States as it was in the sugar plantations of the Caribbean and Brazil. The system would not have arisen but for the crucial lack of labour and the elimination of the large labour supply of Indians in the Caribbean by disease and violence. Viewed continentally, what happened was that Europe robbed Africa of its people to exploit and develop the Americas.

Peninsulares and creoles came to fear the possibilities of a mulatto-led Negro slave revolt, or a mestizo-led Indian uprising. The latter was unlikely; the former did happen in Brazil. In addition the white groups distrusted each other and creole resentments helped to stimulate the growth of an 'American' consciousness, a vision of ultimate separation from Europe. Changes took place in Spain and Portugal in the 18th century which led to reforms of the colonial system. The trend was to increase Iberian control and thus diminish rather than expand the role of creoles and mestizos in colonial affairs. By tightening its grip the Spanish monarchy eventually lost its hold altogether. The same was true of Britain after 1763, though there the tension between colonial-born and English-born was less evident.

Growing colonial separatism

The last of the Hapsburg rulers of Spain, Charles II, died in 1700. Thirteen years of crises followed while the powers of Europe struggled over who should control the Spanish Empire. Exhausted, they agreed by the treaty of Utrecht of 1713 to allow Louis XIV's grandson, Philip, to remain on the Spanish throne as Philip V, but stripped Spain of her European dependencies and forced her to grant trading rights in Spanish America to English and other merchants. After 1713, Spanish policy was to recover from the humiliation of Utrecht. The nation was to be truly unified, aliens eliminated from colonial trade, colonial defences and administration tightened up and growth encouraged by Colbert-type reforms. Joint-stock trading companies were finally allowed to develop the colonial economy. None of this came about to any degree until 1759, when Spain was taken over by an 'Enlightened Despot', Charles III, aided by an able minister, Esquilache.

A new spirit of economic nationalism, inspired by the ideas of earlier Spanish theorists, *proyectistas*, like José Campillo, now freshened colonial policy. The closed system of privilege operated by the merchant oligopoly families of Cádiz and the colonial cities was to be broken up. A new state bureaucracy, owing allegiance to the Crown and modelled on the French bureaucracy of Louis XIV, was sent out to Spanish America: the *intendentes*, Crown agents with wide administrative and judicial powers. The empire was re-divided into provinces each ruled by an intendente. This cut into the old, decaying local government system, upset the cabildos, and increased jealousy between creoles and peninsulares. The colonial-born bitterly resented the power of these brash newcomers with their French ideas. The cabildos began to demand more real authority.

To encourage trade by Spaniards rather than by aliens, the government relaxed the trade restrictions of earlier decades, opened up more ports and permitted colonies to trade with each other. By 1790 trade was possible from *any* port in Spain to any port in the colonies. Taxes were cut to 6% ad valorem duties. The convoyed fleet system was finally abandoned in 1778. British seizure of the Spanish stronghold at Havana, and also Manila, in 1762, and their capture of Jamaica earlier, helped to shock Spain into these changes. Even so the reforms did too little and came too late, despite the prosperity they helped to produce in the late 18th century. Prosperity, reforms, increased tensions and rising expectations only served to prepare the way for the independence movements of the early 1800s. The American Revolution followed by the French Revolution, provided the final stimulus to discontented creoles and mestizos in South America.

NORTH AMERICA IN THE 18TH CENTURY

Meanwhile the Whig Revolution of 1688 in England, a crucial step in the evolution of constitutional monarchy and government by consent, had great impact in the British colonies. The ideas of John Locke, of 'natural rights', of individualism, of the rule of Reason and Science, all found ready reception in North America. In fact the colonies were more Whiggish in political practice than were the English. New immigration in the 18th century of Germans, Welsh, Scotch-Irish, French Huguenots and others together with a high native birth-rate, boosted population and underpinned growing colonial prosperity. Sir Robert Walpole's colonial policy of 'salutary neglect' or 'letting sleeping dogs lie', as he put it, encouraged the growth of colonial separatism and an 'American' self-consciousness. As usual, the English government thought most of the West Indies and gave its attention to its global struggle with France.

In North America during the 18th century population began to spread west of the fall-line of the Appalachians. As settlers crossed the Appalachians the horizons of colonial Americans were stretched. Britain was insensitive to this westward movement except insofar as it brought confrontations with Indians and the French in the Mississippi valley. Who was to control this vast new frontier, settlers from Canada, or those from the thirteen colonies? This was a major issue in the coming struggle between the colonists and England. Meanwhile, farther east, new towns sprang up and old towns expanded. Boston, Salem and Newport became important cities; in the South, Charleston; and dominating colonial trade and life, Philadelphia and New York. Town influences spread throughout the colonies by way of the growing newspaper press, trade and the professions: law in particular. Cultural and professional societies, colleges, and private organisations all encouraged an independent consciousness, a spirit of confidence and 'American' self-reliance.

Like the Spanish, the English had sought to exclude foreign nations from trade with their American colonies and to make the colonies serve the nation as sources of raw materials and markets for English manufactured goods. To this end the Acts of Trade, or *Navigation Acts* of 1651, 1660, 1663, and 1696 had been passed, though they were less rigidly enforced than was the Spanish monopoly system. The acts restricted trade to and from England to goods carried in English ships; listed 'enumerated articles' that could not be exported from the colonies except to other British colonies or to Britain herself; and established colonial customs houses and admiralty courts. Fish, grain and rum were left free of these restrictions. Gradually, the former private-enterprise freedom under which the colonies were founded receded as the state began to impose some sort of structure on the empire. The *Board of Trade* was created in 1696 to exercise over-all advisory authority, almost two centuries after Spain had established its *Casa de Contratación* (1503). A colonial constitution began to emerge.

Political Structure of British America

By the mid-18th century most of the American settlements were Crown colonies, though throughout the colonial period Pennsylvania stayed in the proprietary form. Connecticut and Rhode Island, too, remained company charter colonies down to the Revolution, able to elect their own governors. Elected or not, the power of 18th century colonial governors was restricted in practice though broad in theory. Their position was ambiguous: they represented and symbolised the King's authority on the one hand, and colonial needs and interests on the other. As chief executive, the governor had to be responsive to colonial desires and even defend them in London. Yet he embodied within his office all the royal prerogatives, and more, as Commander-in-Chief, head of the judiciary and legislature and chief executive. There was no 'separation of powers' in this system.

In practical terms however, Whitehall was thousands of tossing sea-miles away, the colonial assemblies had the power to vote the governor's salary and the tax funds to make his administration possible. So the colonists usually won in any three-cornered battle. They would cry 'no taxation without representation!' and would demand the 'rights of Englishmen'. Some governors were shrewd enough to manipulate colonial interest-groups. They could pack the Council with powerful local men, and intimidate the elected assembly through use of patronage. This method became traditionally 'American'. Walpole's system in England in the early 18th century was of course built on patronage. Intricate disputes among assemblies, councils, governors and the London government prepared the colonists for the Revolution and for nation-building thereafter, by training them in essential political techniques and organisational skills.

Styles of economic life

Training in essential economic skills also came early to the American colonists. They had to make a living within the imperial framework now laid down by Britain. To get around the rules of mercantilism they developed ingenious channels of trade. By the 18th century a roughly three-fold differentiation was to be seen among the thirteen colonies: Northeast, Middle Atlantic and South, each group having different economic problems and serving different functions within the system. New England and New York owed everything to the sea. New England in particular provided cod, lumber and naval stores to Britain, and became a major shipbuilding centre—many of the vessels used against the colonists in the War of Independence were built in New England. The colonies were great shippers of other peoples' goods and had opened up trade with the Orient. They shared in the infamous 'triangular trade' between the West Indies, the North American colonies, and West Africa. Specie, gold and molasses were imported from the West Indies to the colonies, the molasses were processed into rum, and the rum (and metal trinkets) were then sold for slaves on the African coast. The Middle Passage was the dreadful run from Africa to the Caribbean, slaves being packed into eighteen inches of space each, with no head-room, chained together. Many died of disease, fear and shock; some committed suicide.

The Middle Atlantic colonies filled an important American role as grain-producers. These 'bread colonies' helped to meet the growing urban demand of centres like Philadelphia, New York and Baltimore and shipped wheat and other cereals to neighbouring colonies. They also traded grains, flour, fish and meat, cloth and lumber with the West Indies settlements, receiving in return sugar *bills of exchange*, paper bills previously earned by West Indies sugar planters from London and Bristol creditors for exports of sugar to England. Northern and Middle colony traders used these bills to pay for their own import of manufactured and luxury goods from England. This was the mechanism of trade.

The Middle colonies dealt directly with southern Europe also, as did New England, selling its fish. American brigantines traded goods in the Mediterranean, received fruits, wines, spices and salt there, and then sold these in England before returning home with English tools, supplies, books and other products. Clearly, American business was already international and very experienced before the Revolution.

The colonies of the South enjoyed an unusual situation: their exports to England exceeded their imports. While the Middle colonies tended to produce goods in competition with England and therefore ended up trading mainly in the Caribbean and southern Europe, the southern colonies did not compete at all; they provided England with goods she could not easily obtain elsewhere: rice, indigo, tobacco. The South was the richest section of the colonies and of the nation for 200 years or so, with fertile soils and an enviable trading position within the Empire.

The most valuable cash crop was tobacco, grown in Virginia, parts of Maryland and later in North Carolina. Virginia leaf had an absolute advantage over other tobaccos in quality and price. It was cheap to transport, having a high cash value in relation to its bulk. A one-crop 'Tobacco Kingdom' grew up, reaching a peak of output and prosperity just before the outbreak of the Revolution. In South Carolina a high-ground crop, indigo, and a low-ground crop, rice, complemented each other as valuable cash exports. All three of these staples came to depend on African slave-labor, so that by 1763 about half the population of Virginia and perhaps two-thirds of South Carolina were Negro.

American society in the 18th century

Anglo-American society reflected these economic underpinnings. For instance a sizeable class of colonial merchants grew up, independent-minded and forceful, jealous of their rights. They played a large role in the Revolution and customs officers sent out from England were a major irritant to these powerful men. John Hancock was one example. The early fluidity of classlines in the English settlements was now diminishing. Class-lines hardened in later colonial America, as second and third generations began to inherit wealth and groups of merchant, tobacco and planter gentry emerged. The Puritan township system in New England began to crumble, perhaps affected by population pressure within its confines. Sectional tensions produced outbreaks of violence—'Tidewater' coastal gentry v. back country farmers; conflicting interest-groups. These tensions induced by social and economic changes were to be seen in Bacon's Rebellion in Virginia as early as 1676, and Leisler's Revolt in New York in 1689.

There were feuds among colonies and among sections. The colonists fought over irksome taxes and road-building, over boundary disputes and land problems, over inadequate defences on the frontier against the Indians and French. Creditors fought debtors. Backwoods farmers rose over falling crop prices, as in Bacon's Rebellion. Often the luckless Indian became the scapegoat. In Pennsylvania the 'Paxton Boys', backwoodsmen scared of Indian raids, took up arms, massacred a peaceful village of Christian Indians and marched on Philadelphia threatening to kill every Indian they met (1763).

Politically the eastern sections often kept the frontier areas badly under-represented in the colonial assemblies. An East-West civil war broke out in North Carolina in 1771, when the backwoodsmen (called 'Regulators') who complained of political manipulation, were put down by militia and their leaders hanged. Little wonder that in London some men regarded the American colonists as violent, factious, dangerous and ungovernable people; or that the Founding Fathers who wrote the Constitution of 1787 spent so much time considering the problems of anarchy and faction.

The struggle for Canada

The colonists and London were agreed upon one question: that England must win the struggle with the French for control of Canada. For England the North American struggle was but a local part of a global rivalry that began in the late 17th century and did not end until 1815. This rivalry found expression in a complex series of European wars: King William's War, 1689–97 (called the War of the League of Augsburg in Europe); Queen Anne's War, 1702–13 (War of the Spanish Succession); King George's War, 1744–48 (War of the Austrian Succession), and the French and Indian War, 1756–63 (Seven Years' War). All these wars produced local wars in North America, the chief issue there being twofold, the fight over control of the fur trade and the struggle to take over the Ohio Valley. Mainly Protestant English-Americans were pitted against Catholic Frenchmen, and each side feared being encircled by the other.

From Canada the French had explored the Mississippi valley down to New Orleans, established in 1718. The explorer La Salle claimed the whole of that valley area for France, and called it 'Louisiana' after Louis XIV (1682)—a region much larger than the present state. So France claimed an immense empire in North America sweeping round from the Gulf Coast northwards and eastwards to the Gaspé Peninsula in Canada, and hemming in the Thirteen Colonies on the Atlantic behind the Appalachians. As Governor Thomas Dongan of New York said, on hearing the French claim for his colony because it was watered by rivers that rose in the Canadian lakes region, 'He might as well pretend to all the countries that drink claret and brandy.'

The French empire was hollow: a mere geographical framework; a chain of scattered forts and claims held together by shaky Indian treaties. Its total population was about 12,000 French traders and trappers. It looked very good *on the map*, and looked better still as the 18th century wore on and French traders pushed its outer edges to Spanish territory in the Southwest (New Mexico), and to the Black Hills of S. Dakota in the Northwest (Pierre Vérendrye, 1743). Further exploration was prevented only by the Rocky Mountains. This was an 'empire' of canoe-trails and *coureurs de bois*, decades away from settlement or genuine economic development.

The four major wars down to 1763 saw advances and setbacks for both sides. The New Englanders attacked 'Acadia' (Nova Scotia) and threatened Quebec; the French attacked the frontier regions of New York and New England, with Indian help. There were massacres of settlements, military recoveries and guerilla ambushes. In all this Indians suffered the most. Caught between the two rivals they were forced to take one side or the other, alternately debauched by alcohol and gifts or annihilated. Disease and warfare wiped out entire tribes, now lost forever. The treaty of Utrecht that ended Queen Anne's War in 1713 did bring about some real territorial changes. Hudson's Bay territory went to England, as did all Newfoundland and the bulk of Nova Scotia. Now the French had a right to feel 'encircled', at least in their northern possessions. The English claimed sovereignty over the remarkable Indian political grouping, the *Iroquois Confederacy*, a powerful alliance of five, later six, nations mainly in the upper New York region, whose authority spread to the Great Lakes and even down to Tennessee. They numbered only about 15,000 in all, yet played a big part in the last of the Anglo-French colonial wars by keeping the French out of the Mohawk valley. The Iroquois people liked the English, and later most of them supported England and the Loyalists against the colonies in the American Revolution.

After the losses of 1713 the French fortified New France more heavily. They tried to strengthen their grip over Indian lands and fought bloody wars against the Fox Indians (Wisconsin) and the Chickasaws (Louisiana-Tennessee). Loss of their most spectacular fortress, Louisbourg on Cape Breton Island, to the New England troops in 1745, caused them to redouble their efforts. However in the French and Indian War after early victories the French were badly defeated. They lost Fort Duquesne (Pittsburgh); then control of the St Lawrence went to the enemy; and finally, in one of the famous battles of military history, General Wolfe was victorious outside Quebec in 1759. The Royal Navy played its part and three English and colonial armies converged on Montreal in 1760. The French empire in North America was over.

North America becomes British

Large parts of North America were still Spanish in 1763, and the Russians were exploring the Pacific coast. The explorer Captain Vitus

S. WESTON

J.L. SPARP sc.

Bering discovered Alaska and the Bering Strait (1728–41), and Russian fur traders settled in the Aleutians and Alaska. Sitka, founded by Alexander Baranov, was capital of Russian Alaska until the US bought the region from Russia in 1867. British North America was now complete, with the addition of New France. Its territorial extent was much less than that of the later independent USA, which would add the purchase of the vast Louisiana Territory and the large acquisitions from Mexico in the 19th century. After 150 years of struggle and adventure New France had been defeated by superior sea power, by overwhelming economic and population odds (about 3,000,000 British colonials faced about 65,000 French settlers), by inability to attract enough immigrants, and by weaknesses at home. Now the many problems which had been the concern of the French were dropped on the lap of English administrators. Most French *Canadiens* stayed in Canada and took their chances with the new British government. Some of the basic problems remain in Canada today.

'British North America' was short-lived. It survived in this form only two decades. Once the French menace was removed, the English-Americans became even more restive and independent-minded, while the London government became more determined to impose a genuine imperial order in North America. The confrontation of these two irreconcilable attitudes produced the American Revolution.

◀ 5. *Old houses at Point Lévis, Quebec.*

59

3
Independence: the creation of new societies, 1776–1830

A great empire and little minds
go ill together.

(Edmund Burke)

What is usually called the 'American Revolution' was in truth the first of a series of revolutions which created the modern political world and which embodied the ideologies of modern times. Followed by the French Revolution of 1789 and the South American Revolutions of the early 1800s, and accompanied in time by that very different Industrial Revolution, the American Revolution opened up a period of about 50 years in which the world passed through a transformation.

REVOLUTION IN NORTH AMERICA

Colonial relationships are inherently unstable, but some imperial connections have held for centuries. Common interests, or external dangers, or both, will hold together an empire despite the inevitable frictions between colony and mother country. The British Empire in North America fell apart precisely when the external danger, France, was removed, and the community of interests seemed to dissolve.

The British take-over of French Canada after 1763 seemed to clear the way for the Thirteen Colonies to expand westwards without hindrance. But the British government in Whitehall did not see it that way. The assimilation of Canada implied from the London viewpoint an entirely new policy towards North America as a whole, a policy that in some ways seemed to fence in the Thirteen Colonies as much as the French had hoped to do. A *Proclamation of 1763* established provincial governments for former French and Spanish territories (Quebec, East and West Florida), prohibited white settlers west of the Alleghenies and placed Indian affairs under direct royal control. This insensitive and blundering step marked the beginning of a series of moves destined to make it clear to the Thirteen Colonies that the London government intended to sacrifice their interests whenever Canada or the West Indies or the East Indies were involved. It was physically impossible to stop settlers from moving west of the mountains; they had already begun to do so.

From the 'Ministerial' or British point of view the war had been expensive. It had doubled the national debt. Defending the colonies against Indians and French cost money, but the Americans hated taxes and were slow even to provide troops and supplies in their own interest. Some colonists traded with the enemy. A tougher line was needed.

From 1763 to 1776 a series of confrontations heightened the tension between colonists and policy-makers in London. First, the British minister George Grenville stationed permanent military forces in the colonies, ostensibly to subdue Indians after Pontiac's Conspiracy of 1763. To pay the bill for these troops he raised duties, put more products on the customs list and tried to enforce collection which had been very lax. Grenville cracked down on smuggling which cost the Treasury enormous sums each year in revenue losses.

Grenville was more guilty of poor judgement than of malice towards the colonists, but his molasses duties hit the triangular trade and definitely favoured the interests of the West Indies over New England within the colonial structure. The notorious Stamp Act of 1765 hit everybody, especially the most articulate and educated Americans. It placed taxes on newspapers, legal documents, pamphlets and licences. For revenue purposes this was a very poor choice of tax. Passed over solid colonial opposition, the act seemed to be an innovation—a new threat. The American colonists responded with a counter-move of their own: they denied the right of any Parliament, sitting in London, to raise revenues in the colonies without representation. The old political argument often used against colonial governors was now extended against Parliament itself.

Violence and the Stamp Act Congress

Mob action broke out in the colonies. Stamp officials and their buildings were attacked; merchants boycotted English imports; the 'Sons of Liberty' (secret radical groups led by men like Paul Revere and Sam Adams) roughed up Crown officials and burnt the Governor's mansion in Boston. Even the colonial elite became involved, though often at odds with the more inflammatory backcountry politicians, as in the Virginia House of Burgesses.

The first united action of the separate colonies against the new economic policy came when Massachusetts organised the Stamp Act Congress of 1765. It met in New York, 27 delegates from nine colonies drawing up a declaration of rights and grievances. This action, together with the decline of British trade and complaints from London merchants, brought in a new minister, Rockingham, and a placatory policy. The Stamp Act was repealed. The Americans had learned that organisation and agitation pays off. Parliament still bristled at the impudence of the colonies however and passed a *Declaratory Act*, to tell them that its right to legislate on all colonial affairs remained unimpaired by the concession.

Parliament tries again

The new Chancellor of the Exchequer, 1766–67, was Charles Townshend, who as early as 1754 when a junior minister had first proposed sweeping 'reforms' meant to make the colonies pay, along the lines later attempted by Grenville. His aim now was to free colonial governors and bureaucrats from the colonial purse-strings by paying them directly from London out of funds collected in the colonies from taxation. This drastic change of pattern would abruptly overturn years of precedent and sharply reduce the degree of self-government in the colonies. Colonial leaders were enraged. Men like the Adams, Patrick Henry and James Otis cried 'no taxation without representation' and demanded for the colonies the same rights won by Englishmen in 1688. Violence broke out again and a war of pamphleteering and propaganda followed.

The British reacted badly to this opposition. A new American department of state was created under the unsympathetic Lord Hillsborough and a Boston Board of Customs Commissioners were sent out, together with troop reinforcements. The Commissioners were despised. Attitudes polarised and various usually conflicting interest-groups in the colonies coalesced against the ministry. The widely-distributed Massachusetts Circular Letter of 1768 took up John Dickinson's idea ('Letters from a Pennsylvania Farmer') that taxes for revenue should be separated from taxes for normal regulation of trade, and should be opposed. Lord Hillsborough foolishly declared the circular to be seditious and ordered all colonial assemblies to ban it or to suffer dissolution. They all promptly supported it in open defiance.

First blood: the Boston 'Massacre', 1770

The bloodshed at Boston on 5 March 1770 arose directly out of these tensions and popular hatred of the British troops. A black (or partly-Negro, partly-Indian) seaman, 47-year old Crispus Attucks, led the crowd, crying: 'The way to get rid of these soldiers is to attack the main guard!' He knew what he was doing and paid the price; he is claimed as the first to die in the American Revolution. Perhaps Attucks had hopes that independence from England might bring abolition of Negro slavery. It should have, in view of the rhetoric of the radicals. At least one white leader, James Otis, demanded abolition as one of the rights of the colonists in 1764, and Boston Negroes themselves petitioned the Massachusetts assembly for manumission as a 'natural right'. Perhaps Attucks had no such hopes; as it turned out, he might have been better off under English rule, since they led the anti-slavery movement a few years later. Four men died with Attucks—something less than a 'massacre'. But the radicals made much of it, especially one master of agitation, Sam Adams.

During the next three years the radicals had to fight the apathy produced by prosperity and by the replacement of Townshend with the more pragmatic Lord North. All duties were removed except tea. What could they do to keep the pot boiling? Sam Adams, working from the Boston Town Meeting which he dominated, established 'committees of correspondence' in each town. The planter radicals of Virginia picked up the idea. These committees became the basic machinery of revolution, waiting to seize the initiative. The British could be relied upon to provide another occasion, since colonial policy was less the product of rational study than of inner Parliamentary manoeuvres on issues largely irrelevant to American affairs.

Lord North opened up a new round of confrontations in May 1773 with the Tea Act. Passed in unthinking innocence to help out the British East India Company the act made it clear once more that American interests came last in the hierarchy of demands from Britain's colonies. Tea would cost the American consumer less now that the Company could export it directly from India; but American traders and middlemen, to say nothing of smugglers, would be cut out of the trade. The merchant class in the colonies were up in arms. Tea shipments to Boston, Charleston and other ports were blocked by mobs. In the Boston Tea Party of December, 1773 men dressed as Mohawk Indians dumped tons of tea into the harbour. The British immediately closed the port of Boston, reduced civil liberties and restricted the role of the assembly. Said George III: 'The die is cast. The colonists must either triumph or submit.'

Canada and the Quebec Act, 1774

Meanwhile the government moved to implement its Canada policy beyond the measures of 1763. Early hopes simply to 'Anglicize' the Quebec French Catholics came to nothing after 1763, and successive English governors sympathised with French demands to the annoyance of the tiny but growing band of English merchants who now controlled Quebec's economy. Lord North took a reasonable attitude towards the French and refused to impose English court procedures (trial by jury) upon them. In 1774 the Quebec Act—the great charter of French *Canadien* civil rights—admitted Catholics to office (not permitted in England until 1829), recognised the Church's tithes, maintained the land rights of the *seigneurs*, and kept French law in civil matters, English in criminal. The Governor's Council had French-speaking members. Alarmed by growing dissent in the Thirteen Colonies, the government hoped to win over French Canada by generosity.

The establishment of the Catholic Church bothered New Englanders. The worst fear was that the Quebec colony was now to include the whole territory between the Ohio and the upper Mississippi. The northern

6. *'The First Blow for Liberty'—the Battle of Lexington, Mass.,
19 April 1775. (F. Darley).*

English colonies were formally cut off from their western outlets. Again
the Americans had been sacrificed for some other interest-group in the
Empire. The Quebec Act produced the first Anglo-American war, before
the War of Independence really got under way: colonial forces (helped by
some *Canadiens*) besieged Quebec in 1775, but were forced to retreat and
leave Canada in the Spring of 1776.

Delegates from all the colonies except Georgia met extralegally in the
Philadelphia Congress of September 1774. A radical *coup* and take-over
produced a tough anti-British set of resolutions, the creation of revolutionary committees in the colonies and the training of troops. Fighting
broke out on 19 April 1775 at Lexington, Massachusetts, when a party of
troops was sent out to arrest the merchant John Hancock and Sam

Adams, and was routed. Gage was surrounded in Boston by colonial forces and throughout the colonies royal governors and councils crumbled.

The first federal government, the Second Continental Congress, of May, 1775, created the army of the 'United Colonies' under George Washington. General Gage escaped from Boston with heavy losses (battle of Bunker's Hill) and Congress petitioned George III but he ignored them. The last links of loyalty to the Crown evaporated for many Americans.

The Declaration of Independence

Various colonies began writing new state constitutions for themselves (like the South Americans, they seemed to be forming separate nations) in the spring of 1776. On 4 July 1776 the Declaration of Independence brought the colonists to the point of no return and declared, quite unfairly, that George III was a classic tyrant and the English, villains. From now on it was win the war or die as traitors. ['We must indeed all hang together, or, most assuredly, we shall all hang separately.' *Benjamin Franklin to John Hancock*, 4 July 1776]. There was no time for subtleties of interpretation. The Declaration, a classic charter of freedom and human rights written in beautiful style, was the embodiment of existing English ideas about natural rights and government by the consent of the governed. Its words were deeply influential in the French Revolution a few years later and stood as a model for the South American revolutions.

The war ebbed and flowed, witnessed various atrocities and reprisals and was ultimately decided by sea-power and the aid of the French. In the west several settlements were burnt and Indians allied with Loyalists to attack the frontier. Such guerilla activities went on throughout the war down to 1782, when the colonists finally defeated the Shawnee in Ohio. American and French land forces converged on Yorktown in August 1781, a French fleet controlled Chesapeake Bay, and Lord Cornwallis finally surrendered in October 1781. The *Peace of Paris* of 1783 was a complex negotiation but skilful American diplomats cut out the French and signed separately. London recognised the independence of the United States with the Mississippi as its western boundary—overturning the Quebec Act and robbing future Canada of what was to become the rich American Midwest. Cutting Canada off from the fertile Ohio valley lands forced that nation to develop the territories north of the Great Lakes, thus shaping future Canadian history.

John Adams estimated that at least one-third of the American colonists did not favour the war with England. Many settlers were simply too busy with their day-to-day battles against the environment to care. After the war 100,000 colonists emigrated to Britain, the West Indies and Canada. About 40,000 of these 'Loyalists' helped to make Canada a bi-cultural nation, strengthened Canadian suspicions of the new nation further south, and buttressed a growing Canadian nationalism. The result of this

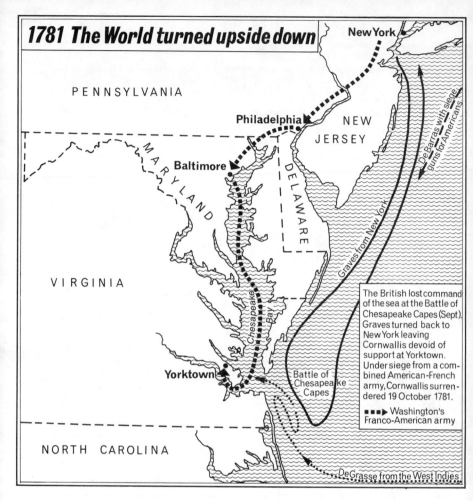

1781 The World turned upside down

PENNSYLVANIA

New York

Philadelphia

NEW JERSEY

Baltimore

MARYLAND

DELAWARE

VIRGINIA

Chesapeake Bay

De Barras with siege guns for Americans

Graves from New York

Yorktown

Battle of Chesapeake Capes

NORTH CAROLINA

De Grasse from the West Indies

The British lost command of the sea at the Battle of Chesapeake Capes (Sept). Graves turned back to New York leaving Cornwallis devoid of support at Yorktown. Under siege from a combined American-French army, Cornwallis surrendered 19 October 1781.

■■■▶ Washington's Franco-American army

outmigration was the Canada Act of 1791, which divided the colony into Upper (English) and Lower (French) Canada, with separate assemblies and styles of government and law.

The American Revolution reviewed

The American colonies were part of the British Empire for so long (as long almost as the US has since been an independent nation) that it is not easy to estimate what the colonists gained or lost through the imperial connection. The rules imposed on colonists by British mercantilism were less rigid and restrictive than those imposed by Spain and they were not adhered to until after 1763. It was economically advantageous for the young settlements to be part of a large trading empire in which they enjoyed a protected market for their products with no outside rivals allowed. However this advantage was felt more strongly in New England and the southern colonies than in the middle Atlantic settlements, whose economies were not complementary to England's but competitive with it in products. The idea of standing alone outside the Empire was not seriously considered before 1763. After that year with the French now gone from the scene the question soon arose: would the colonies be better off free of the London Parliament? One can see why the 19th century US historian Francis Parkman claimed: 'With the fall of Quebec began the history of the United States', though this exaggerates the situation. There is ample evidence to suggest that the Americans would have broken away from Britain in any case sooner or later.

In purely economic terms no definite answer can be offered as to whether the Americans were better or worse off under the British. Virginia lost on the tobacco crop through the colonial system because she was allowed to sell tobacco only through British ports, a routing which raised the world price. In contrast, colonial indigo and rice planters were paid bounties by the British government which also guaranteed the sale of the crops. They were better off under the Empire. Colonial shipping declined after 1783: no longer a part of the protected British global market, American merchantmen now faced the restrictions of the Navigation Acts of *other* nations as well as of Britain, and shipbuilders lost a major customer, the Royal Navy.

On the other hand the British prohibition on manufacturing in the colonies, though irksome, had cost the colonists little since they would not at this stage have been manufacturing in quantity. Their imports however did have to come through British ports and probably cost more than was necessary. Above all, colonial merchants hated the taxes on their trade with the West Indies. The arrival of independence made the situation even worse: they were now legally excluded altogether from such trade. The burdens of the colonial system and of British mercantilism have been exaggerated.

Americans resorted to violence mainly for political and intellectual reasons. Cultural motives too were significant—the growing self-awareness, the sense of being different, of being 'American'. The polarisation of hostilities was accelerated by the rich pamphlet literature of the age which built up a fear among the colonists of a British 'conspiracy' to take away all the political rights the Americans had accumulated over almost 150 years. Pamphleteers asserted there was a sinister plot in England, worked out by the king, Commons, Lords, ministers and bishops to destroy American liberties and to 'enslave' the colonists. The core of this evil plot was allegedly the group of sycophantic men surrounding George III, ministers and court favourites, a corrupted cabinet of self-seeking cabalists. The missionary activities of the Anglican *Society for the Propagation of the Gospel in Foreign Parts* (begun in Maryland in 1701 by Thomas Bray, a commissary of the Bishop of London) were regarded with great suspicion and hostility. The English, it was said, hoped to impose an entire episcopate, a structure of bishops, on America. Moreover colonial judges had never been permitted life-tenure (which British judges were granted from 1701) and this was viewed as a plot against the sacred liberal principle of an independent judiciary.

Americans were also deeply affected by such events in England as the Whig Revolution of 1688 and they took these ideas further than the London government was prepared to allow them to be developed in the colonies. By the time of the first Continental Congress of 1774 the issue for Americans was no longer freedom from allegedly arbitrary taxation or from standing armies, but self-government. Joseph Galloway's compromise Plan of Union would have united the colonies with Britain in a sort of federal system with their own president and Congress. This idea was narrowly defeated by the radicals. The ideal of totally independent, republican government for America had emerged. After the convention John Adams wrote the *Novanglus Letters* which claimed that the colonies were not part of the 'realm' of England and were therefore not subject to the London Parliament. Each individual colony was an independent realm and owed direct allegiance only to the king. In some ways this theory was a preview of the later English 'dominion' theory of the Commonwealth, the notion under which Canada and Australia for example gained autonomy without leaving the Empire. The Spanish Empire in Central and South America had also been constructed on the idea of direct allegiance of each colony to the crown of Castile.

Perhaps, as the French commentator De Tocqueville said in the 1830s, the Americans were 'born mature' so far as politics was concerned— born in the revolutionary upheavals of the 17th century and politically tempered in the long history of 150 years of political management and negotiation among assemblies, governors and the London parliament. Certainly by 1776 there was nothing theoretically novel in their political ideology. What was new was their determination to see their beliefs implemented, to go beyond Lockean theory to Lockean practice, as in some ways the colonies already had. Meanwhile the English government tried to hold fast to the colonies, fearful to lose a great empire so soon. They need not have feared. Soon their second empire would surpass the first, and the Industrial Revolution would make them the world's dominant power for over a century.

REVOLUTION IN THE SPANISH AND PORTUGUESE COLONIES

America is ungovernable. He who serves a
revolution ploughs the sea.

(Simón Bolívar)

The independence movements of Central and South America were delayed until after the American and French Revolutions to which they owed much inspiration. The North American Revolution created the first 'new' republic under liberal auspices. But the South Americans were even more influenced by the French upheaval and remained deeply affected by French ideas throughout the 19th century. The French Revolution, by giving birth to Napoleon's military dictatorship based on popular plebiscites, was also an indirect *cause* of the South American revolutions. They sprang out of Napoleon's seizures of power in Spain and Portugal.

Haiti: black republic

The first revolution took place against the French or against the French white elite in the colony of Saint Domingue at the western end of the Spanish island of Española. It was a black slave revolution, led by a self-taught ex-slave, Toussaint L'Ouverture (1743–1803), a brilliant commander. On Saint Domingue, a sugar island, about half a million slaves were ruled absolutely by about 35,000 whites and a lesser number of mulattoes. Slavery was particularly cruel in the Caribbean. Many slave uprisings took place on the islands during the 18th century and were put down with savagery. In 1791, after the frustration of their high hopes that the Revolution in France would extend to them, the slaves rose, began a murderous campaign exterminating whites and burning the sugar crops, and took over the colony. Toussaint stayed within the French orbit and governed the colony until 1801, when Napoleon sent out 25,000 troops to get rid of him. Bonaparte was temporarily interested in creating a new French empire based on Louisiana; the Negro republic was in the way. Toussaint died in a French jail in 1803.

Napoleon's recapture of Saint Domingue was short-lived, as were his troops, killed off by tropical diseases and counter-attacks by Toussaint's followers. He abandoned his plans for empire in the New World very abruptly, and in fact, sold Louisiana for very little to the United States in 1803. The ex-slaves and the climate were too much for the French.

In 1804 a brutal successor who had fought alongside Toussaint, but was much less cultivated, Dessalines, declared the colony an independent 'Empire' called *Haiti* (land of mountains), with himself as Emperor Jacques I. He was assassinated in 1806 but not before he had murdered about 10,000 mulattoes. Negro-mulatto tensions ran high in the island: some mulattoes had been slave-owners. A. S. Pétion established a more moderate, liberal dictatorship from 1808 to 1818. He was a French-educated mulatto. In 1816 he intervened in the history of South American independence when he allowed the great liberator Simón Bolívar to stay over on Haiti and re-equip an army there to invade Venezuela. The later history of Haiti has been one of isolation rather than international consciousness; the rulers have had an uninspiring record of tyranny, cruelty, corruption and incompetence. For a few decades, down to 1844, the Haitians also ruled over the eastern end of Española, long neglected by Spain. The white Spaniards emigrated or were forced out and the popul-

ation became basically one of Spanish mulattoes. They threw out the French-speaking Haitians in 1844 and declared themselves to be an independent republic: *Santo Domingo*.

Revolutions in South America: origins

In 1807 Napoleon invaded Spain and placed his brother Joseph on the throne. Spain's American colonies would not accept this French intruder as king and began the movements that led to independence. Meanwhile, in Brazil the pattern was slightly different: there the Portuguese monarchy transferred itself to Brazil to escape Napoleon, but on its return home to Portugal after the war, independence for Brazil soon followed—conceded bloodlessly because demanded by the king's own son. There, in a nutshell, is the story of *how* South America became independent.

Answering the question How? does not always satisfy the bigger question: Why? Superficially, the South American pattern seems so different from the North American, with its tale of mounting grievances, royal blundering, inter-colonial jealousies, clever radical scheming and finally the outbreak of violence and foreign intervention to help the colonials. Yet behind the events of 1807 and the years that followed, lay similar divisions and grievances in the South American colonies. Frustrations of creoles and mestizos, hopes of slaves and castas, demands of merchants and professionals, the intrusion of liberal and radical ideas from France and the United States, disaffection among military men—all these, sooner or later, would have produced the revolutions in South America even if Napoleon had never invaded Spain and overthrown the monarchy. The colonial reforms of the 18th century helped to exacerbate and sharpen differences rather than soften them and the prosperity of recent years raised the level of expectations of all South Americans. So often in history, revolutions have arisen not out of hopelessly depressed circumstances, but out of improving conditions of life.

British role: invasion of Rio de la Plata: 1806–7

Generally Britain favoured the South American wars of independence. She blockaded the coasts of Spain and Portugal in the course of her own war with Napoleon, thus throwing the colonies more on their own resources and opening them up still further to the influence of British, United States, and non-Latin trade and ideas. British blockade strengthened the hands of the creoles against the Spanish-born peninsulares. British policy and the ancient Anglo-Portuguese alliance brought direct Royal Navy intervention when Napoleon threatened the Portuguese crown: the Navy provided escort ships while John VI and his court escaped from Lisbon to Brazil. The ports of Brazil were then opened up to world trade, in which Britain was dominant.

◀ 7. *Toussaint L'Ouverture (1743–1803), engraved after F. Philippoteau.*

In what is now Argentina however, the British exerted a *negative* influence. An adventurous Commodore, Sir Home Popham, on his way home from conquering the Dutch in South Africa, invaded the estuary of La Plata, took the city of Buenos Aires and sent home tons of prize money. The Spanish Viceroy fled inland, leaving the creoles to work out their own defence and counter-attack against the British. This they did, and defeated two British occupation forces—the second a reinforcement expedition of 10,000 men. The British, beaten by fierce urban guerilla warfare, gave up and went home. The *porteños* (townspeople of Buenos Aires), left in the lurch by Spain, had taken over and defeated the invader themselves. There was an obvious lesson in this and news of their victory spread rapidly throughout the colonies.

Meanwhile for seven months the British had also occupied and administered Montevideo, on the north (or east) bank of the Plata. In liberal, free-trade fashion and with the help of eager British traders and industrial goods, they had brought a brief taste of modern life and prosperity to this *Banda Oriental*. Unwittingly they had also implanted the seeds of future Uruguayan separatism from Buenos Aires (Argentina). Montevideo, future capital of Uruguay, would be in the lead in throwing off Spanish authority.

Formation of juntas

The *junta*, or self-constituted revolutionary committee of local government, was the basic building-block of the revolutions. The first juntas began in Spain, to organise resistance to Napoleonic occupations. This resistance was very effective and a French army suffered defeat at Bailén in July 1808. A junta at Sevilla took upon itself the power to govern the colonies and sent out agents to the Americas to arrest local radicals and suppress any movement for independence from Spain. Local *colonial* juntas were prohibited. Freedom *for* Spain did not imply also freedom *from* Spain. When a Regency emerged in Spain dominated by the old clique of Cádiz merchant monopolists, the Spanish colonies finally gave up all hope of justice from that quarter.

The essential change had now taken place. The creoles were finally radicalised. The cabildos, no longer content with merely denouncing French usurpation in Spain, became independence-minded. Supported by the mestizos who were their natural allies, and whom they now allowed to have minor power as subordinate officials and N.C.O.s in the revolutionary armies, the creoles assumed control of the revolution against Spain.

Revolution and independence in Mexico

By restricting colonial self-government to the cabildo level, Spain had created a strange situation wherein when royal authority suddenly collapsed all over the Americas, the only legitimate political power was in the cabildo. Thus from the start the revolution was broken up into local centres. No 'Continental Congress' came into existence in South or Central America; no single army of the 'United Colonies'; no single George Washington, to take over as President of a 'United States of South America' after the revolution. The various local risings, usually in capital cities, were of course connected in general aims and ideas; but they did not agree on any *one* form of government after the revolution. Some remained monarchists, others were republicans like the North Americans and French, or even tried to re-establish the Inca Empire, but could not find a suitable Inca.

In Mexico the revolution was different in pattern. It was more radical in origin, closer to the masses than elsewhere; and it did not begin in the city, but in the small village of Dolores, near Querétaro. The village priest, Father Miguel Hidalgo y Costilla, was a poor farm-boy turned scholar who had risen to be dean of a college but ran foul of the Inquisition for his liberal, French ideas. Hidalgo demanded land reform—the perennial theme of South American revolutions ever since—and sympathised with the mass of Indian peasants. Independence Day in Mexico is 16 September, because on that date in 1810 Hidalgo uttered his famous *Grito de Dolores* (Cry of Dolores):

> My children, will you be free? Will you make the effort to recover from the hated Spaniards the lands stolen from your forefathers three hundred years ago?

Hidalgo's caste war

The ancient fears of peninsulares and creoles alike now came true. Unwittingly, Hidalgo had unleashed a bloody caste war, mestizos, Indians and castas against Latins. Joined by about 80,000 he failed to capture Mexico City in October 1810 and was taken himself in 1811 near Guadalajara. Cruelty on both sides was immeasurable. 'Death to the *gachupines* (Spanish-born)!' was the cry of Hidalgo's uncontrollable peasant mob as it attacked the granary of Guanajuato where the *Ladinos* were hiding out. About 600 men, women and children were hacked to pieces. Joined by the city castas and poor, Hidalgo's men sacked the town for two days and left it a bloody shambles.

The Spaniards responded with the bestiality born of race-fear. Any town found aiding the revolutionaries was put to the torch. Mass executions were common, and sometimes had to be halted in the middle, to allow the mess to be cleaned off the streets before recommencing the murders. This was a long way from the so-called Boston Massacre. Yet Hidalgo was a gentle, pious man, a dreamer. Himself a creole he had hoped that his movement would unite creoles, mestizos, Indians and castas against the peninsulares, remove them quickly from power, and establish an essentially creole government, paternalistically looking after the lower orders, like a priest and his flock. Creoles, he hoped would 'govern with the sweetness of parents, treat us as brothers, banish poverty.' Instead his 'army' could see no difference between Europeans: they all looked alike. They murdered and robbed both creoles and Spanish-born and were murdered and robbed in turn by them.

Hidalgo was beheaded and his head was stuck on the granary wall at Guanajuato. It stayed there until 1821.

Indian nationalism: Morelos

The Indians and castas had taken centuries of abuse from the Spanish, with their rigid concept of 'race' that limited all privileges and rights to the 'pure'-blooded, Spanish-born. Hidalgo had released the pent-up bitterness of generations. It could not be silenced now even by the most severe repression. The Indian movement continued and gave Mexican radicalism its major principles for decades to come. The man who made this possible was a disciple of Hidalgo, the younger priest-soldier, José María Morelos y Pavón.

Morelos was in some ways the antithesis of his master. Disciplined, cool, a fine general, perhaps he should have led the revolution. As an ex-labourer and mestizo, Morelos was even more angry than Hidalgo about the caste hierarchy of Mexico, but he approached the problem as a more scientific reformer. His aims included the break-up of the large hacienda system, abolition of special privileges for the clergy and of compulsory tithes, distribution of Church lands to the poor and representative government. These goals would not have made him especially 'radical' in the United States, but they infuriated the Spanish elite.

Like Hidalgo, who worshipped the *Mexican* Virgin of Guadelupe, Morelos was a Mexican nationalist. For him a new society had arisen in Mexico, not a European fringe culture. The *Chilpancingo Congress* which he called in 1813 to draft a new Constitution for an independent Mexico, based on universal suffrage, race equality and an independent judiciary, was the inspiration of future generations. But the tide of war turned, the radicals were overcome and Morelos was executed by the royalists in 1815. For a few years *Indianism* evaporated.

The Mexican revolution subverted: Iturbide

The revolution that began under radical auspices ended up very conservative. A creole elite replaced a Spanish-born elite. Some mestizos tasted power as minor functionaries. The restored monarchy in Spain after 1814 was despotic and repressive. But when Ferdinand VII was forced into abdication by a military coup in Spain in 1822, the colonial creole elite in Mexico, anxious to undercut any radical movement, quickly opted for Mexican independence. Spain was becoming too liberal for them!

Agustín de Iturbide, a creole adventurer and soldier of fortune, was supposed to head the Spanish army in the colony in 1820. He simply made an agreement with the independents, the *Plan of Iguala* (1821), and after a *coup* emerged as Emperor of Mexico. 'Agustín I' reigned for one year, was exiled, returned with an army and was executed in 1824. Various Central American regions broke away from the Mexican Empire, formed the 'United Provinces' and later split up into the separate nations we now know as Guatemala, San Salvador, Nicaragua, Honduras and Costa Rica (1838). A somewhat smaller Mexico was launched upon its career of independent nationhood.

Revolution further south: Bolívar and San Martín

The short-lived, genuine *social* revolution of Mexico did not even occur further south, where the creoles remained in control most of the time. Without any central organisation, two revolutionary armies engaged in a vast pincer movement against the royalist forces. Bolívar's army, after some false starts, swept southwards from Venezuela and Colombia down the Pacific side of the Andes to Peru: it followed the route of Pizarro's conquistadors. The army of San Martín actually crossed the Andes from Argentina—an amazing feat—entered the Chile region, and turned north. With the aid of Chilean patriots, and the British Navy, San Martín moved by sea up the coast of Peru. Lima fell in 1821. The final battle of the wars was at Ayacucho in Peru in 1824. It marked the end of the Spanish American Empire.

'The Liberator', Simón Bolívar, was a Venezuelan creole born in Caracas in 1783. Rich, landed, educated, handsome, a ladies' man, horseman, swimmer and dancer, Bolívar played the role of the Romantic hero idealised by the poets and writers of his day. He stepped out of a poem by Lord Byron. Unfortunately, despite his liberal ideology, learned in European travels and by expensive private tutoring in the works of Rousseau, Locke and Spinoza, Bolívar became a forerunner of strongman rule—*caudillismo*—in South America. Lesser *caudillos* who followed him were far more cruel, despotic and illiberal.

Bolívar was preceded as leader of the independence movement of Venezuela by Francisco de Miranda (1750–1816), another European-educated liberal creole. Miranda lived in London, the centre for South American revolutionaries in exile, and was a friend of the Founding Fathers of the United States revolution who regarded him highly. He planned a United States of South America, to be called 'Colombia', and successfully invaded Venezuela in 1810. With Bolívar he wrote the Venezuelan Declaration of Independence in the Congress of 1811, but after making an agreement with the Spanish royalists, who let him down, he earned Bolívar's suspicion and was betrayed to the Spaniards. Miranda died in a Spanish jail in 1816.

In exile at Cartagena, Bolívar now reassessed the situation in his *Cartagena Manifesto* of 1812. The Spanish were back in power in

Caracas, he said, because the radical junta had failed to assert strong central control over the countryside. Its republican constitution of 1811 was too vague, idealistic and federalised. Modelled on the US constitution it did not fit the Venezuelan situation. The provinces were too autonomous and the Spanish had no difficulty in regaining power. What was needed, in Bolívar's view, was strong, central government buttressed by a reliable army. Much of later South American history is contained in Bolívar's Manifesto: the independent role of the army in politics, caudillo leadership, and city-state type of government.

Bolívar reinvaded Caracas in 1813, lost it again in 1814–15 (defeated by the royalists aided by the mestizo horsemen of the plains—the *llaneros*), and after exile in Haiti, invaded for the last time in December, 1816. Now he carefully avoided Caracas. He invaded much farther east, at the delta of the Orinoco. The llaneros cowboys under José Antonio Paez joined his army. By way of dense jungle valleys and mountains he reached Bogotá, which fell in August 1819. In the Andes of Colombia he called for the creation of 'Gran Colombia' (a state that would cover present Colombia, Venezuela and Ecuador). Bolívar was elected President of Gran Colombia in 1819 by the Congress of Angostura, his capital on the Orinoco.

The idealism of San Martín

Bolívar's personal ambitions and role-playing would not keep him long in Bogotá. Soon he would be off to Ecuador and Peru in pursuit of greater glory. Meanwhile a different sort of liberator, José de San Martín, had already brought independence to Chile and was moving north, where he would neet Bolívar at a historic moment in South American history.

San Martín (1788–1850) was an Argentine creole, about the same age as Bolívar, educated in Spain and an officer in the royal army for twenty years. Returning to Buenos Aires from Europe in 1812 he supported the rebels, led the army against the Spanish and then moved to Mendoza in the far west of Argentina (as it now is), a town in the foothills of the mountains bordering Chile. For many months he organised and trained the 'Army of the Andes'. In January 1817 he crossed the high cordilleras, joined with the Chilean patriot, General O'Higgins, and smashed the royal forces at the battle of Chacabuco (1817). Chile became independent under the liberal dictatorship of O'Higgins from 1818–1823.

San Martín did not pursue personal honours or wealth. He was a professional soldier, who liked to win but left the pomp and glory to others. Helped by the English Lord Cochrane, he now built the fleet that took his international army of men from Argentina, Chile, Spain, England, and France (it was later to contain men from Ecuador, Peru, Venezuela and Colombia) to Peru. After the capture of the City of Kings, Lima, in July 1822, San Martín did agree, temporarily, to be made 'Protector' of Peru. His brief rule was not successful; the Peruvians were

CARIBBEAN SEA

Puerto Cabello

B. of Carabobo 1821

Angostura

Orinoco

BRITISH GUIANA

DUTCH GUIANA

FRENCH GUIANA

VENEZUELA

Panama

Battle of Boyaca 1819

Bogota

COLOMBIA

BRAZIL

B. of Pichincha 1822

ECUADOR

Guayaquil Conference

Bolivar smashed Spanish resistance to New Granada and Venezuela with his victories at Boyaca and Carabobo – although some Spaniards held out at Puerto Cabello until November 1823. His general, Sucre, destroyed the Spaniards at Pichincha in 1822 and went on to win the decisive victory at AYACUCHO in 1824.

Spanish power effectively ended with the surrender of Callao on 22 January 1826.

PERU

Callao

Battle of Ayacucho 1824

BOLIVIA

PACIFIC OCEAN

PARAGUAY

C H I L E

ARGENTINA

Two Liberators
BOLÍVAR and SAN MARTÍN

⇨ Bolívar's liberation of New Granada & Venezuela

▪▪▪➤ Bolívar in conference with San Martín

➡ San Martín

➤ General Sucre's most important victories

Battle of Chacabuco

Santiago

factious, and some did not like his idea that a European prince should be chosen to govern them as a constitutional monarch. In ill-health and low in spirits, this honourable and courageous man now sailed for Ecuador, where a strange fate would overtake him.

For two days Bolívar and San Martín conferred at Guayaquil (July 1822). We do not know what was said. Bolívar opposed the idea of a monarch for Peru. In the middle of a ball given in his honor, San Martín slipped out quietly into the night and sailed away. In September San Martín resigned as Peruvian Protector and left the field to Bolívar. He emigrated to Europe in 1824. When he returned to Buenos Aires in 1829 San Martín felt such coldness towards him that he did not even disembark but sailed back to Europe on the same boat, and died unknown in France in 1850.

South American liberators did not enjoy the fruits of their victories for very long. Unlike the men who liberated the United States and subsequently became its leading political figures, most of the South American liberators died in obscure exile or were killed at home.

Bolívar as dictator

Several battles were still to be fought against Spanish forces in Peru, but Bolívar's able General, Sucre, finally brought the whole war to an end at Ayacucho in 1824. Upper Peru became an independent republic (Bolivia) and Sucre was its president, 1826–28. He was murdered in 1830. This greatly disturbed Bolívar, who had already suffered several political setbacks. His Pan-American Federation idea failed to attract support at a conference in Panama in 1826. In Colombia after 1826 he was forced to apply dictatorial rule, repress provincial unrest, and suspend his own Constitution of 1821. Sucre's assassination seemed another blow aimed at Bolívar himself. Finally he knew he was powerless to stop the breaking-up of his cherished Gran Columbia into its separate parts. He narrowly escaped assassination in 1828.

Bolívar died in 1830, a failure in his own eyes despite his magnificent achievements in attempting the impossible, 'ploughing the sea' as he put it so beautifully. He and his companions liberated the subcontinent from Spain but left it tied to its own past history and its implacable geography. Separatism, nationalism, race problems, poverty and instability plagued the hemisphere. The newly-independent nations soon engaged in bloody wars against each other. All power seemed localised and wielded by local caudillo bosses.

The Monroe Doctrine, 1823: Britain v. the United States

Foreign powers, namely Britain and the United States, did not want to see a 'United States' develop in the southern hemisphere. They were rivals in South America, though Britain had played a much larger role in the revolutions, as she would in the economic development of the area in the years afterwards. Once the United States had signed the treaty with Spain covering American purchase of Florida, President Monroe had no need to fear alienating the Spanish government and so he immediately recognised the republics of Chile, Peru, the United Provinces of Rio de la Plata, Colombia and Mexico in 1822. The British government hastily followed suit, not wishing to be left out of any trade agreements.

The next step was for the two powers to hammer out a common policy on the area, but the United States in an artful stroke, out-smarted the British by suddenly announcing the Monroe Declaration of December 1823. Appearing to act alone, the US unilaterally declared its 'Hands Off!' policy in the western hemisphere, warning foreign powers not to intervene there any more. This was a trick, because the United States realised that Britain would use her navy to stop any aggressions by other European powers in Central and South America. Without the backing of the Royal Navy the Monroe Doctrine was a 'paper tiger'.

Bolívar resented the whole affair. He saw through the US stratagem. The Doctrine, after all, did not guarantee the new republics from interference by the United States itself. So at Panama in 1826 Bolívar fought hard to get the republics to associate, and to counterpoise the Anglo-American assumption of control over the area with a strong cooperative organisation by the South Americans themselves. This failed, and 'Pan-Americanism' has for decades seemed a tool of North American interests. A new colonialism was about to replace the old.

Brazil: sleeping colony of Portugal

In Brazil, a region bigger than the continental United States, two hundred years of Portuguese control had produced very little by 1700 except a few sugar plantations. The Dutch had come and gone and settlements along the coast grew but slowly. Three main towns, Bahía, Rio de Janeiro and Olinda, did not compare with the great cities of Spanish America. No university, no printing-press appeared in Brazil until the 19th century, long after those of the other Americas, South and North. The Jesuits played some role in economic development and teaching the Indians, but the Church as a whole was weaker than in Spanish settlements; there was no Inquisition; the Church hierarchy did not grow so wealthy on colonial exploitation, and consequently there was less anti-clerical feeling and less tension between Church and State.

The Portuguese Viceroy had certain defined powers. The *câmaras*, like the Spanish cabildos, were partly elected local authorities, manned by creoles who resented peninsular appointees to higher offices. Mercantile restrictions were evaded by widespread smuggling (still practised today). Control from Lisbon was much laxer than control from Madrid.

The bandeirantes

The Brazilian economy has passed through various boom stages, rather like the Canadian economy. Its gold boom came in the late 17th and early 18th century with strikes in the hills of Minas Gerais, followed later by diamond strikes. The gold rush came precisely when Brazilian sugar was beginning to feel competition from the Caribbean. Rio de Janeiro, with Minas Gerais as its hinterland, increased in population. Meanwhile the bandeirantes pushed the borders of Brazil outwards and developed parts of the interior in their avid search for Indian slave-labour. We have seen that they destroyed the Jesuit communes of Paraguay. Many of the bandeirantes of later years were *mamelucos* (mestizos) from the growing region around São Paulo. Up on that plateau land they developed cattle ranches, and grew maize, rice and cotton for export. They were in constant need of labour. In the 19th century São Paulo cotton was urgently needed for the textile mills of an industrializing Europe. Further north, around Rio, coffee plantations emerged, and coffee became in the 19th century the basis for another boom cycle in Brazilian economic history.

Like the Spanish colonies, Brazil saw attempts by the crown to 'reform' colonial administration in the 18th century, and these reforms merely served to stimulate feelings of independence and self-confidence in the colonists. Under the Marquis of Pombal, brilliant minister for King Joseph from 1750–77, the policies of 'enlightened despotism' were applied to Brazil as Charles III of Spain and Esquilache applied them to Spanish America. Liberal and anticlerical, Pombal failed to see the value of the work of the Jesuits and expelled them in 1759. On the other hand he encouraged agriculture, raised the Indians to fuller citizenship and gave more outlets to the political energies of the creoles. Rio was made the capital of Brazil in 1763, displacing Bahía. For all this, and for rebuilding Lisbon after the earthquake of 1755, he was rewarded with dismissal and exile.

Revolution by consent

The French occupied Lisbon in November 1807, and a Portuguese royal party of about 2,000 escaped with treasure and ships escorted by English naval vessels. The monarchy was simply transferred to Brazil; Rio replaced Lisbon, as a temporary capital and royal residence.

John VI determined to live as well as possible in Rio. He stayed there for over 13 years and the centre of political balance stayed with him, for Portugal, even after the French were ousted by the English late in 1808, was placed under a Regency. The real power was in Rio: an upside-down colonial situation! Taxes now went to Rio, not Lisbon; the elite and merchants took up residence there to be near the court and the centre of power. The city went a long way towards becoming the metropolis it is today: theatre, press, the symbols and realities of culture now sprang up. Perhaps all this was a major reason why in the end Brazil did not need a real 'revolution' or bloodshed. An irritation of colonial status, as we have seen in the case of the British colonies to the north, is the inability to be understood at Court, to have a sympathetic ear. But in Brazil, the court sat in Rio and was always ready for consultation. Indeed, any jealousy worked the other way: Portugal, and its English allies, felt left out.

In 1815 Napoleon was defeated. John VI gave Brazil equal status with Portugal in the imperial structure: two equal kingdoms. John did not appear at all anxious to return to Lisbon but was forced to do so when the growth of a liberal movement there demanded it. He left in April 1821, and put his son Pedro in charge of Brazil as Regent. A movement for Brazilian independence had been growing for some time. In the Pernambuco region a military rising was suppressed in 1817. Brazilian creoles did not care for John's dependence on peninsulars. But it was the narrowness of the so-called 'liberals' in Lisbon that energised the Brazilians. The Portuguese who demanded John's return and his submission to the rules of constitutional monarchy had no intention of liberating Brazil; they wanted to turn the colonial clock back and reassert control from Lisbon. This parallels the colonialist attitude of the liberal junta in Spain.

To undercut any radical movement that could destroy the authority of the royal House of Bragança in Brazil, the Regent Pedro promptly declared himself a revolutionary and in his own *Grito de Ypiranga* of 1822 ('Independence or death!'), made himself Pedro I of the Empire of Brazil. There was not much chance that his aging father would have put him to death; but Pedro's reign was an unsettled one. As early as 1823 he dismissed his assembly. His liberal Constitution of 1824 made no progress, as Pedro became more involved in Portuguese affairs, and Brazil was busily engaged in a war with Argentina (1826–27) and the loss of Uruguay (1828). After John's death the Regent Miguel made himself king of Portugal. Pedro wanted the Portuguese throne for his own daughter and therefore abdicated as Emperor of Brazil (April 1831), sailed to Lisbon, defeated Miguel, and placed his daughter Maria on the throne in 1833. After some confusion his son became Pedro II of Brazil and ruled until 1889.

Brazilian society: African slavery and race-mixture

This analysis of an unusual almost bloodless 'revolution' by consent, should not obscure the deep tensions that lay within Brazilian society. The rule of John was far from perfect and in addition to the Pernambuco revolt, earlier examples of armed uprisings had been known, led by whites and by blacks. In 1788, 'Tiradentes' (the dentist) José da Silva Xavier had led a movement for independence from Portugal in Minas Gerais. He was executed in 1792 and is known as the 'Father of Brazilian independence'.

Deeper tensions were revealed in Negro slave uprisings and the creation of the 'Republic of Palmares' much earlier in the 17th century. There were many slave insurrections in Brazil over the years. Escaped Negroes formed *quilombos*—remote refuges, like those of the *maroons* in the Caribbean in the 17th and 18th century, or in the southern United States in the early 19th century. Maroons and quilombos, being self-governing communities of escaped slaves sometimes so powerful that they gained political recognition from colonial authorities, were a contant invitation to unfreed slaves, and were greatly feared by owners.

The *Republic of Palmares* was a cooperative of several Negro settlements in northeastern Brazil, with Cerca Real do Macaco as it capital, from 1620 to 1697. The black republic resisted many attempts to destroy it launched by Dutch and Portuguese forces in turn. Numbering perhaps 20,000 it successfully fused African, mainly Bantu, ideas with Western culture. Its final destruction did not end the resistance of Negroes to enslavement, which continued right down to the abolition of slavery in 1888. Quilombos were a constant in Brazilian history, and slave uprisings did not cease. Notable examples in the 18th century occurred in 1756 and 1772.

Nineteenth century Negroes rose in anger in the urban riots of Bahía, 1807–35. They were mainly Moslem Negroes—Hausas with their own secret societies and Moslem temples, fighting serious battles among themselves as well as against the whites. The abolitionist movement itself had Negro leaders like Luiz Gama and José de Patrocino, a leading journalist of the later 19th century. Such movements had little impact on the Brazilian elite perhaps; but Brazil was becoming increasingly racially mixed, and African influence was felt more here than in most South American cultures—in folklore and popular culture, in village religion (the fetishistic *Candomblé* of Bahia, the *Macumba* of Rio), in music and dance (the national folk-dance of Brazil, the *samba*, has direct African origins), in sculpture (the school of Aleijadinho) and painting (the work of Sebastião), and in literature. Brazil has its own 'Uncle Remus' character, *Pae João*.

. Brazil was racially very complex. Growth of race-mixture and increasing proportions of castas, mulattoes and mestizos in the total population, did not necessarily mean a softening of racial attitudes. It did mean that it became very difficult to distinguish who was of what race in Brazil. The very definition of 'Negro' was hard to make.

The aftermath of revolutions: differentiation in the Americas

Both Brazil and the United States built their economies and societies on African slave-labour. The comparison goes little further than that. As the years passed by after the achievement of independence, the various nations of the Americas seemed increasingly dissimilar. Even within South America, differentiation was marked, though those nations shared a common relationship to the outside world, one of neo-colonialism.

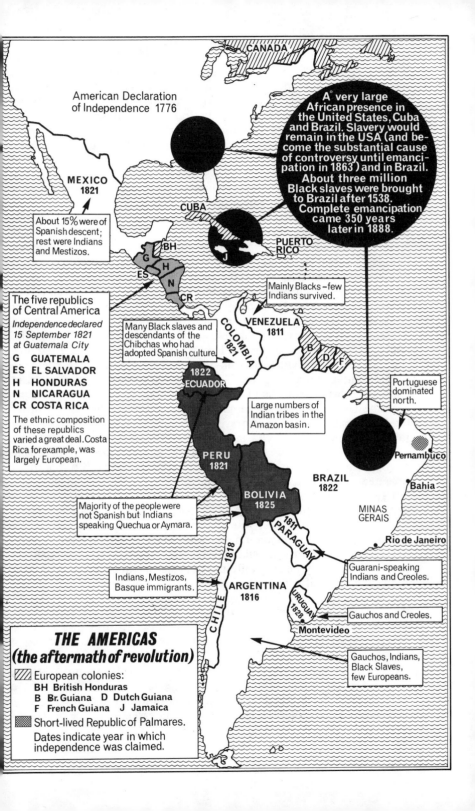

American Declaration of Independence 1776

A very large African presence in the United States, Cuba and Brazil. Slavery would remain in the USA (and become the substantial cause of controversy until emancipation in 1863) and in Brazil. About three million Black slaves were brought to Brazil after 1538. Complete emancipation came 350 years later in 1888.

CANADA

MEXICO 1821

About 15% were of Spanish descent; rest were Indians and Mestizos.

CUBA

BH

G
ES H
N
CR

PUERTO RICO

Mainly Blacks – few Indians survived.

The five republics of Central America

Independence declared 15 September 1821 at Guatemala City

G   GUATEMALA
ES EL SALVADOR
H   HONDURAS
N   NICARAGUA
CR COSTA RICA

The ethnic composition of these republics varied a great deal. Costa Rica for example, was largely European.

Many Black slaves and descendants of the Chibchas who had adopted Spanish culture.

COLOMBIA 1821

VENEZUELA 1811

B
D F

1822 ECUADOR

Portuguese dominated north.

Large numbers of Indian tribes in the Amazon basin.

Pernambuco

PERU 1821

Majority of the people were not Spanish but Indians speaking Quechua or Aymara.

BOLIVIA 1825

BRAZIL 1822

Bahia

MINAS GERAIS

1811 PARAGUAY

Rio de Janeiro

Guarani-speaking Indians and Creoles.

Indians, Mestizos, Basque immigrants.

1818

CHILE

ARGENTINA 1816

URUGUAY 1828

Gauchos and Creoles.

Montevideo

THE AMERICAS
(the aftermath of revolution)

///// European colonies:
BH British Honduras
B Br. Guiana **D** Dutch Guiana
F French Guiana **J** Jamaica

▓ Short-lived Republic of Palmares.

Dates indicate year in which independence was claimed.

Gauchos, Indians, Black Slaves, few Europeans.

They also shared a common external problem within the Americas, namely the preponderance of the growing economic power of the United States in the hemisphere. In the early 19th century however this mainly affected only Mexico to any extent. In Brazil and Argentina the economic influence from the outside was still likely to be British. By 1830 there were few European possessions left in the New World except Canada, a special case, and several much smaller territories. Cuba and Puerto Rico remained Spanish down to 1898, when the US dealt the final blow to the obsolete Spanish Empire. The British, French, Dutch and Danes maintained small settlements in the Caribbean and the Guianas.

Central and South America had been liberated in the space of about twenty years. It has been said that little changed as a result: 'only the Spanish were gone'. Racial and economic hierarchy remained, though in many places mestizos as a class had made gains. No real social revolutions had occurred despite the attempt to create one in Mexico by Hidalgo and Morelos, which was suppressed with fury. For many years, power in South America would be *local* power: the authority of caudillos and land-owning families, like the Terrazas of Chihuahua (Mexico) or the Rosas of Argentina (who did grasp national power for a while). The feudal rules and rites of the Big House and hacienda, or the caudillo's rule of the gun, provided law and order. Except for Chile these new republics had little real national unity until the later 19th century, in Mexico for instance not until the Revolution of 1910.

In the United States the rule of the gun also provided law and order over large stretches of territory, at least until statehood. The annihilation of Indians accelerated with economic progress; the Negro became more firmly enslaved in perpetuity as the demand for cotton rose in Europe. But in contrast, the United States Revolution did not produce seventeen independent and often hostile nations (nor even thirteen), but one federal nation, soon bound together even more by canal, railway and early industrialisation. By 1830 the United States had already had seven presidents, from Washington to Jackson, and had seen eleven national, presidential elections, and twice as many Congressional campaigns. The miracle of the peaceful transfer of political power was no longer a miracle in the United States but was taken for granted, at least until 1860.

The United States Constitution and political cohesion

Many times in seeking to explain the political maturity and cohesion of the newly-United States, writers will point to the federal constitution adopted in 1789. It is true that the constitution is most ingenious, with its compromises between large and small states, its checks and balances, its independent judiciary so essential to freedom, and its additional ten amendments, the Bill of Rights. The US constitution was a remarkable achievement, a distillation of known lore and past experience of government. But few can believe that a mere document can hold together a vast nation. Mexico, for example, has produced some remarkable political documents, like its brilliant radical Constitution of 1917, which have remained largely on paper. Political cohesion must *precede* formal political association. Quite apart from the success of the looser Articles of Confederation in enabling the 'United Colonies' to wage the war against England, the North Americans shared a British colonial political past that was rich in experience and ideas. There was a general consensus among them, and at this time a greater racial and social homogeneity than in the southern hemisphere.

The American Dream

What bound the people of the United States together in one enterprise, more than any political consensus about parliamentarism or individualism, was the knowledge and the fact of *economic opportunity* in that land. Liberal land-settlement policies, a relatively open, fluid class-structure (certainly compared with the class systems further south), lack of any permanent castes (outside Negro slavery), little government interference with private profit-seeking: all these elements helped. South American nations inherited a tradition of 'statism' and central government interference, while at the same time, ironically, those central (city) governments were too weak to defend the provinces from local caudillos. Wealth was tied up in land which remained controlled by large landlords. None of this was true in the United States except in the cotton states, and even there the large plantation was the exception rather than the rule. Would-be feudal landlords vanished from the North American scene, though the French *seigneurs* persisted in Canada.

The 'American Dream' of material advancement, which was for many immigrants no mere dream but a reality, was based fundamentally on land and property ownership, the very things denied to the European and South American masses. Capitalism, individualism, and political maturity thus combined together, with a large dash of good fortune, to produce rapid economic growth in the United States. This 'Dream' operated elsewhere, for instance in Argentina in the 19th century, but nowhere to such effect as in the United States. The North Americans were wrapped up in business and in their internal empire; nobody and nothing was allowed to step in the way of rapid exploitation of the US interior—not Indians, not the Mexicans, who lost a vast territory to the US in 1848, not qualms about Negro slavery. This was a special sort of *internal* colonialism to replace the old.

Part Two

Containment and Growth
(About 1830 to 1920)

By about 1830 the ex-colonies of the western hemisphere had all achieved independent political status and were undergoing varying degrees of containment after a release of revolutionary tension. In Central and South America they formed themselves into separated, independent republics often hostile to each other, while in the USA the ex-colonies became federated and underwent a rapid economic transformation, pushing out their borders on the northern continent. The new republics of the West were differentiated among themselves by at least five groups of factors:

1. Great geographic and climatic variety and consequent differences in what economists choose to call the 'resource-mix' available to each society.
2. Ethnic and racial composition of the populations, which varied widely from the almost purely European stock of Costa Rica to the almost purely Indian stock of Ecuador and parts of the Andes region, or the large African presence in Brazil, Cuba and the USA.
3. Different pre-Conquest historical inheritances and varying patterns of colonial development before independence.
4. Removal of the colonial authorities, British, Spanish and Portuguese, which left no over-all controls—particularly noted in South America.
5. Internal differences created by the rise of rival pressure-groups and economic or regional interests, including not only ethnic or religious groupings, but specific interest-groups such as miners, cattle ranchers, farmers, exporters and shippers, all with their own aims and organisations.

Yet similarities of experiences persisted too, mainly among the ex-colonies of Portugal and Spain. These were: a traditional struggle between Church and secular authority; between the larger latifundia and the peasantry; between creole élites and mestizo, casta and Indian masses; between city and countryside; between 'conservative' and 'liberal' politicians often associated with centralist or 'federalist' ideas. In South America 'federalist' had the opposite meaning (anti-centralist) to its meaning in the USA. These internal struggles are seen working themselves out in the post-independence years. Britain and the USA vied for economic influence in Central and South America in the 19th century, the British retaining dominance for a long time. Spain made a feeble attempt at a come-back with a war against Peru in the 1860s.

From independence to the period of the First World War (from about

1830 to about 1920) a break can be made for convenience in the history of the western hemisphere roughly around the 1880s. At that time the USA, having witnessed the triumph of capitalism and individualism, even over a tragic and bloody Civil War (1861–65), passed to a different phase of its economic and social history. Thereafter mass immigration, the growth of large cities and huge corporations, reform movements like Populism and Progressivism, and a new quest for world power (since the continent was subjugated), brought the USA onto the world scene as an imperialist nation. Its influence in Central and South America, and to some degree in Canada, began to replace that of Britain which had reached its climacteric. The US began to intervene, South Americans would say interfere, in affairs south of the Rio Grande. In Canada the important breaking-point came earlier, with the British North America Act of 1867 which created the confederation of four small colonies out of which a strong and rich nation would grow in the next hundred years.

For the central and southern hemisphere the eighties can represent a stopping-station. By that time the ex-colonies had begun to stabilize their economies, for good or evil, around particular export crops: neo-colonial staples such as coffee, meats, grains and later on rubber, tin and essential minerals. The demeaning and ugly phrase 'banana republic' was becoming a reality—meaning a small nation thoroughly dependent on the export of a single tropical crop to a more advanced nation or nations. Political changes also occurred in the 1870s and 80s which help to mark off the subperiod. In Mexico, Díaz gained power in 1876; regimes began and ended in Venezuela, Colombia, and Central America. In the south (Chile, Argentina, Paraguay and Uruguay) two major wars ended; and political changes took place in the Andes nations (Ecuador, Peru, Bolivia). Yet little fundamental alteration was made in the social and political structures of these nations and their history became a continuum of separatism, local jealousies and violence, and petty dictatorship, punctuated by the doomed attempts of liberal reformers to throw off the dead-hand of the colonial past, the hacienda, the weakened Church, the rule of the caudillo and the racial elite. Thus Central and South American nations built up their unhappy reputation for political instability, rapid changes of regime with little real significance and military *coups*. Yet underneath this instability was a more serious and more dangerous stability or inertia: major social institutions did not change. Hidalgo's much-desired El Dorado of genuine land-reform was not attained. The lower classes remained illiterate, poor, exploited and ignored, the victims of violence from local caudillos and bandits. Though a majority of the population in all these nations, the peons remained outside the mainstream and outside the market economy. Some southern nations did win periods of prosperity, calm and economic growth. Indeed, the beginnings of welfare states are to be seen in later years; but as a whole they entered into a new colonialism, heavily dependent on foreign markets, export of raw materials, and foreign capital investment. Together Central and South America represented an economic colony of the more developed western world and operated in a 'neo-mercantilist' world system as the underdog.

4
Capitalism

CAPITALISM IN NORTH AMERICA

While Central and South America experienced political instability and social inertia, North America experienced the opposite: relative political stability with great social and economic instability, mobility and change. This is true, despite the near-revolution in Canada in 1837 and the intermittent sectional political struggles in the United States.

As a new nation, the United States achieved the miracle of peaceful transfer of political authority between opposing regimes by the election of 1800. This brought Thomas Jefferson to power, after years of political in-fighting and inflammatory rhetoric. *Factions* or political interest-groups had evolved naturally out of the many divisions that made up the debates over ratifying the federal constitution and out of the earlier sectional and interest-group struggles of the late-colonial years. Under Washington's two administrations, the battle roughly polarised around two men: Alexander Hamilton and Thomas Jefferson. They represented constellations of ideas and interests that would form political battle-lines throughout 19th century US history.

Two visions of America: Hamilton v. Jefferson

Hamilton's comprehensive vision for the future United States was of an economically diversified, commercial and industrial nation, respected abroad for its probity, credit and power, and sustained by a great merchant marine, protective tariffs against foreign imports, and a solid national banking system. Jefferson stood for an agrarian ideal, a suspicion of central government; free trade in the world; a minimum of law and regulation for the individual. He would have preferred a United States made up of small farmers and pioneers, and distrusted banks, merchants and the influences of city life.

In practice, as is often the case, these two visions of the future, often quite inaccurately called 'conservative' (Hamilton) and 'liberal' (Jefferson), tended to merge as the United States evolved. Hamilton and

92

Jefferson shared many things: above all, nationalism, pride in the United States and determination that it should command respect abroad. Jefferson, in his search for foreign respect, did much to implement the policies of his great rival. To protect the national interest he would set aside his support of states' rights and use federal power, as in 1803, to buy Louisiana from France and double the size of the nation, or as in 1807, to impose a crippling Embargo Act, commanding US merchants not to trade with foreign ports.

These themes, central versus local or state power, farming versus city and commercial interests, strong foreign policies versus relative isolationism, government intervention (to encourage the economy to diversify) versus *laissez-faire*, are also to be found in the early national period of Central and South America. In North America their conflict did not produce political breakdown.

The United States nevertheless passed from crisis to political crisis in the early national period, and party propaganda could be shrill, the Jeffersonian 'Republicans' investigating Hamilton's sex-life and claiming that he was a secret monarchist and Anglophile ('monocrats', Jefferson called the 'Federalists' who clustered around Hamilton). For Federalist journalists on the other hand, Jefferson was said to be a dangerous French-style anarchist! The nation owed much to the brilliant and calm James Madison, who passed from a moderate Hamiltonian position (he helped design the first organs of executive government) to a moderate Jeffersonian position.

Foreign policy for the young nation was the basis for much political disagreement. This was a vital matter, because the Anglo-French wars which continued to 1815 gave the United States the opportunity it needed for its merchants to step in while the Great Powers fought, and to capture international trade. This windfall was an enormous help in early economic growth for the United States. Profits from foreign trade went into many investments at home. Foreign policy—which side the nation supported, if any—had direct impact on the prosperity and chances of survival of the American people. The US tried to be a neutral trader, but sometimes this could not be sustained without economic or military conflict, as with Jefferson's Embargo of 1807. As the nations fought out the war, the US suffered 'war scares', alternately with France and with England, even with Spain in 1790.

Growth of 'party' organisation: Federalists v. Republicans

The controversial Jay Treaty with England (1795), which Jeffersonian Republicans hated because they thought it was unfair to the United States, helped bring disagreements to a head and spurred the growth of grass-roots 'party' organisation, from precinct to federal level. The two-party system that was slowly emerging was to be the foundation of the American political system and the essential mechanism that made possible the miracle of peaceful transfer of power. In the 1790s Americans were still far from understanding how to behave in a two-party system. Partisanship bordered sometimes on treason and treating with foreign powers to defeat a political enemy at home. After all, the American nation was still a very new concept. Hamilton certainly played a dangerous game with the English very briefly; and under President John Adams civil rights were threatened by the Alien and Sedition Acts of 1798, which tried to cut off Republican criticism by silencing the press. At that point Jefferson almost carried his reaction to the point of disunion (as would often happen in South America). But he remained calm and resorted to working through the electoral system. He won in 1800, and called his victory a 'revolution'.

Expansion and material growth

These were not the last threats (or mild hints) of breaking up the American Union; but after 1800 it was generally accepted by Americans that political differences should be resolved in periodic elections. It was not necessary to over throw the whole system; one could wait four years and try again. Like the English, Americans seemed to accept a two-party grouping or constellation very readily, with occasional third parties when issues arose that seemed unanswered or needs that were unmet. A major reason why they drew back from political violence was their growing absorption in the many activities of rapid economic growth: trade, shipping, farming, advancing the frontier, fighting Indians and building towns. In material growth and territorial expansion across the continent Americans found sufficient outlets for their exuberance and energies. Many Americans did not know who was president and more than other peoples they took no interest at all in foreign affairs, even at the time of the Civil War in the 1860s.

Thus 'politics' became merely a system of obtaining aid to farm, to hold land, to build a canal or railroad, or to stop your rival from doing these things. From the outset the federal government took a large role in encouraging rapid economic growth. It gave generous land grants from the public lands to private enterprise, with few or no strings attached. It used subsidies, tariffs to keep out foreign goods, and other devices. And even before the federal government entered the railway business (in 1850), state governments were donating vast stretches of land and subsidies and guarantees to private corporations and individuals to get canals, railways and other developments built as soon as possible. In all this the Indians suffered badly and the institution of Negro slavery hardened.

Frontier nationalism and the War of 1812

Growing United States self-confidence was greatly bolstered by victory over England in the 'Second War of Independence', the War of 1812. A younger generation of nationalist politicians with Western backgrounds, men such as Henry Clay, a Kentucky lawyer, and John C. Calhoun, a southerner born on the frontier of South Carolina, came to the fore. As the great European war continued it became difficult for the United States to save face when treated arrogantly by French and English naval authorities. As irritations mounted with England, the younger politicians, called 'War Hawks', began to demand retaliation. No doubt some of them had personal economic interests at stake and hoped for territorial gains in Canada.

The expansionist Americans pushed into Florida and annexed West Florida in 1810. In the Northwest they pushed back the Indians and claimed, with some justice, that the English from Canada had incited them to rise. An Indian religious revival, led by Tecumseh and his brother, 'The Prophet', tried to unite the Indians against white land-grabbers. The revival was moralistic and separatist. Tecumseh believed in *peaceful* negotiation with the whites, but was forced into conflict by Governor W. H. Harrison of Indiana and was defeated at the battle of Tippecanoe (1811). Harrison went on to win a presidential election in 1840 on the strength of this action. Tecumseh, the great Shawnee chief, died in 1812 fighting for the British.

Canadian nationalism

American control of Lakes Erie and Champlain gave Harrison a free hand in the 1812 War to lay waste much of Upper Canada and American troops also pillaged the Niagara area. The fledgling centre of Upper Canada, York (later called Toronto) was burnt. In retaliation, the British burnt Washington. This American-Canadian violence made a deep impression in Canada, tied her more securely to England, and helped to create a stronger Canadian nationalism and hostility to the United States.

Victims of white expansion: Indians and Negroes

The 1812 War was a useful occasion for General Andrew Jackson to complete the slaughter of the Indians of Florida: the Creeks (1814) and the Seminoles (1816–18). He went on, brashly, to occupy Spanish Florida. It was purchased from Spain in 1819 and he was its first governor. Such deeds helped to put Jackson in the White House in 1828 as the representative of the 'Common Man'. He was the first 'backwoods' or 'Western' type to make it, though he was an uncommon man and a fairly well-to-do Tennessee slave owner.

The impact of American individualism and rapid growth was also felt by Negro slaves. Slavery as an institution bothered the 'revolutionaries' of the War of Independence, but in the federal constitution a shameful compromise allowed it to continue. This coincided with Eli Whitney's perfection of the cotton 'gin' (1793) on a Savannah plantation, and with a stream of technical changes in the English textile industries of Lancashire which were to increase the demand for raw cotton manifold. Slavery rapidly became an essential labour-system for the southern states who specialised in cotton culture. The erosion of tidewater lands in the South-east, and the expansionist spirit encouraged by the 1812 War, now sent southern cotton-growers westwards, sometimes bag and baggage, with their household, slaves, and tools. The rich-soiled states of the Missis-sippi delta lands and flood-plains were now settled and admitted into the Union as swiftly as possible: Louisiana (1812), Mississippi (1817), Alabama (1819). The Cotton Kingdom was founded in the Old Southwest and the hopes of slavery abolitionists were shelved for decades to come.

The political compromise of 1820 safeguards slavery

Sectional conflict came to a head over the slave-state issue in 1819, when Missouri applied for admission. At that time 11 slave states balanced 11 free states. Since 1802 slave and free states had been admitted to the Union alternately, maintaining the political balance. The North was outstripping the South in population growth and already had more votes in the House of Representatives. Seeking to limit the expansion of slavery, the Tallmadge Amendment suggested banning slavery in Missouri if that state were admitted. After a furious debate on the powers of the federal government to do this or not, a political compromise was reached. Maine was also admitted in the north to balance Missouri; slavery was to be allowed in all states carved out of the Louisiana Purchase region, south of the line 36°30′. In this case the developing American genius for political moderation and compromise merely put off a terrible decision to a future bloody Civil War.

Economic Revolution

In the years that followed, and especially in the 1830s, 40s and 50s, the United States underwent massive economic and social change: the economic revolution. This was a revolution in transportation (turnpike highways, canals, railways), in commerce and banking, in manufacturing, and in agricultural techniques and productivity. By 1850 what was called 'the American system of manufacture' was on show for the whole world to see, and at the Great Exhibition in London in 1851, American mass-made items such as the Colt revolver, were much admired. Traditionally a labour-scarce, high-wage economy, the United States had already developed the reputation for technical ingenuity and labour-saving innovation that was to be its hallmark for some decades.

Such swift economic growth brought with it de-stabilising social changes and that sense of breathless haste and confusion which foreign observers have experienced in the United States up to the present day. It was accompanied, from the 1840s onwards, by growing immigration from Europe and by greater demands for political and social equality, at least among whites. In politics the caucus system, whereby the estab-lishment maintained control over party nominees and selections through a party committee was challenged in 1824, and in 1828 Andrew Jackson, the outsider with a larger popular following, was elected.

The coming of majoritarian politics

The election of 1828 brought to an end government by the talented and landed wealthy, inherited from colonial and Jeffersonian days. The 'Virginia Dynasty' produced its last president in Monroe, who went out in 1825. With Jackson came professional politics: party managers, full-time political organisers, bringing in the mass vote of an enlarged, if not always well-informed, electorate. Jackson allegedly stood for the needs and prejudices of small farmers, business entrepreneurs and workers. Ironically, as a Jeffersonian he was opposed to many of the economic innovations such people needed for their long-term welfare. Many of his hostilities—particularly against the central bank which the nation so badly needed, the Bank of the United States—were inimical to long-term economic growth.

Jackson's hatred of the Bank was understandable however, when seen as a traditional American distrust of 'privilege' and 'monopoly'. Rich money-men, some of them foreigners, did make profits out of the central bank system. Meanwhile stable banking, adequate currency and credit supplies, and firm prices were what a growing nation required. Jackson destroyed the Bank in 1833–34; his own use thereafter of 'pet banks' (selected state banks, which were given federal deposits) did little more for the 'common man'. Jacksonian democracy does not seem more 'democratic' in retrospect than dynastic politics, except in the way politics were managed. Jackson believed in 'rotation in office', but he did not rotate many men out. His record with labour disputes was ambiguous, and he was the terror of the Indians.

President Andrew Jackson bore much of the responsibility for carrying out the policy that Jefferson, among others, dreamt up for the Indians, 'Indian removal' to reservations further and further west, ahead of white expansion. Thousands of Indian families were forced west and thousands died of violence, hunger and disease on the way. Superior fire-power put down all resistance—as in the Black Hawk War (Illinois, 1831). The removal of the advanced and settled Cherokee Nation from Georgia, 1831–32 (the tragic 'Trail of Tears') was one of the worst episodes in this history of liberal individualism and the search for profit. Jackson's administrations ignored maybe a hundred paper 'treaties' with the various Indian tribes and helped to destroy their cultures. The trauma of culture-contact was still to be felt in the future by Plains Indians in the farther West. Jackson's egalitarianism was the freedom of the mainstream or majority: a frontier 'democracy' you had to be *for*, or you were automatically considered *against*. But Jackson at his most confident was aware that an even bigger issue, what he called 'the Negro or slavery question', was not to be put aside so readily.

8. *'The Trail of Tears' by Robert Lindneux.*
From the original oil painting of Cherokee Indians in Woolaroo Museum,
Bartlesville, Oklahoma.

Cotton culture and black slaves

Like the sugar plantations of Brazil (the *engenhos*), southern cotton estates in the USA depended fully on African slave labour. Slavery ran counter to the expressed and implied philosophy of the American Revolution and Bill of Rights and it was severely opposed by liberal early 19th century Britain. Many Americans too, opposed it, and the abolitionist movement became a sustaining branch of radical and reformist thought in the 1830s and 40s. Cotton was the chief southern interest by 1820; output doubled every ten years up to 1860. By that year about four million black slaves lived in the South with about seven million whites. The racial mixing already found in Brazil by 1800, was almost entirely lacking in the United States. Mulattoes were not considered 'white'. Americans, unlike Brazilians, did not fondly hope that the colour problem would vanish with the further 'whitening' of mulattoes through complete mixing.

Southern slavery of course was not simply a labour-system but a way of life. Large plantations did not dominate the scene as much as they did in Brazil, Venezuela or Cuba. The typical unit was small, using five or six slaves. Under 3% of whites living in the South came from families that owned twenty or more slaves. It took about 500 acres to use economically about twenty slaves and an overseer; yet under 3% of southern farms were bigger than 500 acres. The large units could be very large—industrial-type plantations, on which conditions for the slaves were the worst. Sugar plantations in Louisiana were of this variety: up to 2,000 acres, with large numbers of slaves, overseers and steam-powered machinery. The large majority of southern farms were smaller, with a few slaves. They followed the ideas and life-style set by the big plantations and in doing so, helped to create the myth of the 'Cavalier' South. Up to the 20th century the South, like Mexico, Brazil and other nations with large concentrated land-holding systems, did not have a sizeable, unintimidated white middle-class.

The North American slave had fewer legal rights than say, the Brazilian slave, being a complete possession or 'chattel' of the owner in perpetuity along with his children. When the slave-trade was cut off for Americans in 1808 the practice of breeding increased, along with a large domestic slave-trade: usually slaves from Virginia, Maryland and North Carolina (which needed them less as cotton growing in the area declined), were sold farther south to the growing cotton regions of Alabama, Mississippi, Texas and Louisiana. Here families were sometimes split up (they had no recognised legal existence), incentives were given to breed (promise of freedom, clothes for the mother) and the stamp of permanent inferiority reinforced at public auction. The termination of international slave-trading also meant that a higher proportion of United States slaves were *born into* slavery than elsewhere. This fact did not seem to make slave-revolts fewer, as witnessed in Gabriel's Revolt (Virginia, 1801), Denmark Vesey's Plot (South Carolina, 1822), the bloody Nat Turner Insurrection (Virginia, 1831) and others.

Legal discriminations against *slaves* became discriminations against *Negroes* in many respects, for in the United States the 'free Negro' was neither fish nor fowl. This, with the degradations of public auctions, lack of basic rights to sue in courts against whites, and the crushing paternalism of the master-class, presented a brick wall to any Negro hoping to better his position, free or slave. Negro leaders did emerge nevertheless and several abolitionist spokesmen and organisers were black.

The South as a region paid many times over for the sin of slavery, not only by losing the Civil War and by being physically devastated in the process and colonised by the North thereafter. Slavery tied up capital in the South: lack of liquid assets made it hard for planters ever to diversify if the cotton market or sugar market slumped. Many plantations were poorly equipped because all the cash was tied up in slaves. When slavery was abolished without compensation in 1863, thousands of southern farmers were simply ruined.

Plantation slavery was ill-adapted to a growing economic situation of fluctuations in world demand for staples. Its labour-force was narrowly trained, though many slaves were very adaptable and had good general skills. Education of slaves was not allowed. European immigrants would not go to the South because of slavery. Who would want to compete as a worker with slaves? So the South had little chance of building up a reservoir of skilled artisans suitable for any future manufacturing. Under slavery, she was to be a colony of the North, exporting raw materials and at the best only semi-finished goods. Like any colony of earlier years under traditional mercantilist rule, the South exported staples, like cotton, sugar, tobacco and rice; imported finished goods; and managed most of this trade through banks in New York City or other northern ports. She was not much better off than the colonies of Spain in the 17th century, and slavery kept her in that position.

The American as reformer

Meanwhile the American value-system associated with the Jeffersonian-Jacksonian political tradition did not die with Jackson. Democratic, republican individualism stretched on, to 1860, the Civil War, and beyond. It was strengthened by the writings and influence of great thinkers like R. W. Emerson, and the Concord School of idealist philosophers, the *Transcendentalists*. It may seem strange to pair Andrew Jackson and Emerson, but politics make strange bedfellows, and the transcendentalists' notions of human perfectibility, anti-institutionalism and reliance on intuition, and their view of the 'infinite worthiness of man' fitted well with Jackson's fairly negative view of human freedom as freedom from. He would have agreed with them that one only needs to *remove impediments* to improve the quality of American life.

One massive impediment was human slavery. Among the cluster of ideas which made the second quarter of the 19th century an age of radical reform, abolitionism stood out. It began as essentially a religious matter. The Quaker preacher Benjamin Lundy was, before about 1830, the leading abolitionist. American religion has undergone a sort of 'Second Great Awakening'—a wave of religious revivalism like that of the 18th century—which had left far behind the old formal Calvinism that Emerson called 'corpse-cold Christianity'. By the revivalists of the famous 'burnt-over district' of New York State and the western camp meetings, by theologians like Lyman Beecher and C. G. Finney, theology was simply democratised; the 'Elect' seemed to vanish. 'God is Love' was the message. *Communitarianism*, an old colonial tradition, reappeared for a while in such communities as Brook Farm, or the Shaker religious communes, or the daring sex experiment of Oneida. A continuing search for radical new alternatives in private and public life characterised the reformism of the 1830s and 40s.

And what of slavery? If feminism, prison reform, treatment of debtors, insane asylums, Children's Aid, temperance, and a galaxy of other matters should energise the American middle classes, sooner or later Negro slavery would overtop them all. It became the one dominating issue up to 1860. Black leaders were not slow to take advantage of the tide of reform. As early as 1829 David Walker's *Appeal* (Boston) blasted slavery; long before, even in colonial days, articulate blacks were demanding abolition and petitioning assemblies. Frederick Douglass was perhaps the best-known black abolitionist and was elected president of the New England Anti-slavery Society in 1847.

By 1827 slavery was abolished in the North, where it was economically unprofitable. In the 1830s a new generation of more radical leaders denounced Lundy's moralism and gradualism and demanded immediate action of various sorts. Religious persuasion was now ousted by outright denunciation. The new abolitionists, led by Theodore Weld, Wendell Phillips, Theodore Parker, and William Lloyd Garrison broadened their attacks into a vilification of southern society. Garrison's paper *The Liberator* announced: 'On this subject I do not wish to think, or speak, or write with moderation. ... I will not equivocate—I will not excuse— I will not retreat a single inch—AND I WILL BE HEARD.' Harriet Beecher Stowe's super-sweet novel *Uncle Tom's Cabin* (1852) became a world best-seller and was dramatised for popular theatre thousands of times. Abolitionist groups sprang up all over the North and West and by 1840 one federation, the American Antislavery Society (Garrisonian) had 2,000 societies under it and claimed about 175,000 active, proselytizing members. The abolitionists were opposed by many Americans, regarded as fanatics by others, and soon had martyrs of their own to show.

Some fanatics did exist, like John Brown, who ran a station on the 'Underground Railway' to smuggle escaped slaves out of the South (contrary to the Fugitive Slave Laws of 1793 and 1850), then moved to Kansas where he and his sons were involved in bloodshed in 1856 in a fight between pro and anti-slavery men. Brown captured the *Harper's Ferry* (W. Virginia) federal arsenal in 1859, was defeated and later hanged. But the bulk of abolitionists were not fanatical or bloodthirsty; they were deeply troubled Americans, black and white.

Coming of the civil war

As the American economy accelerated with the spread of railways and growing manufacturing and specialised farming belts, the nation headed full-tilt towards separatism and Civil War. This was to be a war for the Union, a war that involved many of the basic political issues about the nature of the American Union going back to the Constitution of 1787 and never fully resolved. These were similar issues to those that divided federalists and centralists in South America, *unitarios* and provincial leaders in Argentina for example, though there the struggle was more extreme, against the bloody dictator and *gaucho* leader Rosas. But more than this was involved; for without slavery, there would have been no Civil War. The War was not only a constitutional issue.

The war was technically fought not over slavery as an institution, but over its possible extension into new western territory as this became politically organised. So the war was also a sectional issue, even though sectional disputes were not particularly tense in 1860–61. These quarrels typically centred on public land policies, tariff levels, the role of the national bank and federal aid to 'internal improvements'. The last issue went back at least to Hamilton and Jefferson. None of these four problems were dominant in 1860. Each had caused trouble in the past—the tariff question brought South Carolina to the brink of civil disobedience in 1833 when she threatened to leave the Union. In 1861 she led the secession of the southern states.

Escalation I: the Mexican–American War

The main issue of 1860 was slavery-extension. Every time a new state was admitted the threat to the political balance between the sections created a new crisis. The crisis deepened as the South came under increasingly bitter attack over slavery, and became more defensive. John C. Calhoun of South Carolina could bring himself to declare that slavery was 'a positive good'. The abolitionist Garrison came to demand *northern* secession from the Union—the constitution, he said, since it accepted slavery, was 'A Covenant with death and an agreement with Hell'. Between these extremes were a growing number of Americans who were prepared to fight over the extension of slavery, if not over slavery itself. The consensus on political solutions was eroding and the situation was escalated by the results of the Mexican-American War.

The United States expanded into the Southwest in the 1840s at the expense of Mexico. The vast territories explored by Spanish conquistadors in the 16th century became part of the US when Texas was annexed in 1845, and after the war with Mexico, 1846–48, the whole of California and 'New Mexico' were ceded. This included present New Mexico, Arizona, Utah, Nevada, parts of Wyoming and Colorado. How would these enormous additions affect the sectional political balance? Could the 36°30' line of 1820, dividing slavery in the Louisiana Purchase lands, be extended to the Pacific?

Henry Clay, who politicked the 1820 compromise line along with Stephen Douglas, managed a new Compromise of 1850. This again shattered the hopes of Negroes and abolitionists. The 'New Mexico' region was divided into two, to be admitted into the Union, with or without slavery, when sufficiently populated. California was admitted immediately, as a free state. A stronger Fugitive Slave Law was enacted, to please southerners, and slave-trading was abolished in the nation's capital in order to placate abolitionists. The trick worked for a while. But future events would show the hollowness of such compromises.

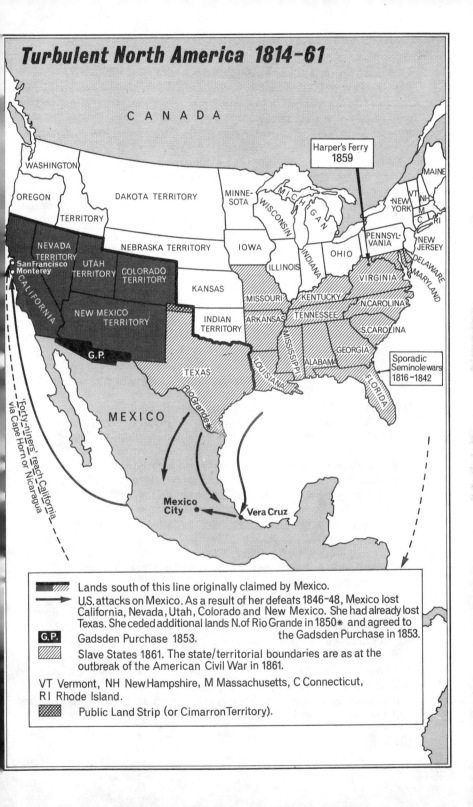

Turbulent North America 1814-61

CANADA

WASHINGTON
OREGON
TERRITORY
DAKOTA TERRITORY
MINNE-SOTA
MICHIGAN
WISCONSIN
MAINE
VT NH
M
NEW YORK
C RI
PENNSYL-VANIA
NEW JERSEY

Harper's Ferry 1859

NEVADA TERRITORY
San Francisco
Monterey
UTAH TERRITORY
COLORADO TERRITORY
NEBRASKA TERRITORY
IOWA
ILLINOIS
INDIANA
OHIO
DELAWARE
MARYLAND
VIRGINIA

CALIFORNIA

NEW MEXICO TERRITORY
KANSAS
MISSOURI
KENTUCKY
N. CAROLINA
TENNESSEE
S. CAROLINA

G.P.
INDIAN TERRITORY
ARKANSAS
MISSISSIPPI
GEORGIA
ALABAMA

Sporadic Seminole wars 1816-1842

TEXAS
LOUISIANA
FLORIDA

Rio Grande

MEXICO

'Forty-niners' reach California via Cape Horn or Nicaragua

Mexico City
Vera Cruz

Legend

Lands south of this line originally claimed by Mexico.

→ U.S. attacks on Mexico. As a result of her defeats 1846-48, Mexico lost California, Nevada, Utah, Colorado and New Mexico. She had already lost Texas. She ceded additional lands N. of Rio Grande in 1850* and agreed to the Gadsden Purchase in 1853.

G.P. Gadsden Purchase 1853.

Slave States 1861. The state/territorial boundaries are as at the outbreak of the American Civil War in 1861.

VT Vermont, NH New Hampshire, M Massachusetts, C Connecticut, RI Rhode Island.

Public Land Strip (or Cimarron Territory).

Escalation II: the miracle no longer works

The election of Abraham Lincoln, a western lawyer and opponent of slavery-extension in 1860 confirmed the South's worst fears on the outcome of the sectional struggle. Lincoln led a new party, the Republicans, a specifically anti-slavery-extension party, whose creation was stimulated by two events of 1854. Pro-slavery Democrats in 1854 issued the quixotic 'Ostend Manifesto', warning Spain that the US would take Cuba, and openly linking territorial growth with expansion of slavery. Not content that slavery existed at all in the American Republic, it seemed that some southerners wanted it to grow more and more. Then the Kansas-Nebraska Act, embodying Stephen Douglas's idea of 'popular sovereignty' (local people to decide on slavery), nullified the compromise line of 1820. Slavery could now exist *north* of 36°30′. Migrants, pro- and anti-slavery, rushed in; the area became 'Bleeding Kansas' as they fought local battles.

Meanwhile the old Whig Party had died out, torn apart by the slavery issue in 1848 after the Mexican War. By 1860 the Democrats also were badly split. The Republicans gained power, though narrowly. Could the American consensus hold? Could the losers, the South, simply wait for four years and try again? Or would it be too late by then? For once, for the first time since the election of 1800, the miracle of peaceful transfer of authority did *not* work. The underlying consensus was broken. The American Union broke down and a bloody, long civil war followed.

Impact of the Civil War at home

The American Civil War was a total war, the first major war of the age of industrialism, involving civilian populations and national physical resources. Its impact on the South, where most of the fighting took place, was terrible. General Sherman's deliberate act of psychological warfare, in cutting a broad swath through the South, destroying all before him, was but one aspect of the great destruction. By 1865 the South was reduced to near-morbidity: its credit gone, its paper money worthless, its plantations destroyed along with many of its cities, and its chief assets—ownership of human slaves—lost. Inevitably, and with careful northern planning, it became even more of a colony of the North and growing Midwest than before. Northern capital and business moved in.

What of the Republicans and the North? The war gave the region and the party the opportunity they needed for growth and consolidation of power. The Congress of 1860 ironically, could have had a Democratic majority, but the angry southerners walked out and went home. This left the Republicans in total control of the government and they immediately took steps to encourage and protect business and industrial interests. Two days before Lincoln took the oath of office the Republicans had passed a high Tariff Act (1861) to protect native American industrialists and workers against foreign competition. Other acts, held up by southern and Democratic opposition, were now pushed through without dissent.

The pro-western Homestead Act to speed up land sales on the frontier; the Pacific Railway Act to give huge land grants to private corporations to extend the railways across the Plains to the Pacific; the Legal Tender Act to allow the issue of federal currency notes ('Greenbacks'); the National Bank Act to facilitate credit for businessmen and strengthen banking; the Contract Labor Law to allow companies to bring in foreign labour; the creation of the US Department of Agriculture. The message was clear: capitalism was in the ascendant and the new Republican party was its political arm.

The Negro was liberated in 1863 but the end of the war two years later did not bring the end of racism or discrimination against black Americans. Emancipation was not accompanied by the other reforms needed to make it work: education, assurance of jobs or land and full civil rights. President Andrew Johnson was unsympathetic to Negro needs. He allowed the South to re-enter the Union on its own terms. By the end of 1865 this sort of 'Reconstruction' meant that white suprema-cists were in control of the ex-rebel state governments and Negroes had been given no political rights. In fact the Black Codes passed by these states deprived blacks of many social and civil rights: they were segre-gated, discriminated against, and put under rigid labour laws.

The 'radicals' in Congress, like Thaddeus Stevens and Charles Sumner, were angry. Authority passed to Congress, mainly to the Senate, where Stevens dominated. Johnson's reconstruction was wiped away; the south-ern states had to re-apply for admission, abolish the Black Codes, accept the 14th and 15th Amendments and submit to oaths of loyalty. The radicals then impeached the President—almost winning their case. This period of so-called Radical Reconstruction saw real achievements in Negro education and material advancements (mainly through the 'Freed-men's Bureau'). But only 700,000 out of four million ex-slaves were qualified to vote by the Radicals. Negroes never gained control of any state government; those who went into politics were not very radical in outlook.

After 1868, when war hero General Grant became president and the nation launched on a program of full-scale capitalist growth, even the radicals waned in enthusiasm. When the 15th Amendment was watered down, allowing escape-clauses, Negroes were cheated of the right to vote. Gradually white supremacy and conservative strength came back to the South. The radical experiment at Reconstruction came to an end. The freedmen had not been given any permanent or lasting help to assimilate into free society.

While the federal government saw fit to give to one railway company alone as much as forty million acres of public land, no land was given to the freed Negroes. This one grant, if transferred to them, would have meant ten acres each. The freedmen were betrayed by the North and enserfed (if not re-enslaved) by the South. They moved from legal slavery to debt-peonage. Lack of opportunities and general rural poverty turned them into a mass of generally docile, available cheap labour—share-croppers, poverty-stricken tenants, labourers. The landed white elite came back in the South, and a fate similar to that of the Negroes befell the poor whites after the war. But white supremacy also brought a re-creaction of the Black Codes in the 'Jim Crow' laws and segregation. The US Supreme Court supported discrimination in the Civil Rights cases of 1883, and in 1896 the Court invented a new doctrine to safeguard segre-gated facilities—the 'separate but equal' rule.

By the late 1870s and early 80s the South was thus similar to large parts of Central and South America in its social structure and economic condition. It was a colony, producing export staples, subject to unstable world demand. Economic control was exercised from outside the region. Communications were bad. One-crop regions were without security. A few large owners and a social-political elite was in power over a broader mass of semi-peasants, tied to the land by heavy debts and by the vicious cycle of poverty, illiteracy and servility. These debt-peons in the South were black and 'poor white'; in the southern Americas they were Indians and castas (blacks still being fully enslaved in Brazil until 1888).

The North, Midwest and the Far West of the United States became modern, urbanised, industrialised, and prosperous. This ex-colony, the United States, became the world's richest nation by the 20th century, and within itself it contained a backward, rural, colonial region: Dixie.

Creation of modern Canada

The impact of the Civil War was felt outside the United States within the western hemisphere. Napoleon III of France took the opportunity of US involvment to invade Mexico and to impose on that nation as Emperor, Maximilian of Austria. In Brazil the slavery abolitionists were heartened by the US measure of Negro emancipation declared by Lincoln in 1863. Brazilian reformers were also under heavy British anti-slavery influence. The greatest impact of the Civil War elsewhere was on Canada, where it hastened the movement towards unity and Canadian identity and helped to bring the British North America Act which is the constitutional foundation of modern Canada.

The nation, Upper and Lower Canada alike, had seen modest economic and population growth after 1791. So-called 'late Loyalists' continued to migrate from the US into Canada. By the 1820s and 30s the pace of development had accelerated with the advent of early manufacturing enterprises as well as of the production of new staples—timber and grain. Canal ventures, like the great Welland Canal of 1829, and later on the railway boom of the 1850s, provided the vital east-west linkage needed in Canada, particularly in view of its geographical shape (described by critics as a 'four thousand mile Main Street' or more bitterly sometimes,

9. *An accident on the Great Western Railway, near Hamilton, Ontario.*

as a 'geographical absurdity'). The essential linkages were provided by lines like the Great Western Railroad of 1860 and the Grand Trunk of 1861.

Economic growth brings social change and upheaval. The Canada of the early 19th century was markedly more élitist and class-conscious in tone than US society. Internal tensions among the colonists as well as between Canada and Britain brought the great Rebellion of 1837. The Canadian rebels wanted firmer government controls over monopolies and privilege, and popular command over revenue and the judiciary. In Ontario the English-American Canadians were divided by a class system. The leading Toronto families (the 'Family Compact') controlled the political scene. They were Anglican, anti-French and anti-Catholic but they stood for economic growth and diversification and the construction of banks, canals and railways, like the US Hamiltonians or Whigs. These Tory imperialists were opposed in the province by a larger number of lower-class small farmers and artisans, usually Methodists, who fought against the 'Clergy Reserve' system of public land grants given to maintain the Church of England. They were anti-bank, anti-internal improvements, anti-monopoly and anti-Family Compact. The radicals of upper Canada were Jacksonian in spirit.

In French Canada the major issue was control of trade by the English minority and inadequate political representation for the French-speaking colonists. French radicals, too, opposed use of public taxation to pay for internal improvements. Led by L. J. Papineau (Quebec) and W. L. Mackenzie (Ontario), the radicals stimulated armed uprisings and violence around Toronto and Montreal. The movement was easily subdued. This was the closest that Canada ever came to an 'American Revolution' against the London government. The mass of Canadian settlers were torpid and did nothing. Too close an imitation of the actions of the United States, and full Canadian independence from Britain, could bring the threat of future absorption into the US.

The Rebellion caused London to send out the young, Radical Lord Durham to study the Canadian problem for five months. His famous *Report* of 1840 told Parliament to give the colonists a wide latitude in self-government in order to keep them loyal. As for the French, Durham said, 'I found two nations warring in the bosom of a single state.' His attitude was one of moderate but inevitable assimilation of the French into a dominant English culture. This has never happened. The *Act of Union* of 1840 rejoined the provinces of Quebec and Ontario, gave the single assembly a wider-based franchise and allowed the Governor-General to choose his government from among the majority party, thus making possible the gradual evolution of 'responsible' and not merely 'representative' government.

As Canada's Governor-General, Lord Grey pursued a policy of trying to enlarge the rights of Canadians over a wide range of areas. He warned the Governor of Nova Scotia to give the local assembly there its head, because:

> it is neither possible nor desirable to carry on the government of any of the British provinces in North America in opposition to the opinion of the inhabitants.

Perhaps an enlightened Durham Report for the 13 American colonies in the 1770s, followed by such a policy, would have made the American Revolution and the creation of the United States unnecessary. A later Governor-General of Canada (Elgin) said with triumph in 1852:

> it is possible to maintain on this soil of North America and in the face of Republican America, British connections and British institutions, if you give the latter freely and trustingly.

It appeared that one historical lesson had been learned.

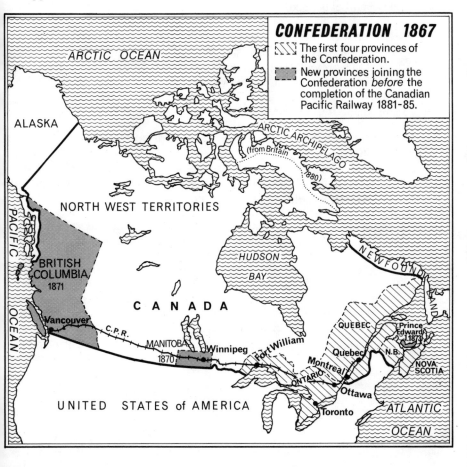

CONFEDERATION 1867

The first four provinces of the Confederation.

New provinces joining the Confederation *before* the completion of the Canadian Pacific Railway 1881-85.

The immediate impact of the US Civil War was to encourage Canadians to strengthen their defences and to form a stronger government, with the British North America Act of 1867. This bound together the heartland with the maritime provinces and with the vast Canadian West and created a nation larger than the United States. Within the British Empire, Canada assumed a special status as a 'Dominion'. This somewhat ambiguous title was chosen (rather than the title 'Kingdom of Canada' favoured by the chief Canadian architect of the new confederation, John A. Macdonald) so as not to irritate the USA or to appear to give Canada too much separate status from London. But in practice the Confederation of Canada had wide autonomy which would be enlarged each decade. The Dominion had a federal structure with a much stronger central government than that in the USA and a British 'parliamentary' rather than a 'Congressional' structure, in which the Governor-General's cabinet was responsible to the House of Commons. Macdonald sturdily opposed the US formula of strong local power and pointed out in 1866 the dangers in the US brought by 'states' rights' protagonists. The very recent Civil War was his witness. Macdonald explained:

> Ever since the [US] was formed the difficulty of what is called 'State Rights' has existed, and this had much to do with bringing on the present [sic] unhappy war in the United States. They commenced, in fact, at the wrong end ...

The Canadian Confederation would not begin 'at the wrong end':

> We have given the central legislature all the great subjects of legislation.

The new nation of Canada was thus an unusual fusion of British and North American political practices and needs.

5
Caudillismo

In Central and South America the independence wars were not true mass movements and did not produce social revolutions. Led by creoles who sometimes found it politically wise to threaten the Spanish peninsulares with the fearsome visions of mestizo, Indian or casta violence, the three aims of the wars were: to kick out the colonial powers, to open up the ex-colonies to free world trade, and to maintain intact at home the existing and inherited social hierarchy. The overall theme of post-independence years was thus creole containment: how the creoles kept their 'revolutions' within safe bounds. Certain inevitable consequences flowed from their goals and policies.

The creole elite faced three social groups: Indians, Africans and mestizos. The first two were kept under control by indebtedness, violence and slavery, the last by co-opting members into the establishment—the lighter-skinned ones by marriage, the darker ones by admission into the bureaucracy and the army. The social and economic status of mestizos improved visibly over the 19th century and in several nations they became the dominant population group. Indians however declined in status as concentration of white land-holding took place at the expense of their communal lands, particularly in Argentina and Mexico. Due to medical improvements (smallpox vaccination) the Indian population grew while its dependency and poverty increased. Like Jackson or W. H. Harrison in the USA, General J. A. Roca launched a military campaign to clear Indians from the southern *pampas* (plains) of Argentina in 1878–9. Subsequently he became president. Like the American Dream, the Argentinan Dream of growth would let nothing stand in its path.

Indians often fought back against the white expansionists, as in Peru and Mexico; sometimes they enlisted the aid of local caudillos. In Mexico the Yaqui Indians were uprooted and shipped to distant plantations in Yucatan. Those who later fought for the revolution under Obregón in 1914 remembered such treatment. Against the forces of economic expansion, monopoly of the army, and racism, the Indians could not prevail. Mestizos who rose in the system were as bad as creoles towards Indians.

111

In Mexico the Yaquis were persecuted by the mestizo, Díaz (who used to powder his face as white as he could). Liberal reformers of the 19th century considered communal lands to be feudal survivals. Under the cover of liberal 'modernisation' Indian communes were broken up, and countless Indians became landless labourers, domestic servants, debt-peons. As such, illiterate and powerless, they were not allowed to vote under the new liberal constitutions. The gap between the Indian country-side and the white cities widened.

Creole containment: the rise of caudillos

The outcome of creole policy was thus the rise of caudillismo. Geography and colonial separatism also played their part in this rise, as did the influence of European ideas of the early 19th century, especially of the Romantics who worshipped charismatic leaders and individualistic 'heroes'—like Napoleon I for instance. Caudillos were rural strong-men, who provided the real local government. Supported by the class of large land-holders, these caudillos (*coronéis* in Brazil) maintained their own troops and were the supreme law of the countryside, as the creole elites of the old colonial cabildos were the supreme law in the cities. Creole containment and the rigid, aristocratic class-system it supported, retarded the emergence of a sizeable middle class of property-owners and businessmen in South American nations, which could have held the caudillo system in check. Between the mass of peasants and slaves and the small landed oligarchy there was no real buffer-group.

The sectionalism that plagued the United States and helped to produce the Civil War was even more severe and constant in South and Central America. The creole-caudillo system of rule exaggerated city-rural tensions. In Argentina for example, the city of Buenos Aires engaged in open war against rural leaders in a struggle for control of the nation's government. This was a much more intense and bloody version of the city-rural hostility found in the United States in the 19th and 20th centuries (New Orleans versus upstate Louisiana; Chicago versus suburban and downstate Illinois).

United States or Canadian-type political parties did not develop. In-stead, *leaders* had followings, or lost followings. So South American political history in textbooks is often a mere cataloguing of names of leaders and administrations. Despite this emphasis on personality (*personalismo* is an essential concomitant of *caudillismo*), certain themes were common. Federalists (local provincial, 'states' rights' types) opposed Centralists; 'liberals' opposed 'conservatives'. Liberals when in power had a tendency to become centralists; as did local *gauchos* (like Rosas of Argentina), if they took over the reins of national government. Ideology always gave way before personality and circumstances.

The many constitutions written by the creole liberals came to little because they were not ready to share political rights with the lower classes who made up the bulk of their populations. In South American history constitutions came and went, but the ruling elites continued in power. Liberal constitutions, though often based on the US model, tended to legitimize 'Napoleonic' dictatorships, giving strong executive powers to the president, the right to declare a national emergency ('state of siege') and to impose military rule at any time. Liberals agreed to such powers out of fear of separatist factions and lower-class uprisings. The peaceful transfer of political power rarely took place; countless regimes were begun by *coups*. The role of the army was crucial—it was the only *national* institution capable of bringing order out of separatist chaos. Uruguay, Chile, Costa Rica were exceptions to this general rule. Most early presidents were army men: eight out of ten in Peru. This is why 'revolutions' were mere palace coups, younger officers, perhaps from the provinces, replacing older officers. While some nations, under strong enlightened despots, enjoyed longer periods of calm, perhaps even as long as thirty years or so (Mexico, Guatemala), others experienced bewildering changes of government. This was an accelerating process for some nations: it was worse in the 20th century than in the 19th. Ecuador had 12 foreign ministers in two months in 1933.

Lack of formal parties

Swift change of regimes reflected weakness of the party structure and the personalism of South American political life. In Uruguay, a more homogenous nation and one where representative government has also had a better chance of survival, the *Colorados* opposed the *Blancos*. The latter party, representing the rural and clerical, conservative interests of the 1830s (under Manuel Oribe) opposed the liberal *colorados* (under José F. Rivera, first president of Uruguay). The *blancos* received help from the Argentine dictator, Rosas, who besieged Montevideo on and off for nine years (1843–51) until Rosas himself was overthrown in Argentina.

The Uruguayan situation was unusual. Generally, 'liberals', whether moderates or more extreme *exaltados*, stood for greater decentralisation and provincial power; for secular state education; for separation of Church and State, direct election of presidents, and wider suffrage. 'Conservatives' would preserve the Catholic Church with its special privileges, restrict the vote, spend little or nothing on education for the masses, and centralise power in the capital city. On the other hand, like the Hamiltonians of the United States they also wanted economic growth, diversification, capital investments. Neither group was well-defined, and neither really believed in popular democracy. It is doubtful if over 4% of the male population of any Central or South American nation was allowed to vote during the 19th century, and the liberals and conservatives were at one in their policy of oppression towards the Indians and Negroes.

113

Mexico: counter-revolution and tyranny

After the hideous bloodshed of the independence years counter-revolutionary Mexico settled down to about thirty years of political instability, division, and economic decline, presided over by General Santa Anna (1797–1876). Eleven times he took over the central government of Mexico, and in between his influence was strong. Usually conservative and pro-Church, Santa Anna had few political principles and low administrative ability. Rushing north to crush the independence movement begun in Texas by United States cattlemen and cotton-planters, Santa Anna wiped out a small US force in the San Antonio mission—the *Alamo*—but was defeated and captured by Sam Houston at San Jacinto, two months later (April 1836). The Republic of Texas became independent and was then annexed by the United States.

This ignominious defeat did not put down Santa Anna. In 1846 he was recalled from one of his exiles to fight the Mexican-American War, and was trounced in two battles and chased out of Mexico City by US forces in 1847. Yet by 1853, after another exile, he was dictator of Mexico again. Exiled for the last time in 1855, he travelled about the world for almost twenty years and returned to die in Mexico City in poverty and obscurity. He had seen Mexico's demeaning losses at the hands of the United States, the forfeiture of vast territories in North America. Mexico was cut in half. Yet nationalists remembered his stand against the Americans, against the French, who invaded Veracruz in 1838, and against the Spanish, who tried to retake Mexico from Havana in 1829. His amputated leg, lost at Veracruz, was buried with full military honors under a monument in Mexico City. This handsome, sallow, Romantic hero of a failed General was corrupt, despotic and prodigal of the nation's wealth; but he was constantly returned to power. Santa Anna was the classic example of a caudillo.

'La Reforma': Juárez and mestizo rule

The revolution of Ayutla, 1855, overthrew Santa Anna and produced an era of reforms—'La Reforma'—led mainly by middle-class mestizos and liberals. Concentration of land-ownership in a few hands had speeded up under Santa Anna. No alternative to the large hacienda was offered. Mining declined after 1810 and did not return to its old levels again until 1880 when foreign capital was introduced along with European technology and railways. Government encouragement to textile mills through high protective tariffs and development loans, brought poor results.

Though successful in some ways, the liberals were hindered by the Church which controlled public education, resisted the immigration of non-Catholics (despite the obvious example of the contribution of immigrants to US and Canadian growth to the north), and through its large properties and lands wielded great inertial force throughout Mexico.

Meanwhile, classic sectional problems kept Mexico backward. Small-town and provincial leaders did not want cheap foreign imports to ruin their local artisans; they fought the merchants of Mexico City. Guadalajara resisted the capital over economic policies. There was demand not only for tariffs against foreigners, but for *internal* tariffs and tolls between regions. Long before this, the US constitution had abolished all internal barriers to trade, and had created one large market: the secret of US internal growth.

The liberals of the 1850s tried to overcome some of the impediments to rational economic growth in Mexico. They aimed to break up large estates, put the Army and Church under the civil authority, and stop any more territorial depredations by the expanding United States.

The *Ley Juárez* of 1855 (Juárez Law) abolished the *fueros*, or special legal privileges of the Church and Army in Mexico. But in the following year the *Ley Lerdo* hit the Indian communes. Intended to take away Church lands and redistribute them, the act included as 'civil corporations' the ancient Indian communal village lands, respected for three hundred years by the Spanish conquerors, and called *ejidos* in Mexico. The ejidos were now to be partitioned and owned by the Indians tilling them. In practice, as with the Church lands which were to be sold to existing renters (or auctioned off), speculators stepped in and most of the Indian lands passed rapidly into the hands of surrounding *hacendados* albeit in the name of liberal reform. Concentration of land-ownership was boosted still more. Land monopoly remained. The Indians were cheated, and their way of life destroyed.

In 1857 a liberal congress wrote a federal constitution that contained these individualistic ideas. Civil war broke out between liberals and conservatives (1858–60), and Benito Juárez, a full-blooded Zapotec Indian and liberal leader, emerged victorious.

Juárez, though Indian, did little for his people. He identified with the mestizo-creole liberals and anticlericals and was especially radical about Church matters. He confiscated monasteries and Church property without compensation (1859—the earlier law had allowed them to be sold), and made marriage a civil ceremony. He established freedom of the press and of speech. When he moved to clear up the chaotic national finances of Mexico and suspended payments of interest on the national debt, foreign powers took the opportunity to invade, in defence of the investments abroad of their rich citizens.

The US was busy with its own Civil War when England, Spain and France sent ships to Veracruz. The French stayed, marched on Mexico City (June 1863) and installed the choice of Napoleon III, Maximilian of Austria, as Emperor of Mexico in April 1864. Maximilian, an amiable, good-natured and weak man who knew next to nothing about Mexico, could not keep control. He alienated even the Mexican conservatives and clericals, while the liberal forces under Juárez had moved to the north to prepare a counter-offensive. When the American Civil War ended the US warned France off and Maximilian was abandoned to his fate, a Mexican firing-squad, in June 1867. Juárez resumed his reformist rule until his death in 1872. He gave Mexico a few years of prosperity, though some of his ex-guerilla forces became bandits and he resorted to authoritarian rule and fixed elections. An even firmer and more conservative dictatorship was established in Mexico when General Porfirio Díaz overthrew Juárez's successor in 1876. Díaz ruled until the Mexican Revolution (1911).

Central America: federation and independence

Modern Mexico has seven near-neighbours to the South. Tiny British Honduras was ceded to England in 1859. The others are: Guatemala, Honduras (a 'banana republic' today, dependent on the US market and US corporations), El Salvador, Nicaragua, Costa Rica, and Panama (created in 1903 with US military help, in a revolution against Colombia). Costa Rica is racially unusual, almost entirely 'white'. Guatemala is preponderantly Indian. The rest are heavily mestizo and other racial mixtures.

The colonies of Central America became part of Mexico after independence (1821) and then formed their own Central American Federation (1823–38) for fifteen years. After 1838 when they separated, these nations all became subject to foreign intervention and to boundary wars among themselves. They developed export economies, selling staples to Europe and North America, such as bananas, and coffee. They were virtual economic colonies once more. The clash of interests between England and the US was temporarily resolved in 1850 with the Clayton-Bulwer Treaty which promised that neither great power would exert an exclusive control of any part of the Isthmus to build a canal to the Pacific. Trading with Asia without having to go around the tip of South America was the great issue.

The mountainous and volcanic land of Guatemala was ruled by an ultra-conservative dictator, Rafael Carrera, from 1839 to 1865. He was a casta: Indian-European-Negro. Illiterate and a pious, Church-loving Catholic, he brought little economic change to his people. He signed away British Honduras and fought wars with Honduras and El Salvador to little effect. Like subsequent rulers of Guatemala, Carrera fancied himself as leader of a united Central America.

A more reform-minded dictator took over in 1873, Justo Rufino Barrios. This tough anticlerical hated the Church and attacked it so strongly that it never recovered in Guatemala. Church tithes were abolished, the hierarchy sent packing, Jesuits evicted, and education secularised. Barrios was educated and intelligent: his plans for the economic growth of Guatemala included encouraging the coffee, rubber and cotton plantations while insisting on crop diversification for balance. Barrios

116

built highways, encouraged railways, and gave his country good credit abroad. Like Carrera however he had no respect for the Indian masses. He thought the only hope was *white* European immigration. He had ambitious ideas about federating Central America. Barrios was killed in an invasion of El Salvador in 1885. Though he was authoritarian (his orders were carried out in the provinces by local bosses, not unlike the colonial intendentes, called *jefes politicos*), Barrios was among the most able leaders of this period of Guatemalan history.

Costa Rica and Nicaragua, like Guatemala, left the Central American Federation in 1838. Both countries were torn apart thereafter by internal dissension: in Costa Rica, between two landed *families*; in Nicaragua, between two *cities*. A measure of order came to Costa Rica when Tomás Guardia took over in 1870. He exiled opposing politicians, and ruled with army help until he died in 1882. US businessmen, the Keith brothers, built a railway across the nation and shipped bananas. The Keiths were progenitors of the later United Fruit Company of 1899. Like many South American reformers, Guardia introduced a constitution in 1871 but did not follow its rules himself.

In Nicaragua the problem was hostility between 'liberal' León and 'conservative' Granada. In 1838 the liberals, still in power after independence, made León the capital. Harassed by the conservatives, they accepted the aid of a US mercenary, William Walker. This adventurer had recently failed to wrest Lower California from the Mexicans. He willingly invaded Granada in a 'filibustering' raid, put down the conservatives, and ended up making himself president of Nicaragua in 1856. Ludicrously, the US government recognised him. The great American capitalist, W. H. Vanderbilt, did not. Walker had seized his ships, so Vanderbilt's money supported an invasion from Costa Rica and Honduras. Walker was kicked out; he was shot while attempting yet another raid on Honduras in 1860. Few young nations have had to suffer the indignity of seeing two foreign adventurers fight it out on their native soil.

The 'Spanish Main': Venezuela and Colombia

While the once-magnificent colony of Mexico was suffering under the incompetent Santa Anna and Central America was subject to the whims of foreign powers, what was happening to the lands of the former 'Spanish Main'? In Venezuela the wars of independence were prolonged and destructive. Autonomy was not fully guaranteed there until the battle of Carabobo in 1821. Bolívar had liberated Bogotá earlier, in 1819. This difference in timing was due to Bolívar's flanking movement in going up the Orinoco valley into Colombia, and by-passing Caracas. Both nations were united with Ecuador in Bolívar's Republic of Gran Colombia until 1830.

Venezuela lost at least 25% of her population in the bloodletting of the independence struggle and did not make up that tremendous loss until 1850. The Spaniards had paid little attention to this colony, not realising of course that Venezuela was a *true* 'El Dorado'—fabulously rich in underground lakes of oil (one of the globe's greatest oil producers today). The plains of the east and south make up three-quarters of the nation; the cowboys of these llanos swung the balance in favour of Bolívar. But 90% of the people live in the small plateau region and cities of the Northwest. Venezuela has had a classic history of caudillo rule, which reflects its geography.

The first dictator of Venezuela was a cowboy from the eastern llanos, a superb horseman and guerilla fighter who had brought his men to Bolívar's side and decided the outcome of the war in 1821: José Antonio Páez. From 1830 to 1846 Páez ruled, sometimes using a frontman as president. His early years were modestly reformist. The Church's role was restricted but not eliminated. Páez encouraged some educational and economic advances; he permitted a degree of intellectual and political freedom. Five armed revolts were suppressed, but in 1846 he was replaced by the harsher Monagas brothers. After several attempts to stage a come-back, Páez returned in 1861, aged 71, and governed much more despoti-cally. He was overthrown in 1863.

A second dictator emerged from the confusion and civil wars following the fall of Páez, a man entirely different. Antonio Guzmán Blanco was no llanero cowboy, but a sophisticated, well-travelled diplomat and suc-cessful representative of Venezuela in European capitals. He obtained government loans from European bankers in the 1860s. The son of a liberal Caracas journalist, Guzmán was the *urban* figure, where Páez was a classic *rural* caudillo. Together they represent two basic modes in the political life of South America.

Guzmán had some economic imagination. He encouraged railways, he began a compulsory system of secular national education, he put Venezuela's finances on a solid footing and won international credit. Unfortunately, his own hedonism and moral laxity let him down. Guzmán lived off the national treasury and travelled constantly on public funds. While he was living high in Paris his puppet president in Caracas turned the tables and took over real power in 1888. Wisely, Guzmán stayed where he was, living off his profits to the end (1899). At home, students tired of his vanity, corruption and despotism, tore down his statues and public portraits. Guzmán is remembered most for his bitter attack on the Catholic Church in Venezuela. He was not only heavily influenced by French anticlericalism, but was himself a leading freemason.

An extraordinary geography has dictated Colombian history: the east-ern two thirds, with about 2% of the population, are all jungle, forest and plains, watered to the east by two of the world's greatest rivers (Orinoco and Amazon). The people live in the western third—high Añdes moun-tains and steep valleys. The 1,000 mile Magdalena river penetrates the huge range, linking the interior capital, Bogotá, to the Caribbean at Cartagena. Colombian politics and society has therefore been even more regionalised and fragmented than other South American nations. The nation is heavily mestizo but the tiny 'Latin' white minority has insisted on its racial purity and links with Spain, giving Colombia an exaggerated Spanish culture: a very conservative 'Spanish' Church, for example, giving rise to an exaggerated anticlerical movement in reaction. So Colombia's history has been one of intense ideological battle and unusual regional tension.

Each 'department' (province) became a city-state, with opposing economic and political interests and no sense of national unity. Civil wars between city-regions were common. Meanwhile liberals and conservatives divided over the Church issue, the liberals winning control after nineteen years of bloodshed in 1849. They were never supreme though a federal constitution was drawn up in 1863. Order came to Colombia only as late as 1879 with the election of Rafael Nuñez, the 'Regenerator', an ex-liberal who became a centralist dictator in 1884. He restored the Church to power and imposed truly centralised *national* government with the Constitution of 1886, Colombia's tenth. Like all his predecessors he achieved little for the mass of the population, but did manage to die in office in 1894. Nuñez was an intellectual, a poet, and a student of the English philosopher of *laissez-faire*, Herbert Spencer.

Argentina: gaucho versus city

The persistent theme of Argentine history has been the conflict between city and countryside. In typically Spanish colonial fashion, the centre of the Plata colony was the town of Buenos Aires. The wealth of the area was not precious metals but something more lasting that makes Argentina one of the world's greatest agricultural nations today, the rich soils of the pampas. The interests of Buenos Aires and those of the provinces that surrounded it were not always the same.

So, Argentina's first dictator, Juan Manuel de Rosas, perhaps South America's most infamous caudillo, was a powerful local gaucho, a rich grain and cattle man from the southern part of Buenos Aires province. Rosas was born in Buenos Aires but left the city at the age of sixteen to take over his father's *estancia* and make a fortune on the rich, black, fertile soil of the pampas. By the age of 25 he owned thousands of acres, and was known as a perfect horseman, expert with the lasso and *boleadoras*, a harsh master who identified totally with provincial values and resisted the city. He organised a group to build a local processing-plant and evade the duties imposed by Buenos Aires. Like Russia's cossacks of the steppe-lands, North America's prairie cowboys, or Venezuela's llaneros, the Argentine gaucho created a horseback subculture at variance with metropolitan values. This was the source of Rosas' early power.

The 'United Provinces of La Plata' which declared their independence from Spain in 1816 were anything but united. The Banda Oriental on the other side of the La Plata river seceded and became independent in 1828 (Uruguay); the *junta* of Buenos Aires also failed to annex Upper Peru (Bolivia) and Paraguay. Anarchy reigned up to 1829, when Rosas took over after a successful foray into politics with his armed gauchos behind him. He stood for the federalists against the *unitarios* or centralists.

Rosas ruled bloodily until 1852 by suppressing all opposition, and by brain-washing the people about the 'filthy, savage' unitarios through the school-system, press and pulpit. His portrait, like Guzmán's in Venezuela, was everywhere, even in Church. Only the Jesuits resisted, and he re-expelled them in 1847. But Rosas, like many a caudillo who attained national power, became centralist in practice. His spies, his soldiers in scarlet *ponchos*, and his secret police, were free to enter homes, destroy the contents, rape and murder. If other local caudillos rose, they were promptly decapitated and their heads displayed. For three years, 1832–35, Rosas played coy with the junta, staying out of office until they were willing to grant him total power, but using the time to push outwards the southern and western boundaries of the province, wiping out Indians in the process. During his absence his politically-active wife organised a campaign of the *mazorca* (a terrorist group used even more bloodily in later years) in Rosas' favour. The junta broke down and gave Rosas total power: 'toda la sumer del poder'.

The foreign policy of Rosas was not markedly 'provincial' in tone: no Buenos Aires centralist could have been more nationalist. He prohibited river traffic to Paraguay, in an attempt to control that country. He besieged Montevideo for nine years, unsuccessfully, trying both to subdue Uruguay and to capture his political enemies hiding across the river. He became disastrously involved in an undeclared war with England and France, whose commercial interests wanted Uruguay to remain free. In 1845 these powers blockaded Buenos Aires; they had gone home by 1848. Rosas turned this event into victory by appearing as his country's saviour against foreign powers. The 72-year old San Martín, for example, an idealist to the end, died in exile in 1850 and willed his sabre to Rosas. Never was a gift more inappropriate.

At home Rosas killed Indians, encouraged concentration of land ownership in fewer hands, and continued the old Buenos Aires, city policy of taxing the interior by levying heavy duties on goods going in or out via the port of Buenos Aires and the great rivers. Rosas squared this with his earlier resistance to Buenos Aires by giving special preference to his *own* hinterland province. His old friends, the great estancieros of the Buenos Aires province paid very little in tax, while the farther interior was made to pay heavily to make up the difference. Rosas also placated ranchers with a cheap money policy. He abolished the central bank of his predecessor, Rivadavia, and favoured inflationist measures, as did the US Jacksonians.

Not even Rosas could keep the provinces down forever. He was defeated in battle by a provincial gaucho leader and exiled to England, where he died 25 years later in 1877. The nation now broke apart. The victor, Justo José de Urquiza, a moderate and fair-minded man (he even gave an allowance to his rival Rosas, in England), could not satisfy the *porteños* of Buenos Aires that he was more than just another gaucho boss. They seceded, refusing to join his 'Confederation' created by the Constitution of 1853. For ten years or so the Argentine Confederation existed without the city which was its very heart.

Urquiza amnestied everyone, produced the constitution strongly influenced by the great exile Argentinian intellectual, Juan Bautista Alberdi, and gave the provinces a few years of peace and economic growth. His new capital was at Paraná, three hundred miles inland on the Plata. From there he genuinely tried to carry out Alberdi's brilliant proposals for the economic and political growth of Argentina: European immigration; greater self-government; religious toleration; abolition of internal trade barriers; a large educational program; and encouragement of public investment in railways, telegraphs and education. The basic problem faced by the Confederation was that classic one: the man-land ratio. The provinces were underpopulated. As Alberdi said: 'Gobernar es poblar' (to govern is to people). Urquiza could do little without Buenos Aires.

Creation of the new Argentina

Urquiza resigned in 1861, having been forced to war with the turbulent Buenos Aires province. He retired to his cattle ranch in an act of statesmanship that saved Argentina from further chaos. The new leader, uniting the nation once more under a new federation, was Bartolomé Mitre, who promptly moved the capital back to Buenos Aires. Mitre was a porteño intellectual and soldier, a pamphleteer, biographer, and *rococo* poet. He governed according to the new constitution, put down the last of the caudillos in distant provinces, extended the economic growth and educational measures begun by Urquiza and brought in 100,000 European migrants. These were real achievements. The last three years of Mitre's rule threw much away because he became involved in the wasteful Paraguayan War in 1865. His profound nationalism was Mitre's undoing.

In 1868 Mitre allowed a free election and was defeated by yet another intellectual and writer of even greater stature, Sarmiento. Mitre entered the senate and founded one of the most influential newspapers in South America, *La Nación*. He had *not* made himself a rich man at public expense; he had believed in constitutional government and in the peaceful transfer of political power. Urquiza and Mitre led Argentina down a new path altogether. Meanwhile, Argentina's economic development was bringing her into world trade in a larger way. From the mid-1840s wire fencing came to the pampas, and therefore arable farming of wheat, corn and other grain crops. Immigrants brought new skills and trades: Irish and Basque shepherds established the vast sheep industry in the wastes of

Patagonia in the south, Italian sailors and boatbuilders, and above all, English merchants and bankers, laid the foundations of future prosperity.

Sarmiento: the intellectual in office

Perhaps the most famous South American intellectual to wield political power was Domingo Faustino Sarmiento. He believed in two panaceas in particular: popular education and European immigration. Yet his regard for the 'people' was low. The masses he found to be 'loafers, drunkards, useless fellows.' Immensely snobbish (he was particular about blood-lines and proud of his own part-Arab origins) and unpleasantly egotistical, Sarmiento was not very attractive as a man.

Sarmiento was a poor boy from the far western province tucked against the Andes, San Juan. He hated provincialisms and worshipped Europe. He wore full-dress European uniforms, as a 'protest against the *gauchesque* spirit,' as he put it. For him the poncho was a symbol of caudillo barbarism and backwardness. Self-taught in several languages and a prolific writer, he had much to feel egotistical about. He lifted himself up out of San Juan and into international fame as a writer by sheer hard work. He hated caudillos, bitterly opposed Rosas, and was exiled to Chile four times, often for several years. His impact on the *Chilean* education system was considerable—wherever he lived, Sarmiento studied local conditions, wrote at length, and proposed reforms. He wrote texts and started Chile's first Normal School for teacher-training. Travels in the United States and Europe convinced Sarmiento of the need for mass immigration from Europe to solve Argentina's population needs and cultural backwardness. Mitre and Alberdi, both exiled in Chile along with Sarmiento at one period, held similar views.

Sarmiento directed the Buenos Aires province education system during the secession and when Mitre assumed power he was sent to the United States as Argentine ambassador (1865–8). Naturally, he then wrote a study of the USA. Elected president of Argentina in 1868, Sarmiento started a large reform programme the heart of which was educational. In six years he doubled school enrolments and buildings, brought in a host of ladies from the United States, selected by Mrs. Horace Mann, to start teacher-training, and began adult education classes. These ideas of book-learning and scientific training were extended outwards to the armed forces, the general public (he created 100 libraries), and the nation, through the Academy of Science, a national observatory, a beautified Buenos Aires, applied science in agriculture and state-encouraged humanitarian endeavours.

'Facundo': civilisation or barbarism

In his own terms Sarmiento was successful. His greatest book, *Facundo* (1845) posed two alternatives for Argentina—civilization or the barbarism of life under Rosas. It was based on the life of a local tyrant of a neighbour province to San Juan, Facundo Quiroga of La Rioja (murdered in 1835). Sarmiento brought Argentina a long way from barbarism. Besides his cultural and social reforms he encouraged economic growth, built railways over the pampas to colonise empty lands, created a new national bank, and saw the immigration of another 300,000 Europeans. At the end of his regime (1874) Argentina had a population of about two millions, 25% of these in Buenos Aires province. Sarmiento finally won the Paraguayan War, and at least until the very end, governed Argentina by the rule of law.

The three rulers who 'civilised' Argentine politics, Urquiza, Mitre and Sarmiento were all three remarkably tough and resilient, even Sarmiento, despite his schoolmaster's approach and his emotionalism. Urquiza's reward was to be cruelly murdered in his own home, in retirement, by a local rival in 1870. Mitre and Sarmiento acted badly over the election of 1874. Mitre ran for president and lost; he accused Sarmiento, rightly, of election fraud, and organised an armed uprising for three months. Sarmiento was too anxious to have a successor to his liking and imposed his education minister, Avellaneda, on the electorate. It was not a bad choice, but the method was not in keeping with Sarmiento's high principles. The action was not 'barbarism', but not real constitutionalism either. Argentina had come further than many South American nations, but still had far to go.

Paraguay and Uruguay: a study in contrast

No South American nation has suffered as much as Paraguay, from her small population, isolation in the land-locked heart of the continent, and tyranny from outsiders and from her own dictators. An economic colony of Argentina and Brazil, and more distantly of the US, Paraguay has lived by her farms and forests: grain, cattle, maté and quebracho (for tannin). Her first dictator after independence (1811) was the infamous Dr. José Francia (1814–40), who for thirty years *literally* cut off Paraguay from outside trade and contact by the simple military act of banning river traffic, the only real outlet. A theologian who turned lawyer, Dr. Francia became anti-clerical. He broke with Rome and appointed his own clergy, and scorned the rule of law in his utterly cruel and absolutist regime. He murdered and exiled the Spanish elite and stole their lands and businesses; he forced a harsh labour code on the mestizo masses. It was a strange, if effective, way to attain 'law and order'—at the cost of keeping the economy on a purely subsistence level.

Francia's successor was fat and ugly, Carlos Antonio López (1841–62). His main disadvantage was not his looks, but his setting up of his degenerate son to succeed him in 1862–this was the López that fought the Paraguay War. The father introduced some mild reforms and opened up the river for external trade and human contact; in fact he got over-involved in comic-opera disputes with great powers. There was nothing comic about his evil son's war, which cut the population to about 221,000, a mere 28,000 men remaining! The Paraguayan War of 1864–70 was horrible and entirely unnecessary. It was brought on largely by the intemperance of Paraguay's third and worst dictator since independence, Francisco Solano López, the one who more than *halved* Paraguay's population, killed off most of the males (he forced all to fight—old men and boys as well, or tortured them to death) and brought foreign occupation. Brazilian invaders shot López the younger in 1870. He left behind him a nation of women and little children, brutally occupied for six years by free-living Brazilian troops.

The contrast with Uruguay is great in many ways. While *El Supremo* Francia cut off Paraguay, Uruguay was in contact with the world's great trading powers, particularly England, which was liberal and capitalist. Paraguay was physically isolated; Uruguay commanded a great and beautiful estuary on the Atlantic with the port of Montevideo, which was given an economic boost by the British occupation of 1806–7. Paraguay was mestizo (Guaraní-Latin), Uruguay mainly European. But Uruguay was too small to 'command' the estuary, was constantly invaded—a football between Brazil and Argentina, and was so torn apart politically that most of its early advantages for economic growth and stability were lost until the 20th century.

The politics of Uruguay in the 19th century were astonishingly complex. A local cattleman, José Artigas, began the fight for independence in 1811 but had to face not only the Spanish but the Brazilians and the porteños from Buenos Aires. He lost in 1820 to Brazil and the area was annexed to Brazil for five years. War broke out again in 1825 with the Argentines supporting the independence movement, expecting to annex Uruguay at the end. Britain intervened in 1828 to protect its trade interests. The final political settlement, agreed to under British pressure, created an independent Uruguay as a tiny buffer-state to keep Brazil and Argentina from each other's throats. The trade of Montevideo was to be kept free from monopoly, that is, open for English merchants to develop and manage.

After 1828 and on into the 20th century the division between *blancos* (conservatives) and *colorados* (liberals) dominated Uruguayan politics. Neighbouring states have often been drawn in. Rosas beseiged Montevideo for years; he supported the blancos. In the Paraguayan War, López supported the blancos, Brazil the colorados, until the colorados won and brought a temporarily united Uruguay into the conflict against López. Such patterns of intervention and the essential defencelessness of Uruguay—geographically a northern tongue of the open pampa grassland—badly retarded the nation's economic growth. A small number of large ranchers dominated Uruguay, which was still over 90% a cattle country even in 1900. Britain built and owned the railways, controlled much of the trade, and sold the country her own cheap, mass-produced manufactured goods. There was little hope of domestic investment in manufacturing under these quasi-colonial conditions, quite apart from the political instability of Uruguay which remained chronic up to 1903.

Chile: stability and oligarchy

Chile, 2,600 miles long and about 110 miles wide, stretched out along the Pacific coast of the Andes from the tropics towards the Antarctic, from stony northern desert to saturated southern forests. It did not begin to develop economically until the later 19th century. This growth took foreign entrepreneurs, British capital and the nitrate deposits of the northern deserts. Before the 'nitrate era' began, Chile was mainly a pastoral economy. The bulk of the people lived then as now in the central third, supported by the farm products of irrigated valleys. Here grew the chief towns of colonial and post-independence days, and here most of the fighting took place, after San Martín crossed the Andes to link up with the Chilean patriots under O'Higgins in 1817.

San Martín virtually installed O'Higgins, but the latter's liberal dictatorship failed in 1823. A series of conservative presidents kept Chile stable for thirty years after 1831 and drew up the Constitution of 1833 which emphasised strong central authority. In contrast to the political confusion and ideological battles of Uruguay, or the drawn-out independence wars of Venezuela, Chile was quickly liberated and was soon taken over by representatives of its landed oligarchy. The illiterate and landless naturally could not vote. The president controlled congress, the elections, the courts, the army, and the provincial administrations, but he was the landowners' creature. Chile was not torn apart by rival caudillos and local toughs.

Unity and control from the capital enabled Chile to be aggressive in foreign policy and to expand its territory at the expense of more divided nations. President Manuel Bulnes (1841–51) pushed south to the Straits of Magellan in 1843. Later, in the War of the Pacific (1879–83), Chile took the rich nitrate lands of the north from Peru and Bolivia, actually cutting off Bolivia from the sea altogether and leaving her land-locked. Chile, despite her conservatism and relatively unchanging nature for over half a century, was a haven for dissidents and intellectuals from neighbouring dictatorships. Men like Bulnes did introduce social reforms, especially in the field of education. This explains the welcome given on several occasions to Sarmiento.

The new 'Indian' nations of the Andes

Three new nations—Ecuador, Peru and Bolivia—emerged from the independence wars in the Andes. Though mainly Indian they were governed by racial elites for some years.

Ecuador, with its mass of poor Indians tied to the hacienda and to the upper-class minority by debt, and its economy of balsa wood, cacao and banana exports, underwent little fundamental social change over many decades. In the later 19th century Ecuador's present neo-colonial export-

125

economy and crops began to appear. Most of the population lived in the temperate mountains on the western slopes, then as now, where the capital Quito is located. The trans-Andes area and the tropical coast were underpopulated, except for the port outlet of Guayaquil.

The independence struggle began in 1809 but did not end until 1822, when Ecuador became part of 'Gran Colombia'. After total autonomy (1830) the nation suffered thirty years of great political and social instability and low economic growth. The highland city of Quito battled with Guayaquil; local caudillos played havoc in the provinces; personalismo rather than party or principle was the issue. The two-city struggle reminds one of Nicaragua, the caudillismo of several other nations. In the 15-year period, 1845–1860, Ecuador had eleven governments, three constitutions, several wars with neighbours, and civil uprisings. Slavery of Negroes was abolished, but the Indian masses saw little improvement in their lives. Local bosses grew so strong that one of them made a deal of his own with Peru and actually gave away the nation's only major port, Guayaquil.

This erratic act brought in strong central dictatorship under García Moreno in 1860, which lasted 15 years. Under Moreno's fierce rule, the Church gained many privileges, for Moreno was a religious fanatic. He dedicated the republic of Ecuador to the 'Sacred Heart of Jesus' in 1873 and gave Rome control over all education, literature and publishing. All non-Catholics were stripped of civil rights. While Moreno built his wall between the true God and the Devil, he gave Ecuador modest material improvements, encouraged trade, established good international credit and built schools for the Jesuits. Ecuador's Catholic dictatorship ended when Moreno was stabbed to death in 1875.

Meanwhile in Peru, centre of the once-great Inca Empire and of Spanish mining wealth, British capitalists had begun to develop the rich *guano* nitrate deposits of the coast—centuries of bird-droppings, piled in enormous mounds and untouched by rain, which would have leached away the valuable salts. The 'Manure Age' began in the early 1840s. Farther south explorers, again with English capital, developed the nitrate deposits of the deserts, which they blasted and crushed on the spot and shipped to Europe. The desert nitrates were lost to Chile in the Pacific War, precisely when the guano deposits were becoming harder to harvest.

After independence Peru was ravaged by caudillo wars and pillaging troops. In turn Argentine and Chilean armies invaded. Then in 1845 a strong man, Ramón Castilla, seized power and managed to hold Peru until 1862. Castilla, though a soldier by profession, ruled moderately and did not treat his liberal opponents badly. He abolished Negro slavery, eased the forced tribute system under which the Indian masses suffered, and abolished Church tithes. The peace and calm he brought to Peru was supported by the quick wealth being made from manure, nitrates and European loans.

Two decades of confusion followed upon Castilla's retirement in 1862 and foreign individuals and nations plundered Peru. Spain tried to re-capture part of its lost imperial glory in the years 1862–66, by grabbing the manure islands; but she could not hold them even against Peru. An adventurer from the US, Henry Meiggs, made and lost a fortune by building railways in Peru under corrupt contracts which outdid those by which railways were constructed in the United States in the 1850s and 60s. He used Chinese labour, bribery and politics, and built many bridges and tunnels in the Andes at extravagant cost to the Peruvian nation. Quick wealth made Peru very corrupt and when Chile launched the 'War of the Pacific' in 1879, Peru was without defences.

Shattered by the war and by Chilean occupation, bereft of rich terri-tories, and bankrupt, Peru survived for seven years after the war. She then allowed a British-organised corporation to take over all her national railways, the shipping line on Lake Titicaca, most of the guano industry and seven ports, in return for accepting responsibility for the national debt of Peru (1890). Under this unusual arrangement, the London capital-ists virtually managed the Peruvian economy and paid its debts: they ran Peru like a private enterprise.

Bolivia: cholos and caudillos

The third Indian nation of the Andes, Bolivia, is over 90% Quechua, Aymará or *cholo* (mestizo). 'Upper Peru', as it was to the Spanish, suffered especially from that gold-fever the conquerors inherited from Columbus. The Spanish were interested only in the immediate wealth of the silver-mines of Potosí, for which countless Indians paid with their lives. The potential agricultural and forest wealth of the *yungas* (mountain valleys) and *selvas* (hardwood forests) was left undeveloped. Even today most of the population live on the high *altiplano*, 12–14,000 feet up, where the capital, La Paz, and the mining centres are. Tin has replaced silver as Bolivia's major mineral export to the world.

Bolivia's weakness left it a prey to foreign invaders and internal caudil-los in the early 19th century. Independent from 1825, Bolivia was ruled first by Bolívar himself, then by General Sucre, and for ten years of relative order, 1829–39, by a mestizo from Lake Titicaca, who claimed royal Inca descent, Andrés Santa Cruz. Santa Cruz's Napoleonic ambi-tions led him to conquer Peru and establish a short-lived confederation in 1836. Chile, ever expansionist, invaded and put down the empire of Santa Cruz in 1839. He was exiled to Europe.

Throughout the 1850s and 60s Bolivia was ravaged by wars between cholos and the land-owning elite. One temporary dictator, Mariano Melgarejo (1865–71), a debauchee and drunkard, illiterate and bestial, imposed a savage regime on the Bolivian people. Using the national resources as his personal estate he sold Indian communal lands, sold part of the country to Brazil, and gave Chile the rights to exploit the nitrate deposits of the Pacific. In the War of the Pacific, Bolivia lost for-ever her Pacific coast and was left with no outlet.

SPANISH–AMERICAN WAR 1898
Cuba became independent.
U.S.A. annexed Puerto Rico.

1844–45 A general war
involved Guatemala, Honduras,
Nicaragua and El Salvador.

Rivalry and War in Central & Southern America

Panama Revolt 1903.
Washington Treaty gave
US chance to build canal.

1899–1902
COLOMBIA
suffered an
appalling
civil war.

Boundary
dispute
1895–99

VENEZUELA

Br. Fr. Du.
G U I A N A

ECUADOR
(total autonomy
after 1830.)

B R A Z I L

PERU

Ancón
Lima

SECRET ALLIANCE 1873

Lake
Titicaca

B O L I V I A

Attacks on Paraguay
by Brazil, Argentina
and Uruguay.

PARAGUAY

Asuncion

Antofagasta

WAR OF THE PACIFIC 1879–1883
Settled by
Treaty of Ancón 1883
Bolivia lost her valuable nitrate coast
to Chile.

Chilean
army

CHILE

ARGENTINA

URUGUAY

Buenos
Aires   Montevideo

PARAGUAYAN WAR 1864–1870
1865 More than 500,000 in Paraguay
1871 Census: 221,079—and of these
192,333 were women and
children !

Havana

CUBA

PUERTO
RICO

G
H
ES
N
PANAMA

The Portuguese heritage: Brazil

> Brazil grows at night, when the
> politicians are sleeping

(Brazilian saying)

Brazil became an independent empire almost bloodlessly. But how did she survive economically after 1810, when a preferential treaty with England, the godfather of her independence, allowed British manufactures to flood in, and made it more difficult for Brazilians to diversify their economy? Lack of a large middle class at home to serve as a market and as a source of managerial and professional skills, poor transportation and communications, and capital-shortage plagued the nation. After the dyewoods, sugar and gold booms, Brazil needed a new export crop. Cotton played some role on the São Paulo plateau lands. Farther north, around Rio, the coffee crop emerged and came to dominate economic life.

Coffee was suitable as a new export. It involved only minimal capital and primitive tools; a cheap labour-force was available through the existing African slave trade; soil and climate were compatible; the Rio area had a good port and short haulage distances to the harbour; and above all, world demand for coffee was very elastic. Demand was fast-growing, not merely in Europe but in the large market of the United States. By mid-19th century coffee took up at least 40% by value of Brazil's total exports.

The coffee plantation gave new life to slavery in Brazil. In the last decade of legal slave traffic, the 1840s, about 370,000 slaves were imported. Perhaps one and one-third millions came between 1800 and 1850. It took British gunboats to force Brazil to restrict this trade in human beings. As in the United States earlier, abolition of the legal slave trade resulted in the growth of a *domestic* slave-trade—declining sugar and cotton estates in the North made extra cash by selling slaves to the coffee plantations of the South, just as Virginia and North Carolina, suffering from economic decline, began selling slaves to the new lands of the American Southwest.

These developments, and other ways of getting around regulations, made the Law of Free Birth (*Lei do Ventre Livre*), 1871, almost a dead letter. In 12 years under 20,000 slaves gained freedom under the law, by which children of slave mothers were supposed to be born free. The planters simply disobeyed it and the abolitionists led by the tough activist from Pernambuco, Joaquim Nabuco, in Congress awoke from a temporary slumber in 1879. Negroes and mulattoes dominated the abolitionist movement in the country, including José Patrocínio, an eloquent ex-slave, and Luiz Gama, a mulatto lawyer, once sold into slavery by his own Portuguese father. As in the United States of the 1840s, antislavery now became an intensely moral, emotional issue. Economic arguments were swept aside: the stain of human slavery must go.

In 1888, the *Lei Aurea* or 'Golden Law' gave immediate liberty to all slaves in Brazil. About 700,000 human beings were liberated at a cost to the owners of about a quarter of a million dollars. This was uncompensated; earlier halfway measures had experimented with compensation but had been evaded. As abolitionism reached its fulfilment countless owners freed their slaves ahead of the law, while many slaves ran away from the *fazendas* and were not chased; army men refused to go slave-hunting. This immediate liberation of 1888 was the last blow to the Brazilian Empire and to the Bragança royal connection. In 1889, Brazil became a Republic.

Pedro II and the Republic of Brazil

Pedro II, who had taken over from the regency in 1840, was a moderately enlightened ruler, constitutionally minded, though often bothered by federalist provincial uprisings in his first decade. Interested in currents of modern thought and science he often visited Europe. Pedro reigned over a Brazil that saw continued economic expansion, the coming of railways, educational reforms, universal suffrage and the metric system, in addition to abolition of slavery. After the Paraguay War his nation settled down to years of peace and calm. Nevertheless the worldwide spread of republican ideas, and ironically, his own alienation of the upper classes, the landlords and the army, rather than a mass republican movement of the 'people' brought his downfall.

The great *fazendeiros*, with family fortunes built on sugar, cotton and coffee, all involving slave-labour, or cattle, clung to the monarchy as a protection against abolition. Once slavery was wiped out, along with many of their fortunes and some of their political power, the upper classes abruptly abandoned the Empire that had let them down. The small but growing urban middle class and the new European immigrants disliked slavery, but also found the monarchy to be obsolete and unnecessary. Even the Church, whose survival seemed tied to the royal house, was offended by Pedro's liberal and rationalist views. So Pedro lost, both for being an anachronism and for being too liberal!

Pedro, who shared the zeal for educational programmes of so many South American liberals, would just as soon have been a school-teacher as an emperor. He had supported abolition, and when he heard the news that the Golden Law was passed in 1888, he wept with the words: 'What a great people!'

In 1889 an army revolt led by an ambitious general, Deodoro da Fonseca, demanded Pedro's abdication. Pedro moved to France, where he died in 1891 in modest circumstances, lonely, sick and sad. He refused a pension from Brazil. Deodoro, of course, did not replace this 'obsolete' constitutional monarch with an up-to-date parliamentary democracy like Britain or the USA, but with his own personal dictatorship.

Abolition was a financial blow to a sector of the Brazilian economy and society; but freed of the incubus of unfree labour, Brazil expanded more rapidly after 1888. The major reason was the real beginnings of large-scale European immigration, held off for decades by hatred and fear of slavery. Now the European workers flooded in, especially Italians, who provided the free labour needed to man the coffee fazendas.

In the 1890s coffee growing moved to the Southeast, to the São Paulo plateau where most of the Italians gathered. The plantations seemed just as profitable, perhaps more, as under slavery. The soils of the former Rio area were now badly eroded and the English, as usual, seizing the main chance, built a railway from the coast to São Paulo to ship the crop. New estates were begun on virgin lands, with free immigrant workers, often working as sharecroppers.

Immigration and race in South America

While the ex-slaves became tenants and sharecroppers themselves and intermixed and mingled into the mulatto and white population without many of the discrimination and segregation problems felt in North America by black freedmen after 1863, millions of free Europeans came in to Brazil to work. They had previously gone to the United States and to Argentina; now they came to Brazil also, a million and a quarter in the decade 1888–98 alone. In the more temperate south, German pioneers transformed Brazilian farming methods. Others included Portuguese, Spaniards, Russians and in the 20th century, Japanese—the largest group coming in the 1920s: 110,000 in the decade 1924–33. One could now hear many languages spoken in major Brazilian and Argentine cities.

In about 1880 many of the descendants of the creole leaders of 1810 were still around and in control, mixed with mestizos. Creole containment had worked for some time, though the mestizo was now a greater political influence in Central and South America. Mestizos absorbed the racial and social outlook of the creoles and political, economic and social evolution widened the gap between mestizo and Indian. Even in heavily Indian countries like Guatemala, marriage between mestizos and Indians became improbable as the years wore on. The original Americans, the so-called 'Indians', remained the vast peasant multitude of the countryside, the beggars and casual workers of the cities.

Where the impact of European immigration was felt, these white newcomers were fairly easily absorbed into the social structure, co-opted, if they were rich and successful, into the governing classes. The growth of cities in South America gave hundreds of new opportunities for an expanding middle class: white collar, professional, legal, medical and educational. In Argentina and elsewhere 'society' (meaning upper-class society) remained very stuffy and exclusive, even towards European immigrants of good birth. In time well-placed merchants, predominantly English, but also Swiss, French and German, could intermarry with landed creole families. The whitest mulattoes and mestizos could also rise socially, but the chief device for keeping back such social intruders was public education. Inadequately financed by the upper classes, who sent their children to private schools, often in Europe anyway, education was not used as a social ladder or as a deliberate device for the acculturation of citizens of different ethnic and racial backgrounds as in the US. Public schooling was restricted, in order to limit upward social mobility. Liberal reformers fought to keep the issue of mass public education alive politically but with little success in South America. Mass education supported by public taxes as in the US and Canada, and, somewhat belatedly, in Britain, is a function of a given type of social structure, one with a middle-income group large enough and willing to pay the taxes. This was lacking in Central and South American nations.

6
Immigration, Reform and Imperialism, 1880–1920

THE UNITED STATES: IMMIGRANTS AND CITIES

In countries like Brazil and Argentina immigration was a significant element in social, economic and political history; but in the US it was much more—a massive, shaping force. The US became a nation of immigrants, especially in the years 1890 to 1920. Between 1850 and 1920 about 30,000,000 foreigners entered the US as immigrants. This was twice the total population of Mexico or of Brazil and seven or eight times the population of Argentina as of 1900. The immigrants became producers and consumers: in their great numbers they enlarged and transformed the American market economy. Though some groups settled in rural areas of the US, the vast bulk of immigrants moved from the European countryside to the American cities. The American urban market of workers and middle-class people capable of buying standardised products of the machine age, increased in size from 6,000,000 to 54,000,000 in the post-Civil War years (1860–1920). This huge home demand was the secret of US economic growth.

The Europeans, Asians, Canadians and Mexicans who migrated to the US in the late 19th and 20th centuries were all predominantly young people of working age. Few of the very old or very young made the journey. Raised abroad, these eager young adult workers were in effect a free gift of human capital to the US. They came precisely when the industrial economy was passing through a later stage of its evolution and needed thousands of unskilled factory hands for its mass-production sectors. It did not matter that the new workers spoke many different tongues, professed several religious faiths, and possessed mainly rural skills. In the cities they formed the vital home market as well as the labour-force, and their housing, education, feeding, clothing and general care was itself a major task which involved the physical growth and construction of a new urban America. The building of cities added another chapter to that long story of extended real-estate boom which is known as US history.

In the immediate post-Civil War decades, the so-called Gilded Age of the great industrial 'Robber Barons' like Andrew Carnegie (steel and railways), John D. Rockefeller (oil refining), Gustavus Swift (meat-packing) and others, the framework of the US economy was mapped out. The continent was rigged with telegraph wires and linked by railroad lines; the mines were dug, the forests and ores exploited, the cities laid out. By the later 19th century this 'heroic' age was virtually over. The phase of 'industrial capitalism' when the emphasis was on heavy industries and producers' goods, was being supplanted by a later stage of development based on new energy sources and mass-consumption industries.

Problems of production were not all entirely solved, but problems of distribution and of marketing became more dominant. During the 19th century the capitalist system suffered classic crises of boom-and-slump, usually thought of as crises of 'over-production'. From the 1890s onwards reformers and economists began to think of economic crises as caused by 'under-consumption' (an idea that eventually matured in England in the 1920s and 30s in the theories of J. M. Keynes, which stressed the need for mature industrial economies to maintain 'effective demand'). Responding to such changes the American corporation evolved, replacing the family firms of the early enterprisers and the informal corporate structures of the Robber Barons. By the 1920s the business corporation was impersonal, staffed by trained personnel from law, banking and the new university schools of business administration, and had developed large marketing, market research and dealership organisations. This new form of corporate enterprise achieved miracles of productivity and sales in the 1920s, the peak decade of US business. Fundamental and hidden weaknesses in the economy caused massive breakdown after the great stock-market crash of 1929.

The mass-production, corporate, immigrant, urban America was very different from that other America south of the Rio Grande. Its essential basis was the urban market, the urban labour-force, with its high degree of powered technology and high productivity per man-hour, and its relatively high wages. American firms spent more on research and on tools than those of other nations, and their workers out-produced them. Soon the US even surpassed Great Britain as the world's chief industrial power and after 1914 New York City replaced London as the world's financial centre. The US, which in the 19th century had consumed its own manufactured products and sold abroad its raw materials like cotton, meat and wheat, now began to export manufactures also. Economic growth brought higher living standards for all Americans, greater longevity, a high degree of home-ownership and of extended public education, and many other benefits. These benefits were still unevenly distributed within the nation itself, both regionally and socially though living standards in general were higher than in advanced European nations. What type of society was supported by, and in turn supported, this economic system?

The myth of the 'melting-pot'

Urban America was no true 'melting-pot' of ethnic, racial and religious groups in the sense that people of very different origins would intermarry. The white, Anglo-Saxon Protestant ('W.A.S.P.') view of the melting-pot had envisioned the 'melting' not of native-Americans but of the immigrants, who would emerge from the process speaking English and conforming to Anglo-American ways. This 'Anglo-conformity' was not fully realized as millions of immigrants from central and eastern Europe and from the Mediterranean flooded into America—Catholics, Jews, Orthodox Christians and others. Very few Americans genuinely believed in a true melting together of all types to make a new American. Before World War I a British playwright, Israel Zangwill, put on a well-known play in New York called 'The Melting Pot' which sang the praises of such a new society and demanded intermarriage. People went to the play but its influence was minimal. An entirely opposite view was taken by an American philosopher Horace Kallen, who thought the melting-pot idea was *un*-democratic, since it implied that immigrants should lose their peculiar ethnic identities in the democratic mass. He argued against 'Americanisation' and in favour of the notion of *cultural pluralism*, each group maintaining its own cultural identity within the American framework. In practice neither the Zangwill nor the Kallen solution came about.

Immigrants from particular villages would often settle on particular streets of American cities like Chicago or New York or Boston, and strive to live, get married, work and be buried among their own kind. In practice complete separation was never possible and as the influx of immigrants was reduced and eventually almost cut off by law in the 1920s, and little fresh blood was coming in to keep alive and renew ethnic customs and languages, the new generations of American-born immigrant children began to drift away from traditional practices and beliefs. Gradually America became a triple-melting pot: Catholics, Jews and the rest (known as Protestants for want of a better word). Old animosities among Catholics (Poles, Irish, Italians for example), broke down: Catholics married Catholics. Americans were divided largely by race and religion rather than by ethnicity at the time of World War II. What *united* most Americans was the persistence of the ideology of the 'American Dream', the deep belief in equality, mobility, opportunity, individualism and economic growth, a belief held even in the face of depression and often overt inequality in the cities. Whatever the US was at present, most American believed, it was in a state of constant change and improvement and the future outlook was good.

Workers and radicalism

Higher living standards in the US were a relative matter. Within the nation such standards had to be fought for and the lot of the worker was not always happy. To protect himself against the tremendous power of the

'Robber Barons' of industry and the later large corporation with its impersonal and sometimes inhuman labour practices, the worker organised. Labour unions fought a bitter struggle for legal recognition. The courts sided with the employers. The general public, hardened by a philosophy of opportunity and egalitarianism and influenced by mass newspapers, usually opposed the unions when they went on strike. There was violence, though most of it was on the employers' side and produced by the forces of 'law and order'. The corporations armed themselves with weapons, built up great private armouries, and used thugs and Pinkerton men (private police) to break strikes forcibly. They sometimes brought in fresh immigrants or Negroes as workers, to keep the plants going and ruin the union finances. After several large strikes, as in 1886 (on the railways and in meat-packing plants), 1892 (steel) and 1894 (Pullman), some gains were made; but more often the unions were destroyed. There were 24,000 strikes between 1880 and 1900; only one third were successful for the men.

When radicalism only seemed to produce repression, the unions became more respectable and business-like. Under the leadership of an immigrant cigar-worker, Samuel Gompers, the American Federation of Labour was created at Pittsburgh in 1881. The idea was to keep account books, take regular dues, build up strike funds, start mutual benefit systems for sickness and death and avoid politics and ideology. Gompers simply aimed for a floor under wages and a ceiling over hours. He wanted, as he put it: 'More!—Now!' This was far from socialism, or redistribution of income, or any of the other radical notions that so frightened the businessmen and the general public of the day. Gompers' system worked, and the AFL became an economic force.

The AFL was exclusive; it was interested only in federating skilled trades and craftsmen. The mass of the immigrant unskilled were left out in the cold.

Radicalism returned in the early 20th century when the Industrial Workers of the World (IWW—known as 'Wobblies'), was formed from various splinter groups of socialists, miners, lumbermen and others (1905). The Wobblies did not want a mere federation of skilled craftsmen and aristocrats of labour like the AFL, but 'One Big Union', uniting all workers, skilled and unskilled, men, women, and all ethnic groups. Such an organisation could bring massive pressure to bear on the nation's economy.

The IWW won the support for a while of leading socialists, like the head of the Socialist Labour Party, Daniel De Leon (a Marxist from the Dutch West Indies), and Eugene V. Debs. After managing two strikes (Lawrence, Massachusetts: successful, 1912; Paterson, New Jersey; a failure, 1912–13), the Wobblies fell apart in an aura of factionalism and violence. Socialism itself, of any variety, failed to gain a strong grip on the United States public as a *political* movement. The influence of socialist ideals and ideas however, was more lasting, and is to be seen for instance in movements of wider appeal like Populism and Progressivism.

Moderate reform: the power of the middle-class conscience

Short of socialism, other reform movements expressed the needs and demands of particular groups, and often appealed to the conscience of the large middle class of United States cities and small towns. Radicals ran for office like the well-loved Henry George, who demanded the return of profits from rented land to the public whose growth had made that rent rise (taxation of land-values: *Progress and Poverty*, 1879). He almost became mayor of New York City in 1886. Edward Bellamy, through the technique of a best-selling futuristic novel, *Looking Backward* (1887), even made some socialist ideas respectable. Theology softened and ministers of various sorts adopted the 'Social Gospel'. Some called themselves Christian Socialists. Journalists and muck-raking writers stirred up the public conscience about meat-packing, city government, the doings of large trusts like the Standard Oil Company and a host of reform issues. The roots of this activity were urban, as were the new magazines that now spread a literate mass popular culture.

Rural reform was also significant and arose directly out of the changing economic conditions faced by the farmer of the United States. North American wheat and meat fed Europe while that continent industrialised; it kept alive the eastern part of the US itself, while that area developed its great metropolitan industries. Yet the more the farmer produced, and the more efficient and modern he became, with use of combine-harvesters and other miracles of ingenuity, the lower prices he received for his crops. This sad irony, and recurrent droughts and fluctuations in world agricultural prices, brought forth radical protest from farmers, often aimed at those nearest to them—the 'middlemen' wholesalers, the grain storage elevator companies, the railways, the local country store at which they owed so much credit.

Populism: the farmers get angry

For ten years or so after 1886, agricultural depression hit the United States, and drought came to the Great Plains. Kansas corn production, for one example, was cut to one third, 1885–90. Previous farmers' movements like the Grangers of the 1870s, who won legislation regulating railway rates, and the more social and cultural Farmers' Alliances of the 80s had not appealed directly to urban workers for their support. In 1890 the 'People's Party' which emerged in Kansas, Nebraska and South Dakota, did so. It stood for currency inflation, easy money policies, and agrarian reforms, and won a couple of state governorships. A large St Louis Convention of the Populists in 1892 sounded a radical clarion-call that seemed very close to socialism:

> The people are demoralised ... The newspapers subsidized or muzzled; public opinion silenced; business prostrated, our homes covered with mortgages, labor impoverished, and the land concentrating in the hands of capitalists ... *From the same prolific womb of governmental injustice we breed two great classes—paupers and millionaires.*

Sectional wings united in 1892 also on the Omaha Platform: currency inflation through monetizing silver ('Free Silver'); nationalisation of transportation; and prohibition of further land grants to private corporations. Populists also wanted a graduated income tax, ballot reforms, new legislative techniques like the Initiative and Referendum to give direct *participation* of the people in the political process, and federal loans to farmers based on crops stored in government warehouses awaiting better prices. Many of these ideas were tried later, as in the New Deal of the 1930s.

Populism was particularly radical in the South, where the poor whites and blacks suffered under the pseudo-gentry value-system and tenancy. But 1892 was its high tide everywhere. The party took Nevada, Idaho, Colorado, Kansas and parts of Nebraska and Wyoming in the presidential campaign, with a million popular votes and fifteen seats in Congress. A bad political decision in the 1896 campaign, to support the Democrats under William Jennings Bryan, and the waning of rural radicalism through improving market conditions and climate, wiped out the party before 1900. Populism was a deep expression of the farmers' anger at their discovery that the much-vaunted 'competition' of 'free enterprise' meant deprivation for them, while industry and transportation organised themselves into huge monopolistic blocs and were fixing prices.

City reformers: Progressivism

The cities came to the reform movement a little later than the countryside. 'Trust-busting' became the central theme of city reformers, though their aims were many, ranging from 'clean' government to near-socialism. The Progressive reform urge of the years 1890 to World War I was the second of four major periods of reform in US history (the others being the 1830s and 40s, the 1930s, and the 1960s). Each has been dominated by a major issue, with a surrounding of many other movements. Trust-busting eventually entered presidential politics with the administrations of the Republican Teddy Roosevelt and the Democrat, Woodrow Wilson—both Progressives, though of entirely different personality types and belonging to different parties. These two men, largely through their Progressive aims, put the presidency back on the political map after its decline and long quiescence in the decades after the Civil War. Strong executive government returned to the United States.

The Progressives were usually well-to-do 'WASP' men of middle age who devoted themselves to reform. Naturally they could not have succeeded without the support of wider groups such as the working-class reformers and the trade unions. Through all this, Negroes saw little improvement in their conditions. Segregation was severe. Advances in education through Negro self-help and white benevolence always meant segregated Negro institutions. The bulk of the Negro population had merely passed from legal slavery to debt-peonage. From the 1890s onwards, accelerated greatly by the World War and the 1920s, an increasing number of Negroes left the South and moved to northern cities like New York and Chicago. There they lived in segregated ghettos, such as Harlem or the South Side. These blacks, and many more later, passed through peonage into urban ghetto existence, the third great mode of Negro life in the United States.

What did the Progressives achieve? A mass of social legislation and many private philanthropic ventures. Trust-busting, with the Sherman Act (1890) and Clayton Act (1914), tariff and currency reforms, central banking (the Federal Reserve System, 1913), the federal income tax, farm credit measures, railroad labour and child labour acts, and many other reforms. Also Teddy Roosevelt brought to a head the growing ecology-conservation movement, the first in US history (another came in the 1930s and a third in the 1960s). Outside Congress and the White House—through the courts, through private business (many businessman saw the value of reforms), and independent agencies like settlement houses in the slums, the National Urban League (1911: to help Negro migrants adjust to the city and find jobs), the National Association for the Advancement of Colored People (NAACP, 1910: chiefly to fight legal cases, against discrimination and lynching)—Progressivism touched every aspect of American urban life.

'Social imperialism'

The Progressives brought the urban 'frontier'—for it was like a new frontier—into the mainstream of American life. Some Progressives however were nativists who regarded mass immigration with suspicion and feared the racial and social consequences of admitting millions of poverty-stricken, illiterate, polyglot peoples from peasant Europe and Asia. This fear or low regard for peoples of different cultures also expressed itself in a growing United States nationalism and feeling of superiority. The nation emerged onto the world scene as a great power in the 1890s. Encouraged by theorists like the naval enthusiast, Captain A. T. Mahan, the United States began to 'look outwards' and flex its muscles internationally. In 1890 the frontier was officially (if somewhat meaninglessly) declared 'closed' by the US Census Bureau. The nation had accumulated sufficient capital to begin lending and investing abroad.

Under pressure from some congressmen and politicians like Theodore Roosevelt, a navy was developed. The ex-colony and republic was about to become a colonial and industrial power.

The combination of social reform at home and imperialism abroad is not uncommon in history. In England in this period even the *socialist* intellectuals—the Fabians—supported the Anglo-Boer War. Arguments and rationalisations about expansion abroad helping the worker at home and keeping up living-standards, were easy to think up. Some argued that states with advanced social systems and welfare reforms should expand in order to spread the benefits of *reforms* to more peoples. Others talked of the 'white man's burden' or 'Manifest Destiny'. In the 'Grab for Africa", England, Germany and France, and even Belgium, carved up that vast continent between them in the space of very few years in the 80s and 90s. Clearly there was a great power differential in the world. The gap between the nations of the world was made wider by the coming of industrialism and new technologies. Those nations that possessed such power advantages used them. The United States, despite its allegedly anti-colonial heritage, was no exception.

The Spanish-American War, 1898

US aggressiveness against the nations of the New World was already an established fact well before the 1890s and the so-called '*New* Imperialism'. Canada and Mexico in particular had experienced its impact. In future years however Canada was likely to remain the object mainly of US *economic* penetration; other nations were open to both economic and political penetration, and even to the use of American force.

Cuba had long been an object of desire for the United States, because it strategically commands the Gulf so well, and because of its rich sugar-plantations. President Polk tried but failed to buy it in 1848. Filibusters and adventurers from the US made occasional quixotic raids on the island during times of tension there, as in the long anticolonial war, 1868–78, which Spain put down very brutally. A US tariff of 1890 took the duty off Cuban sugar; another tariff of 1894 reimposed it. Such changes brought economic havoc to Cuba—rapid growth followed by collapse. The island depended heavily on the US outlet for its products. US tariff policy thus created the violence and unemployment in Cuba that brought in Spanish repression in 1895, atrocity reports in the growing 'yellow press' of the United States, and ultimately war between the US and Spain.

America's investments in Cuba totalled about $50 million and her annual trade was worth about $100 million at the time when war broke out. War psychosis built up rapidly as events escalated: the De Lôme letter (stolen by a reporter from the Havana post-office and published by the New York *World*) in which the Spanish ambassador violently, if justly, criticised the US president, McKinley; and the unsolved sinking of the US battleship *Maine* in Havana harbour. But Congress declared war *after* Spain had sacked De Lôme, had begun enquiries into the *Maine* sinking, and had abjectly given way to a strong US ultimatum which had demanded instant armistice in Cuba, abandonment of camps for prisoners, and acceptance of US mediation. The yellow press campaign had something to do with popular excitation over the war. Several leading figures however totally opposed President McKinley's action, including Andrew Carnegie, the steel millionaire, Mark Twain, William James, and others. At first, businessmen (except the sugar interests) feared the war would cost too much and disrupt trade and the economy. But the war came.

The war was over in 113 days; after all, the Spanish were in no condition militarily to fight for long. They had even been beaten by Peru in the 1860s. The US did not win the war (its planning was atrocious); the Spanish lost it. Two months *before* war broke out over Cuba, Assistant Secretary of the Navy Teddy Roosevelt sent a cable to the friend whom he had helped to appoint as naval commander in the Pacific, Admiral Dewey, warning him to prepare for 'offensive operations' in the Spanish-owned Philippine Islands. There was obviously more to US involvement than Cuba.

The war in the Pacific gave the US her first and most bloody experience of acting as a hated and unwanted colonial power. Dewey plotted with the Filipino independence leader, Aguinaldo, encouraging him to start a revolution in the islands; but then Dewey himself invaded Manila and occupied it. Aguinaldo took to the hinterland and began a long and horrible war, with atrocities on both sides, that did not end until 1903. The conflict was much worse than the Cuban revolt against Spain which was the alleged moral reason for the US involvement to begin with. The US also finally annexed Hawaii in 1898, after several years of interfering in her politics and economy. Other islands in the Pacific were taken as stepping-stones to the mirage of great trade with China: Midway, Guam, Wake. In China, the US supported the 'Open Door' policy imposed by the Great Powers to force China to trade with them.

US imperialism: the Caribbean

Nearer home, the US occupied Cuba after the war, staying there for four years. Marines helped the great Cuban scientist Dr Carlos Finlay to prove his theories that yellow-fever was carried by the mosquito. The scourge of yellow-fever was eliminated by spreading oil in breeding-grounds in 1900. But the US degraded Cuba before leaving, by imposing arrogant terms: the Platt Amendment to the Cuban constitution gave the US the right to intervene militarily in the island at any time to protect 'life, property and individual liberty', *whose* was not clear. This demeaning clause was not abrogated until 1934.

The treaty of 1898 also allowed the US to colonise Puerto Rico, which was placed under the marines for a couple of years, and then given ter-

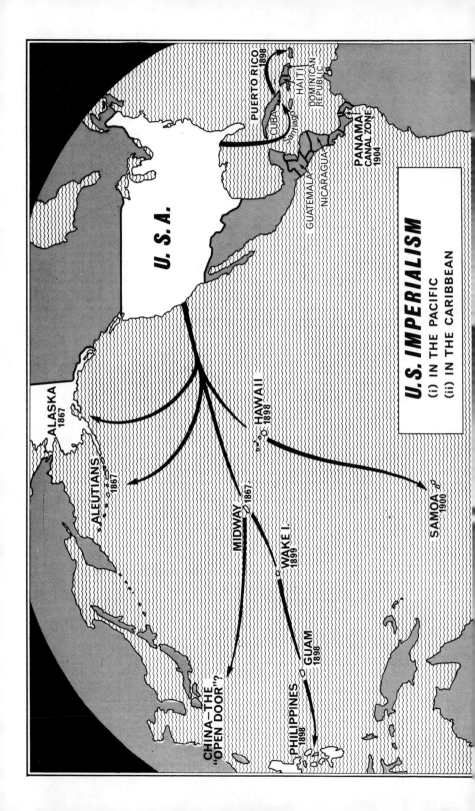

U.S. IMPERIALISM

(i) IN THE PACIFIC
(ii) IN THE CARIBBEAN

U.S.A.

ALASKA
1867

ALEUTIANS
1867

CHINA—THE
"OPEN DOOR"?

PHILIPPINES
1898

GUAM
1898

WAKE I.
1899

MIDWAY
1867

HAWAII
1898

SAMOA
1900

PUERTO RICO
1898

CUBA
Santiago

HAITI

DOMINICAN
REPUBLIC

GUATEMALA

NICARAGUA

PANAMA
CANAL ZONE
1904

ritorial status, of a special sort, in 1900. US capital moved in, developed the major industries for export to the mainland, tobacco and sugar, and drained off most of the profits, leaving little for native economic development: a classic colonial situation. Farm consolidation under absentee corporations in the Great Depression of the 1930s created a large landless peasantry. The Puerto Rican landless began to emigrate to New York City and formed a new substratum in the ethnic hierarchy of the United States. This was the fate of the island discovered by Columbus in 1493, conquered by the conquistador Ponce de León, and given political independence by Spain just before the US took it over.

To protect US investments and presumably to keep out Europeans the US established 'protectorates' enforced by marine detachments, over Nicaragua (occupied by the US 1912–33), Haiti—the first nation to have declared its own freedom after the American Revolution (occupied 1915–34), and the Dominican Republic (occupied 1914–24, with US management of its national finances). The US bought the Danish West Indies (Virgin Islands) in 1917 after bickering for them since 1900. The Caribbean was converted into a United States lake.

Creation of Panama, 1903

US capital was by 1900 heavily invested in Mexico and in the minerals and oil of Venezuela, Colombia, Peru and Chile. She also needed a communication and shipping short cut across the Isthmus to the Pacific. The British were willing to relax existing treaty rules and to allow the US to build a canal across Panama. A new Anglo-US treaty was drawn up in 1901. The government of Colombia did not like the terms of a proposed treaty with the US requiring it to cede land for canal construction. A swift 'revolution' created the secessionist state of Panama, instantly recognised by the US. The US gunboat *Nashville*'s presence on the scene of this revolution of 1903 was no accident. The new republic of Panama gladly ceded all the land the US needed, in perpetuity, though later Panamanians had second thoughts and in the 1960s demanded renegotiation.

The Panama Canal was built by US engineers. Its impact on trade flows and economic growth has been incalculable not only for the US and the Caribbean nations, but for England and Europe.

US intervention in Mexico

US investors were increasingly part of the scene in Mexico, in ranching, mines, oil and transportation after 1880. There was fierce international rivalry for such investments, but those of US capitalists became three times as big as those of the next largest nation, England. The US connived in the Madero revolution in Mexico, 1910–11, and Woodrow Wilson who became president in 1912 supported the democratic land-reform ideas of Madero. The counter-revolutionary government of Huerta, installed after Madero's murder, was overthrown with President Wilson's public moral approval and its successor regime, that of Carranza, had his initial support. Wilson had interfered in Mexican internal affairs. He demanded of Huerta a cease-fire in the civil war, and a free election in which Huerta would not stand. He offered in return the possibility of US loans for the new government. Here Wilson, the moral Progressive reformer, was telling Mexicans how to behave. Huerta refused and Wilson sent arms to his rival, Carranza and ordered the navy to blockade Veracruz (1913). The US support embarrassed Carranza, who was not sure he needed it or could live with it.

An operetta-like series of events then occurred, with tragic consequences. US sailors ashore in Tampico strayed into a restricted area and were arrested by Huerta officials. They were immediately released, but the US captain demanded more—he told the Mexicans to fly the Stars and Stripes over Tampico and give the US flag a 21-gun salute. They refused and Congress gave Wilson authority to use force against Mexico to gain respect. While this 'Tampico Incident' was going on, the worst had happened. Fearing the landing of German supplies for Huerta, the US had actually bombarded Veracruz and occupied the port. About 200 young Mexican cadets were killed in the action.

The Mexicans were temporarily united behind Huerta, against the United States. Mexico and the US were on the edge of war. Wisely, Wilson accepted mediation by the ABC powers (Argentina, Brazil, Chile) at a meeting in Canada. Huerta did not, though his prestige was weakened and his government fell. Carranza did take over, but with no love at all for his would-be helper, Wilson and the United States.

Two years later Mexican-US relations reached a new crisis. Carranza was unable to control local caudillos and freebooters like Pancho Villa, who made border raids into New Mexico and Texas and also killed US civilians travelling in Mexico, 1913–15. In March 1916 Villa shot up the town of Columbus, New Mexico. Wilson ordered General Pershing to invade Mexico on a punitive expedition, searching for Villa. Pershing failed to find Villa, and his expedition was withdrawn as the US came closer to war with Europe. Again US intervention brought the Mexican people together against a common foe, the colossus of the North.

Carranza's radical 1917 constitution for Mexico proceeded to nationalise the land and subsoil, or at least to declare national ownership of them. Titles to lands and rights to exploit the subsoil could still be transmitted to individuals, but only to native Mexicans. The clause was aimed against economic imperialism and the foreign exploitation of Mexican resources. Despite its radical rhetoric however, this clause was not made retroactive, and in practice it was easily circumvented. Mexican owners were used as fronts for example for foreign companies and individuals, and US economic control remained. Woodrow Wilson himself fought against pressures

144

at home to deny Mexico diplomatic recognition unless the radical clauses of the new constitution were changed. US-Mexican relations were deeply embittered for generations.

Canada: survival and growth

To the North, Canada also struggled to maintain its national identity and economic independence from the giant power of the United States. Physically larger than the United States and rich in natural resources, Canada was also deeply rooted in British political institutions, and developed a British-model 'parliamentary' system rather than a US-model congressional form. Yet as a nation Canada was divided between French *Canadiens* and Anglo-Canadians, and its growth rate was retarded by relative lack of population (compared with the United States). In 1867 its population was only 3,500,000, and in 1967, 100 years later, about 21,000,000. After the mid-19th century, the United States posed no real military or territorial threat to Canada; the problem was one of economic power and influence, and whether the London government would protect Canadian interests in negotiations or give way to the United States for diplomatic reasons.

The *British North America Act* of 1867 created the 'Dominion' of Canada, composed at first of four provinces (ten today). Upper and Lower Canada were united, and to these two, Ontario and Quebec, were added New Brunswick and Nova Scotia. In 1869 Canada bought from Hudson's Bay Company the vast territory of the Midwest (Rupert's Land and Northwest Territories). The Arctic Northwest has remained a Territory up to the present day, while the rest eventually became the provinces of Manitoba (1870), Alberta and Saskatchewan (1905). As in the United States, the Far West was developed before the large, intervening mid-continent: British Columbia, already settled, was added to the confederation as a province in 1871. Prince Edward Island, in the Gulf of St Lawrence, joined in 1873. Not until 1949 did Newfoundland decide by popular plebiscite to become a Canadian province. Clearly this Canadian process of territories becoming provinces is not dissimilar from the US pattern of territories becoming states of the Union. In Canada also the railroad served to unite and settle the middle regions. The transcontinental *Canadian Pacific* linked the east and west coasts of Canada for the first time in 1885. The Canadian Midwest, like that of the US, soon became a vast granary and cattle region, helping to feed the world. Great differences remained, for Canada had emerged from colonial political status gradually, not by revolution. Canadians rejected the American Revolution, as French Canadians rejected most of the ideas of the French Revolution a few years later. Both resisted any assimilation by the United States.

Up to the first World War the Canadian economy was largely dependent upon the British market. After that war, and especially from the 1930s onwards, it became increasingly dependent on the US market and

145

on US investments. Canadians were dependent because they mainly exported staple products to industrialized nations, first fish and furs, later wheat, and in a later stage lumber and paper too. This was a neo-colonial pattern, as seen in South American nations, and it was dictated not by US policy but by force of Canada's own economic and geographic circumstances. The economy grew in spurts, not continuously, with bursts of growth in the 1850s, the late-19th century and pre-World War I years, the wheat era, and the post-World War II years.

Politically Canada was dominated by the Conservative party of Sir John A. Macdonald from 1867 to 1896—a long stretch of time during which the opposition held political power only in the years 1873–8. Macdonald, who died in 1891, fought for greater independence from Britain, but was staunchly conservative at home. He was aided by an alliance of the three chief English-speaking groups and the conservative French *Bleus*. What united them was desire for national economic growth and preference for pro-business policies, not unlike those of the US 'Gilded Age' and 'Robber Baron' era. They wanted government encouragement for canals, railways, and business in general, and protective tariffs. The *Bleus* meanwhile demanded protection of the French language and customs in Quebec. There were more radical forces at mid-century, such as the Quebec *Rouges*, and the English 'Clear Grits' who stood for agrarian democracy, universal suffrage, the secret ballot and the election (rather than the appointment by the Crown) of the Governor-General and lesser officials. A growing moderate group, led until 1880 by George Brown of Toronto, stood for constitutional liberties and representation by population. What evolved in Canada was the present-day system in which the Governor-General is the nominal head of government, appointed by the Queen but only on the advice of the Canadian government. The elected cabinet and Prime Minister, who leads the majority party, form the true government.

The Conservatives gradually lost their grip on the country after the late 1880s, and from 1896 to 1911 Canada was governed by the Liberal Party led by a French Canadian, Sir Wilfrid Laurier. A major crisis the Conservatives had to face was growing tension with the French *Canadiens* and their demands for cultural independence, as in the matter of Catholic education. The execution of Louis Riel in 1885, a rebel who had twice raised forces to attack the Canadian government (the last time in Saskatchewan), made him an instant hero in Quebec. In addition Canada suffered from the depression of the 1890s as did the United States, and therefore the Liberals were triumphant in the election of 1896. A period of rapid economic growth followed up to the outbreak of World War I. Two million emigrants swelled Canada's ranks and helped to develop the West, and the vast wheat prairies were settled. Industrialization came to Canada with the beginning of the mining frontier and the establishment of large iron and steel, textile, newsprint and other concerns. The two major cities of Montreal and Toronto emerged and a flood of British capital (and US technology—the reaper, the grain elevator, the steel plough) boosted the rate of growth. The Canadian nation remained badly divided by regional differences and above all by the constant threat of tension and violence between French and English cultures, now added to by the immigration of Ukrainians and other Europeans.

NEO-COLONIALISM AND DOMESTIC POLITICS IN CENTRAL AND SOUTH AMERICA

For the southern half of the New World the last thirty years before the outbreak of World War I illustrate clearly how the former *political* imperialism of the European powers was simply replaced by *economic* imperialism. In contrast with Canada, *cultural* imperialism emanating from Europe and the United States was far less significant at this time. The United States was not principally a territorial imperialist power in Central and South America any more than she was in Canada, though she did acquire territory and dominion in some regions after 1898. Her chief territorial expansionist phase had come earlier, with the acquisitions of the Mexican-American War in the 1840s. By the 1890s the US was chiefly interested in trade and investments, not territory, and she would support this interest with political intervention where necessary, particularly if her non-intervention would threaten action by some other Great Power. Britain, for example, also lacked territorial ambitions in the region at this time; but her economic goals were expansionist too. Central and South American leaders were well aware of these trends and of the dangers their republics faced. These dangers were often hidden by the immediate economic advantages that foreign investments offered to poor and underdeveloped nations. The foreign powers could easily divide South American opinion, and many a government was supported by shrewd alliance with foreign capitalists. Thus geographical circumstances and local politics helped to create the system of neo-colonialism in Central and South America.

Neo-colonialism was certainly the burning issue of intellectuals at the end of the 19th century. The Uruguayan modernist writer José Enrique Rodó, a Montevideo intellectual who tried to reject material, industrial values for spiritual, cultural norms, produced the best-known South American critical analysis of the United States in his essay of 1900: *Ariel*. He contrasted Latin American spiritualism and North American utilitarianism and materialism: Shakespeare's spirit, Ariel, versus his brute, Caliban. There was little spiritual freedom however for the Indian masses and the oppressed castas and blacks of Central and South America. They, and the middle classes, probably would have preferred more of the 'materialist' benefits to be enjoyed north of the Rio Grande. Rodó, the intellectual and aesthete, sneered at the immigrants and the 'rabble'.

147

Yet, these, in considerable numbers, could save the economies of the southern hemisphere and help to bring a little comfort and prosperity to the masses after years of neglect and cruelty.

Mexico: Porfirio Díaz

In Mexico after 1876, Porfirio Díaz ruled sternly but did see some of the real economic possibilities for his nation. He listened to his *científicos* advisers who pushed for economic growth by stabilizing national credit and finances, modernizing wherever possible and encouraging better communications, manufacturing and mining techniques. The cientificos took exactly the opposite stand to Rodó's *Ariel*. They rejected idealistic, spiritual considerations, and concentrated on scientific, positivistic methods. José Limantour, finance minister to Díaz (1893–1911) typified this school of thought. He established central banks in each state, nationalised the railways, abolished the ancient sales-taxes inherited from the Spanish (the *alcabalas*), funded the national debt, and put Mexico on a solid gold standard. His internal improvements schemes included harbours, communications and buildings.

The científicos thought no better of the lower classes than did Rodó. Their reforms delivered Mexico into the hands of foreign capitalists and benefited the rich upper classes, bureaucrats, the Church and the army. Indian peasants lost more communal lands to hacendados. A renewed burst of Indian land-grabbing took place as the result of railway construction in the 1880s and 90s. The government, to speed up construction, gave foreign survey companies the right to keep one third of all public lands they surveyed for subdivision. The Indian *pueblos* and helpless small property-owners were cheated unless they had the help of a venal local judge. In Oaxaca alone, four grantees received almost six million acres. By 1910 50% of the Mexican people were landless. The process of concentration of ownership into few hands had accelerated enormously under Díaz. The ideal of 'land reform' seemed further away than ever. The científicos in their haste to catch up with the United States, or approach it, had prepared the way unwittingly for the Mexican Revolution.

Argentina: boom and slump

Meanwhile, among the large 'ABC' nations, Argentina witnessed territorial growth and a great economic boom based on exports of farm products to Europe. This boom collapsed in 1890, along with the political system. Two corrupt presidents, General Roca and Juárez Celman held power in the 1880s. Julio A. Roca was the man who marched against the Araucanian Indians of Patagonia (destined to be great sheep country) in 1879. The aggressive Chileans had tried to claim the same territory but Roca declared the Andes chain and the ocean as the only true boundaries of southern Argentina. Marching south like a Crusade, or a band of *conquistadores*, complete with priests and religious trappings, Roca over-came the unarmed Indians (2,000 of them) and sent them to Buenos Aires to be jailed or given as indentured servants to porteño households to 'civilize'.

Concentration of land-ownership continued throughout the 80s and 90s and the lands opened up in the south by Roca added to this process. Export demand for wool, beef and hides from the growing urban centres of England and Continental Europe pushed up Argentine land-values to highly inflated levels. The nation was fully integrated into the system of international division of labour as a major food source of the world. She was now part of the world economy. Roca and his lieutenants received large grants of lands in the south; the rest went to speculators who cut out small landowners. Powerful political families grabbed millions of acres. A Ministry of Agriculture, created in 1898, was astonished to cal-culate that the caudillo governments had virtually given away 150 million acres of Argentina to private persons, all large estancieros.

Immigrants from Europe continued to come in larger number, over 200,000 in 1889 alone. Mainly Italian and Spanish, and usually farmers, they had to become sharecroppers and tenants, as they did on the coffee plantations of Brazil. But the monetary rewards made it worthwhile. A typical *golondrina* ('swallow': seasonal laborer who migrated for a period to make money, then took it back home to Europe), could make enough in only two weeks to pay for his round-trip passage from Europe by the 1890s. Some immigrants, badly-advised, ended up in the cities. In Argentina, unlike the United States, the economic opportunities were not normally in the cities, where few factories had sprung up, but in the provinces. An official Immigrants' Hotel in Buenos Aires gave five days free board and lodging to enable the workers to settle in. Transportation to the farm lands was improved for immigrants after 1900. By 1900 Buenos Aires, federalised as the official capital since 1880, was heavily immigrant and had reached about 300,000 in population.

The boom in land-values and in cattle, grain and sheep, stimulated by the coming of the refrigerated ship in the late 1870s and the spread of alfalfa over the pampas as cattle food in the 80s, created several large fortunes for stockmen serving the English market. But the Argentine nation itself went bankrupt in 1890 and reneged on debts after borrowing wildly at ruinous rates of interest, and printing more and more paper money, each *peso* worth less than the one before it. A few became rich; food prices rose very high; the poor and the masses suffered. A national uprising overthrew the regime, organised by an entirely new group, the *Unión Cívica*—political unknowns, middle-class, led by a lawyer, Leandro N. Alem. A year later Alem broke with his own *Unión* and moved to the left with a new *Unión Cívica Radical* (1891).

A new era in Argentine politics began in 1890–91. The traditional oligarchy of landed wealthy and urban rich (bankers and merchants) was challenged. They had run the nation like a private enterprise for their own profit; Argentina had prospered and become a united country. Now it was the turn of the new middle-class, though a 26-year political battle was to ensue. The Radicals came fully to national power in 1916 and survived their many mistakes until 1930.

For a few years Alem's *Unión* was out-manoeuvred politically. The election of 1892 therefore did not bring Alem to power, and he led a new revolt in 1893, along with his nephew, Hipólito Irigoyen. This failed, and Alem's suicide in 1896 left Irigoyen as party leader. Irigoyen built the Radicals into a national party, and was twice president of Argentina in the 20th century. Meanwhile in 1898 General Roca returned to power as dictator (to 1904).

Chile: the coming of parliamentary government

In 1891 the aggressive and expansive Chileans suffered a short civil war which overthrew the presidency of Balmaceda, allegedly 'liberal' but barely distinguishable from that of the 'conservatives'. Thirty years of parliamentary rule followed, with a multiplication of political parties and a complexity of coalitions and cabinet changes. The old two-party system had gone. Its basis, the land-owning oligarchy, was suffering from the rivalry of a rising class of middle and lower groups: extractive workers, urban types and *inquilinos* (agricultural labourers). The first parliamentary president was Jorge Montt (1891–6). He wanted to put Chile on the gold standard and build up good international credit. Such things were of great consequence to the economy, developed as part of it was, by British capital. Parliamentary opposition prevented him from doing much. The Chileans developed a political system like that of late-19th century France—a moral advance over caudillismo, but not very capable of getting things done. Parliamentarism was a radical step forward for Chile, but one must remember that the franchise was still heavily restricted, literacy qualifications were imposed, and the masses did not vote. The many parties existed only among the élite. The range of political opinions was now wider, and more attention was being paid to the needs of the lower orders, even if they themselves were not participating.

Meanwhile the nitrate resources brought prosperity to late 19th century Chile and a new boom—copper discoveries, made in 1911 and 1915—added to national income. US capital soon moved in to exploit the copper mines in the 1920s.

Brazil: Os Sertões

In Brazil, the third of the large ABC countries, the story was more violent but equally the product of foreign interventionism and the economics of national dependency. The paper constitution of 1891 had made Brazil a federal republic with a bicameral congress and four-year presidential term, separation of Church and State and some extension of the franchise. Under this constitution, modelled theoretically on that of the US, Brazilians who could vote elected Deodoro da Fonseca, who as we observed, rapidly became an authoritarian ruler. After his fall a period of political upheaval and violence included a full-scale naval uprising in Rio and a monarchist counter-revolution in the south during the autumn of 1893. A rebellious Admiral, De Mello, threatened to bombard the defenceless city of Rio until prevented by the intervention of British and US warships. Nevertheless thousands died in the civil war until peace was restored in 1894. A series of civilian presidents did manage to govern Brazil from that year until 1910, the first three all coming from São Paulo—a clear reflection of that city's economic growth and new political importance as the centre of the coffee industry and nesting-place of Italian and other European immigrants.

The political life of Brazil became more orderly and predictable except for occasional attempts at revolution or *coup*. One of these, a strange hill-billy sort of uprising, took place among the poor folk of the arid Canudos region of Northeast Brazil and inspired Brazil's most famous book, *Os Sertões* by Euclides da Cunha (translated as *Rebellion in the Backlands*, 1920). A religious fanatic calling himself Anthony the Counsellor, António Conselheiro) ruled his own private community in the Bahía backwoods. In 1896–7, after mysterious spirit-rappings with one Sebastian, a king of Portugal who had vanished in Africa in 1578, Anthony decided to march against the 'sinful' republic of Brazil. Conselheiro was killed by Brazilian government troops, and the movement of his followers, called *sertanejos*, was suppressed.

The inheritance of the late 19th century was thus a marked pattern of neo-colonialism, political instability, and foreign intervention for the nations of central and South America. Where railways were built or city services multiplied (sewage lines, highways, lighting and other utilities) the capital and technology were usually British. Towards the end of the century the US began to assert its dominance over some sections of the hemisphere. Within this pattern it was difficult for individual national economic systems to diversify or develop themselves, but given the political and social conditions of the period British capital did at least bring a measure of economic growth to selected regions.

The latifundia or concentrated land-holdings dominated the rural economies even more by 1900 than in earlier years. The Mexican hacienda, the Brazilian fazenda, the Argentine estancia perpetuated a way of life for the upper and lower classes alike in South America that had entirely disappeared or was rapidly vanishing in other parts of the globe. In Brazil and Argentina these large units and élites throve on economic booms based on particular crops or minerals and changing over time. In the late 19th century for example, large rubber plantations were built under incredible conditions of work and life in the Amazon jungles of Brazil. The large estate and the family system of economic control was to be seen everywhere, in Cuba, for instance, as well as in Brazil, Mexico and Argentina.

By 1900 in some nations local caudillo power-structures based on regional geography and the support of the latifundia were giving way to national or quasi-parliamentary systems, but there would be many relapses to forcible rule by men-on-horseback and to localism. In many areas mestizo groups were in the ascendant where they existed. Slavery no longer survived formally in the western hemisphere, though blacks and Indians were very poor and the Indians of the provinces were still exploited, resistant to white culture, and illiterate.

Part Three

The Building of Plural Societies
(From the 1920's)

Two World Wars brought massive changes in the world balance of power after 1917, but within the western hemisphere the relative positions of the nations were remarkably unaffected. The United States continued to dominate the hemisphere in the 1970s as she now partly dominated the globe, economically and militarily. The Central and South American nations still had dependent, staple-exporting economies. Even Canada, though it was no longer agrarian but a modern industrial society with three-quarters of its people living in towns and cities and only one-tenth on farms, was tied to and penetrated by the US economy and US culture. Yet the world outside the Americas had witnessed the traumatic events of the Russian Revolution of 1917 and the rise of Soviet power, the post-1945 liberation of the Indian subcontinent and parts of Asia and the crumbling of former empires, the creation of new nations all over Africa, and the emergence of Communist China with its massive population increasing rapidly and racing towards the billion mark.

In such a setting the history of Central and South America seemed relatively unchanging. The newer politics of the 'Third World' nations might offer some promise of faster change in what the rest of the world still called 'Latin' America. But as a concept, 'Third World' was still vague in the early 1970s and tied more to Middle Eastern, Arab and African problems. The phrase could hardly embrace such diversities of potential and history as Africa, parts of Asia, and Central and South America. Perhaps the last could form a 'Fourth World'. More likely, South Americans could adopt as their model post-World War II Western Europe, with its so-called economic 'miracles' of growth and its increasingly powerful Common Market. A Central and South American Common Market could perhaps be formed, a sort of *Pan-Americanism without the United States.* The signs of such cooperation were still meagre however as late as the mid-1970s. Pessimistic observers felt that these societies might never be able to throw off the influence of a long colonial past; others despaired of US policy ever changing towards the rest of the Americas, despite the greater interest in the southern continent showed in the 1960s by the short regime of President John F. Kennedy. America's involvement in Europe and Asia was massive; at different periods it gave more aid to South Vietnam or Korea than to all the nations of Central and South America. Still others began to feel that any hoped-for US aid, even if it came without strings and in sufficient quantity and was well-spent by the authoritarian governments of the region, was a snare. Aid, like investment, would not alter the basic structure of South American economies and would leave them still dependent on the North. Meanwhile various types of socialism became increasingly popular. In particular the churches of South America began to awaken as if from a long and deep sleep. Catholic Marxists, so-called 'Third World priests' and other movements disturbed the equilibrium in the 1960s and 70s. It was unlikely that in the years ahead the US model would be followed so readily in the western hemisphere. In Canada too, the impatience of French *Canadiens* and the restiveness of Canadian political leaders generally, indicated a strong desire to separate that nation from American foreign policies, such as the war in Vietnam, and to take stronger steps to assert Canadian independence in cultural and economic affairs.

In the years since World War I some nations of the southern hemisphere had begun to experience the genuine social and economic revolutions denied to them so many times after the wars of independence and the success of the creole policies of containment. Mexico led the way in 1910, its revolution in fact preceding Russia's. Later major examples were Brazil (1930), Argentina (1945), Bolivia (1952), and Cuba (1958–59). Guatemala attempted a late revolution but it was successfully suppressed by the right wing, admittedly aided by a ubiquitous branch of the US government, the Central Intelligence Agency (1954). In the 1950s, and 60s the US frowned on revolutions south of the border, whether they were democratic, nationalist or economic in character. The fear that they might become communist, and the general US dislike for any sort of radical disturbance of the equilibrium anywhere in the world at this time (a dislike shared by that other great power, Soviet Russia) helped to explain this CIA intervention. Both great powers were counter-revolutionary if they feared the revolution or change in question might upset their own view of the balance of power or their own strategic and economic interests. The Guatemala intervention did not improve America's bad image in Central and South America, even though conservative, right-wing regimes predominated in that region. National pride was also involved. Nevertheless, day-to-day relations with border nations—Mexico and Canada—were generably tolerable.

After World War I the history of the American and Canadian peoples became more than ever a part of world history. The Great Depression of the 1930s, the Second World War and the ensuing Cold War, real and imagined, linked North America not only with Europe but with Asia. Both Canada and the US became highly industrialised and urbanised, high-consumption mass societies, variants of a model which saw other national variants emerge, as in Japan, Britain and elsewhere, in the post-1945 decades. South of the Rio Grande, caudillismo, the usual technique for 'revolution' or effecting changes of rule, underwent its third stage of evolution. Stage One had been the emergence of the local caudillo system supported by the landed aristocracy. Stage Two saw caudillismo allied with business interests and foreign capital in the later 19th century, as with

Díaz in Mexico. Stage Three came out of 20th century revolutions and changes: caudillo rule supported by mass labour groups like the tin-miners of Bolivia, the rural labourers of Cuba who supported Fidel Castro and the urban workers of Argentina who were the backbone of the movement led by Perón.

7
Growth and Depression in North America

The United States developed a mature industrial economy by 1914, with Canada following a few years later. Such economies are increasingly dependent on demand for their mass-produced, standardised products. They have to maintain purchasing-power and the level of investment in industry. This economic pressure partly accounted for US expansionism in the Caribbean, Mexico and elsewhere, and for growing US investments in the Canadian economy too. Expansionist policies had an economic basis whether couched in the moralistic, idealistic and superior rhetoric of Woodrow Wilson, or in the franker 'Big Stick' pronouncements of Teddy Roosevelt in earlier years, though often it seemed that the US stepped in *to keep other powers out*. The logic of the economic and foreign policies of the Roosevelt-Wilson years carried the US towards Great Power status, and subsequently into World War I.

North America and World War I

Canada's involvement in that war was taken for granted from the moment of its outbreak by Canadians and British alike, although Canada had taken no part in the complex diplomatic manoeuvres that had led to the European conflict. The nation was still governed by the terms of the British North America Act of 1867, which left foreign policy matters to the London government. Also, according to the Colonial Laws Validity Act of 1865, the House of Commons in Westminster had the authority to nullify Canadian laws which it found 'repugnant' to the United Kingdom. Canada's intervention in World War I did much to further the cause of its independence from England.

The United States showed great reluctance and internal indecision over the European war, yet gradually it drew closer to Britain and was alienated from Germany. The Anglo-American 'mystique' of kinship, language and common institutions, together with clever British propaganda and inept German policies, especially cruel submarine warfare, brought the US into the war against Germany in April 1917—quite late. By contrast the Canadian Expeditionary Force was in England before the end of 1914. Almost half a million men were mobilised in Canada, and 60,000 were killed in heroic and bloody engagements in France like Ypres, Passchendaele and Mons. While the US contribution was chiefly the threat of her great economic power, the number of US men involved greatly exceeded the Canadian total of course. In the last-push battle, the Meuse-Argonne offensive (September–November 1918), 1,200,000 US troops fought. The US mobilised well over 4,000,000 men and lost almost 131,000 dead. Comparative total population figures at this time were: Canada, about 8 million; the United States, over 100 million.

The US economy however was never fully geared to fight the war, and US men went to war in Allied ships and fought with Allied guns. At home the war was viewed in moral terms, as fully in keeping with Wilson's concept of a league of large industrial powers, allied together to enforce international morality and to impose a moral and economic order on world society. This view did not survive the post-war enthusiasm, and Wilson's 'League of Nations', though founded, was not joined by his own nation. At home the war had great social and economic impact on both Canada and the United States.

Wilson's government saw the war as a popular, moral crusade for democracy. The president appealed to the German people over the heads of their government, and caused the more conservative Allies some concern with his rhetoric of political and social reform. The French, English and other allies were not certain that they fully shared Wilson's views of what peace should bring under US leadership. It was ironical and tragic that in the US itself, Wilson's war policies brought a curtailment of civil rights, federal control over an efficient propaganda machine run by George Creel, and a high degree of economic centralisation. Radical activities and anti-draft agitation were stamped out hastily. The offices of the IWW were closed down; journals were harassed; films censored. Though one leading jurist, Justice Oliver Wendell Holmes Jr., invented a dogma to protect civil liberties—the concept that there must be a 'clear and present danger' before suspension of rights—in practice this idea did not prove strong enough during the war. (Decades later, in World War II and again in the 1950s, the doctrine was proved to be weak yet again). War production brought better conditions and wages for labour, especially in essential war industries with government contracts, such as meat-packing, munitions, metal-working and shipbuilding. Industrial unions grew to power (as against the more conservative, old-fashioned craft unions of the skilled, favoured by the AFL). General trade union membership also rose. Wilson strongly favoured women's rights and tried to persuade industry to adopt equal pay provisions through the War Labor Board, with little real success.

Similar labour advances occurred in Canada as the economy expanded in such crucial areas as steel production, minerals, wheat, and other raw materials needed in the war. The post-war years saw an outbreak of radical labour organisation, the attempt by western Canadian labour leaders to organise 'One Big Union' for all workers, white-collar and manual alike, in 1918–19. From 15 May to 25 June 1919 the bitter Winnipeg General Strike brought this movement to a climax until it was suppressed by troops and police. Despite the violence, Canadian Progressives and reformers did win political successes in the early 1920s, in strong contrast to the situation in the United States.

The most important outcome of World War I for Canada was a greater degree of national independence. Prime Minister Robert L. Borden felt confident, in view of Canada's spectacular war effort, in demanding from England in 1916 a Canadian representative on the Imperial War Cabinet. In 1919, independent Canadaian representation was allowed at the Versailles peace conference. Canada joined the League of Nations as an independent nation, and after 1919 nationalist-minded writers and politicians pressed for greater Canadian autonomy. In the 1920s, Prime Minister Mackenzie King pursued an independent line in diplomacy (for instance he signed a treaty with the United States in 1923); and finally in 1931 the *Statute of Westminster* made the British Commonwealth of Nations a grouping of equal partners, not subordinate to each other. This group included Canada, Australia, New Zealand, South Africa, the Irish Free State, and Newfoundland (separate from Canada until 1949). The legal doctrine of 'repugnance' was abolished. Thus the gradual evolution of Canadian independence was brought to conclusion, hastened by the events of World War I.

Black Americans and World War I

While the war further divided French and Anglo-Canadians, and led to bitter French Canadian anti-draft riots in Quebec city in March-April 1918, in the United States the tension between black and white Americans also reached a new climax. Negroes, largely forgotten by the northern liberals since the end of Reconstruction in the South (1877), and abandoned in their civil rights by the Supreme Court, had been re-subjected to racial discriminations by white supremacist southern state governments. Nevertheless, war expansion brought some job gains for Negroes, and blacks enlisted in the army in the early days of US involvement in the war.

Retrogressive steps included President Wilson's deliberate segregation of federal employees in Washington in the enlarged wartime bureaucracy. Congress was flooded with anti-Negro bills; lynchings increased—even a public burning before cheering crowds (in Waco, Texas in 1916). Negro soldiers were mobbed in their uniforms. This continued while the US public was shocked by press tales of German atrocities in Europe. Blacks could serve their nation only as messmen in the Navy; they were totally banned from the Marines. In the Army, black protest finally forced the creation of a (segregated) Negro Officer Training School. Army camps were strictly segregated, and racial friction was common. Yet black Americans fought valiantly, 100,000 of them serving in Europe. They ignored German propaganda leaflets that tried to persuade them to desert.

At home many blacks experienced the 'Great Migration', an acceleration of the movement from the southern countryside to northern cities. With the war a great impetus was given to a new phase of black history, the rise of urban ghetto life. Blacks brought to great cities like Chicago (the 'Top of the World' as Negroes who moved up the Mississippi called it), their labour, their deep religious faith, and their music and dance. 'Jazz' in its various phases, moved up the river with the migrants, passing through various styles—New Orleans, Memphis, St. Louis, Chicago—and, of course, Harlem in New York City. The two great centres of the northern black subculture became Harlem and the South Side of Chicago. Race conflict now broke out in the North. It was no longer a mainly southern problem. Black and white Americans seemed to be competing for living-space and jobs, and cruel real-estate manoeuvres forced the blacks to crowd into restricted, high-priced slums. Violence occurred in the savage East St Louis race-riot of 1917, and in the more evenly matched war between black and white youth gangs in Chicago in 1919. These were the deepest hostilities of a mass society, built on promises not always fulfilled.

The dictated peace of 1919

The victors imposed peace terms on a humiliated Germany in 1919 and Woodrow Wilson's hopes for a democratic peace between equals came to nought. It was US military intervention in the war which had made this dictated peace possible. Terrified by the spectre of Communism in the successful Russian Revolution of 1917, and eager for vengeance on the 'Hun', the English and the French demanded that Germany be branded with 'war guilt', stripped of her colonies, and forced to give up the rich Saar coalfields and industrial regions of Alsace-Lorraine. Thus were sown the seeds of another conflict, World War II. The United States squirmed a little, but agreed. Wilson mishandled his Congress and the League of Nations, an American brain-child, was not ratified by the Senate. The US remained mainly outside the world-order it had helped to create. Canada was committed to the League, with Britain.

The twenties: consumer capitalism

In the US the 1920s began in a negative spirit as the civil-rights deprivations of the Wilson government continued. The president's Attorney-General, A. Mitchell Palmer, a one-time Progressive reformer, was now hysterically anxious about 'Bolshevism', feminists, radicals, and what he called 'alien filth'. His 'Palmer Raids' and deportations were the core of the Red Scare of 1919–20. Trade unions were harassed; teachers and others forced to take loyalty oaths; syndicalists and even democratic socialists repressed. Palmer used widespread wire-tapping of private telephone conversations.

Meanwhile the United States turned inwards and rejected the Europe from which many Americans came. Despite the inescapable fact of the make-up of the US population by 1920, laws were passed to cut off further European immigration, aimed at those from Central, Southern and Eastern Europe. This doctrine of 'Nordicism', that those from Northwest Europe were racially superior, was of course, but one aspect of a wider racism and exclusiveness based on fear and anxiety. The Quota Laws of 1921 and 1924 imposed strict limits on who was to come to the United States—based on ethnic and racial standards. The US overturned its traditions of over three hundred years. Over a century before, Spain had sought occasionally to restrict immigration to its colonies to Catholics, but had failed. The democratic republic of the North had now imposed a selective filter that was more humiliating, and far more effective. A more brutal aspect of racism was seen in the rise of the Ku Klux Klan from 1915, in popular hatred of Negroes, and in race-riots and lynchings in the years 1917–19. The year 1919 saw 26 recorded race-riots and many attempts by black Americans to defend themselves at law. Lynchings continued throughout the twenties.

The hands of the employers and corporations were strengthened by popular phobias about radicalism in the early 1920s, and as a result of this unions lost many of their wartime advances. The violent strikes of 1919, as in steel and coal, were soon left far behind, as the employers developed employer associations, use of repressive private police and spies, and started to undercut the appeal of unions by creating their own 'company unions' and offering limited company benefits. The 'American Plan'—enforcement of the 'open shop' (no union employees to be hired)—cut deeply into trade union membership and income. In the prosperous consumer-boom years of the 1920s the US trade unions actually declined in membership, despite the overall increase in the population and labour-force. These were the 'lean years' for organised labour. Union leaders themselves became cautious and t imid, led by the AFL hierarchy. Much of this happened under the presidency of Calvin Coolidge, whose rapid rise from relative obscurity to the White House had been given a large boost through his tough if belated opposition to the Boston police strike of 1919: an early example of an American 'law and order' political stand that paid off.

Prohibition: legislating morality

The regime of President Warren Harding (elected in 1920, promising a return to 'normalcy') was noted for its extensive corruption, graft and scandals. Yet under the 18th Amendment (ratified January 1919) it was supposed to enforce personal morality—abstention from alcohol—on all United States citizens. The task was impossible, the borders of the nation too vast, and the Prohibition Bureau too small and understaffed. The result was the exact opposite: a great increase in drinking, often of inferior and downright poisonous liquors, and the creation of perfect conditions for the application of corporate techniques of organisation to crime. Crime syndicates, based mainly on bootleg beer and liquors, became a semi-permanent feature of US life. Perhaps more important, the general disregard for the prohibition laws practised by thousands of otherwise normal Americans, did not encourage automatic respect for the law.

The 'New Era': moral rhetoric and Big Business

The death of Harding in 1923 put his vice-president Calvin Coolidge in the White House where he was returned by the election of 1924. There was no break in the *laissez-faire*, pro-business policies already established. A huge consumer boom, based on the application of science and technology to industrial production and great strides in management and labour productivity, boosted several old industries and created new ones. A great urban building mania brought the skyscraper skylines now familiar in Chicago, New York and elsewhere. Urban land values shot up. In Florida rapid development of the coast as a resort area produced over-speculation and eventually a collapse in 1926.

Coolidge worshipped 'business' in this 'New Era'. 'The man who builds a factory builds a temple', he once said. As chief executive he hated executive power in government and did as little as he possibly could—the reverse of Teddy Roosevelt or Woodrow Wilson, with their eager centralisation of power in the President's hands. He tried to save money, cut the budget and give tax relief to rich men, on the theory that the benefits would eventually 'trickle down' to the masses through extra business investments bringing greater productivity. This was a complacent theory, an economics of success totally unsuitable if a downturn should come. Fortunately for Coolidge no recession occurred until his successor took over.

Coolidge was intensely moralistic, the nation less so. While he applied his simple prescriptions business was rushing ahead and becoming very complex. The trustification movement of the turn of the century now revived: huge concentrations of business power emerged in oligopolies that divided the market among them as they saw fit and fixed prices to their own advantage. Despite the Sherman Anti-trust Act (1890) and other measures, there seemed to be little effective attempt at public control. Giant corporations dominated the mass industries: for example, steel, automobiles, meatpacking and tobacco. Labour was weakened and lacked the *countervailing* power to balance off such huge blocs. Meanwhile, intense speculation on the exchanges began to build up a wild 'bull'

163

market. Many people bought stock 'on margin', borrowing cash to buy shares, expecting a quick profit from resale in a market that seemed to be permanently rising. When the Crash came in 1929 such investors had nothing to protect them from total bankruptcy.

The perils of uneven growth

The boom of the 1920's was based on a large upsurge in the general *purchasing-power* of US consumers. The demands and buying ability of this growing middle and lower-middle class pushed up the Gross National Product (total output of goods and services) and stimulated industry. Older groups benefited, like real estate construction and highways, steel, and rubber, as did brand-new sectors like automobiles, kitchen gadgetry, radios, electronics. The sale of the latest appliances, called 'consumer durables' by economists, such as refrigerators, radios, washing machines, electric irons, stoves and vacuum cleaners, brought with it a growth of consumer advertising and a large expansion of consumer credit. The US economy began to assume the features it has today. It still lacked built-in controls and legislative restraints. Credit piled up, but demand for the new products was very 'elastic': in bad times, people could still do without such items, and the bottom could fall out of the market as it did in the market for stocks.

The new consumer industries were doubly dangerous, being founded on credit sales and elastic demand. Their role in the general economy could spread the ill-effects of any collapse. Cars for one example, used up 15% of total national steel output, as well as great quantities of petrol, lead, glass, rubber, nickel. The industry was worth about 13% of national manufacturing output. If it were to crash many other sectors would be dragged down with it.

Farmer radicals

While some parts of society flourished, others lagged behind. The older industries, on which the industrial revolution of the early 19th century had been based, now found themselves out-paced and obsolescent, with a heavy burden of ancient capital construction. The coal industry, leather, lumber, railways, textiles, and shipbuilding could not attract sufficient capital to renew themselves, while money flowed readily into more glamorous areas. The workers in these sectors suffered badly while they witnessed general prosperity for most of their colleagues. Farmers, above all, suffered from this dilemma, and were not always prepared to stay silent. The Grange had survived from the 1890s and grew steadily. Political groups for organised lobbying in Washington included the Farmer's Union, which demanded nationalisation of railways, taxation of land-values (following the ideas of Henry George), cheap farm credit and many other reforms. Less radical were the Farm Bureau Federation and the 'farm bloc' of Congressmen organised to vote together in the

1920s. These pressure-groups achieved some successes including controls over stockyards and over grain speculators. But a major reform, the McNary-Haugen scheme for federal control of farm surpluses in order to manipulate the market, was defeated five times.

North Dakota farmers were most restless. Their Non-Partisan Political League (1915) spread into 15 western states. North Dakota took over its own grain elevators, banks and warehouses; it created a state hail-insurance fund, exempted farmers from taxation on improvements and gave them easy loans for home-buying. Pacifist during World War I, the Dakota radicals lost favour and in the early 1920s they declined. Out of the League grew the Farmer-Labor Party, which sought to achieve that old, honoured goal of radical movements, a unity between rural and urban workers. In the 1924 election it threw its support to the reformist La Follette of Wisconsin who ran on a Progressive ticket, along with AFL trade unions and Socialists. But traditional divisions among the American left prevented any genuine or long-term cooperation. For the rest of the decade and on into the depressed 1930s, the farmers continued to suffer from tenancy, sharecropping, falling farm prices and bankruptcies. Technology advanced further. The tractor and the large farming corporation split the farm community apart.

Social class in the Jazz Age

Class cleavage was seen in the cities with their ethnic and racial complexity, even more than among farmers. Many positive features of the economic growth of the decade should not be overlooked: the doubling of high-school and of college enrolments; the decline of stuffiness and relaxation of regulations for women and children within the family and at work; the impact at the popular level of 'Freudian' ideas in personal relationships. Yet, although the central theme of social history was the rise of a large, more educated, wealthier and more liberated *middle* class, social differentiation was more acute.

The gap is seen if one reads Richard Wright's *Black Boy*, for example, and contrasts the life-style it portrays with that of Scott Fitzgerald's *Great Gatsby*. This is to take a wide extreme. In between one could read the novels of Sinclair Lewis, excoriating and yet drawing in some detail that must connote a sort of affection, the small-town United States of the Twenties. The ambiguity of intellectuals like Lewis was reflected in the rise of two separate cultures: 'popular' and 'serious', seen most clearly in music. Popular tastes were heavily swayed by the new movie industry, by radio and dance-halls and the doings of popular 'stars' and entertainers of the 'Jazz Age'.

The High Culture of the Twenties

Some intellectuals and writers, disgusted by what they called the 'materialism' of the age, echoed the earlier criticisms of the United States made by the Uruguayan, Rodó in *Ariel* (1900). They exiled themselves to France, or inhabited little 'Greenwich Villages' in US cities, living as psychological emigrants from their own nation. These people nevertheless put US literature on the map; their writings have lasted and have given the nation the literary and artistic status they felt it lacked in the 1920s. T. S. Eliot, John Dos Passos, Scott Fitzgerald, and many other brilliant names are among them. In painting, the twenties was also a crucial period. The growth of middle-class purchasing-power, whatever scorn Sinclair Lewis and others might heap upon bourgeois tastes, did begin to create a sizeable native market for works of art. The artist could now begin to make a living in the United States, though President Coolidge was such a philistine that he rejected a French government request for US paintings to be shown in Paris, on the grounds that there were not any. He seemed not to have heard of the Ash Can School of the early 1900s, the Armory Show of 1913, and the coming of the American Modernists in the 1920s—Marin, O'Keefe, Weber and the cubist-realists like Demuth and Sheeler.

The growth of Harlem, the Negro ghetto in New York City, brought together all sorts of black Americans and more recent West Indian immigrants. Harlem became the Mecca of the black intellectual, artist and writer. With the spread of jazz clubs and cabarets it also became a white tourists' showplace, where black entertainers played to white audiences, out for a thrill in the ghetto. The white readers expected black writers to meet certain pre-conceived notions of what Negro life was all about. Black poets were supposed to have a 'jungle beat'. Trying to overcome these stereotypes, while at the same time not repudiating their own background and the Negro masses, was a subtle and difficult problem for black intellectuals in the twenties.

Out of their struggles for self-identity came a flood of creative writing, called the 'Harlem Renaissance'. The major writers like Claude McKay, Langston Hughes, Jean Toomer or Countee Cullen, both adopted and rejected 'primitivism' and exoticism in their work. Through difficult paths of race-pride, folk-writing, and rejection, black writers moved towards that *full* liberation reached in later decades by James Baldwin, acceptable to himself and to others as a writer, not purely a *black* writer.

Black nationalism: Marcus Garvey

Most ghetto inhabitants of Harlem did not know there was a 'Renaissance' going on. More significant for them was the mass religious movement of Marcus Garvey, the 'Black is Beautiful' movement of the 1920s. 'I am the equal of any white man,' Garvey told the Negro masses, 'I want

10. Marcus Garvey parading in New York.

you folks to feel the same.' A West Indian immigrant, Garvey dreamed of a new African empire and of the unity of Negroes the world over. Though he had never been to Africa himself, Garvey was painfully aware of the way the African Negro had been written out of history and not mentioned. He insisted on emphasizing the cultural wealth of the African past, and great Negro contributors to world history—such as Toussaint L'Ouverture, the saviour of Haiti.

Garvey's appeal was direct, and went to the heart of the Negro masses in a way that the intellectual NAACP and the middle-class, social-work oriented Urban League could not. Yet he was a rigid separatist who could see no hope for blacks living among whites. Like the white racists of the pre-Civil War years, Garvey advocated the mass emigration of Negroes 'back' to Africa. His open talks with southern white extremists and Klansmen angered other black leaders like W. E. B. DuBois and A. Philip Randolph. Randolph, the socialist and trade union leader, stood for cooperation between blacks and whites in trade unions. Garvey attacked such views with great bitterness. He said 'The NAACP want us all to become white by amalgamation!', and he satirised other leaders as 'Uncle Tom niggers'. The 'Empire' of Garvey, with its bright uniforms, orders and regalia, collapsed under charges of fraud over his Black Star Steamship Line. But Garvey dealt in dreams: dreams for the black urban masses. They would need something to live by in the cruel years of depression which lay ahead.

The twenties in Canada

The 1920s were also years of prosperity and growth for many people in Canada. The national economy was still in the midst of a great wheat boom which lasted from about 1900 to about 1930. Major economic flows were still east-west and directed towards Britain and the European market. However, newer industries were developing away from the great Canadian prairies, in Ontario and Quebec. Electricity, paper and pulp factories and other manufactures were emerging which would change the balance of the entire economy. Politics were controlled by the Liberal Party under W. L. Mackenzie King, the leader of the Canadian unity movement and of the struggle for Canadian autonomy from England. The years of the wheat boom were already numbered, and the coming of the 1930s would see a massive shift in economic flows, north-south, rather than east-west, as the United States gradually began to replace Britain as Canada's major outlet, and as her chief capital source. Producers of Canadian exports moved towards meeting the US demands for forest and mineral products.

Meanwhile the population of Canada had altered. Mass immigration even before World War I had brought thousands of Germans, Ukrainians, Poles, and Russian Dukhobors (many of whom moved in the 1890s to Saskatchewan). The Canadian West began to take on the ethnic plural

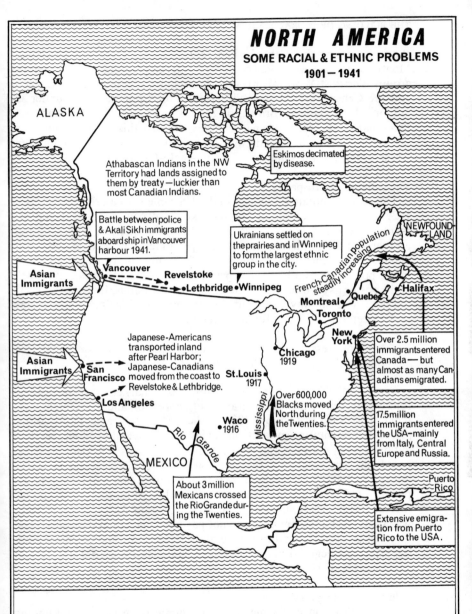

NORTH AMERICA
SOME RACIAL & ETHNIC PROBLEMS
1901 — 1941

ALASKA

Athabascan Indians in the NW Territory had lands assigned to them by treaty — luckier than most Canadian Indians.

Eskimos decimated by disease.

Battle between police & Akali Sikh immigrants aboard ship in Vancouver harbour 1941.

Ukrainians settled on the prairies and in Winnipeg to form the largest ethnic group in the city.

NEWFOUND-LAND

French-Canadian population steadily increasing

Asian Immigrants

Vancouver • Revelstoke
• Lethbridge • Winnipeg

Halifax

Montreal • Quebec
Toronto

Japanese-Americans transported inland after Pearl Harbor; Japanese-Canadians moved from the coast to Revelstoke & Lethbridge.

New York

Chicago
1919

Over 2.5 million immigrants entered Canada — but almost as many Canadians emigrated.

Asian Immigrants

San Francisco

St.Louis
1917

Los Angeles

17.5 million immigrants entered the USA — mainly from Italy, Central Europe and Russia.

Waco
• 1916

Over 600,000 Blacks moved North during the Twenties.

Mississippi

Rio Grande

MEXICO

Puerto Rico

About 3 million Mexicans crossed the Rio Grande during the Twenties.

Extensive emigration from Puerto Rico to the USA.

Both Canada and the United States restricted Asian immigration during this period – partly due to the fear of the so-called 'Yellow Peril'. The Canadians passed the 1923 Chinese Immigration Act which successfully reduced the number of legal Chinese immigrants between 1923–41 to fifteen ! American discrimination against Japanese children in San Francisco during 1906 caused an international crisis; but by the time of Pearl Harbor (7 December 1941) there were about 140,000 Japanese–Americans living in the United States.

character of much of the United States. Later, Canadian cities like Montreal also saw many newcomers of different nationality and religious groups. The Post-World War II years brought fresh immigrants to Canada and the Census of 1971 showed that, of a total population of under 22 million, 48% claimed British origin, 31% French, 4% German, 3% Ukrainian, and 14% other nationalities. Despite this growing pluralism the major division in Canada was still considered to be the bi-lingualism which separated the *Canadien* and the Anglo-Canadian.

The collapse of prosperity

The first economic downturn in the US came with a brief recession in 1927. Prices fell, the building boom slackened off causing some unemployment and the car industry was cut back by one quarter. Wages, output and the standard of living for some people all fell. The recovery was swift and reassuring and people shrugged it all off. One could not readily believe in the possibility of a massive depression after almost ten years of growth and booster psychology. Moreover, in 1927 dividends, interest and rents did not suffer the way wages did. So President Coolidge's annual message of 4 December 1928 was full of confidence:

> No Congress ... has met with a more pleasing prospect than that which appears at the present time.

Ten months later came the greatest stock-market crash in history, followed by ten years of long drawn-out depression and mass unemployment. The crash of October 1929 on the exchanges dragged down other prices in a downward spiral. Companies could not sell products, so they cut back on investment and jobs and laid off workers. The people in turn could not buy, and thus the spiral was self-reinforcing and hit rock-bottom in 1933. The results were tragic. Families that had never known poverty and lack of work now saw hunger, loss of mortgages on homes, loss of businesses, and little hope for the distant future. Savings were wiped out, as banks simply could not pay back the money deposited. The New Deal would later bring federal and state insurance of most bank deposits, to safeguard people's savings, but such things did not exist in the America of 1929.

What did the Depression mean?

The Depression could mean coming home from school and finding your father at home, out of work, and your mother out scrubbing floors to earn money to pay for the next meal or rent. It could mean graduating from high school and waiting as long as two or more years before finding your first job. In Chicago, the citizens grubbed around among the waste dumps for scraps of rotten food; school-teachers taught as long as they could without pay; the city was without funds. A cabinet member suggested that restaurants save scraps from diners' tables to feed the workless. Young people stopped getting married: the marriage rate fell 30%, 1929–32, as did the birth rate. Gangs of unemployed youths roamed the countryside seeking work, avoiding home where they would be a burden. Former business-men sold apples on the street and begged for work.

These experiences, which hit the middle classes, had for a long time been the life-experience of American disadvantaged and minority groups. Such people were now depressed even further as out of work whites and skilled workers took their jobs. Some people tried to drift to the countryside. Plans to settle urban workers on farms usually failed. Meanwhile, the federal government, tied down by a narrow philosophy that feared government 'interference' and hoped for a sharp but short recession followed by a quick upturn, did very little.

Coming of the New Deal: pragmatism

Herbert Hoover, elected President in 1928, was a brilliant self-made man and philanthropist of international reputation. Many of his ideas were taken up by his successor in the New Deal, including the Reconstruction Finance Corporation, a federal body to help businesses regain credit and start investing again; farm relief; enouragement to trade unions; and federal spending on internal improvements, like the massive Boulder Dam. But he could not bring himself to spend federal funds in a large way, and what he did do was simply not enough in face of the drastic nature of the economic problem.

When army veterans demanded the full repayment of their service bonuses and marched on Washington, they were cleared out of their ramshackle huts on Anacostia Flats in the capital by an unnecessarily large and over-armed force of troops using fixed bayonets and tanks. Such events, and the depressing shanties that grew up in city parks all over, called derisively 'Hoovervilles', made Hoover a much hated man. He was blamed for the depression itself. The election of 1932 brought in the confident Democratic aristocrat, F. D. Roosevelt, who proclaimed that the nation had 'nothing to fear but fear itself', though at the time he did not have much idea what he was going to do about the depression. 'FDR' was no intellectual and his grasp of economics was poor. But he was flexible, a supreme pragmatist, tied to no ideologies or theories. His character became the character of the New Deal, a bewildering mass of reform measures and authorities with alphabetical names, often working at odds with each other, but somehow getting the country moving again. The New Deal was not 'socialism', as its enemies sometimes claimed; but it did change US capitalism in certain definite ways.

New Deal: recovery and reform

Roosevelt's main problem was to start up the economic system again. Beyond that, he wanted to enact some reforms that would help to prevent such a depression recurring, or at least modify its impact. For industry the National Recovery Administration (NRA) was created, based partly on World War I experiences. 'Code authorities' for each industry were to administer 'fair' competition and had precedence over antitrust regulations to allow agreed pricing policies and industrial consultation. The NRA was administered by a tough, ebullient General, Hugh Johnson, amid big publicity and splash. Its Blue Eagle sign was plastered all over— even worn on the backs of chorus girls. In truth the NRA was a rather modest attempt at reform, a self-policing by industry. The committees were supposed to represent labour and the consumer as well as the industry concerned; in most cases this did not happen. The NRA cost the federal government only the finance of its administration. It did not pump much extra needed money into the economy.

FDR's agricultural policy, the Agricultural Adjustment Administration (AAA) was even more conservative in tone. Based on earlier reform ideas put forward by farmers, the AAA tried to maintain farm prices by the simple capitalist expedient of destroying crops, and keeping goods off the market until prices improved. It was a strange sight in a hungry nation, to see over six million pigs slaughtered and wasted, ten million acres of cotton destroyed, fruit crops left to rot on the trees and wheat lands taken out of production. Prices of such crops did rise and national farm income increased substantially. But the system was insane to the common observer. Like the NRA, the AAA did not cost the federal government much at all; the farmers' subsidies for restricting output were paid for out of a processing tax on farm products.

More to the point in stimulating demand was the government-spending part of FDR's programme. Like a farm pump that needs to be 'primed' with water before it will start to pour forth, it was argued in the 1930s that the national economy needed to be primed with federal funds. The idea was for the government to spend more than it took in—deliberately. This 'new economics', an accepted policy by the 1960s and 70s, seemed heretical to many in the 1930s. FDR himself always wanted to balance his budget, like a good housekeeper. When finally convinced of the need for federal spending he split the budget into two parts. The unbalanced part was extraordinary, and, he hoped, a temporary matter.

It would be an error to call the New Deal 'Keynesian': the British economist Keynes had not yet fully worked out all his ideas, and FDR certainly would not have grasped them. The basic idea of spending over income to stimulate a sluggish demand, was well-known before Keynes, and was pushed by the English radical J. A. Hobson as well as by American writers. More important, FDR did not become fully converted to 'deficit spending' until very late—1937–38. In fact the New Deal was not a clear success because FDR simply did not spend *enough* on public works and employment.

The second half of the Act that created the NRA in 1933 also authorised deficit spending. While the flamboyant General Johnson led the NRA, the spending section was given to a cautious, penny-wise Republican, Harold Ickes, who tried to get 100 cents back on every dollar. This over-caution did much to soften the economic impact of Part II. A contemporary said Johnson and Ickes should have been switched in roles, and the New Deal would have worked better. It was typical of FDR however to divide the authority between two men.

The new ecology: conservation

A spectacular part of the spending programme was in the field of youth employment on conservation projects, a second conservation movement in US history following on that of Theodore Roosevelt. The Civilian Conservation Corps (CCC) gave work to about three million young people who reforested, built dams, roads and telephone connections, developed fish hatcheries, prevented fires and soil erosion and checked animal diseases. The Public Works Administration (PWA) and similar Works Progress Administration (WPA) spent billions on conservation, roads, flood control, direct relief, loans and grants, slum clearance, health, education and cultural programmes. Parks, playgrounds, housing projects, reservoirs, theatres, power plants—all were created by these agencies. In the public housing area however, real estate interests, entrenched then as now, prevented any substantial progress in the pro-vision of cheap housing for the poorer income groups despite efforts by FDR's Housing Authority (USHA).

The outstanding achievement of the New Deal in conservation-ecology was the Tennessee Valley Authority reclamation project (TVA), inter-nationally famous and highly regarded. The great Tennessee river and its tributaries were dammed to create flood regulation, power plants, navi-gation, and irrigation for 40,000 square miles of land in seven states. The largest fish hatchery in the world was established there, along with count-less other amenities for farmers, sportsmen and industry. It brought an entire geographical region to economic life and was a triumph of geogra-phical planning over merely political divisions. In later years TVA came under heavy political fire from private vested interests especially in the power industry, and the scheme was cut down and greatly dimin-ished.

These major measures do not begin to cover the mass of reforms achieved by the New Deal and the many more attempted. In its com-prehensiveness and energy and in its sheer quantity, the New Deal was entirely unprecedented in US history. Only President Lyndon Johnson's reforms of the 1960s came close to (or surpassed) the New Deal in scope. Conservation measures multiplied; the National Youth Administration in particular caught the spirit of the New Deal in this area. One third of all the unemployed were young people; they suffered badly from missed education, malnutrition and uprooting. Like the work-study provisions of the Great Society of the 1960s, the NYA gave money for student work on campus. The amounts earned were small; but together with CCC work, this helped a proportion of students to keep going somehow, though not on the scale of later years.

Labour and the New Deal

FDR was not initially very sympathetic towards labour. The pressure from pro-labour advisers like Senator R. F. Wagner, and the growth of violent industrial conflicts, finally convinced him to do more to encourage trade unions and to put the federal authority behind the workers to balance their weakness in the struggle with giant businesses. The Wagner Act of 1935 created the National Labor Relations Board to regularise collective bargaining and listed 'unfair practices' of employers used against unions. The Fair Labor Standards Act of 1938, pushed by Hugo Black of Alabama, aimed to put a ceiling on hours and a floor under wages. Black had hoped for a national six-hour day and thirty-hour week, to spread the work. The Act established a forty-hour week and minimum federal standards of 40 cents an hour.

Labour violence did not cease. There were 5,000 strikes in 1937 alone, and a more determined and radicalised trade union leadership refused to give way then as they had in the 1920s. Union membership, encouraged by Section 7(a) of the NRA Act of 1933, shot up. The AFL was forced to move with the times and allow 'federal' unions into its organisation, on an industry-wide rather than craft-wide basis. Eventually men from these industrial unions, being more radical, broke away and formed, under the leadership of the fiery John L. Lewis of the United Mine Workers, the Congress of Industrial Organisations (CIO). By mid-1937 the CIO was already a tough rival to the AFL itself and its membership was larger, four as opposed to three million men.

Tougher union methods were adopted by the CIO, including the sit-down strike, in which workers occupied the plant. This idea, used in France, was to come up again in the 'sit-*in*' demonstrations of the civil rights movement of the 1960s. The idea was to prevent normal business from going on. In earlier years, employers had merely brought in strike-breaking workers—immigrants or Negroes desperate for work—and continued production. Now the boot was on the other foot; workers at automobile plants sat down on the job and refused to allow anyone in. Violence ensued; but the CIO won some victories, including a crucial one over US Steel in 1937. Ford held out until 1941. The Memorial Day Massacre at the Republic Steel plant in South Chicago (June 1937) was one example of violence and police brutality. Ten strikers were killed. The workers were also violent, but Republic Steel was the largest buyer of tear- and sickening-gas in the United States and kept a large armoury and a small army of 400 armed 'police', according to a Senate investigation.

Belated arrival of the welfare state in the US

In addition to redressing the balance for labour, the New Deal, with the Social Security Act of 1935, finally brought the 'welfare state' to the United States. Other advanced industrial nations had begun to provide welfare measures much earlier: old-age pensions, unemployment insurance, accident and sickness benefits and the like. Germany began some schemes in the 1880s, Britain mainly in the early 1900s. Liberal individualism, fear of federal intervention in the economy except to encourage private business, and the conviction that poverty was the fault of the individual in America, kept such ideas away from the United States until the massive breakdown of capitalism in the 1930s. State accident compensation laws protected some workers from accidents on the job, but old age was unprotected before 1935 and unemployment insurance was unheard of. One state alone had unemployment insurance covered by state law (Wisconsin, 1932). American labour unions often opposed state insurance schemes, along with the private insurance companies.

The Social Security Act of 1935 began the true history of federal welfare in the United States. It provided *social insurance* in the form of old-age and survivors' benefits, and unemployment insurance paid by the federal government through the states. Also *categorical aid* was given to specific cases: the needy aged, the needy blind, and dependent mothers and children. A third section governed *health and welfare services*—federal grants to the states for services to crippled children, orphans, rehabilitation of the disabled, and public health services. Many later amendments have added millions more beneficiaries, and have broadened the scope of the act of 1935. Since 1965 the act has included 'Medicare' programme for those over 65.

The New Deal and minorities

More Americans found space in the sun because of the New Deal, though racial minorities were not its major concern. The act of 1934 gave a 'New Deal for the Indians' by putting a stop to federal attempts since the late 19th century to destroy tribal culture and Indian religion, and by ending the forced sale of communal lands to individuals (as happened in Mexico and South America). The Dawes Act of 1887 was thus overturned and Indian communal ways were reaffirmed. The reform owed much to the US Indian Commissioner (1933–45), John Collier. Though Indians had been granted US citizenship in 1924, renewed attempts at forcible assimilation of Indians to the white man's world had continued. In 1923 a struggle to transfer Pueblo land titles to whites was prevented in Congress only after vigorous protest by the Indians themselves. In 1926 the Indian Bureau began to attack the Pueblo religion. The 1934 act terminated sales of common land to individuals, and tried to protect Indian folk-ways.

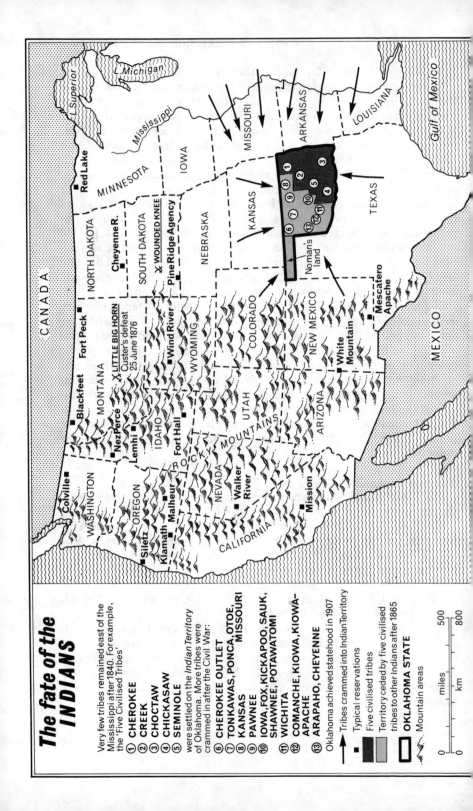

The fate of the INDIANS

Very few tribes remained east of the Mississippi after 1840. For example, the 'Five Civilised Tribes'

① CHEROKEE
② CREEK
③ CHOCTAW
④ CHICKASAW
⑤ SEMINOLE

were settled on the *Indian Territory* of Oklahoma. More tribes were crammed in after the Civil War:

⑥ CHEROKEE OUTLET
⑦ TONKAWAS, PONCA, OTOE, MISSOURI
⑧ KANSAS
⑨ PAWNEE
⑩ IOWA, FOX, KICKAPOO, SAUK, SHAWNEE, POTAWATOMI
⑪ WICHITA
⑫ COMANCHE, KIOWA, KIOWA–APACHE
⑬ ARAPAHO, CHEYENNE

Oklahoma achieved statehood in 1907

→ Tribes crammed into Indian Territory

■ Typical reservations

Five civilised tribes

Territory ceded by five civilised tribes to other Indians after 1865

☐ OKLAHOMA STATE

Mountain areas

miles   500

km   800

CANADA

L. Superior
L. Michigan
Red Lake
MINNESOTA
Mississippi
IOWA
NORTH DAKOTA
SOUTH DAKOTA
Fort Peck
Cheyenne R.
Pine Ridge Agency
✗ WOUNDED KNEE
MONTANA
Blackfeet
✗ LITTLE BIG HORN
Custer's defeat
25 June 1876
Nez Perce
Lemhi
IDAHO
Fort Hall
Wind River
WYOMING
NEBRASKA
KANSAS
Noman's land
COLORADO
ROCKY MOUNTAINS
UTAH
NEVADA
Walker River
CALIFORNIA
Mission
ARIZONA
White Mountain
NEW MEXICO
Mescalero Apache
TEXAS
MEXICO
Gulf of Mexico
LOUISIANA
ARKANSAS
MISSOURI
Colville
WASHINGTON
Siletz
Klamath
Malheur
OREGON

Federal encouragement of a revived corporative and communal identity among the Indians brought mixed results. Many tribes were so thinned out, and most had been so intermingled by white policy-makers that distinctive tribal traits had almost vanished. A result was the emergence of *Pan-Indianism*. This was a cultural and eventually a political movement to span tribal differences and unite Indians in a common struggle for identity and survival in the white world. By the 1960s and 70s the 'Red Power' movement was one illustration of Pan-Indianism. Increasingly, Indians were prepared to take action to defend their rights and customs. Sometimes violence ensued as when Indians took over federal property or organised a sit-in in Washington, D.C. In February 1973 some Indians at Custer, South Dakota, rejected what they considered a too-light sentence on a white who had stabbed an Indian. The result was a raid on the courthouse, the burning and stoning of some buildings, and a long Indian occupation of the Wounded Knee village site.

While the 'Native Americans' (a title some preferred to the word 'Indian') faced a long struggle in the years ahead, by the Census of 1970 it was clear that their numbers had increased since the New Deal and had reached roughly the same total that historians have estimated for the 17th century. The 1970 estimate was over 790,000. Of these nearly a half were classified as *urban* Indians (almost 356,000). In a big city like Chicago they were to be found among the poorest Americans.

Eleanor Roosevelt, the president's wife, was a greater champion of minority and especially Negro rights than her husband. She socialised with black leaders and tried to change white attitudes by her own example as First Lady. Black Americans were covered in most of the relief measures of the New Deal which made no distinctions based on race, creed or colour. Since they were among the most heavily depressed and unemployed Negroes gained much from federal aid. By the election of 1936, in northern big cities where they could vote without intimidation, Negroes swung strongly away from the party of Abraham Lincoln to the party of Roosevelt and the New Deal. They formed thenceforward a part of the 'Roosevelt alliance' which made the Democrats the majority for so long— blacks and city minorities, farmers, labour and liberal intellectuals. But apart from the general relief measures offered to all poor Americans, the Negro population did not receive any specific help from the New Deal. Indeed, during World War II, or at its outset for the US in 1941, Negro leaders had to threaten Washington with a massive march on the capital in order to make Roosevelt issue his executive order against job discrimination in the expanding war industries.

The New Deal was a deliberate attempt to save American capitalism from self-destruction and to help democracy survive at a time of severe economic and social crisis. It was not 'radical' in the sense of wishing to overturn American economic institutions or to institute any sort of 'socialism' in the United States. Yet, in conserving capitalism, Roosevelt was forced to change it in several ways. The result was the introduction of certain structural alterations—for instance welfare and strong unions—which were unlikely to be reversed. Did the New Deal achieve what it set out to do, to end mass unemployment and recharge the American economy? This seems doubtful. Unemployment remained high until 1941, when war orders from Europe, and eventually, US entry into the war brought huge federal contracts. War spending made the spending of the New Deal seem trivial. *War* was the ultimate form of 'deficit spending'. In 1937–38 a renewed recession seemed very dangerous for the nation and for FDR. That recession was wiped out by war demands, noticeably after Pearl Harbour was bombed by the Japanese in 1941. Students still debate whether the nation would have enjoyed an economic recovery without World War II.

The Depression in Canada

The depression hit Canada badly, partly because of the neo-colonial nature of her economy in which at least one third of total national income came from the export of basic raw materials and other products to foreign nations. World prices fell sharply and Canadian farmers felt the impact, as did lumbermen and producers of newsprint and minerals. Many sectors of the economy and society—the transportation system and factories—were locked in to dependence upon export markets. A large proportion of investment capital had come from abroad, mainly from England and the US. Alberta and Saskatchewan were two provinces that suffered heavily. Wheat producers were bankrupt and a federal government board stepped in to control wheat sales after 1935.

In truth the geographic limits of wheat expansion were already reached by 1930, depression or no depression. The collapse of the European market and the growing magnetism of US demands drew Canadian resources away from wheat. The US needed raw materials like pulp, paper and minerals, as its maturing economy encountered depleting natural resources. Meanwhile Britain had lost economic leadership in the world to the US and by the first World War, New York had already replaced London as the global money market. US purchases brought US direct investments in Canada. Even the US labour unions came to dominate in Canada, calling themselves therefore 'International' unions. These changes were most felt in the 1940s and 50s.

The Canadian 'New Deal' was led initially by the Conservative party Prime Minister, R. B. Bennett, after his first attempts to control the depression, mainly through a combination of public optimism and higher tariffs, had no visible effect. In 1935 he brought in a programme of social welfare legislation, but this was too late to avoid political defeat in the elections of that year. A long period of Liberal party rule followed and in 1939 a Plains Farms Assistance Act began a system of farm aid through quotas and subsidies not unlike that adopted earlier by FDR. In the long-run the striking of oil in the West transformed the prairie economy and introduced pipelines and refineries into the heartland of Alberta. Wheat farmers turned towards dairying and livestock, particularly hogs, though Canada continued to produce excellent crops of wheat.

At least two major economic-political movements grew out of Canada's experience in the depression: the Cooperative Commonwealth Federation and Social Credit. The CCF was basically a socialist party, a combination of radical farmers, labour men, urban socialists from western cities like Vancouver and Winnipeg, and established Independent Labour Parties on the English model. It was founded at Calgary, Alberta in August 1932. The Regina Manifesto, adopted in 1933, tried to unite farmer-labour appeals by demanding security of farm ownership while at the same time advocating nationalisation of the means of production, financial machinery, transportation and public utilities. A National Planning Commission was to begin a new, more rational economic order. The CCF was important locally and on the provincial level in Saskatchewan, British Columbia and part of Ontario. Not until 1944 did the party come to full power even in Saskatchewan; 28 members sat in the federal House of Commons in 1945.

The Social Credit party grew up in the early 1930s also in the West, in Alberta. Its chief inspiration was the British theorist, Major Clifford H. Douglas, who believed fervently that lack of purchasing-power was the major source of economic sickness. Maldistribution of income made it impossible for society to purchase all the goods it could produce. By the issue of 'dividends' to each citizen, purchasing-power could be spread and demand could be maintained at the proper level. The party gained power in Alberta in 1935, led by William Aberhart, a radio evangelist. Douglas's Social Credit ideas were lost, buried in the conservative evangelism of Aberhart and his followers and Major Douglas repudiated the party. Finally in 1937 as provincial Prime Minister, Aberhart did attempt some Social Credit reforms in Alberta, but the federal parliament revoked them. In fact, in Alberta and in British Columbia the Social Credit party, far from being radical, emerged as an anti-socialist force. Social Credit members of the national House of Commons tended to be more radical. Douglas's ideas remain alive in Canada today. Suggestions for a 'guaranteed income' or 'negative income tax" in the United States in the early 1970s parallel such notions.

By contrast, the growing popularity of French Canadian nationalism in Quebec during and after the depression years was not associated with liberal or radical economic ideas. The chief party, *L'Union Nationale*, led by Maurice Duplessis, tended to be right-wing and depended on the support of business groups, those who stood for provincial rights as against the federal government, and those who opposed trade unions. Duplessis won control of Quebec province in the election of 1936. His separatism was deeply-rooted.

8

Revolution and Intervention

Nineteenth century radicals in Central and South America fought for the 'liberal freedoms' already hammered out and defined in Western Europe since the struggles between Crown and legislatures in the 17th century and won by the United States largely at the time of the American Revolution. To these ideals, equality before the law, free elections, freedom of the press, speech and opinion, they attached universal education. This was a US ideal; the English did not begin to pursue it seriously until the education act of 1870.

Revolutions of the 20th century were less political, more economic and social in tone. Countless liberal constitutions had already been written, usually to no effect. Freedom from arbitrary arrest, for instance, remained meaningless in nations beset by military *coups*. Radicals now began to feel that the underlying economic and social structure must go. The class-caste system and the economic dependence on outside powers must be eliminated before any real 'democracy' could survive in the southern Americas. In fact democracy itself seemed secondary as a goal in view of the never-ending material suffering of the masses. The demand to put an end to this suffering, the demand for social equality, was now harnessed to nationalism and xenophobia (hatred of foreigners), in an explosive combination that was to produce real revolution.

The Mexican Revolution

The 'Pax Porfiriana' established by Díaz in Mexico after 1876 was a rigid system of law and order coupled with economic growth that benefited mainly the upper classes and foreign capitalists. Díaz kept 'peace' in the countryside of Mexico with his *rurales*, a tough, professional gendarmerie, many of them ex-bandits themselves. The infamous *ley de fuga* (prisoners could be shot while 'escaping'), dispensed with the apparatus of trial and evidence, within a 'constitutional' system that was purely formal. Díaz packed his Congresses and was automatically 're-elected' whenever this was deemed necessary. The Juárez Constitution of 1857 was a mere façade.

Meanwhile nowhere in the Americas was the gap between rich and poor wider than in Mexico. Nowhere had the process of land concentration in the hands of the few gone further. Nowhere were greater concessions and privileges given to British and US capitalists. By 1910 Mexico was one of the world's great oil-producers and the oil-fields, discovered about ten years before, were owned and exploited by foreigners—along with mines, public utilities, and vast stretches of territory, especially in northern Mexico, where US citizens had bought land. The policies of Díaz and his científico advisers like José Y. Limantour, brought deep popular xenophobia and nationalism. In the United States in the 1950s, left-wing and radical ideas were associated by conservative opponents with lack of patriotism or love of country; in contrast, foreign exploitation of the southern Americas in the 1900s made the *radicals* the patriots. Nationalism and radicalism fused.

The Mexican revolution began modestly in 1910 with the demand that a genuine election be held, no automatic 're-election' of Díaz as in the past. A wealthy, European-educated, northern Mexican, Francisco I. Madero, led this move. The Díaz political élite was aging and calcified; there was no room at the top for new blood. As Mexicans said, wryly, the bus was full (*carro completo*). From 1905 Madero began to oppose the political machine and in 1908 Díaz made the tactical error of relaxing his controls. He hinted that he would begin to allow legitimate opposition parties in Mexico. Madero's group, the Anti-Re-Electionists, soon became a national party.

Realising his mistake, Díaz jailed Madero during the 'election' of 1910. The results were declared to be millions in favour of Díaz, 196 for Madero. Díaz contrived Madero's 'escape' to the United States, without making use of the ley de fuga to remove him permanently. This was his second error. From the US Madero organised the revolution, which became a military uprising in November 1910. The political revolution passed out of Madero's hands as radical leaders took over: the bandit chief, Pancho Villa, captured Ciudad Juárez; the Indian radical land-reformer, Emiliano Zapata, took the southern city of Cuautla. Díaz was exiled to France and died there in 1915.

The mild and vacillating Madero became president in 1911 but immediately faced a widening of the revolution with the demands of peasants and urban workers. Zapata denounced Madero as a traitor. From his rural headquarters he issued a powerful revolutionary manifesto: one-third of all large estates should be taken over for the peasants; the deprived Indians should take back their lands by force. Zapata's troops ravaged haciendas, burning and killing. Meanwhile the small number of organised workers found a mouthpiece in Pascual Orozco, who attacked Madero for selling out to 'Washington gold'. From the right wing, Madero was also pressured by various counter-revolutionaries and Díaz types.

181

Madero asked a blood-thirsty general, Victoriano Huerta, to put down the Díaz counter-revolution in Mexico City. For ten awful days, *la decena trágica*, the city centre was bombarded in February, 1913. Huerta then imprisoned Madero and later had him murdered. He imposed his own counter-revolution on Mexico, running the nation by decree for 17 months, from his den, a Mexico City saloon.

Civil war, 1913–14: Carranza emerges

Apart from the fact that Huerta was no Díaz, the revolution had gone too far to restore that sort of law and order. Mexico had altered, irreversibly. The old establishment was broken. An astonishingly confused period of civil war and bloodshed followed in which the loss of life was so heavy that the graph of Mexican population growth was not only retarded, but actually fell absolutely. The population of 15.2 millions of 1910 *fell* to 14.3 millions by 1920, after a rapid rise from 13.6 million in 1900.

The United States gained an indelibly bad name in Mexico through the foolish actions of its ambassador, Henry Lane Wilson, who openly supported the dictator Huerta as the saviour of law and order and approved the arrest of Madero. Woodrow Wilson, elected in 1912, detested Huerta, but he only made the situation in Mexico worse by intervening militarily against the dictator. Wilson had wanted to help the man who did finally restore the revolution, Venustiano Carranza, though US aid only embarrassed Carranza, and he never asked for it.

While Huerta waged a war of extermination against the peasant rebels of Zapata and Pancho Villa's bandits raped the north, a group emerged under Carranza that demanded the enactment of Madero's original plans for lawful government: the 'Constitutionalists'. Carranza was tough-minded, an ex-Governor under Díaz. He was able to forge a temporary military alliance with Villa and other bosses and overthrow Huerta. His victory of 1914 was almost ruined by US intervention and the occupation of Veracruz.

With the help of an able general, Alvaro Obregón, Carranza maintained a shaky government in Mexico. The popular appeal of the radicals was undercut by Carranza's promises to concede most of their demands. While Villa and Zapata alternately controlled the capital, Carranza issued decrees and promises from his headquarters at Veracruz. He offered land redistribution, municipal self-government, protective laws for labour, outlawing of peonage and easy divorce. People came to accept his constitutionalist position. The revolutionary idealist Zapata was assassinated in 1919 and the Indians were deprived of their hero. The bandit Villa survived until his murder in 1923.

By March 1915 Carranza was in charge of the nation and governing from Mexico City. A constitutional convention met to drew up the radical and far-reaching *Constitution of 1917*, the main achievement of his

11. A group of rebels after capturing Mazatlán in 1913 during the Mexican Civil War.

regime. The Constitution was modelled on earlier ones of 1824 and 1857, with their French and US antecedents, but it went much further. To their 19th-century liberal freedoms and rights of the age of individualism were added the doctrines of a later age: national ownership of natural resources; equal pay, guaranteed collective bargaining, and wage and hour regulations, built-in as part of the Constitution; common welfare to be held above private interest. This was before the Russian Revolution got under way, though that revolution went much further in practice. Carranza himself was not a revolutionary; he had merely grasped the radical temper of the nation. He was overthrown in 1920 by one of his own generals, Obregón. This happened despite his strong stand against the US and his political accomplishments. Foreseeing the end, Carranza filled a train with bullion and escaped with his family. The train was attacked and he was murdered in the mountains.

José Vasconcelos and popular culture

Obregón proved more conservative on some economic issues than Carranza, and less antipathetic to foreign capital. His brilliant minister of education, José Vasconcelos, proved to be one of Mexico's leading intellectual figures. Vasconcelos built hundreds of rural schools and tackled the problem of Indian illiteracy. He reformed the universities and built up libraries. Through deliberate state patronage he stimulated a great revival of painting. Vasconcelos had been one of Madero's original Anti-Re-Election Party men. Exiled in the US as an opponent of Carranza (1915–20), and again in 1929 after failing to win the presidential election, he eventually became head of the National Library. Among his writings the most famous was *The Cosmic Race* ('La Raza Cósmica', 1925), which claimed for the Americas the creation of a new race, based on the melting-pot of races in the New World. *Indianismo* runs through his work, and the creative fusion of Indian-Aztec and European-Christian ideals. Racial fusion was more a reality in Mexico than in his place of exile, the United States, but in practical terms the Mexican Indian masses gained only moderate advances in 1920s.

Vasconcelos gave government contracts to mural artists to decorate with frescoes the inside and the outside of public buildings. This released the creative energies of several major artists, and produced a painting 'revival' (in the sense that murals had been an attainment of the Aztecs). The state gave work to major artists like Diego Rivera, José Clemente Orozco, and David Siqueiros. All three were revolutionaries. Rivera at times supported the Communist Party, though its ideology could not contain his artist's temperament. Siqueiros fought not only in the Mexican Revolution but against Franco in the Spanish Civil War (1936–39). The works of Orozco, Siqueiros and Rivera in Mexico City–for example Rivera's magnificent education ministry murals, and his works elsewhere, as in the Cortés Palace at Cuernavaca—all express the radical ideals of the Revolution. Ugly foreign capitalists oppress the nation, *hacendados* exploit the peasant masses, the Catholic Church looks on, or wields the sceptre like the sword. Spanish and later US imperialism, nationalism, anti-clericalism, Indianism—these are the themes of the murals. In a society that was still heavily illiterate, no words were needed to convey the message.

Many Mexicans did not like the political content of this artistic revival, but the artists themselves became internationally famous, and created great interest in Mexican culture in the 1920s and later. So they came to little harm,* and their frescos were accepted as part of the Mexican national heritage. Love of art and nationalism combined to overcome political hostilities.

---

* Siqueiros was jailed, 1964–68; but it did not halt work on his vast, multimedia building, the *Polyforum*, completed in Mexico City in 1971.

'Christ the King!': religious warfare, 1926–29

In the frescoes of the 1920s the Church is always an evil force: counter-revolutionary and oppressive, linked with great landowners and foreign capitalists. Altogether lost in the radical view of history is the role of the colonial church, of men like Las Casas, of the Jesuits in education and communes, of the cultural achievements. Later history swallows up earlier deeds. The Revolution did not need the stimulus of Marxism or events in Russia to be anticlerical; it persecuted the Church along lines set down by Juárez and earlier radicals.

When Plutarco Calles, the successor to Obregón in the 1924 election, closed the parochial schools and ordered the deportation of all foreign priests (to be replaced by Mexicans), the Church went on strike for three years. From 1926 all priests were told by the hierarchy to stop working. No Masses were said until 1929. This was the first break in the giving of Mass in Mexico since 1519. The strike was accompanied by real warfare and was brutal on both sides. *Cristeros*, fanatical Catholic peasants crying 'Cristo el Rey!' ('Christ the King!'), burnt and pillaged state schools and mobbed teachers. The Cristeros were put down by troops and the western part of Mexico suffered badly. The Church lost in the end. Church buildings stayed open and Indian peasants continued to burn their candles, hold their rituals and dances and keep their fiestas, which long pre-dated the coming of Christianity to Mexico. In truth, Christ was *not* King for many Indians; Catholicism was a veneer. The strike showed that they could manage without priests and Masses. The excesses of the *Cristeros* and the whole notion that priests could go on strike and deny Mass to the people, did the Faith more harm than good in Mexico.

The Revolution is institutionalized: the PNR

Calles called himself a socialist. He did continue land redistribution and many Indians received plots, though large slices went to his military friends. He listened to organised labour, and in 1925 he ordered foreign 'owners' of oil-fields to sign 50-year *leases*. The English and US capitalists were made to accept the Constitution of 1917: the prohibition of outright foreign ownership of the Mexican soil and subsoil. In 1929 an official, one-party state emerged. The Revolution was institutionalised in the PNR: *Partido Nacional Revolucionario*. Thereafter, reform slowed down. By the mid-1930s the Revolution had ground to a halt. In this one-party system, which bound together local groups and *caciques* into a national organisation, differences of opinion were expressed only as 'wings' within the party. No one questioned the Revolution itself any more. That long struggle, at least, was over.

Lázaro Cárdenas, elected to the presidency in 1934, brought new life to the Revolution after ten years of domination by Calles. Calles selected Cárdenas, an honourable revolutionary veteran of mixed Indian background, partly to placate the left wing of the PNR, but also expecting

him to be easily controlled. Once in power, Cárdenas swept into a programme of radical reform, exiled Calles, and gradually supplanted (without
violence) the leading *Callista* front-men. By careful use of patronage
and shows of force Cárdenas was in total control of the nation by the
summer of 1935. But the secret of his success was not such techniques,
it was his immense popularity, based on what he stood for. Cárdenas came
from a poverty-stricken village, Jiquilpan, in Michoacán, without adequate water, roads, or services. There was no school, no doctor. The land
was stony and arid. This he never forgot.

Cárdenas was a most unusual president. He spent little time in Mexico
City but travelled constantly throughout the nation with a small retinue,
living very simply with the people. Wherever he happened to be was
the centre of government. In the capital itself the luxuries of the governing
classes were now tempered. The Cárdenas example affected all government workers. A new revolutionary zeal produced better work, less
corruption and a government that really cared for the people of Mexico.

Land reform: the ejido revived

By 1940, in a surprising acceleration of land distribution, Cárdenas
had redistributed twice as much land to the peasants as all previous
Mexican governments: about 45 million acres. The Indian communal
ejido lands which had suffered from partition in the individualistic
Reforma years under the Ley Lerdo of 1856, now experienced a revival.
Land was given to 12,000 villages. The hopes of Zapata were partly fulfilled: now over half the population lived on ejido communities and controlled over half the nation's cultivated land. Not all the land was well
used, given the educational levels and poor technology of the Indians. But
Cárdenas *personally* supervised many land transfers from large haciendas
to village communities: a remarkable event to witness in the history of any
nation.

Scarcity of capital impeded the success of the ejido system. Cárdenas
encouraged a new direction for the ejido lands—cooperative organisation
for commercial crop production. Previously the villages had been concerned with subsistence farming; selling commercial crops would bring
in needed cash to be split on a profit-sharing basis. A National Bank of
Ejido Credit was created, like New Deal farm credit experiments at the
same time in the US, and the government supplied seed and machinery,
though this was never adequate.

Cárdenas encouraged organised labour. Led by its Marxist secretary,
Lombardo Toledano, the Confederación de Trabajadores Mexicanos
was established in 1936. Toledano patterned his leadership on the industrial unionism model of other nations—in the United States on the
CIO. Cárdenas openly encouraged the Confederation to strike against
employers, as it did in 1935. Two years later he nationalised the railroads,
expropriating the mainly foreign owners, and in 1938, when the oil com-

panies refused to accept his demands for better wages and hours in the oil-fields, he took over the oil industry altogether. Compensation was later paid to the US and British companies. *Expropriation Day* (18 March 1938) became a national Mexican holiday.

US and Mexico: the Good Neighbour Policy

In earlier (and perhaps in later) decades such action by Mexico would have brought prompt invasion by US troops or blockade, despite the open lawlessness of the foreign companies and their disrespect for Mexican institutions. Nationalisation of the oil industry brought no US intervention in 1938. F. D. Roosevelt's 'Good Neighbour' policy, part of the New Deal, placed men in power in the US diplomatic service who actually knew something about Central and South America and who sympathised with its problems. The vigorous Under-Secretary of State Sumner Welles, would not think of intervening. The Ambassador to Mexico, Josephus Daniels, was genuinely admired in Mexico and he personally favoured the oil expropriation.

The big British and American international oil companies attempted to crush the newly-nationalised industry by boycotting Mexican oil and refusing to supply essential machinery. This plot backfired: the militant Germans and Japanese, arming for world war and eager for fuel, were only too happy to barter for any surplus Mexican oil. Roosevelt could not allow this dangerous strategic situation to develop. In fact the momentous Cárdenas decision to expropriate the foreign oil companies in 1938 marked the crucial turning-point in the history of Mexican-US relations. Instead of embittering those relations, expropriation was ironically the true beginning of a long era of friendship and cooperation between the two nations. While Britain's diplomatic relations with Mexico were temporarily severed (the novelist Evelyn Waugh called expropriation *Robbery Under Law* in a book of that name in 1939), America's were not. Angry feelings were soon overwhelmed in the greater emotions and concerns of World War II. FDR's wise decision to accept expropriation as a given fact was well received in Mexico. A peaceful, economically stable and friendly Mexico was essential not only to Roosevelt's Good Neighbour policy and to the demise of the old, openly imperialistic Dollar Diplomacy of the 1920s, but to America's own security in a world on the brink of war.

Cárdenas rapidly suppressed an attempted right-wing coup in Mexico led by General Saturnino Cedillo. Under the friendly eyes of the US administration the nationalised oil industry PEMEX (*Petróleos Mexicanos*) survived a shaky start and grew to success as a large gas and oil producer. Expropriation also marked a true beginning for the industrialisation of Mexico. By the 1950s and 60s the chief demand for the fuels of PEMEX was at home rather than abroad, from a semi-industrialised Mexican economy. By-products and subsidiary industries were emerging in Mexico itself and great hopes were pinned on a domestic petrochemical industry. Full compensation had been paid to the foreign oil companies, as President Roosevelt had demanded in 1938.

During World War II, Mexico and the US drew closer together. The new president after 1940, Avila Camacho (1940–46), a one-time general in the Revolution and ex-War Minister for Cárdenas, led the nation away from the radical changes of the Cárdenas era into a long period of retrenchment. The Camacho-Roosevelt agreements brought Mexico into World War II against the Axis powers in May 1942—in contrast with other South American nations, like Chile or openly pro-Hitler Argentina. Camacho avoided social experimentation and cut the funds for rural collectives. Emphasis was placed on industrialisation instead of rural reform, a natural change of direction in view of the large World War II demand. The ancient Revolutionary veterans died out one by one and a new generation of leaders took over command of Mexico. These lawyers, professional administrators, party men and economists were like the *científico* advisers of the dictator Díaz, though their political regime was very different. Cárdenas lived on until 1970 but took no part in national affairs except that in 1959 he expressed strong enthusiasm for the Cuban Revolution led by Fidel Castro. The Mexican economy however was by now fully embracing capitalism.

The ABC nations: Argentina

Since the political upheavals of the 1890s and the emergence of the new national Radical party led by Irigoyen, Argentina had undergone years of rapid economic growth based on grain and meat exports to Western Europe. She saw the rise to power of a sizeable middle class who now dominated Argentine society and politics down to the 1940s. As in other Central and South American nations, it was easy in Argentina to accuse the old, conservative, landed aristocracy of being unpatriotic and opposing the national interest, which demanded reform. The Radicals, the party of the middle classes, combined their own personal drive for power with nationalism. Argentina's first Radical president, Irigoyen, governed on and off until 1930. A major Reform Act of 1912, passed by an idealistic conservative president, Sáenz Peña, gave Argentina the secret ballot, universal male suffrage, and compulsory voting. Under this Act the Radicals were swept to power in 1916, Argentina's first genuinely democratic election.

Irigoyen's years were an anticlimax as far as reform was concerned. Though worshipped by the masses he did little directly for them. His reforms were timid and cautious: limited labour laws (maximum hours and minimum wages). Despite his own democratic style—he rode to his inauguration by tram-car and gave away his professional salary for charity—Irigoyen did nothing to disturb the rich commercial middle class of Buenos Aires. Perhaps he was too old and had governed too long. The Radical years were corrupt and administratively confused. Irigoyen tried to do all the governing himself, interfered with the provinces, and failed to delegate power effectively to get things done.

The great reform of Sáenz Peña failed to establish a working two-party system in Argentina and Irigoyen was returned to power in 1928 by his *personalista* followers. Though the rule of the gaucho had long ago been curbed in Argentina personalism remained. This problem the Soviet Russian critics of Stalin in the 1950s would call the 'cult of personality'. With no effective two-party system, Argentina in the late 1940s was ruled by a popular dictator.

What kept the Radicals going was a continuing economic boom. Argentina attracted about 200,000 immigrants a year by 1914, when her population numbered about eight million. During the First World War when she remained neutral, the nation gained great profits on the increased demand for meat and grains. She had many advantages for economic growth, being more fortunate than most of her neighbours. Argentina was free from racial strife; along with Uruguay, she was the only nation that could truly be called 'Latin' American. She had the best educational institutions, and was the most literate nation in the southern Americas. She attracted mass immigration, like the United States, if not on the same scale. In fact there was an 'Argentine Dream', like the North 'American Dream', based on the opportunities of the fertile pampas. As Ortega y Gasset, the Spanish philosopher, wrote in 1930:

> The *pampa* promises, promises, promises. The horizon is for ever making gestures of abundance.

Economic growth continued in the boom years of the 1920s, and Argentina soon led all the nations of Central and South America in her rate of economic development and her general living-standards. She lacked any large, permanent class of poor peasants or Indians. She enjoyed the largest *per capita* income.

The pampa and the city have not yet kept their promises. Argentina did not grow as expected after 1930. Many things went wrong, beginning with the great depression of the thirties. No leader emerged in Argentine politics like Cárdenas of Mexico, capable of modernising and reforming the nation in the midst of a world recession. The muddle-headed Irigoyen could not cope with economic disaster. His Radicals went under with the evaporation of the boom that had sustained them.

Argentina suffered *arrested* development. She approached economic 'take-off' into what economists call 'self-sustaining growth', but then faltered. The economic breakthrough did not come. Cut off in the middle of her boom curve, Argentina stagnated, with virtually negative growth rates, and around 1950 the international market turned against her sort of exports. She began to face unfavourable world terms of trade.

Though Argentina was governed under the oldest continuously operating constitution in the southern Americas, that of 1853, she did not fulfil her early *political* promises either. Past historical traditions, confusion of factions and great instability in the 1930s, helped to put the army in power. The two main power groups in Argentine politics became not Radicals and Conservatives, or centralists and federalists, but the Army and organised labour. In 1946 an army man, Perón, became dictator by basing his techniques partly on ideas he picked up in the Germany of the 1930s: he united the army and labour in a populist, authoritarian, nationalist regime. People have called Perón's rule 'Fascist'; but its roots lay deeper in South American traditions—in caudillismo and personalism, in violent class and group-interest feelings, and in nationalism.

In 1943 Colonel Juan Domingo Perón, leader of a 'Group of United Officers', supported a nationalist *coup* in Argentina. He became vice-president and secretary of labour and welfare. On this power-basis he built his own national constituency by enacting sweeping pro-labour reforms. Feared by the regime for his growing mass popularity he was jailed, but released very quickly in October 1945 after mass demonstrations in Buenos Aires. Crowds of workers—*descamisados* ('shirtless ones')—supported his election to the presidency in 1946.

Justicialism: the rule of Perón

Perón's final and full accession to power meant more than another military dictatorship masked by compulsory voting in a theoretical constitutional framework. It came to mean the transfer of political power in Argentina from the middle and upper to the mass of the working-classes. Even more than the Radical success of 1916 it represented the power and the concentration of population in the city, the domination of the city over the countryside, factory over estancia, worker over gaucho. It represented the power of Buenos Aires, which by 1970 numbered seven millions and housed almost one-third of Argentina's 23 million citizens. The city's population in 1946 was already about three million.

Perón's personal ideology was confused. Like other military men of South America he had tended to favour Hitler during World War II, indeed the manifesto of the Group of United Officers issued in May 1943 was avowedly Fascist in tone:

COMRADES

The war has fully demonstrated that the nations are not able now to defend themselves alone ... Germany is making a titanic effort to unite the European continent. The strongest and best-equipped nation should control the destinies of the continent in its new formation. In Europe it will be Germany.

In America, in the north, the controller will be, for a time, the United States of North America. But in the south there is no nation sufficiently strong to accept this guardianship without discussion. There are only two nations that could do so: ARGENTINA and BRAZIL.

The simplistic, junior-officer philosophy of this 'might makes right' appeal to Argentine nationalism went on to praise Nazi Germany as an example for Argentina. 'In our time Germany has given life a heroic meaning. . . . Hitler's fight in peace and war shall be our guide.' Mere 'civilians' should be 'eliminated' from the government and forced to accept a philosophy of 'Work and Obedience'. By allying with Paraguay ('We already have Paraguay'), Bolivia, Chile and Brazil, Argentina could command the continent. The manifesto demanded a large armaments programme and public sacrifice to make Argentina great:

> With Germany's example, the right spirit will be instilled into the people through the Radio, by the Controlled Press, by Literature, by the Church, and by Education, and so they will venture upon the heroic road they will be made to travel.

The harsh puritanism and demand for national austerity in this manifesto did not become part of Perón's programme, and Germany's example in many respects was not followed though post-war Argentina became a haven for escaped Nazis from Europe. In practice Perón came to embrace the cause of industrial labour. With support from the Church hierarchy (the Catholic faith is the established, official church in Argentina, though not in other, more anticlerical nations of South America), and with military control of the electoral process and press censorship, Perón hoped to bring about a radical transformation of Argentina.

The central goal was simple: *industrialisation*. Nationalism was expressed in the rejection of British and US investors, in the creation of state monopolies and in the enhancement of state power. Perón shared the traditional Argentine dream of dominating the continent and creating a strong South American community of nations. In reality economic affairs at home engaged most of his energy. Perón called his atypical military-labour dictatorship 'justicialism'. Other strong rulers have sought justifications in high-sounding political theory, like Mussolini, whose regime Perón had admired while he served as Argentine military attache in Italy, 1939–41. But most people called his system simply 'Peronism'. It was a variant of state-guided capitalism, with heavy worker-welfare overtones.

Perón's personal pro-labour sympathies were not really very deep. It was his popular, attractive radio-star wife, Eva Duarte, who pushed him in that direction. After her early death, considered a national tragedy in 1952, Perón again veered away from labour. In the 1950s he even allowed the US California Oil Corporation the right to exploit Argentine

191

oil-fields—in his haste for Argentine economic development to pay for the many social schemes of earlier years. The US was at first hostile to Perón, which was hardly surprising, in view of Argentina's pro-Axis sympathies during the war and Perón's military background. American policy-makers however soon came to appreciate Perón's ability to instil a measure of stability in Argentina in post-war years. The US gave diplomatic recognition to the regime.

Another change of heart after Eva's death was Perón's bitter break with the Church in 1954. He legalised prostitution and divorce, banned religious education in state schools, and separated Church and State. This policy arose partly out of his fear that the Church was secretly opposing his regime.

Perón finally brought Argentina out of the 19th century and into the world as a welfare state, on the West European rather than the United States model. He created programmes for the workers, the aged and infirm; built blocks of cheap apartments; nationalised railways and public services; established new unions and collective bargaining, and provided compulsory vacations with pay. Yet by the mid-1950s his hold over the nation, magnetic at its height, was waning. The main problem was Argentine economic stagnation, rising prices, and gross corruption in his administration. When a rumour was spread in 1955 that he intended to quiet his opponents by arming the trade unions in the cities, the navy blockaded Buenos Aires and troops from the provinces marched into the capital.

No 'miracle' of peaceful transfer of power would have been possible. Perón had controlled all the elections, muzzled the press (closing down the world-famous newspaper, *La Prensa*), and strictly controlled the schools and universities. He was now exiled to Paraguay by the counter-revolutionaries.

The failure of civilian government: Frondizi

The new military right-wing government of Argentina held no elections for three years, dismissed all peronista men from office in a massive purge, and militarised the trade unions (a military leader for each union—the *interventor*). Politics in Argentina were deeply fragmented. Perón supporters remained strong, but increasingly divided among themselves. The old Radical party was splintered into various factions, 'Intransigent Radicals', 'Popular Radicals' and others. An election of 1958 brought in Arturo Frondizi, a leftist Radical with peronista support. The army was divided between *legalistas*, who feared Frondizi's reputation but still favoured using constitutional forms and allowing him to run his six years in office, and *golpistas*, who thought they should intervene forcibly at any time if they did not care for a political regime. Frondizi was allowed to remain in office to 1962, but his rule was chaotic. He fought a running political battle with the military as he tried to stabilise the economy and to amnesty political prisoners. His liberality towards the peronistas led to an overwhelming pro-Perón vote in 1962, so the anxious golpistas simply annulled the elections and sent Frondizi into exile.

Though a leftist, Frondizi was plagued by the need to rejuvenate the economy. His stabilisation and tight-belt economic policies to counter inflation and to improve industrial efficiency alienated many groups in Argentina. These policies did make Frondizi popular with the United States under John F. Kennedy, and even earlier under Eisenhower. Frondizi forced the nationalised oil industry to reform itself; he devalued the *peso*; he tightened the national budget and tried to balance it better than in the past. Few groups, including his own supporters, were ready to accept the costs and sacrifices necessary for genuine economic reform of this sort. Against his own beliefs Frondizi was forced by the military to break diplomatic relations with Cuba. His dependence on the army was sometimes total as seen in the disorder and terrorism during the election of 1960. Frondizi followed a long line of political leaders into exile when the golpistas took over in 1962 and brought any pretence of civilian government to an end in Argentina. The economy continued to drift, and inflation mounted.

In truth Frondizi had inherited severe economic problems. They arose not only out of past Argentine history, facts of geography and the nation's resource-pattern, but out of changing world terms of trade which did not favour exporters of primary products; population pressure on resources at home; and the past mistakes of Perón. With their heavy emphasis on the cities and on industrialisation, Perón and his followers had neglected agriculture and had failed to encourage the adoption of improved farming technology. It was a short-sighted policy, since for some years to come farm products would remain the chief source of Argentine export income. Industrialisation could not be paid for without a foreign trade balance.

Meanwhile in the 1950s the terms of trade turned against Argentine food exports and population growth, combined with Perón's efforts to improve urban living standards at home meant that an increasingly larger proportion of Argentine meat output was needed for home consumption rather than for export. Meat output did not increase fast enough to keep up with population growth. By 1960 Argentina's population numbered 21 million. The cattle stock had increased from 32 million head (1930) to 43 million head, but the proportions going to export and for home use had altered. In 1930, 654,000 tons of beef were exported and 872,000 tons used at home. In 1960 560,000 tons were exported (an *absolute* fall in exports) and 1,650,000 tons consumed by the larger Argentine home market. The dollar value of Argentine exports fell drastically from $1,613 million (1947) to $929 million (1955). Meanwhile inflation hit the very worker to whom Peronism had appealed. A cost of living index for Buenos Aires workers (1953 = 100) revealed increases each year—to

156 (1957), 229 (1958), 438 (1959) and 515 (1960). The economic unrest of Perón's later regime and of the years that followed was thus of deep-seated and structural origin.

Uruguay: democratic success story?

Argentina's small neighbour Uruguay enjoyed for many years a stable 20th-century political experience that contrasted with Argentina, with most nations of Central and South America, and even with its own highly unstable and politically complex 19th-century past. We have observed how defenceless, largely flat Uruguay, a nation that numbers under three million even today (nine-tenths of them first-, second- or third-generation Spanish and Italian stock), became virtually an economic enclave for British capitalists. The nation somehow kept its independence from its larger neighbours, Brazil and Argentina, and in this century settled down to modest economic growth, genuine democracy, the creation of the subcontinent's first welfare state, and great stability.

No nation owes more to one leader than Uruguay does to José Batlle y Ordóñes (1856–1929). Batlle, founder of the reform newspaper *El Día* (1886) and leader of the *Colorado* party, shaped the history of modern Uruguay. An earlier military dictator, Latorre, had resigned in 1880, saying flatly that Uruguay was 'ungovernable'. From 1903 however, Batlle took his nation into the first economic and social revolution in the subcontinent, preceding that of Mexico. Batlle was president of Uruguay from 1903 to 1907, and then refused to be re-elected. He went to Europe for study and became enamoured of Swiss democracy. Four years later he returned home, was easily re-elected (1911–15), and continued his thoroughgoing programme of economic and social reforms. Batlle's model was thus European rather than US. He established the eight-hour day, social security, unemployment insurance, public owner-ship of major industries and services (petroleum, alcohol, meat-packing, insurance, electric power, banking and others), greater women's rights (including easy divorce at the request of the wife, with no questions asked), free and clean elections, and elimination of foreign controls in the national economy. Twenty or thirty years *before* the more limited New Deal of the United States, Uruguay had become a democratic, par-liamentary, welfare state, a 'mixed economy', between capitalism and socialism.

Batlle was a confirmed democrat who believed that the chaos of the 19th century in Uruguay had been the result of excessive *executive* govern-ment. He wanted Uruguay to abolish its presidency altogether and, on the Swiss model, govern through a committee. Thus would the dangers of the cult of personalism and of caudillo or army rule be eliminated. His ideas were embodied in the remarkable Constitution of 1917 which divided political authority between the president, in charge of foreign affairs, the small armed forces and the police, and a National Council of nine members. At least three Council members were to represent the minority party. This idealistic document had to be rescinded for five years during a troubled period of the 1930s, but it worked well thereafter. By the Constitution of 1951 the presidency of Uruguay was finally abolished completely. In future, members of the National Council would each act as chairman for one year in turn, on a rotating basis.

Uruguay thus enjoyed constitutional government throughout the 20th century, except for a brief break under Gabriel Terra in the 1930s, and for much of this half-century or so the executive branch was deliberately kept weak. An active two-party system helped to make the constitution work, though Batlle's Colorados dominated. More important still as an underpinning of Uruguayan constitutionalism was its rich economy. By the 1960s Uruguay was over 90% literate, had relatively high per capita income and had a considerable urban middle class living in Montevideo, the only major city and the home of about 45% of the entire population. The nation was one of the best-fed in the world. Its 1970 population of only three millions, in a state not much larger than South Dakota, was outnumbered at least 10 to 1 by the cattle and sheep population—about 22 million sheep and 8 million cattle. Uruguay did not suffer from too-rapid population growth, in fact the growth rate was almost low compared with other nations of the region, about 1.3% a year.

What happened to this rich welfare state? First, like Argentina, this food-exporting nation suffered from the changed world market conditions of the post-war decades and the unfavourable terms of international trade for primary producers. Second, the universal enemy, inflation, hit Uruguay. By the 1960s the rate of increase of prices was phenomenal: over 85% in 1965, another 50% in 1966 and an incredible 136% in 1967. Nothing is more certain to cause deep helplessness and widespread discontent among any population than inflation of this sort. Viewed against its economic background the sudden outburst of terrorist violence in Uruguay in the late 60s is more explicable. The urban guerilla movement with its kidnappings, bank robberies and arms raids, gained world attention. (Soon the idea had spread, and encouraged by the results of the Arab-Israeli war of 1967, was taken up by Arab nationalists, Irish dissidents, and many other groups as well as by individuals).

American observers usually blamed Uruguay's financial problems on the large welfare payments made by the government. The deeper cause was continued Uruguayan dependence on its meat and wool exports in a world market which saw increased competition for wool from man-made, synthetic fibres, and falling prices for hides and meat. Unlike Argentina's, Uruguay's home demand for meat—and more important, for its small but growing industries, food-processing, construction and metallurgy for example—was necessarily tiny. The nation could hardly transform and diversify its economy on the basis of its own home demand. Among Uruguay's European customers Britain still took a large chunk of exports (13% in 1967) followed by West Germany and Italy (about 10% each). These outlets were threatened by European Common Market policies. The US remained Uruguay's chief supplier of industrial goods (14% of imports). These goods must be paid for, and as the economy went into decline even the cattle industry failed to keep pace with modern methods and to increase productivity. The number of the animal population, though high in relation to humans, was in fact static. Ranchers were conservative and slow to change. Some areas began to see diversification and the introduction of crops, rather than total dependence on the pastoral agriculture of sheep and cattle. This development was too slow. Poor weather in 1967 did not help the financial crisis of that year, when overall agricultural production actually *fell* in a year of massive inflation.

In 1966 the nation voted to restore executive government and the presidential system to Uruguay. The 15-year experiment with the Constitution of 1951 came to an end. Two presidents came and went in rapid succession and in December 1967, in a crisis year, the helm was taken by Jorge Pacheco Areco. President Pacheco faced extremely grave economic conditions. It was unlikely that he could soon reverse the trend of very low growth rates (under 1% a year, 1955–61), followed by actual decreases (under 1% falling-off in growth each year, 1961–67). The morale of the nation was low. The effects of economic decline were to be observed in the once-brilliant city of Montevideo where public buildings were shabby and in disrepair, urban services were slow and inefficient, and there was a generalized feeling of hostility and helplessness among the people. A violent urban guerilla group, the *Tupamaros*, shocked the nation from 1968 with their acts of terrorism; in 1970 they kidnapped and then brutally murdered a US economic aid adviser, Dan Mitrione. The Uruguayan government had refused to meet their ransom demands. President Pacheco was soon threatened with impeachment and had to bring in the military to maintain order. Top military leaders, thoroughly disgusted with the young terrorists, pressed strongly for tough executive action against them.

The presidential election of 1972 was bitter. Pacheco's chosen successor Juan M. Bordaberry, came to power with a tiny proportion of the total popular vote. Bordaberry faced almost immediately a general strike which shut down the country's economy. He survived politically and met another crisis in January and February 1973—an army revolt—by giving still greater influence to the military. Uruguay, once the showcase of democracy and of the welfare state in South America, was now on a perilous course. The fundamental and unmet challenge of changing world markets and the new exclusiveness and rivalry of the European Common Market, clearly pointed to the pressing need for South Americans to organise themselves. It was unclear whether the Latin American Free Trade Area (LAFTA) or a hemispheric Common Market would really

196

solve Uruguay's problems however. She produced goods that competed with those of large neighbour states like Argentina.

The ABC nations: Chile

Another democracy with hopes for continued responsible, constitutional government was Chile. Its parliamentary structure was somewhat like that of France or of Argentina in later years, mainly one of many parties and factions. Economic prosperity and growth depended on the fortunes of the nitrate industry and after 1900 on the large number of copper discoveries, developed by American capitalists. Nitrates and copper brought to Chile a genuine, classical, Marxist-type working-class or proletariat of miners and factory-workers to supplement the numbers of the *inquilinos* who laboured in the fields. With this enlarged and more radicalised working-class the token nature of the Chilean parliamentary system of the 1890s and 1900s (with its limited suffrage) became apparent. The system was no longer as acceptable to the Chilean masses as in the past.

Modern industry also brought boom and slump to Chile. World War I inflated the world price of nitrates and copper and these sectors of the economy boomed, only to suffer from recession, falling prices and unemployment once war demand came to an end in the 1920s. In Germany during the conflict scientists had, out of necessity, developed acceptable substitutes for nitrates, for use in making explosives and fertilisers. These substitutes (part of a rising chemical industry in several parts of the world) now rivalled Chile's own nitrate exports. Losses in nitrates were later replaced to some extent by the development of sulphur mines in the high volcanic mountain areas of Chile, and she did remain the world's greatest copper producer. Three large corporations of US origin controlled Chilean copper output.

Post-war misery and unemployment helped to bring to power a former Liberal cabinet minister, Arturo Alessandri, in 1920. The son of Italian immigrants to Chile, Alessandri promised his country a 'revolution'. Tough conservative opposition, a split between the two Houses and inertia in the Senate made his task impossible. Each of the two Houses was controlled by opposite parties. The reforms Alessandri was able to suggest, very much watered-down, included separation of Church and State, welfare measures, votes for women, the income tax, government control of the nitrate industry, and a greater measure of local government. Alessandri also had difficulties with the army, who ousted him in 1924 but brought him back again the following year. The new Constitution of 1925, designed as a solution to such unrest, gave strong executive powers to the president of Chile. It failed to keep order, however. Military distatorship and further confusion followed until Alessandri was re-elected in 1932. He then managed to govern a full six-year term and brought relative calm and order; but he could achieve little in the way of fundamental structural change. In the first place, these were necessarily years of only modest economic growth and budget retrenchment at the depth of the world economic depression of the 30s. In the second place Alessandri himself had grown old and cautious, and was most concerned with merely maintaining the government in bad times.

In 1938 a mixed group of radicals, communists and reformers elected Pedro Aguirre Cerdá to power. They called themselves a 'Popular Front' in keeping with the phrase that was common in western nations at that period, though in Europe it meant a unity of reformers of all shades against Fascism. Aguirre Cerdá was a rich wine-grower, lawyer and dean of a business school, a Radical who finally turned Chile into a welfare state. The state intervened in industry; welfare and labour legislation was enacted; the nation (like Uruguay) followed the Western European-Swedish model of a mixed economy rather than the US capitalist mode. Through a national development corporation (CORFO) the process of industrialisation was accelerated, especially of the steel and hydroelectric power industries. Large landowners were aided by irrigation projects in grain and wine areas though the poorer farmers were virtually ignored. In January 1939 Aguirre Cerdá had to face a terrible national calamity when the great earthquake struck at Concepción-Chillán, killing at least 25,000 people and demaging economic progress. He died in office (an unusual circumstance) in 1941.

The Popular Front and socialist and communist opinions remained powerful in Chile thereafter. González Videla was elected with such support in 1946 though he broke with the communists two years later and they resigned from his cabinet. In the years 1948–58 the Communist Party of Chile was officially outlawed. Economic troubles, falling copper prices and declining exports to the US, inflation and violent labour strikes in the 1950s, which created a virtual state of siege in 1954, kept economic radicalism alive in Chile.

Socialism in Chile

The 1960s brought socialist policies to Chile at a time of severe economic difficulty for the nation as a whole due mainly to world copper fluctuations and over-dependence on that industry for the government's revenues. Outside Cuba no avowedly socialist party controlled any nation in the Americas. The 1958 election in Chile was a three-way fight among the Liberal-Conservatives, led by Alessandri's son Jorge, the Christian Democrats of Eduardo Frei Montalva, and the Popular Front of former years—the *Frente de Acción Popular*—under Salvador Allende. Alessandri won in 1958, and did little but face another disastrous earthquake (1960). In the next election, 1964, Frei won, and in 1970, Allende. The electorate it seems became increasingly radical.

Certainly the times would explain this. Chile's economic and social problems were overwhelming. In 1964, Frei took over a nation that was bankrupt. Rampant inflation, 46% in the year 1964 alone, wiped out surpluses. Interest on the national debt consumed over half of all Chile's export earnings. The city slums, *callampas*, were among the worst to be found. In the countryside three quarters of the best land was held by 4% of the landholders, the large *fundos*.

The Christian Democrats led by Frei dated from the 1950s, though their roots went back to the 1930s. Like parties with similar names in post-war Europe, they hoped to combine deep religious, but not clerical, feeling with demand for radical social reform. Frei, president of Chile, 1964–70, stood for Catholic social action. His socialism was parliamentary and democratic, like that of the Scandinavian nations of the 'Middle Way'. He was anti-communist, but also out of sympathy with capitalism. The Christian Democrats, to be seen in Venezuela and in Peru also, were greatly heartened by Frei's major victory of 1964. It seemed to point a new way altogether for Central and South America, uniting ancient religious traditions with the new socialist determination.

Frei tackled the landholding problem head-on, as previous Chilean reformers never did. After two and a half years of struggle in the legislature his sweeping land reform act was passed (1967). This expropriated, with compensation, most estates of over 200 acres, for redistribution to the poor *inquilino* peasants of Chile. About 15 million acres was to go to about 100,000 families.

The Christian Democrats then 'Chileanized' the copper industry. They insisted on a percentage of Chilean stock ownership, and got the large Kennecott Corporation to agree to its underground mine, *El Teniente*, the world's biggest, becoming a Chilean government corporation. The US company continued to manage the plant, but 51% of the stock was nationally-owned. US owners thought this preferable to the outright confiscation which the *Frente* opposition were demanding, while Frei was glad to get a large measure of control over a mine that produced 40% of all Chile's copper exports. Controlling the mines did not solve the problem of world production levels and prices, however. By 1967 the major world producers, Chile, Peru, Zambia and Congo, had outstripped world demand and falling copper prices caused Frei great anguish. His national budget depended on Chilean copper receiving a certain world price. He was made acutely aware that even a nationalised industry could still be an economic 'colony' of the world economy.

Like other leaders, Frei bitterly resented President Lyndon Johnson's military intervention in the Dominican Republic in April 1965. He leaned towards Western Europe, and spoke of a different sort of 'Alliance for Progress' than that of the late J. F. Kennedy, an alliance between Latin America and Europe. But he resisted pressure and infiltration from Fidel Castro in Cuba and tried to keep his own political independence from communist influence. Frei's political appeal in Chile began to slip nonetheless, despite his great energy. His deeply religious philosophy was partly derived from Papal encyclicals such as Leo XIII's *Rerum Novarum* of 1891, and the later *Mater et Magistra* of John XXIII and *Populorum Progressio* of Paul VI (1968). The growing radicalism of the Church gave heart to many South American Catholics who were also political and economic radicals, and *Populorum Progressio* gave a Papal recognition to the needs of the underdeveloped and exploited Third World, and to South America's place in it.

The election of 1970 in Chile brought in the *Frente* and the presidency of the well-known Marxist lawyer, Dr. Salvador G. Allende. An abortive army coup in 1969 had shocked democratic Chile, which had not known such conspiracies since 1931. It was a three-way election and Allende gained only a plurality, 36.3%, not a clear majority of the votes, on September 4th. The political situation was uncertain for some time, since the legislature had to vote also to make the election legal and final. However the army did not intervene at this stage, and Congress accepted Allende in October. Allende had promised a multiparty government, 'nationalist, popular, democratic and revolutionary, that will move towards socialism.' But he defined socialism as 'a developing social process' rather than as a violent revolution. He would not seek to imitate China, Russia or Cuba. So Allende became the first constitutionally elected Marxist ruler in the New World.

Chile did not escape bombings and violence. Two weeks after Allende's acceptance, the Army commander, General R. Schneider was assassinated. When Allende opened relations with communist nations and toured Peru, Mexico, Algeria, the Soviet Union and Cuba in 1972, and when he completed the nationalization of the copper companies, and took over the telephone operations of the giant US monopoly, ITT, the US began to block international credits to Chile. In March 1972 a Washington journalist, Jack Anderson, exposed an alleged plot by ITT and the CIA to keep Allende out of office at the time of the 1970 election. This evidence was useful to Allende in appealing to Chilean nationalism in support of his regime. Continuing economic difficulties, especially the failures of food production under Allende's socialist reforms in agriculture, would count for more in the long run than any alleged or real US undercover activities. In any case, the big issue in the US was the slow and difficult withdrawal of forces from the Vietnam War. Public opinion at that time was not likely to favour a new intervention anywhere else, whether clandestinely as in Guatemala in 1954, or openly as in the Dominican intervention or the Bay of Pigs invasion of Cuba.

Allende's chief problems were internal cohesion and the survival of Chile in the world of international trade. Despite inflation his regime had managed to reduce Chilean unemployment from 9% to about 3% by the beginning of 1973, and had increased wages considerably. He still only controlled the allegiance of about 40% of the people at most, the middle and upper classes were afraid and hard-pressed, and he felt the

12. *President Allende's last day, 11 September 1973. Wearing glasses, he emerges from a building with a gun in his hand.*

need to take into his cabinet military leaders, in particular the new Minister of the Interior, General Carlos Prats. Dr. Allende remained firm in his determination to push Chile along the road towards greater socialization, until his fall from power and alleged suicide in 1973.

Chile's cultural achievements

Very few nations the size of Chile have produced such a remarkable panoply of writers and creative people in music and in humanistic scholarship. The first Nobel Prize winner for humanities of South America was the Chilean poet, Gabriela Mistral. Her work expresses concern for justice, the Indians, children, and human suffering in general, of which Chile has known a great deal. Another great poet is Pablo Neruda much of whose work is surrealistic and also charged with anger about social injustice and the need for revolutionary change. Chilean letters have been dominated by brilliant social scientists and historians. Like Neruda, the more recent scholars tend towards leftist or communist philosophies, or at least have a Marxist outlook.

The nation of Chile has developed a clearly socialist culture, and the Church hierarchy has not remained unaffected by the rise of a powerful Christian Democratic movement, Catholic Marxism and other varieties of belief. Almost 500 'Christians for Socialism' met in convention in Santiago, Chile, in April 1972. Most were Catholic priests and they included at least one bishop. They called for 'a strategic alliance of revolutionary Christians and Marxists in the process of liberating the continent.' A Jesuit priest, Gonzalo Arroyo, led the *Group of 80*, the most radical of Chile's reformist priests. He organised the Christian Socialist convention.

The elevation to power of Salvador Allende in 1970 was thus not as 'sudden' as it appeared to some European and North American observers but was based on a deep and growing belief in socialism in Chile shared by many of the working-class, the intellectuals and some of the Church heirarchy. Allende fell under the weight of economic failures, widespread strikes and the refusal of some sectors of labour to support his regime. A bloody military coup by the army brought a period of repression and persecution for many of these reformist and radical Chileans, lay and clerical alike. In the long run however the seeds of socialist ideas were now too deeply sown to be extirpated by military repression, and the tragic example of Chile's experiences in the 1970s would serve as an example all over South America.

Brazil and Vargas

Among the three greatest nations of South America, Brazil, the largest remained a sleeping tropical giant. It failed to achieve stable civilian government in the early 20th century. Though racially more democratic than some nations the vast land was divided by deep class and regional antagonisms. The poor were abysmally poor, especially in the uncharted Amazon regions, or in the dried-out Northeast, pictured vividly in *Os Sertões*. As the century wore on, city slums soon rivalled the rural backlands: the misery of the urban *favelas* was almost unrelieved. Economic growth, based on specific boom crops like rubber and coffee, did little to raise general living standards. The nation was inadequately governed by the army at the centre, by political machines in the states, and by bosses at the local level—the *coronéis*. The constitution of 1891 remained a thing of paper. As in Mexico, Argentina and elsewhere, a potent force for real change was to be nationalism rather than the demand for social justice. Yet Brazil remained dependent on its exports of 'colonial' type crops to more developed, industrialised economies. Its ties to British trade continued, with the US gradually taking a larger role.

US and European technical innovations in vulcanisation and use of rubber for waterproofing, as insulation in the new and rapidly-growing electrical industries of industrial nations, and in the bicycle mania at the turn of the century in the US and England, brought tremendous demand

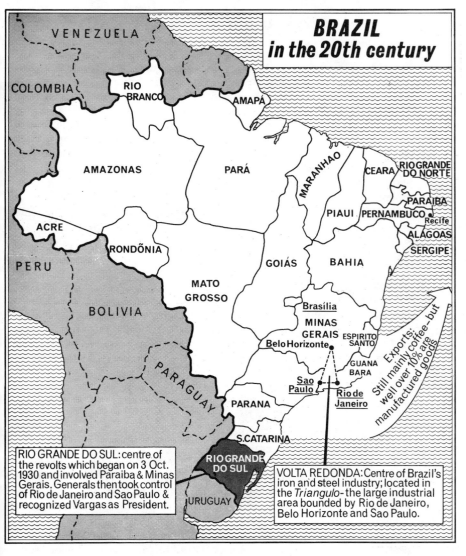

BRAZIL in the 20th century

VENEZUELA

COLOMBIA

RIO BRANCO

AMAPÁ

AMAZONAS

PARÁ

MARANHAO

CEARA

RIO GRANDE DO NORTE

PARAIBA

PERNAMBUCO

Recife

ALAGOAS

SERGIPE

PIAUI

ACRE

PERU

RONDÕNIA

MATO GROSSO

GOIÁS

BAHIA

BOLIVIA

Brasília

MINAS GERAIS

ESPIRITO SANTO

Belo Horizonte

GUANA BARA

Sao Paulo

Rio de Janeiro

PARAGUAY

PARANA

Exports: Still mainly coffee-but well over 10% are manufactured goods

S. CATARINA

RIO GRANDE DO SUL: centre of the revolts which began on 3 Oct. 1930 and involved Paraiba & Minas Gerais. Generals then took control of Rio de Janeiro and Sao Paulo & recognized Vargas as President.

RIO GRANDE DO SUL

URUGUAY

VOLTA REDONDA: Centre of Brazil's iron and steel industry; located in the *Triangulo* - the large industrial area bounded by Rio de Janeiro, Belo Horizonte and Sao Paulo.

for rubber in world markets. For about a decade after 1900 the wild rubber trees of the Amazon were quickly and crudely exploited using labour that worked under terrible tropical jungle conditions.

Land speculators fought it out in the Amazon while poverty-stricken workers came in from the dry Northeast of Brazil. Two thousand miles up the navigable Amazon, the boom town of Manaus sprang to life. Here the rubber kings built an ostentatious Opera House where the great Pavlova danced and the *nouveaux-riches* lived a life of imported French luxury. But they were too eager for profit and killed the trees in their haste to tap them. A wily Englishman had already smuggled out rubber

203

seeds as early as 1876. Subsequently transplanted, via Kew Gardens in London, to Ceylon and Malaya, the deliberately cultivated seeds did much better than the wild trees. Organised plantations in the Far East wiped out Brazilian competition after about 1910. The brief cycle ended. Manaus waned, though its Opera House still stands.

Brazil's major export crop was and is still coffee. As with the rubber crop, the United States is its major buyer. Coffee accounts for up to two-thirds of Brazilian exports in value. Brazil is also a large producer of bananas and has immense reserves of iron ore and other mineral and plant resources. Great wealth lies untapped. Brazil's over-dependence on coffee has brought anguish again and again since 1900. In both World Wars Brazil supported the United States and took part on a modest scale in military campaigns. World War I, for Brazil as for other South American exporters, brought greater prosperity, followed by peace-time recession and deep social unrest in the 1920s.

'Tenentismo': the Revolution of 1930

National humiliation, poverty and stagnation angered the middle classes and workers alike in Brazil. Younger army officers, usually middle class in origin, revolted in São Paulo in 1924 and fought intermittently for three years in the interior led by Luís Carlos Prestes, who later became head of the Communist Party of Brazil. This movement *tenentismo* (translatable literally as 'lieutenant-ism'), was a large factor in the revolution of 1930. Among the conflicting demands of the 1924 group were: states' rights; an independent, unified judiciary; clean government; balanced budgets; free primary and technical education, and some of the classic liberal freedoms. Their nationalist, reformist banner did not attract enough civilian support for a general uprising.

The real revolution came in 1930 when Getúlio Vargas, governor of the southern-most ('gaucho') state of Rio Grande do Sul, overthrew the existing regime. Vargas ruled Brazil from 1930 to 1945, and again from 1950 to 1954. He transformed the nation in many ways. Few of the early *tenentismo* aims were fulfilled by Vargas, least of all the liberal freedoms or states' rights. In 1937 he established a complete dictatorship. In fairness to Vargas, he was not a 'bloody tyrant' but an evasive, devious ruler who played off conflicting interests and regions against each other and managed to survive the calamity of world depression, falling coffee prices (down from 29 cents to 7 cents a pound, 1929–31), and internal revolts without resorting to massive repression. As late as 1938, when a fascist group surrounded his palace and he fought them off with his daughter and a small staff until the army arrived, Vargas did not execute any of the culprits. This fascist group, the *integralistas*, led by a neurotic anti-Semite, Plinio Salgado, believed in a confused mixture of ideas from Mussolini, the 'corporative state' and sun-worship and practiced weird ceremonials and marches. The integralistas were a major political force in Brazil in 1937–38. Thereafter Vargas was unchallenged for seven years.

Depression and misery were the chief causes of the popularity of the integralistas and of the radicals on the left too. Brazil's fate was tied to coffee prices. Serious foreign rivals were competing for the shrinking world market of the 1930s: Central America, Colombia, Venezuela and Africa and the E. Indies. Like Roosevelt in the New Deal, Vargas sought to keep up farm prices by destroying and limiting crops. More than this, he aimed at economic *diversification* and industrialization. In 1940 he began an economic Five Year Plan, on the Russian or German model, by planning a large steel plant at Volta Redonda. Vargas pushed public works and nationalized electricity and steamship lines. To sustain such economic growth measures he reformed Brazilian education and improved medical services. In 1943 he permitted a labour code favourable to urban, industrial workers. Vargas understood the significance, politically and economically, of the growing urban working-class in his plans for Brazil's future, though he did not use it as blatantly as did Perón.

The pro-Hitler military officers of Argentina in 1943 had hoped to attach Brazil to their cause and pointed to the large colony of Germans in Brazil. In fact Vargas saw the war mainly as an opportunity for Brazilian economic growth on the US side of the conflict. As in World War I, Brazil officially supported the democratic Allies, not Germany. Vargas declared war on the Axis powers in August 1942, a couple of months after Mexico and eight months after the Japanese attack on Pearl Harbor (7 December 1941) which brought the US herself into the world conflict. A Brazilian Expeditioniary Force went to Europe late in the war; Brazil's pilots fought with distinction in the Italian campaign. The war encouraged expansion of Brazilian textiles, paper, chemical and other industries. The Volta Redonda steel plant began large-scale operations in 1946, by which date the economy of Brazil was very much altered.

Part of Vargas' campaign of modernization was to stimulate architecture in Brazil. Twentieth century dictators have often taken this role, using public works funds to glorify their regimes. However in Brazil the end-product was not the gimcrack monumental style of Nazi architecture of the 1930s or the quaintly old-fashioned and massive style of Stalinist building, but a significant contribution to the art and science of enclosing space for human use. Brazilians established themselves as major figures in world architecture. The movement stemmed partly from the visit to Brazil in 1936 of the leading French architect and high priest of the modernist, functionalist school, Le Corbusier. He went to consult with the Brazilian architect Lúcio Costa over designs for a new university. The impact of Le Corbusier was enormous in Brazil particularly on the younger men around Costa, one of whom was the future master, Oscar Niemeyer. Modern buildings designed in Brazil, like the Rio Ministry of Education, became world-famous. The Brazilian school of architecture became a matter of national pride, part of a wider cultural renaissance that also included a wealth of new painting, writing and the music of Villa-Lobos, Brazil's first internationally acclaimed serious composer.

13. São Paulo, Brazil.

14. The Candango Monument, Brasília. ▶

Brazil after Vargas

After the suicide of Vargas in 1954 his successor, President Kubitschek, continued the building programme. Despite the pressures of economic adjustment and rising prices, Kubitschek planned and built a brand-new capital city, *Brasília*, 600 miles inland from Rio in the underdeveloped state of Goiás. Brasília cost the nation hundreds of millions of dollars. It was lavishly constructed as an international show-piece. The city was more an expression of the deep and growing Brazilian nationalism of the 1950s than of economic good sense, or of hopes that the underdeveloped central regions would truly be opened up for population settlement by the venture.

Brasília was inaugurated in 1960, the last year of Kubitschek's regime. After his administration, Brazil lapsed into the classic South American mode. It became an unstable military dictatorship, maintained by continuing industrial growth based on heavy investments in Brazil by foreigners. In the 1960s and 70s manufacturing of all sorts came to Brazil, including automobiles, steel, textiles and consumer goods. Americans Germans and Japanese invested heavily in such sectors. Brazil began making its own television sets, cameras and a range of consumer products, and looked around for markets elsewhere in South America. The Latin American Free Trade Area would be of benefit in this respect.

The rapid economic growth of the 1950s and 60s took place mainly in the Southeastern regions of Brazil, and the West and North remained largely unexploited. The growth rates of the 50s, averaging as high as 6% a year, fell sharply in 1962–63 to 1.6%, but recovered thereafter and managed to maintain a satisfactory average rate of 3.6% a year up to 1970. The rate of population growth was consistently high, though not as massive as in Mexico and elsewhere, at over 3% a year. Brazil however was very nearly self-sufficient in foodstuffs (except for wheat), given the enormous size and variety of her terrain. Agriculture continued to support about half the population, which totalled about 95 million in 1970, and to supply 75% of exports and one-third of Gross National Product.

The dictatorship of successive generals in Brazil after Kubitschek was not like the benevolent authoritarianism of Vargas. A Constitution promulgated in 1967 gave wide powers to the executive branch and left the individual states financially weak within the alleged federal system. The following year, the powers of the president were extended still further. The economic policy of the military regimes aimed to shift resources into agriculture in order to try to keep urban food prices down, and at the same time to build up infrastructure and broaden Brazil's industrial base. By 1969 manufactured goods accounted for fully 10% of all Brazilian exports. More foreign investment was being encouraged, usually through mixed corporations, sharing control with Brazilians, and further exploration was taking place in petroleum and mineral regions. However, economic growth was not easy to achieve in a regime of increasing terror and police brutality. The military rulers did not hesitate to use extreme measures and were exposed and attacked in the world press for their abominable tortures of children in front of their mothers, women, nuns, priests and any who seemed to threaten their rule. The historians' ancient myth that Brazil was somehow a gentle land, more humane and sensitive than the countries settled originally by the Spanish or other Europeans in the New World, now seemed a distant fairy-tale. The Catholic Church played a large role as the conscience of this society. Priests often opposed the generals. Among others, the courageous Bishop of Pernambuco spoke out. There was no strong Christian Democratic movement in Brazil as of yet and the outlook in the 1970s was grim indeed for the cause of human liberty.

The Indian Andes: Ecuador

The 19th century Indian nations of the former Inca Empire—Ecuador, Peru and Bolivia—passed into the 20th century with little formality or fundamental change. After the strange religious dictatorship of Moreno, Ecuador experienced years of political struggle between Liberals and Conservatives, coast versus capital, Guayaquil versus Quito. In 1908 British entrepreneurs built an amazing railway up into the high Andes and connected the two rival cities, cosmopolitan, liberal Guayaquil and the conservative, traditional-minded mountain valley capital, Quito. The Liberal party finally broke through to power in 1895 with the election of the anticlerical reformer, Eloy Alfaro, after a brief civil war. Alfaro was in control, in and out of formal office, for 16 years up to 1911.

Under the Constitution of 1906 Church and State were separated in Ecuador, education was secularised, divorce was permitted and Church lands were confiscated. In 1912 Alfaro himself was jailed and subsequently mobbed to death. His regime had begun the slow and painful process of modernisation of the port facilities, the economy and the entire way of life of Ecuador. The ancient so-called 'Spanish' elite remained in power up to the later 20th century and managed to block any major reforms which threatened their family interests. The Indian masses whose plight was described in a moving novel by Jorge Icaza, *Huasipungo* (1934), were simply ignored. The cholos were allowed a very limited role in public life, chiefly in the army, trade and farming.

Amidst constantly changing political regimes the economy of Ecuador passed through a series of 'booms' or phases, developed largely by US investors for American profit. The cacao boom lasted to about 1925 and gave way to a rice phase, followed by a banana era. The banana is today's chief crop in Ecuador. Though she claims to be the world's biggest banana producer, Ecuador faces increasing competition from African and Central American countries. Almost half of her total exports of all products is taken by the US market and fully 40% of her imports come from there. Some light industries were beginning to take hold in the 1950s and 60s (home consumer goods) and two US corporations were exploring for oil in the Northeast Oriente region (Texaco and Gulf Oil). Oil discoveries promised greater wealth for Ecuador in the future in a world suffering from fuel scarcity. The first large oil production was scheduled for 1974. Meanwhile the wealth of the forests remained unexploited and the fertile fishing grounds off Ecuador's coast were still to be developed. Ecuador entered the 1970s as one of the least developed of all nations in the Americas, with a low per capita GNP and a largely agrarian, peasant population.

A recurring president, Velasco Ibarra, who was in power briefly in the 1930s, again in the 40s and then in the 1960s, tried to impose a nationalist, personalist order on the polity and economy of Ecuador. Ibarra called himself the 'National Personification'. His wild rhetoric and gross demagoguery did not have the desired effect in bringing about national unity. Velasco was forced out by a military junta in November 1961 and returned to power yet again in 1968. Adult males were finally given the vote in Ecuador and in 1963 the junta began to distribute land to the Indians. An attempt was made to end their serfdom by insisting that peasants be paid cash wages for work. Reformers in Ecuador placed their hopes on the force of Indianism, on the awakening of the peasant masses, and on the assertion of authority by the better-off cholos. No genuine national unity would appear until the relationship among the different social classes was vastly improved.

Peru: dictatorship and native radicalism

Neighbouring Peru had been defeated and nationally humiliated by Chile in the Pacific War, ending in 1883, an event of long ago which still lived in the minds of Peruvians. Later a British group of businessmen had managed the nation's economy. Out of this trauma came a new national Peruvian literature of criticism and political moves to revivify the nation. British influence was gradually replaced by that of the US as a result of the economic impact of both World Wars. Copper mining became of major significance in Peru, and after World War II the industry attracted American interest and investment.

For most of the years 1908 to 1930 Peru was ruled by the dictator Augusto Leguía. Like many 20th century dictators Leguía brought industrial development together with foreign loans and investment, mainly from the US. Mining, communications, port facilities and irrigation projects were developed; some schools were built. But Leguía crushed all opposition points of view and shut down the ancient University of San Marcos. He left the Church alone, with its great wealth and its alienation from the peasantry; he made no attempt to disturb the large landowners; he had no real feeling for the Indian masses, who, in Peru as in Ecuador, often laboured for no wages at all, in a serf-like condition.

Against this backdrop there developed in Peru a radical political tradition. This native radicalism owed much to the work of Manuel González Prada (1846–1918), one of the disillusioned, post-Pacific War generation, the 'Generation of 1910'. González Prada was a socialist-minded poet whose works, mainly available posthumously, affected later writers deeply. He was a strong anticlerical and pro-Indian writer, who said repeatedly that the ruling-class of Peru was obsolete and dangerous. The intelligentsia and upper classes of Lima lived entirely apart from the rest of the nation; they despised things native and worshipped European culture. Peru and its problems were beneath their attention. The native *radicals* of Peru, in contrast, were true nationalists, who took pride in the

15. *A street scene in Peru, 1923.*

past glories of the Indians (the Incas), and fought for Indian rights in their own day. Their nationalism expressed itself in bitter anti-'Yanqui' feelings and they were usually very anticlerical. These currents of thought were general in South America at the turn of the century. The Modernist move- ment in literature brought them together, cutting across national bounda- ries. Thus the rise of radicalism in Peru was influenced by the Nicaraguan writer Rubén Darío; the Uruguayan, Rodó, whose *Ariel* was mentioned earlier; the Mexican, Vasconcelos, whose *Raza Cósmica* of 1925, and writings on Indianism, extolled the virtues of race-mixture. Nearer at hand, the local Peruvian literary group called the *Cólonida* produced several writers, especially José Carlos Mariátegui—the outstanding radical and socialist thinker in Peruvian history.

Mariátegui's literary group were proudly Indianist. He worked on a play about colonial Lima with one of them, Julio de la Paz, better known for his own play, *El cóndor pasa*, 1916, protesting Indian injustices. But Mariátegui added something to the literary attacks and interests of the Cólonida: economic and social analysis. Born poor, crippled when young, and hacked by tuberculosis, this brilliant man died at the age of only 35 in 1930. By then his propaganda work had sown seed in Peruvian soil and he had many disciples. Curiously, it was the dictator Leguía who gave Mariátegui the money to go to Europe, 1919–23, after closing down the newspaper for which the young radical worked. There Mariátegui met the leading European socialists and became a Marxist. He applied a socialist economic analysis to the problems of Peru in his most famous work, seven essays on the 'real' Peru (1928). Like many South American Marxists however, Mariátegui was no orthodox determinist. He tinged his socialism with mysticism and Indianism, and tried to fit it to Peru: a socialism with spiritual values and with heavy overtones of Inca communalism. He did not live long enough to develop this special national brand of 'Peruvian socialism'.

Meanwhile a political movement had developed among some of his student followers. An exiled college radical, Haya de la Torre, created the *Alianza Popular Revolucionaria Americana* (APRA) in 1924. The *apristas*, as they were called, kept alive the earlier ideas of Indianism. They fought for redistribution of communal lands, for education and farm aid to Indians and for labour laws. Peru was *Indo*-America, the *apristas* insisted, not merely Spanish-America. The Indian masses must enter the mainstream of Peruvian life and the answer to Peru's problems was not, as the elite wanted, to invite mass European white immigrants to swamp the Indians and 'whiten' the race. Neither should Peru follow the *Yanqui* model of capitalism. The land and all industries should be nationalised and foreign capital ousted. The APRA movement fell short of full socialism however, unlike Mariátegui's own organisation, the Socialist Party which he created just before his death in 1929. This party promptly joined the Communist Internationale. In later years *aprismo* made many compromises.

The Aprista compromise: Belaúnde

Haya de la Torre never grasped the reins of power. Leguía fell in 1930 and six years later the APRA won the election but were thwarted by an army coup. In 1945 their support gave the presidency to the moderate liberal Bustamente and some of them gained cabinet rank. They achieved little in the way of reform. Bustamente, who was forced by the right wing to dismiss them, was himself deposed in 1948. Several years of bloody persecution of the aprista left-wing ensued while the new military strongman, General Manuel Odría, covered his tracks in classic fashion by pushing through industrialisation measures—the oil and mining industries, hydroelectric power, steel.

Mariátegui, if he had lived, would by now have been a bitter opponent of APRA, and most likely a supporter of the Communist Party. The surviving apristas made many political compromises: in the 1956 election they went so far as to support the conservative candidate, Manuel Prado, over the radical Belaúnde. In return, Prado was to support Haya de la Torre for office in 1962. The election of 1962 was the low-point: at that time Haya de la Torre, starved of office all his life, threw in his lot with the bloody dictator Odría and opposed Belaúnde. As González Prada, had said bitterly many years before: 'In Peru there is pus wherever you put your finger.'

The decline of APRA idealism was complete. But a new radicalism was born with the successful election of Fernando Belaúnde Terry, a US-educated architect and social planner, who stood for Indian rights, welfare and land reform. From 1963 Belaúnde had a fairly broad constituency among the Indians *and* the Peruvian middle classes. He combined a desire for economic development with social justice, and unlike earlier radical thinkers, was more interested in reforming his country than in isolating certain villains for blame. Pluralist, he tried to recognise the problems of the large coastal farming corporations as well as those of the Indians in the Andes. His Agrarian Reform Act of 1964 expropriated some lands (with compensation) for redistribution to peasant families. Belaúnde tried to abolish sharecropping and planned great irrigation schemes. Andes rivers were to be diverted by tunnels to bring life to desert areas on the coast. The eastern jungles of the Amazon, the *selvas* rainforests, were to be tamed and subjugated (still a dream). In addition the upper Andes valleys were overpopulated, and Belaúnde sought to persuade the Indians to move down. For those who stayed, a programme was begun like an internal 'Peace Corps', with students and others helping the Indian communities to build roads, community centres, schools and other facilities. This idea was cut short by opposition in the Peruvian Congress from the old elite, the conservatives and APRA.

Belaúnde's hopes and what was possible politically were two different matters, but he was determined both to reform the social and economic structure of Peru and to maintain economic growth. The efficient cotton and sugar plantations of the coast were not touched by the land reforms, and Belaúnde also resisted expropriating the US controlled oil industry, though he finally had to give way to internal pressure and do so. Like other socialist-minded reformers in South America he walked a tight-rope: at one end were the Communists and at the other the US companies, and in resisting both he was accused of being a Communist *and* a United States puppet. 'Puppet' or 'Communist', Belaúnde was ousted by a bloodless military coup in October 1968.

213

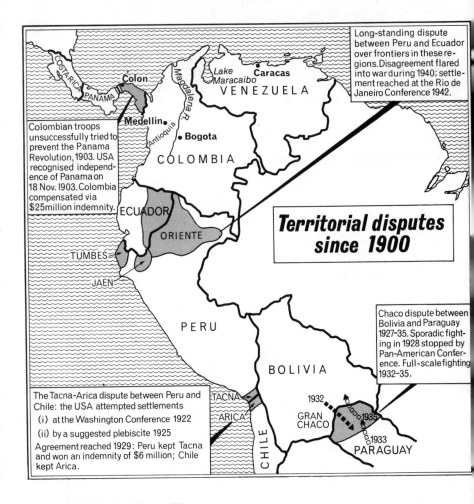

Long-standing dispute between Peru and Ecuador over frontiers in these regions. Disagreement flared into war during 1940; settlement reached at the Rio de Janeiro Conference 1942.

Colombian troops unsuccessfully tried to prevent the Panama Revolution, 1903. USA recognised independence of Panama on 18 Nov. 1903. Colombia compensated via $25 million indemnity.

Territorial disputes since 1900

Chaco dispute between Bolivia and Paraguay 1927-35. Sporadic fighting in 1928 stopped by Pan-American Conference. Full-scale fighting 1932-35.

The Tacna-Arica dispute between Peru and Chile: the USA attempted settlements
(i) at the Washington Conference 1922
(ii) by a suggested plebiscite 1925
Agreement reached 1929: Peru kept Tacna and won an indemnity of $6 million; Chile kept Arica.

Bolivia: the Chaco War

For Peru's neighbour, Bolivia, the War of the Pacific had been a major disaster. Losing her Pacific coast she turned eastwards with dreams of an outlet via the Paraguay River to the Atlantic. In the years 1932–35 this vain hope produced a second military disaster—the futile Chaco War with Paraguay, an extended boundary dispute. Gran Chaco is a vast plain, hot and drought-stricken in the west and often flooded in the east. Stories of vast oil deposits whetted Bolivia's appetite for war, as did the existence of an army trained by a German general and equipped with US arms. Over 100,000 soldiers died in this war and Paraguay was the dubious victor, taking most of the Gran Chaco. The Bolivian army lacked any nationalist morale. The troops were all Indians, forced down from the high *altiplano* to die as cannon-fodder in the oppressive lowlands. Their officers were all white.

Exhausted by its 'victory', Paraguay suffered on, from one military ruler to the next, few of them being genuine reformers, as some South American military presidents have been. In 1954 order was imposed on the nation by General A. Stroessner, successively re-elected into the 1960s. A second-generation German-Paraguayan, Stroessner ruled with secret police and torture and did not flinch at beating up the clergy if they complained. Some internal development took place under this so-called 'last of the dictators' of South America, but economically Paraguay was a colony of Argentina, and increasingly of Brazil and depended heavily on US loans.

The Bolivian national revolution

In contrast, the loser of the Chaco War, Bolivia, had a national revolution in 1952 which brought extensive changes towards a welfare state. While Stroessner's *pyragues* ('hairy-feet': Guaraní for the secret police) prowled around Paraguay, a new radical political party led by a highly educated economics professor and lawyer, Paz Estenssoro, brought revolutionary alterations to Bolivia. His party, the MNR, *Movimiento Nacional Revolucionario*, was supported by organised labour in the mines. Its aims included sweeping land reforms, improved farming methods, road-building (to connect the altiplano with the rich eastern valleys), nationalisation of the three great tin corporations, and extending the franchise to the illiterate. Indians were now to be called *campesinos*, country folk, instead of the often pejorative *indios*. The land they received from the far-reaching redistribution reform at first suffered a drop in food output, but later recovered in production.

Paz ruled in the years 1952–56 and 1960–64. By the 1960s his MNR party was no longer able to hold the nation together. It had achieved one of the most comprehensive revolutions in South America but in 1964 Paz was exiled and replaced by a general. The new personalista ruler, General Barrientos, brought the Bolivian National Revolution to an end. Towards the close of his regime Paz had been authoritarian himself and the political change was therefore not very abrupt. Both administrations received encouragement and aid from the US—Paz, apparently in the hope that his revolution would stave off a Communist coup in Bolivia, an attitude not often adopted at that period of history by US advisors. During the 1960s Bolivia was plagued by roving revolutionaries and guerilla bands. Since Bolivians continued to suffer one of the globe's lowest standards of living, with abysmal nutrition and medical problems, high infant mortality and massive illiteracy, their nation was considered to be fertile ground for revolution. Into this 'Tibet of South America' with its population of about $4\frac{1}{2}$ million (65% of them poor Indians) came various groups of committed revolutionaries from the outside. One of the most famous groups was led by Ernesto 'Che' Guevara, seconded from his work in Cuba after the Fidel Castro revolution there, to organise Castroite

215

16. *Bolivian revolutionaries take shelter in a narrow street on the outskirts of La Paz during the National Revolution, 1952.*

movements in other nations. After six months of activity he was captured and put to death by (US-trained) Bolivian Rangers in October 1967. The dead Che became a hero for revolutionaries and self-styled radicals the world over, particularly students. His practical impact on Bolivia however was infinitesimally small.

Bolivia's legacy

By 1970 it was clear that the National Revolution, for all its triumphs, had made only the merest beginning in Bolivia. Moreover it had left the nation a legacy of severe economic problems. One direct consequence of the Revolution was to bring post-revolutionary chaos and maladjustment in which hyperinflation hit the economy so badly that US economic aid became vital to national survival. It was a numbing and discouraging outcome for any revolution. In the years 1952–58 Bolivian Gross National Product actually *fell* about 10%; over 20% in per capita terms. US aid began to flow in during 1959. Unusually, this American aid was given to bolster the Bolivian budget directly, not merely for long-term development projects. From 1959 the economic stabilization programme solved the immediate financial crisis and produced low but steady economic growth rates thereafter. In 1962, thanks to outside help, the Bolivian GNP managed to exceed the level of 1952 for the first time, and the effects of the Revolution were now left behind.

An internationally conceived 'Triangular Plan', supported by the US, West Germany and the Inter-American Development Bank, was begun in 1962 to renovate and modernise the state-owned tin mines. Falling world tin prices after 1965 did not ease problems of adjustment and innovation. To diversify the industrial and export base and shift away from an over-dependence on tin, oil and gas reserves were developed by foreign private investors with government aid in eastern Bolivia.

General Barrientos was killed in an air crash in April 1969 and a series of military successors struggled with the economic problems of the country. For some years food prices were kept artifically low, but in the early 70s, when foodstuffs were crossing Bolivia's borders into higher-price nations like Chile and Argentina, the government tried to check this flow by doubling prices. Food was said to be actually scarce in parts of Bolivia as a result of price differentials. Urban workers had been allowed wage increases, but this was not extended to farm regions. In February 1974 peasants revolted against the sudden price increases and set up roadblocks. The regime of General Hugo Banzer immediately used military force to suppress the peasant dissidents, and when workers at a shoe factory in Cochabamba also rose they were put down forcibly, with some deaths reported. The government declared a state of siege and blamed 'extremists' and Communists. To some degree however the economic problems of the nation were brought about by badly mistimed policies. The currency had been devalued in 1972 precisely when world tin prices were beginning to rise once more. Imports were thus made more expensive at a time when this change was not really necessary. The future of Banzer's government and of Bolivia itself was once more in doubt.

Colombia: violence without revolution

Of the Spanish Main nations, Colombia remained torn apart by the deepest geographical and ideological divisions and ruled by a tiny, white, self-consciously 'Spanish' élite and a very conservative Church. This nation has produced far more than its share of South America's poets, writers and scholars (especially philologists). The élite, and the small professional and business middle class, has been very distinguished. Even the dictator Nuñez, already mentioned, was a poet and gentleman. However, violence has proved the undoing of many noble schemes for reform and regeneration in Colombia, often senseless and undirected violence—plain banditry and vandalism. Colombia has been a nation of stark contrasts.

After the death of Nuñez in 1894, political confusion produced the bloody 'Thousand Day War', 1899–1902, which wiped out about 100,000 Colombians and solved nothing. The war set back the growth of Colombia's one-crop export economy. A rail connection from the Andes town of Medellín to the Magdalena River (and thus to the Caribbean), made possible the development of plantations of mild coffee on the volcanic mountain slopes of Antioquia. Most plantations were family-sized (large families). The region has produced many of Colombia's entrepreneurs in various fields, textiles, banking and transport. From the early 1880s coffee has been the chief export of Colombia, and it still is, despite the other activities of the aggressive *Antioqueños*.

The trauma of civil war followed by the humiliating confrontation with Teddy Roosevelt and the US and the loss of Panama (1903), produced a period of about thirty years' calm under Conservative party presidents. US capital flooded into Colombia, especially in the 1920s, and was invested in coffee production, oil, textiles, and the service industries. Such foreign capital did not encourage much social change in Colombia; the few upper-class white families dominated the scene. Not until the disaster of world depression and falling coffee prices in the 1930s, did any genuine attempt at reform come to Colombia. A Liberal president, Alfonso López, acceded in 1934 and introduced some land reforms, labour protection, a progressive income tax and welfare measures. The coming of World War II, closer economic links with the United States and improved prosperity for the upper classes did not stimulate further reform measures. After the war, Conservative regimes presided over a declining economy, beset by violence, class tension, inflation and falling living-standards for the now larger working-class.

In 1948 the capital city of Bogotá was plundered and burnt by raging mobs, angry at the assassination of the champion of labour, the leftist statesman, Jorge Gaitán. Four or five years of savage banditry and violence followed. Some say 300,000 people perished. And still no national revolution came to Colombia.

Laureano Gómez ruled dictatorially until 1953, moving towards a corporative, Mussolini-type of state, giving great power to the Church. He was removed by a bloodless army coup and replaced by General Rojas Pinilla, whose government was equally tough and conservative, with the difference that the general opposed the Church. During these

17. The scene in Bogotá after mob riots, 1948.

years after the explosion of 1948, the economy did grow, and living standards rose, while exports doubled. Naturally, foreign capital was the base of much growth.

Rojas Pinilla built a large steel plant at Paz del Río, 9,000 feet up in the highlands, as a sort of industrial show-piece. Poor communications—the essence of all Colombia's economic problems—meant that steel imported from abroad was still cheaper. High tariffs and other trappings of economic nationalism did little to make the steel venture a real economic success. From 1957 the two major parties agreed to form a *National Front* government, an unusual experiment to keep order and restrain the irrational violence of Colombian life. Meanwhile, even the most conservative Colombian Catholic Church saw a growing concern for social action by its younger rebel priests, trying to follow faithfully the social doctrines of Pope John XXIII. By the early 1970s this had not yet become a major political movement, as it had in Chile and elsewhere.

Venezuela: from caudillismo to welfare-state

The experience of Colombia's neighbour, Venezuela, was somewhat different. This nation of classic caudillo dictators and llanero cowboys, did manage to develop a welfare state to some degree in the mid-century. Like Peru, Venezuela was ruled by one dictator for the first thirty years or so of the twentieth century—Juan Vicente Gómez (1908–1935). His regime was of the Díaz type: dictatorship resting on alliance with foreign capital, pushing industrialisation of the oil industry and sound debt-management. Gómez was a brutal, unschooled, Andes cowboy. His military tyranny was frank and savage; the jails were crowded with tortured prisoners; students who dissented were put to hard labour building roads. Gómez openly declared his view of the people he governed: that they were primitive, pastoral, and unfit for democracy. The Indians called him *brujo* (witch-doctor), believing his eyes were everywhere.

Gómez was lucky. Venezuela simply became a rich nation at this time, not only through rising world coffee prices and the deflection of heavy US investments from Mexico to other nations after the fall of Díaz, but because of the Lake Maracaibo oil discoveries. Dutch, English and US capital flooded in to Venezuela, and Gómez played the companies off against each other for the best terms. In 1920 he imposed taxes on them all, and laid aside reserve oil lands for the nation's future. He raked off his own percentage each year, to support himself and his many bastard children. Oil income paid off the national debt entirely. Gone now were the humiliations of the past—the European blockade of Caracas in 1902 because the nation could not pay its debts, the intervention of Uncle Sam in line with the US claim of 1895 to be 'practically sovereign on this continent'. Now Venezuela had the highest *per capita* income in South America. By 1930 she was the world's largest exporter of oil. This owed little to the policies or to the so-called 'democratic Caesarism' of Gómez.

Gómez died in office in 1935 and was followed by a series of army generals, representing the oligarchy of land and business. World War II brought even more prosperity for Venezuela and closer US contacts. The war also brought the rise of *Acción Democrática*, the middle-class, professional, non-communist left led by the famous novelist Rómulo

Gallegos and by the much-exiled student of law and economics, Rómulo Betancourt. They ruled briefly, 1945–48, giving a broad section of the people a say in government for the first time. The *Acción* tried to begin land redistribution, to raise oil royalties, and to investigate corrupt generals. They moved too fast and alienated three power groups: the landed, business and the army. As a writer, Gallegos was distinguished, as seen in his novel of the llanos, *Doña Barbara*, 1929. His rule as president was brief and inept. In 1948 both Rómulos were exiled and the army took over again.

The Gómez-type of military tyranny was re-imposed on Venezuela from 1952 to 1958 by Pérez Jiménez. This was a senselessly brutal, criminal government, using jungle concentration camps, secret police and suppression of all dissent. In Caracas the Central University was simply closed; labour unions were taken over; the press was muzzled. Again, classically, the dictator invited further US capital investments, won the strong approval of the Eisenhower administration, which honoured him with the Legion of Merit, and started a flashy public works programme for the foreign audience: some highways, a sumptuous officers' club overlooking Caracas and modern buildings for the capital. Like Gómez, Pérez took his own rake-off on all government contracts. In 1958 he escaped to hospitable Florida with an estimated $200 million.

What brought him down was a democratic coalition on the left and centre which included the Catholic social action of an awakened Church. As in Chile, and to lesser degree in Peru, Brazil and elsewhere, some Church-members were no longer content to suffer under what Archbishop Rafael Arias denounced as sub-human conditions. The jailing of priests only made the fall of Pérez more certain. A free election in 1958, *assured* this time by the armed forces, brought a swing of the Christian Democrats to the Acción Democrática and the installation of Betancourt, who introduced the Welfare State to Venezuela.

Betancourt: the welfare state in Venezuela, 1959–64

Betancourt found it very difficult to steer a course between violent groups on the left and right, towards what he hoped would be the creation of a Swedish-type middle-road welfare society for Venezuela. The heritage of violence was now ingrained. Plots against Betancourt were organised by various groups, both right-wing and left-wing. The rightist dictator of Santo Domingo, Trujillo, supplied arms for Venezuelan dissidents. One nearly successful assassination attempt of 1960 left Betancourt with bad facial burns. The success of Fidel Castro in Cuba in 1959 despite strong US hostility, gave great encouragement to the communist left in other nations. Castroite terrorists were now added to the various groups of guerillas at work throughout South America. The Marxists were split into Castroites, traditional pro-Soviet communists, Maoists and Trotskyists, but even tiny groups could do much political damage through terror.

Urban violence was common in Venezuela years before the outbreak of Tupamaro activity in Uruguay. Small guerilla groups could combine with disaffected junior military officers to achieve political *coups*. In Venezuela leftist agitators lacked mass support and were usually opposed by organised labour, by business leaders and by most military men.

In 1960 a faction of Betancourt's own party, the Acción, broke away and called themselves the MIR (Movement of the Revolutionary Left). These strong Marxists and Castro supporters could be politically effective when allied with the traditionalist Venezuelan Communist Party and the minority of leftist student leaders who always seemed to dominate student politics. Fortunately for Betancourt their attempted *coup* of May 1962 left them momentarily discredited. Betancourt jailed the leaders and closed their offices. Plotting did not cease: in 1963 the government stopped a large illegal arms shipment from Cuba, sent in preparation for the coming December election in which rebels planned to take over Caracas. In spite of such disruptions the electoral system continued to function every four years. In 1964 Betancourt was followed by an Acción successor as president and in 1968 by a university professor, Rafael Caldera of the Social Christian Party (COPEI).

What was achieved by these administrations? Betancourt himself was forced to maintain huge defence spending whether he liked it or not. Still, he did manage to push through a major land reform in 1960. The trend of concentration in land-ownership had reached the stage in which 2% of all owners controlled about 64% of all land under cultivation in Venezuela by 1950. Betancourt proposed to settle 350,000 landless peasant families on property taken from the huge estates (with compensation to the owners). Also, to make the land redistribution a practical success in terms of productivity, he provided training, seeds, machinery, credit and advice to the newly-landed peasants. This land reform was buttressed by welfare and economic growth measures in a four-year economic plan: public works, health, education and industrial diversification. Oil remained the economic base, bringing in over half of national revenues. Oil and mining together accounted for 98% of exports but employed a mere 2% of the labour force. Venezuela, like Arab oil nations, had large gold and foreign currency reserves, excellent credit and a stable currency; but her major industries did not provide *jobs*. Fully one-third of the employed labour force were still in agriculture in 1970 and produced 7% of GNP. Food output was increasing at about 3% a year, the population at about 3.5%, with rapid rates of urbanisation.

The energy crisis of the early 1970s seemed to ensure future prosperity for Venezuela in gross terms, though how this would affect the real living standards of the people remained to be seen. US private investment in Venezuela, principally in oil, amounted to almost three billion dollars in the late 1960s and represented one of the largest American foreign investment groups. Indeed, 25% of all US private investment in Central and

South America was tied up in Venezuela. The dangers to Venezuelan autonomy had already been faced; in 1959 all future oil exploration concessions to foreign corporations were prohibited. This policy proved to be too extreme: the number of exploratory wells fell rapidly, along with total foreign investment in Venezuela. The government reversed its policy in 1967 and allowed the large loophole of 'service contracts', instead of outright concessions. Special tax incentives were offered for the construction of new plants to remove sulphur from oil.

A more fundamental safeguard to the Venezuelan economy would be its own *home market*, especially for manufactured and consumer goods. With the highest per capita purchasing power of any South American nation and a fast-growing urban population, Venezuela was in a good position to develop home manufacturers. In 1968 manufacturing was only about 15% of GNP and employed about 15% of the labour force. The sector was likely to grow, and as far as power was concerned, in addition to oil, Venezuela's hydroelectric facilities were large and growing: she was already the fourth among South American countries in electric power output, the first per capita. In the near future would come a multiplication of plants to manufacture petroleum by-products, textiles, clothing, foodstuffs and beverages, drugs, paper and wood products, metal goods and a range of consumer products. Automobile assembly plants were already established.

Central America under the shadow of the USA

The replacement of British influence with that of the US is well illustrated in Joseph Conrad's novel, *Nostromo*. Conrad's mythical nation 'Costaguana' is situated somewhere in Central America. There, US pressure, economic and sometimes military, has been a shaping force. That pressure shaped the little republic of Panama, created largely at US behest in 1903. Although the US maintained by treaty-rights the choice of stepping in to preserve order in Panama City, not abrogated until 1936 by F. D. Roosevelt's 'Good Neighbour' policy, the history of Panama after 1903 was very unstable. Half a century after independence, one president was murdered and his successor charged with complicity (1955). Meanwhile, Panama failed to diversify its economy, since the great canal had too easily offered ready income. 'Imperialist' social class distinctions were harsh: the whites lived in fine houses up on the hill, looking down on the natives of Panama, who were mulatto and black, descendants of Negroes brought in to build the canal.

This obvious '*gringo* imperialism', as it has been termed, bred intense dislike for the United States, Panama's godfather and 'protector'. By the 1960s, after several incidents in the past, animosity, arrogance and envy produced the riots of 1964. In response the United States threatened to build a competing canal, at sea-level, though President Lyndon Johnson softened this threat with an offer to renegotiate treaty rights. Increased traffic will probably call for a second canal in any case. The economic future of Panama is therefore very uncertain and the wealthy native élite has managed to delay any real social reforms by using the US presence as a scapegoat for all ills. The North Americans are blamed for everything.

Honduras, Nicaragua and Costa Rica continued their in-fighting, first exemplified in the 19th century. El Salvador tried to keep itself neutral and to preserve the idea of future re-federation for Central America. Increasingly after 1900 the presence and power of the US United Fruit Company was felt. We have observed that US forces landed in Nicaragua to protect investors in 1912 and stayed until 1933. They occupied Haiti and Santo Domingo too.

Honduras and Nicaragua were plagued by classic caudillo dictators like General Carías (1933–49) of Honduras, who named his own successor, and the boss of Nicaragua, General Somoza, who ran the republic like a personal enterprise from 1937 until he was shot by a patriotic poet in 1956. The Somoza family remained in charge of Nicaragua and they owned many of the most profitable enterprises not controlled by the US. The decade of the 1950s brought insurrection and instability to Central America generally. Even in Honduras the banana workers finally revolted against United Fruit and its friends in the government in 1954 and managed to win collective bargaining gains at a cost to the US investors of about $15 million-worth of rotted, unpicked bananas.

Costa Rica, the most purely 'Latin' nation, and after an election of 1889, the most stable and democratic, with more fairly dispersed landholdings, saw only one break in a tradition of peaceful transfer of power and constitutional government, a coup of 1917–19, right down to 1948. Civil war erupted in that year over a disputed election. Five years later the insurrectionary leader, José Figueres, a leftist coffee planter, won a sweeping electoral victory and became president. What he faced was an invasion supported by Nicaragua (1955). Nevertheless Figueres forced United Fruit to renegotiate its contracts and to allow Costa Rica 35% of net earnings. He encouraged economic growth and foreign investment but refused to give special privileges to alien corporations. Figueres wanted the US to stop propping up dictators in Central America and to be more sympathetic to reform governments. His task was difficult in the 1950s, when US fear of the 'Communist menace' was at its height, and many politicians inside the US itself depended on it for their own professional careers—men like Senator Joseph McCarthy of Wisconsin.

Guatemala: the low-point in US relations

Guatemala in 1954 saw the low point in United States relations with Central America, when US preoccupation with the alleged 'Red menace' brought exactly the opposite sort of conduct to that desired by democratic reform leaders like Figueres. The Central Intelligence Agency of

18. *Typical primitive thatched huts in the Indian village of Santiago on Lake Atitlan, Guatemala.*

the US encouraged a minor Guatemalan colonel to launch an invasion from Honduras and overthrow the reform regime of Jacobo Arbenz in 1954.

Arbenz had intended to continue the reforms of his predecessor, Juan José Arévalo (1945–51), who had begun a genuine social revolution in Guatemala by creating the structure for a welfare state, with labour codes, social security, educational reforms and restrictions on the military. Arbenz was elected to enlarge this programme. Naturally, socialism of this middle-road type attracted the attention and built the hopes of communists, and the United States of the 1950s felt threatened by this. Certainly the United Fruit Company was threatened by Arbenz, when his agrarian reform law of 1952 planned to expropriate land to give the means of subsistence to about 300,000 Guatemalan families. The US persuaded the Inter American Conference of 1954 at Caracas to denounce 'international communism'. Since neither Mexico nor Argentina would support the resolution the meeting was no real measure of South American opinion on events in Guatemala.

The new government of Colonel Castillo Armas went back on the projected land reform in favour of the interests of the American company. Assassination removed the colonel in 1957 and brought in an even more frankly right-wing dictatorship. The reform movement had been terminated and the four or five million Guatemalans were left with their one-crop economy, their illiterate Indian masses, and their elite of a few rich families allied to US economic interests. The weak position of the Catholic Church here as in Central America generally provided no hope for the emergence of any Christian Democratic movement of the left of centre that could survive under the shadow of the United States. Rising expectations and unchanging US attitudes seemed likely to bring future upheavals.

9
Plural Society and its Problems

After 1945 external affairs, specifically the Cold War struggle, real and imagined, dominated US and Canadian history. It shaped America's relationships with the neighbouring republics to the south. Canada's policies towards the Soviet bloc nations was slightly less hostile, but of necessity she joined a powerful US-Canadian defence network and was a faithful member of groups like the North Atlantic Treaty Organisation. Canada herself was penetrated still further by US economic and cultural influences after World War II as she grew increasingly independent of Britain. The latter trend was symbolised in the abrupt change in the design of the Canadian flag, eliminating the Union Jack. The ideology of 'Canadianism' was partly driven by the strong desire for Canadians to distinguish themselves from the US as well as, or even more than, from Britain. Canada had to define her own unique national qualities.

Beneath the Cold War headlines, profound domestic social and cultural tensions were at work in Canada and the US as both strove to build plural societies. Canada's pluralism was complicated by her historic relationship with Britain, the cultural pressure from the US, and the existence of a large minority of French-speaking Canadians. Canada's problem of 'bilingualism' did not exist in the US where there had never been any serious question as to which language was the national tongue. For this and other reasons Canadians oversimplified the US and often regarded it as a true, conformist 'melting-pot'—a view which would astonish most Americans. Canadians used the alleged 'melting-pot' example of the US either as a notion to be copied or as one to be avoided. Meanwhile, Americans had even less knowledge of Canadian problems and needs: they fought out their own internal racial and ethnic issues without reference to the example of their northern neighbour.

Distracted by the Cold War and other exigencies the US paid little genuine attention to its neighbours to the south, except to view them as a possible base for 'communist aggression'. The general American public had no knowledge of the attempted land reforms and social welfare revolutions in South America, and no grasp of the impact of late industrialisation in that region and of the part played in it by US corporations. However, when the Soviet Union installed missiles on Cuba in 1962 all Americans were instantly involved. Cuba occupied television screens for several weeks. The final settlement of the missile confrontation between President John F. Kennedy and Nikita Khrushchev paid little apparent attention to the opinions of Cuba's leader, Fidel Castro. Cuba and its problems vanished from the American mass media once more.

The misnamed 'Cuban' missile crisis of 1962 symbolised decades of history and the traditionally inferior position of the nations of Central and South America. US economic aid did flow to the south and was very much increased under Kennedy's 'Alliance for Progress'. In proportion to overall US aid it was not significant—in the 1950s the whole of Central and South America received less aid than South Korea. Meanwhile the rapid evolution of the US and Canada as urban, mass, plural societies with high living standards and middle-class social structures, widened still further the enormous gap that divided the northern and southern parts of the Western Hemisphere. The particular type of industrialisation which had taken place in the south did not necessarily lead to a high degree of modernisation of the societies and polities concerned. In fact several nations, like Argentina as we have observed, had begun to suffer economic retardation in the 1950s and 60s while Canada and the US enjoyed consumer booms.

Social impact of World War II

World War II broke out in Europe in September 1939 with Adolf Hitler's invasion of Poland. This brutal move brought France and England into war against Nazi Germany, but the US did not enter the conflict until the late winter of 1941. On 7 December 1941 the Japanese carried out what would today be called a 'pre-emptive strike' and without declaration of war, bombed the US fleet in Pearl Harbour, Hawaii. This act brought the US into war against Japan and its ally Germany. Even without Pearl Harbour the US would have had to enter the war: the dangers to her economy and security, of a Europe united by Hitler were only too obvious. Hitler had alienated each American ethnic group in turn as he invaded and raped the nations of Europe successively. Though the British were left almost alone to fight the heroic 'Battle of Britain' in the air, and managed to beat off the Luftwaffe and cause Hitler to call off his invasion across the English Channel, it was only a question of time before the Americans would return in uniform to Europe.

The *social* outcome of the war in the northern half of the Americas was to accelerate the coming of mass, urban society. Like all American wars, this one permanently increased the power and influence of the federal government within the US system. War demand saved the economy from further stagnation and created the government-industrial contracting system which favoured the huge private corporations.

The war stimulated all the existing trends towards mass organisation and bureaucracy; it favoured the large businesses; it speeded the economic and demographic growth of the American South, Southwest and Far West, bringing high-capital, high-technology industries to cities like Los Angeles and Seattle. It accelerated the normal population drift from countryside to city, including the migration of black Americans to the North and West, adding nine millions to the urban population. On the farms, still fewer people produced still more food, and they doubled farm income while doing so. More women were released for factory and office work, and freed from the exclusive role of motherhood, if they wished (though after the war some of these changes were seen to be impermanent).

Similar urbanising forces were at work in Canada. A major result of the war was further Canadian autonomy. The nation readily supported England, declaring war on Germany on 10 September 1939, only one week after England—yet this time, unlike World War I, the British war declaration was not taken automatically to include Canada. Like the US, Canada had her pacifists, isolationists and other groups: the leader of the Cooperative Commonwealth Federation party, J. S. Woodsworth, opposed Canadian involvement in the war. French Canada was less ready to fight perhaps, as Prime Minister Mackenzie King feared; but Catholic sympathies for Poland, and still greater feelings for France, were assured by Hitler's successive subjugation of both those nations. The war brought growth of Canadian industry, as well as of her armed forces. Shipbuilding, the aircraft industry and traditional war industries expanded as did newer enterprises like high octane fuel, magnesium and aluminium. Steel output more than doubled. The large contribution of the Canadian army and navy and the Royal Canadian Air Force to the war effort, much larger in proportion to population than that of the US, was made without the use of conscription until the end of the war. Quebec province rejected the draft in 1942. When 16,000 conscripts were to be sent to fight in Europe in November 1944, anti-draft riots broke out in Montreal, as they had in World War I. The war did not heal the wounds of the *Canadien* minority, and post-war prosperity exacerbated the French-English conflict in Canada.

Civil rights in World War II

In the US the impact of total war on civil rights was mixed. Black Americans gained when the March on Washington movement of 1941 finally forced the reluctant President Roosevelt to agree to the demands of black leaders. Inspired mainly by the trade unionist, A. Philip Randolph, Negroes persuaded Roosevelt to issue an Executive Order directing war contract industries not to discriminate in employment on the grounds of race, creed or colour. A Fair Employment Practices Committee (FEPC) was created to oversee this directive which applied to trade unions as well as to employers. The March was never held; its threat was enough. Jobs for blacks did increase and Negro income rose during the war, bringing further migrations of blacks to the industrial cities of the North, Midwest and West. One tragic outcome as in World War I, was a number of bad race-riots, the worst example being the Detroit Riot of 1943. The FEPC, while it lasted, helped to bring more jobs for Negroes; but there was no marked change in other civil rights, or in the widespread segregation and discrimination in public places from which black Americans suffered not only in the South.

For Japanese-Americans the war was a major tragedy. Racism, economic jealousy and anger after Pearl Harbour brought a drastic anti-Japanese movement in California supported by the federal government. Roosevelt allowed the Army to supervise the mandatory removal of all citizens of Japanese ancestry, the *Nisei*, born in the *US*, as well as the *Issei* (Japanese-born) from the West coast to inland camps often in the deserts. Later on they were to be dispersed further East. Sometimes with only 48 hours notice families had to pack up, sell what they could not carry and leave their homes, farms and businesses to live in ugly, guarded camps. No distinctions were made, and many citizens whose talents the nation needed in time of war were forced to live out most of the war in this way. Even veterans from World War I were so treated. The Supreme Court refused to help the Japanese-Americans in this wholesale abolition of their rights (*Korematsu v. the US*, 1944), in spite of the US tradition of respect for private property and individual freedoms. The man in charge of the operation, General De Witt, stated bluntly in his official report:

> The Japanese race is an enemy race, and while many . . . have become 'Americanized', the racial strains are undiluted.

However, German and Italian Americans, present in much greater numbers, were left with their rights intact. Military government in Hawaii, where Japanese-Americans were in the majority in the population, was much less harsh, and civil rights were not damaged so badly.

The Canadian-Japanese fared no better. Resentment, racism and economic jealousies from the majority of the population in British Columbia paralleled the anti-Japanese sentiments of California. In February 1942 the Canadian government ordered all Japanese-Canadian citizens and aliens to be moved inland, east of the Rockies. In this case 76% of the 21,000 who were rapidly moved were Canadian-born citizens. They lost their fishing boats and possessions and were scattered on interior beet farms, road camps and isolated settlements. Worse still, even after the war was over, almost 4,000 were deported *to Japan*—of whom over 2,000 had been born in Canada. Like the US, Canada adopted a dispersal policy for the rest at the war's end, sending the Japanese-Canadians to live in the eastern provinces, on the plains, or at least in eastern British Columbia, in a deliberate attempt to break up the former Japanese communities on the West coast.

Nuclear terror: The US uses the atom bomb

World War II brought the revolution in science and technology a stage further, as illustrated in the breakthrough in atomic research that created the atom bomb. Other successes included radar, sonar, the jet engine and countless medical advances. The US *Manhattan Project*, 1940–45, devised and built the two bombs that were dropped on the high-density Japanese cities of Hiroshima and Nagasaki in the summer of 1945. The project was a highly secret, massive scheme of cooperation among universities and scientists, the army, industries, workers, the military and government—the roots of the 'military-industrial complex' later so named by President Eisenhower in 1961. President Harry S. Truman, who had been in office for almost two weeks before he learned the details of the project, took upon himself the total responsibility for dropping two atom bombs on Japan. Naturally, the full responsibility is not so easy to pinpoint, despite Truman's insistence to his death in December 1972, that the decision was wholly his. Policy-advisers like Secretary of War H. L. Stimson, scientists, and others share the responsibility for the manufacture and for the use of the atom bomb. Some leading military men opposed using this weapon, including Admiral William D. Leahy. But the Interim Committee appointed to advise the government counselled Truman to drop the bomb, without any prior warning, on a Japanese city (a 'dual target': industry or military installations near mass housing).

If the American people had been told, would they have voted to act differently? It is difficult to guess. World War II had seen mounting horror, culminating in the Nazi death camps; the Germans had been forced to an unconditional surrender, and it seemed logical to demand the same kind of total surrender from the Japanese. The nation was in no mood to make distinctions. General Curtis Le May's conventional mass bombing raids over Japan were already destroying cities and fulfilling his stated goal, to bomb the Japanese 'back into the Stone Age' (a phrase Le May repeated, applied to North Vietnam, as vice-presidential candidate in 1968). It seemed that the Allies would be satisfied with nothing but total and unconditional surrender from Japan, though several military experts thought this demand was unreasonable and unnecessary.

By the 1950s, with hydrogen bombs and bacteriological and chemical warfare on the cards, and moon flights planned, the advance of science and technology had created a new world of terror, difficult for the most educated North Americans to comprehend. What were now called 'weapons systems' of mass destruction had irreversibly altered the structure of international politics and made a world of horrifying uncertainty in which

231

it seemed likely that scientists could split the globe by accident or choice. It was a world in which the original atom bomb of Hiroshima would rapidly become old fashioned and relatively cheap to manufacture. Quite small nations could become capable of producing atomic weapons.

This new state of permanent uncertainty was produced in large part by the successes of the US economic system. At home it was accompanied by a huge consumer boom in the 1950s and 60s. The nation witnessed the largest wave of prosperity in its history thus far, comparable to the boom of the 1920s but more solidly based on a population explosion. Like that of the 20s the consumer society of the post-war decades had serious flaws. Too much of the demand which sustained it was dependent upon the federal government. Defence contracts to the large corporations, farmed out across the nation to smaller firms, helped to keep the system growing. This was a Cold War prosperity. What would happen if cold war tensions diminished and if 'peace broke out'? Could the economic growth continue indefinitely?

The anti-communist crusade

The fundamental psychological and political basis of the defence boom was the fear of 'international communism'. Mutual Great Power suspicions after World War II soon hardened into Cold War ideology and abstraction, the world being divided by the 'Iron Curtain' running through Central Europe. President Harry Truman had succeeded to the White House upon the death of FDR in April 1945. He struggled to keep alive the reform ideals of the New Deal but was himself a staunch anti-communist crusader. No doubt his tough, anti-communist foreign policy gained support for his extension of the New Deal at home (the 'Fair Deal' as he called it). Anti-communist feelings ran high as much of Eastern Europe and parts of Asia fell under communist control in the immediate post-war years. Even Truman could not escape attacks from right-wing critics who accused him of being 'soft on communism'. This was an ironical charge tó bring against the president who invented the 'Truman Doctrine' that communism must be somehow 'contained' and its spreading empire checked, by America giving large doses of military and economic aid to endangered nations.

The Truman Doctrine was formulated in 1947 over Greece and Turkey. In order to stimulate Congress to pass an aid bill to these two crippled nations, Truman developed a broad argument the scope of which surprised some of his most ardent anti-communist advisers. It was the duty of the US, he said, to come to the aid of 'free peoples who are resisting attempted subjugation by armed minorities or by outside pressures.' In 1947, a year of financial crisis, Britain could no longer maintain her forces in the Middle East. When she announced her withdrawal from Greece and Palestine, the US stepped into the vacuum. Perhaps out of fear of residual isolationism in the US, Truman 'oversold' his anti-communist policy. He chose to scare the public and Congress into action and to win large foreign aid appropriations on the basis of the communist bogey. Perhaps the president fully believed his message. Certainly there was no question about the communist victories or minority take-overs in Poland, Rumania, Yugoslavia, Bulgaria and Hungary by 1947. Finnish foreign affairs were Soviet-controlled; East Germany (the Russian zone of occupation) was naturally converted to communist organisation. Meanwhile in Asia communists had grasped power in Korea, there was strong resistance to America's ally, Chiang Kai-Shek, in China and active communist dissidence was bringing unrest in old colonial areas such as Malaya, Indochina, Burma and Indonesia. Truman himself put the struggle in simplistic moral terms. Commenting later he said wryly:

> I suppose that history will remember my term in office as the years when the Cold War began to overshadow our lives. I have hardly had a day in office that has not been dominated by this all-embracing struggle—the conflict between those who love freedom and those who would lead the world back into slavery and darkness.

It was a curiously naïve statement in view of the complex inheritance of some of the nations concerned, particularly the ex-colonised, largely anti-western, and deeply nationalist countries of Southeast Asia.

Congress responded to Truman's appeal in 1947 and passed the Greek-Turkish Aid Act. The US was now launched on a long career of global policeman which would take her through the Korean War and into the Vietnam struggle of the 1960s. Truman's ideas dominated American foreign policy for almost thirty years. What he called 'containment' became the justification for use of massive US aid to known right-wing dictators in various parts of the globe. America's traditionally anti-colonial power stance in world affairs seemed hollow; to Third World peoples the United States, for all its generous economic aid, was a counter-revolutionary force. Counter-revolution was never the explicit aim of US foreign policy of course, but some American advisers saw the threat of communism in almost all liberation movements. In Guatemala in 1954, for example, a leftist regime was deposed with American aid, with little or no real evidence that Communists were about to take over that small nation. This containment policy brought the US directly into Southeast Asia, and in Vietnam she inherited the French colonial role.

In Truman's own administration the most forceful example of the use of the containment doctrine was his intervention in the Korean War (1950–53). The Truman Doctrine was made in 1950 to apply to Asia. Originally it was conceived of as a guard against advances of communism in Europe. Now a new communist foe was to be 'contained': Red China. The apparent success of the United Nations, US-inspired action against

19. *John, Robert and Edward Kennedy photographed together at the former's home at Hyannis Port, Mass., when he was campaigning for the Presidency, July 1960.*

North Korea encouraged American exponents of the 'get tough with communism' line. The 'success' in Korea was judged in terms of waging a limited war for limited objectives—the North Koreans were driven back into their own territory and South Korea did survive, albeit under an undemocratic regime. When the commanding general, Douglas Mac-Arthur, sought to expand the Korean war aims into a fight against China itself, Truman eventually dismissed him. The US Joint Chiefs of Staff supported Truman's decision on military grounds. The Korean action widened the idea of containment and the world responsibilities of the US became enormous in the years ahead.

The military-industrial complex

The impact of the Korean war at home was to stimulate economic growth still further, accelerate the rate of suburbanisation, and increase the possibility of social tensions. The 1950s boom and the complacency it sustained, obscured some important statistics. During the Eisenhower years (1952–1960) the number of poor people in the US had increased both absolutely, with population growth, and relatively. In this rich decade of 'consensus' people missed the fact that poverty was increasing in the world's richest society. The election of John F. Kennedy in 1960 (America's youngest president and the first Catholic to hold the office) brought the so-called 'New Frontier' and a younger generation of advisers and office-holders. Social investigations, such as the influential tract by the Catholic socialist, Michael Harrington, *The Other Americans*, brought a massive rebirth of social conscience. The reform era that now developed was comparable with that of the pre-Civil War years or with the New Deal.

After 1960 a whole range of needed reforms, ignored during the 50s, reached the front pages of American newspapers and hit the television screens. Truman's Fair Deal had largely failed despite his appointment of a civil rights committee and his struggle to enact a national health care programme. A recalcitrant Congress and Truman's complete absorption in foreign affairs and anti-Communism vitiated most of his programme. In the hectic 1960s all the old issues reappeared with new vigour: poverty, conservation (now known as 'ecology'), civil rights, the problems of the aged, immigration reform, public education and other issues. This flood was cut short by President Kennedy's assassination in 1963. A potentially great figure was removed from the American scene. However, by November 1963 few of Kennedy's reforms had been enacted; if he had lived it is hard to say how successful he would have been with Congress and public opinion. Kennedy, too, was something of a Cold Warrior, at least at the outset of his administration. After his murder a more willing Congress was pushed by the tough new president, Lyndon Baines Johnson, to pass a great mass of reform legislation affecting almost every aspect of

American society. These reforms of Johnson's 'Great Society' years did more for civil rights, public education and numerous other areas than had ever been done by one president. The Great Society programme was a social revolution, sadly hidden by growing resentment against President Johnson's involvement in the Vietnam war.

In 1964 the US was not yet deeply embroiled in Vietnam, and Johnson won a massive re-election victory, the greatest majority in US political history, though very nearly matched by Richard Nixon's victory in 1972. The vote of 1964 was to a great extent against Johnson's opponent, the arch-conservative Republican Senator, Barry Goldwater of Arizona. Goldwater was the first conservative politician openly and honestly to fight an election campaign with the idea of *reversing* the New Deal. Since 1932 the US had finally joined the majority of Western industrialised societies in adopting the welfare state and managed-economy techniques for overall growth and welfare. The US had not yet gone as far in its mixed-economy as the Swedish or even the British model, but the results of the 1964 election seemed to show that the American shift to the welfare state was irreversible. Four years later Richard M. Nixon was elected as Republican president and he did succeed in retarding the reform movement on many fronts, notably in civil rights and welfare; but he had no intention of 'rolling back' the New Deal as Goldwater had demanded in 1964. After two years in office President Nixon declared his sudden conversion to what he called the 'New' economics, now old-fashioned, of government spending and economic management. The myth of *laissez-faire* capitalism was truly dead in America.

The government spending of the 50s and 60s was unlike that of the New Deal in one important respect: most of it consisted in defence spending. War, or Cold War, proved to be the ultimate 'Keynesian' management technique. After the conclusion of the Korean conflict, defence spending was maintained and when the US began to replace France in Southeast Asia (from 1963) defence expenditures rose to a level of over $80 billion a year. The long and costly Vietnam war did not come to an end for the United States until January 1973. By the mid-60s the public were beginning to complain about the costs of the war, mounting spending, and inflation. In 1968–69 there was a scare that the long post-World War II boom was tailing off into recession—recession *with* inflation, an unusual condition. The government however felt compelled to continue to underwrite the large defence corporations, particularly in the aircraft industry, and to guarantee their profits against failure and incompetence (as in the outstanding case of the Lockheed company).

In 1969–70 President Nixon made small, very tentative motions towards a cutback in defence contracts. The immediate result was unemployment and fear in cities like Seattle, Washington, and Los Angeles, California. Several cities and parts of states and huge sectors of US industry had become dependent on federal contracts for their prosperity.

The Department of Defense was the world's largest corporation and the biggest employer of labour and materials. The recession in Seattle in 1970, directly linked to a diminution of government contract work, brought bitter resentment among the highly skilled and semi-professional workers involved. One board read: WILL THE LAST PERSON TO LEAVE SEATTLE PLEASE TURN OUT THE LIGHTS?

While the Cold War transformed the American economy it also shaped intra-hemisphere relations. In Central and South America, US anti-communism encouraged forceful intervention in the internal politics of small nations. When Fidel Castro's leftist guerillas overthrew the bloody right-wing dictatorship of Batista in Cuba in December 1959 the US at first took no strong action. In the last months of the Eisenhower regime, however, military intervention was planned, a plot in which US Intelligence would train and arm Cuban émigrés and support them in an attempted invasion of Cuba. The plan had not fully matured when President Kennedy took over in 1961. Kennedy decided to allow the invasion to go ahead. The exiles were easily routed by Castro's forces when they landed at the Bay of Pigs in April 1961. The invasion was a humiliating fiasco for America. It would not have happened if many Americans had not been taken in by distortion and wishful thinking about Cuba. They had believed that Cuba was a seething mass of discontented people, ready to rise and throw off the cruel dictatorship of Castro and embrace the CIA-supported counter-revolutionaries. This was not the case at all at that time.

The Bay of Pigs pushed into the political background the large programme of US aid for South America which Kennedy had announced only a few weeks earlier under the grandiloquent title, the 'Alliance for Progress'. Credibility in American motives in this new Alliance was shaken by the Cuban invasion. Cuba in 1961 was not the easy prey that Guatemala had been in 1954. Moreover, many South American leaders respected Castro at first despite the harshness of his regime. His land reforms and economic changes were desired elsewhere. Hostility between Cuba and the US became total. In December 1961 Castro declared himself to be a 'Marxist', a useful claim by which to speed aid from the Communist bloc. Aid was denied to him by the US, which prohibited all trade with Cuba. As a result the island suffered very badly and its suffering was used by American critics as evidence of the failure of 'communism' in Cuba. Castro's friendship with the Soviet Union, begun with a trade treaty in February 1960, led directly to Khrushchev's installation of Russian missiles on the island and to the confrontation of 1962. Cuba failed to benefit from the confrontation except to be assured that the US would not invade her shores. The resolution of the Cuban missile confrontation was brought about by the president's brother, Attorney-General Robert F. Kennedy, who promised the Soviet ambassador that in return for Russian withdrawal of the missiles and submission to the US 'quarantine' of Cuba and search of vessels going to Cuba, American

20. *A Soviet ship carrying eight canvas-covered missiles and transporters,
which are visible on its decks, as it steams away from Cuba,
7 November 1962.*

missiles would be removed from Turkey. This solution was very remote
from Cuba's needs.

These events reverberated throughout Central and South America.
'Fidelista' movements sprang up in various countries, as Cuban agents
infiltrated South America. However, the new Castroite factions fractured
the South American left still further.

American aid and trade

In the 1960s and 70s the US remained the largest trading partner of 20
Central and South American republics. The following table reveals the
size of US trade.

238

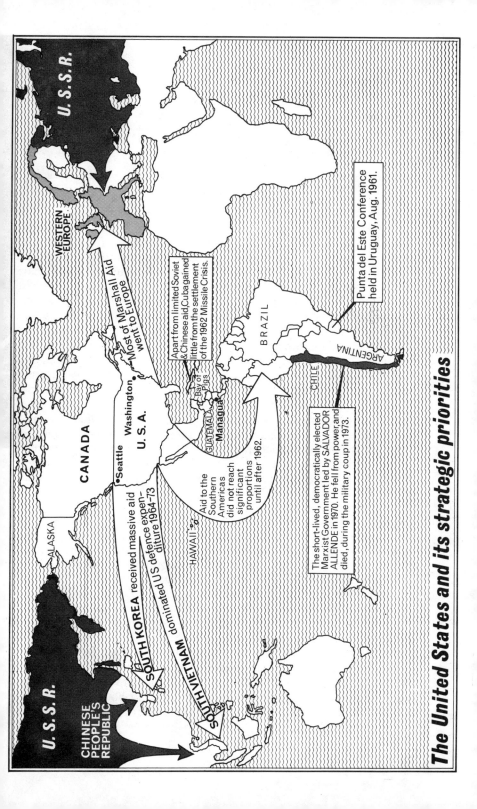

The United States and its strategic priorities

U.S.S.R.

U.S.S.R.

WESTERN EUROPE

CHINESE PEOPLE'S REPUBLIC

ALASKA

CANADA

Seattle

Washington

U.S.A.

HAWAII

GUATEMALA

Managua

Bay of Pigs

BRAZIL

CHILE

ARGENTINA

Most of Marshall Aid went to Europe

SOUTH KOREA received massive aid

SOUTH VIETNAM dominated US defence expenditure 1964–73

Apart from limited Soviet & Chinese aid, Cuba gained little from the settlement of the 1962 Missile Crisis.

Aid to the Southern Americas did not reach significant proportions until after 1962.

The short-lived, democratically elected Marxist Government led by SALVADOR ALLENDE in 1970. He fell from power, and died, during the military coup in 1973.

Punta del Este Conference held in Uruguay, Aug. 1961.

	1960	1970
Total US exports	$20,576 million	43,224 million
Total US imports	14,654 million	39,952 million
Total Western Hemisphere		
US exports	7,684 million	15,612 million
US imports	6,864 million	16,928 million
Canada: US exports	3,810 million	9,079 million
US imports	2,901 million	11,092 million
20 C. and S. American		
republics: US exports	3,577 million	5,695 million
US imports	3,528 million	4,779 million

As for American aid, in the years 1953–61 South Korea *alone* received 2½ times as much aid as the whole of the southern Americas. Under the Marshall plan it was natural for the heaviest outflow of US grants and credits to go to war-stricken Europe. So, in the years 1948–52 out of a total of about $14.5 billion in aid, the southern Americas received a bare $19.5 million. Europe got the lion's share with $12.4 billion. Under the Mutual Security legislation of the years 1953–61 from a total of almost $17 billion, the southern Americas received only $825 million. South Korea alone received over $2 billion, Europe $2.7 billion. By the period 1962–71 the proportions had altered, drastically changed by Kennedy's *Alliance for Progress* programme and other world factors. Out of an estimated aid total of over $22 billion under the AID programmes (as they were now known), the southern Americas were allotted over $5 billion— a massive six-fold increase in US aid over the previous period. Europe now received only $22 million. Vietnam was given $3 billion. The large expenditure in Vietnam is too low an estimate, since from 1966 onwards much of the Vietnam spending was transferred to the Department of Defense appropriation, and this would have to be calculated separately and additionally. (All these figures can be readily checked in US Bureau of the Census, *Statistical Abstract of the United States, 1972.* US official statistics are very reliable.)

In years to come these facts will no doubt astonish students of the region. Yet they accurately reflect US opinions as to the nation's strategic priorities at the time. American aid takes several forms, some of it not direct. The 1960s saw a proliferation of goodwill and humanitarian programmes including *Food for Peace*, the *Peace Corps*, and US financial support of leading international lending agencies such as the Inter-American Development Bank and the International Monetary Fund. Americans underwrote financially many of the programmes of the United Nations and its agencies. Also US private business contributed in various ways to economic development in the nations concerned and paid out an estimated billion dollars a year in taxes to the governments of the southern Americas, according to a 1970 figure. It is difficult to measure quantitatively the value of such programmes as food distribution or the Peace Corps. President Kennedy's idealistic Alliance for Progress ground to a halt, but its goals were sound. The idea of 1961 was to plan a huge investment over a ten-year period of $100 billion in Central and South America, $20 billion of it to come from outside the region, including $11 billion from US tax payers. In return the receiving nations agreed to undertake certain structural reforms—comprehensive agrarian reform, fair wage and collective bargaining laws for labour, tax reform, and large-scale attacks on peasant illiteracy. If public health services, schools, and low-cost housing could be provided, if the larger estates could be more fairly divided into smaller farms and the new owners taught how to increase output, and if the lower classes could be given new hope that one day their children would eat regularly, read and write, and own decent homes, the Alliance for Progress would have been a triumph of American aid. The illiberal, counter-revolutionary stigma would forever be removed from American policies in the Western Hemisphere. This did not come about—or had not done so by the mid-1970s.

In these years the republics themselves were moving closer together. The *Organisation of American States* (OAS), historical successor to the US-dominated Pan American Union of 1890, was created in 1948. Its members were more independent of the USA than before World War II, though the OAS still failed to provide a forum where genuine equality of opinion could prevail. The twenty republics were all members, and all founder-members also of the United Nations Organisation. They rarely came out for strongly independent action in that body. Their combined population of about 300,000,000 by the mid-1970s was not making its presence felt in international councils. A stable, prosperous South America was essential to the peace and stability of the world community. The economic potential of the southern half of the continent was enormous. As a link between Have and Have-Not regions of the globe, South America could play a crucial role in future world development. In the early 1970s however, all this was mere potentiality. Within the region itself the *Latin American Free Trade Association* of 1960 (LAFTA) consisted of Argentina, Bolivia, Brazil, Chile, Colombia, Ecuador, Mexico, Paraguay, Peru, Uruguay and Venezuela. This surely could become an impressive bloc of economic power. The smaller nations were less likely to benefit from intra-South American free trade. Underdeveloped nations were too poor to compete with the richer states like Argentina, Brazil and Mexico. They would need special aid and concessions. A *Central American Common Market* was also created—Costa Rica, El Salvador, Guatemala, Honduras and Nicaragua. What would they sell to each other? Very often they were competitors in world markets.

Mexico: halfway to modernity

Mexico was by 1970 most representative of the midway position between economic maturity and underdevelopment. Her rate of economic growth exceeded her rate of population growth. Real GNP was

241

improving at about 6% a year after 1940, population growing at about 3.5%. She did not suffer unduly from inflation and her currency was valued in foreign exchange markets. Mexican credit was excellent and she had little need of US aid. She was a major supporter of the Alliance for Progress, but viewed it as a programme in which she herself would be a leader in the hemisphere. By 1970 Mexican trade was less dependent on the US than in former years—60% of it was with her northern neighbour as compared with 86% in 1950. Of private investment in Mexico, 74% was still from the US, but it now entered on Mexican terms. In any case fully 90% of Mexican gross investment came from her own internal savings. She was friendly towards the United States but was prepared to act independently in some foreign policy matters, as at the Punta del Este conference of the OAS in 1962 when she refused to vote to expel Cuba from the organisation. There was no legal provision for expulsion of a member-state in the charter. Nevertheless Mexico did not choose to go as far as Brazil or Argentina, who roundly declared that the Cuban question was purely a dispute between Castro and the United States, and did not concern the OAS as a body. Mexico maintained diplomatic ties with Cuba; the relationship was not a warm one. She stood for non-alignment, as far as possible, in the Cold War dispute. According to the Estrada Doctrine, put forward by a Mexican Foreign Minister, Gerraro Estrada, Mexico would recognise and deal with any *de facto* foreign government without regard to its form or origin, and would act in accordance with the national interests of Mexico. In practice these interests were almost purely commercial; Mexico had only a small military establishment. The threat of US intervention by force in Mexican affairs had disappeared since World War I and she had no major security problem.

By 1970 Mexico was semi-industrialised and was beginning to diversify her exports and build a healthier economic base. The massive shift of population to the cities, especially to the Federal District, exacerbated problems of urban poverty. This was portrayed brilliantly in the works of the American investigator, Oscar Lewis, whose *Children of Sanchez* was a family portrait based on taped interviews. The 'culture of poverty' in a Mexico City tenement is described in that book with a directness that strikes home. Because of the existence of what Karl Marx would have called a 'reserve army' of 2 or 3 million property-less peasants who kept down living standards and wage-rates, the problem of improving per capita income in Mexico was difficult. A population limitation programme would help, though family-planning was a thorny problem in a traditionalist, male-dominated, Catholic nation. In the 1970s the Catholic Faith itself was undergoing change. In the cities its hold was enfeebled. Mexico City, which suffered as much from smog and pollution as any major city of the developed nations, had grown from 368,000 (1910) to over 8,000,000 (1970). A quarter of its inhabitants lacked piped water in 1970. The ancient dream of 'land reform' and peasant holdings—individual or communal—was dead in Mexico, where over half the population were now urbanised. Half of all agricultural output was produced by only 5% of the rural labour force by 1970, but that 5% worked on large farms, not on the economically unviable 'minifundia' or small peasant holdings. Productivity could not be improved on tiny farms. Economically, the noble ideal of land reform and the break-up of the huge estates had not proved wise. This is no judgement on its social or political justification.

The miracle of the peaceful transfer of power between administrations had been the norm in Mexico since the emergence of the one-party system of the 'institutional revolution', the PNR, in 1929. Forty years of stable politics ensued, under the direction of presidents like Calles, Cárdenas and Alemán, different personalities who each contributed to the survival of this unique political structure. The PRI (as it became) felt itself to be the virtual representative of all the major groups in Mexican society and differences of opinion were to be expressed *within* the party. Mexico was not a 'police state' and enjoyed a certain degree of freedom of the press and of expression. The political system worked through patronage—what was called in 19th century North America the 'spoils' system. By the 1960s the party was the establishment and a major division appeared, in Mexico as in most nations, between governing groups and the growing number of young people. The issue was not so much ideology as the generation gap. The student movement, or its minority leadership, was deeply influenced by left-wing terrorist ideas and by the widespread violence of the decade. A tragedy occurred before the Olympic Games, held in Mexico 1968, when rioting students, claiming traditional and time-honoured student grievances such as poor teaching and large classes, organised a demonstration. The government alleged that the students were organised and armed by Castroite agitators. Some students did use automatic rifles. As troops advanced on the university plaza to arrest student leaders, sniper fire broke out. In the ensuing mêlée 200 died and many were jailed. It was a bloody spectacle for the Olympic Games and a blow in prestige for the most advanced and politically mature nation in the southern Americas.

Argentina: Perón returns

The most unusual occurrence of the early 70s was the return to political power of the aged Perón in Argentina. This return was made possible by growing unrest and violence in the nation. Yet another military coup dissolved the Argentine Congress in 1966 and eliminated all 25 political parties. A new military president combined in his office all legislative and executive power. The following year a strict anti-communist edict was issued and the press and media were effectively muzzled, as were the universities. Angry, embittered students and workers rioted in 1969 while urban guerillas began a round of kidnappings and terror, as in

243

Uruguay and elsewhere. They murdered ex-president Pedro Aramburu, an anti-Perón leader. After more riots in Cordoba an army chief, Alejandre Lanusse, was made president in 1971. Lanusse allowed political parties to be re-constituted and a court legalised the Justicialista party of Perón. The plan was to prepare for a return to legitimate, civilian government in Argentina in an election set for March 1973. After a long, 17-year exile mainly spent in Spain, Perón was permitted to return home in November 1972. Security was heavy and the visit was preceded by weeks of negotiation with the military junta. Perón announced a new Justicialista Liberal Front to contend the coming election, aided by ex-president Frondizi. He stayed in Argentina 28 days and temporarily rejected the idea of running for president himself. Despite second thoughts by the junta during Perón's absence in Rumania and elsewhere, he did return to Argentina and emerged as the nation's president once more in the autumn of 1973. He died the following summer. None of these dramatic events promised much for the ailing Argentine economy. The depression of the early 1960s had levelled out and economic recovery had been under way since 1969. Large budget deficits and the problem of inflation remained.

The civil rights revolution in North America

The ancient issue of political freedoms came up again in Argentina while in the northern Americas an unprecedented breakthrough occurred in the struggle for racial civil rights. The boom years of the 50s and 60s had brought rising expectations for all US citizens, and they now expected more from their government and their country. Black Americans in particular were restive. The benefits and opportunities of the Consumer Society were made so much of in the mass media and in official propaganda and comparisons with the communist world, yet some minorities were excluded from fully enjoying them. Led by Chief Justice Earl Warren, the US Supreme Court began to take an active interest in discrimination and civil rights, passing in 1954 its epoch-making decision in the case *Brown v. Board of Education of Topeka*. Unanimously the Court overturned the 'separate but equal' doctrine of 1896 and declared that segregation by race in schools was unconstitutional and violated the rights of school-children under the Fourteenth Amendment. One year later the Court also ordered all state and local authorities to put an end to this illegality and to desegregate schools 'with all deliberate speed'. The idea was extended later to all public places, common carriers and tax-supported colleges. Early attempts to enforce the desegregation rulings were not very successful, but soon it was realised that the rules

◄ *21. Perón flanked by bodyguards outside his home in Buenos Aires after his return from exile, November 1972.*

22. *An aerial view of the Lincoln Memorial, Washington, during the massive demonstration for Civil Rights, 28 August 1963.*

must apply in the North as well as in the South, to *de facto* as well as to *de jure* segregation. Even President Eisenhower, with his great respect for the states' rights doctrine and fear of executive power, used federalised troops to enforce the desegregation of Little Rock High School in Alabama in 1957.

Violence mounted in the South, with murders of prominent Negroes, bombing of black churches and schools, lynchings and murders. The Ku Klux Klan reappeared in full force. Pseudo-scientific arguments about Negro racial inferiority came into the open again. Usually, local police forces condoned violence against blacks and civil rights workers. White Citizens' Councils were organised to combat desegregation. Liberals and moderates in the South became embattled. In December 1955 a black woman in Montgomery, Alabama, Mrs Rosa Parks, started a whole new phase of the struggle by refusing to give up her seat to a white in the public bus. Black 'passive resistance' became a force to be reckoned with. The Rev. Martin Luther King preached the Gandhian doctrine of non-violent opposition to oppression and organised the Southern Christian Leadership Conference (SCLC). A more 'radical' group, the Council on Racial Equality (CORE), containing at first mainly white college students, sent 'Freedom Riders' to the South deliberately to test out segregation there beginning in 1961. The CORE volunteers were beaten up by angry and fearful white mobs and Attorney-General Robert F. Kennedy sent federal marshals South to maintain order.

'Jim Crow' segregated seating on public transportation was finally ended in the United States with the rulings of the Interstate Commerce Commission of 1962–3. Discrimination in public restaurants came under fire from February 1960, when a group of black students began the sit-in movement at a Woolworth's in Greensboro, North Carolina. Many sit-ins followed, with some violence. The student movement became more radical, with the emergence of SNCC (Student Non-Violent Coordinating Committee). The year 1962 saw two deaths at 'Ole Miss' (University of Mississippi) when federal forces again had to be used to assure the admission of a black student, James Meredith.

A climax came in 1963, the centenary year of Lincoln's Emancipation Proclamation. Demonstrations and police violence became common. In Birmingham, Alabama the use of electric cattle-prods, heavy water-hoses and police dogs against black demonstrators was seen on world-wide television. A massive March on Washington, like the one threatened in 1941, now focussed public and world attention on the crisis in the United States. A. Philip Randolph was there, as in 1941, and newer civil rights leaders, particularly Martin Luther King, the now acknowledged spokesman for the vast movement. The crowd numbered one-quarter of a million, and its peaceful assembly in Washington was the high-water mark of non-violent demonstration.

Unfortunately, Congress delayed President Kennedy's civil rights bill, murders continued in the South, where four black Sunday School children were killed by a bomb in Birmingham, and white supremacists were voted into office in the South. The frustration of the hopes of 1963 created an atmosphere of violence and stimulated a re-birth of black nationalism and separatism. Blacks took over various civil rights groups. White students were often no longer welcomed. A new black militancy was seen among writers and religious leaders, like Malcolm X of the Black Muslims. President Kennedy himself was murdered in November, 1963.

The middle 1960s were years of upheaval in the cities, climaxing in the grim year, 1968. Long hot summers in the urban ghettos of the North and West now balanced the earlier violence of the South, which did not cease. The Watts riot came in 1965, Newark and Detroit in 1967. Large sections of ghettos were burnt; people were killed, usually blacks, and occasionally white firemen or police. An official government investigation, the Kerner Commission Report of 1968, blamed the urban violence on 'white racism' as the root-cause of all the problems faced by black Americans. Two murders in 1968 made it the most humiliating and shameful year Americans had known in their history—the murder of Dr Martin Luther King on 4 April 1968, and the murder of Senator Robert F. Kennedy a few weeks later on June 4th, when he seemed ready to win the Democratic nomination for the presidency. The immediate results of Dr King's assassination were 125 urban riots. A new civil rights act was pushed through, this time with an open-housing clause. The immediate political results of Robert Kennedy's death were the fragmentation of the Democratic party and the violent convention in Chicago, that, in selecting Vice-President Hubert Humphrey as candidate virtually gave the election of 1968 to the Republicans. Humphrey refused to disassociate himself openly from the Vietnam war policies of President Johnson and did not condemn the police violence in Chicago during his nomination.

One major triumph of Johnson's years however, despite his basic unpopularity over refusing to pull US forces out of Vietnam, was the Civil Rights Act of 1964. The most important measure since the end of the Civil War, the act sought to establish equal rights for all Americans, regardless of race, nationality, religion or sex, in matters of public accommodation, education and other areas. It outlawed discrimination in public places, in federally aided programs and in employment. Buttressed by a Voting Rights Act in 1965, this measure did much to eliminate racial injustice in the US. The effectiveness of legislation depends however on how forcefully the administration of the day chooses to enforce it through the Justice Department and in other ways.

The Canadian crisis

Canadians, unscientifically, continued to regard their central problem of the tension between French Canadians and others as a 'race' question. As is so often the case, prosperity and economic growth did not assuage this bitter division, though major violence and terrorism did not break out until the later 1960s. The Liberal party was in control of Canada from 1935 to 1957, a long stretch of time. W. L. Mackenzie King was replaced as Prime Minister in 1948 by Louis St Laurent. The Liberals were a moderate, middle-road, New Dealish party, though in creating the welfare state in Canada they followed more closely (if belatedly) the thoroughgoing British model—with Unemployment Insurance (1940), Family Allowances (1944) and Old Age Security (1951). They gave price subsidies to farmers and some tariff protection to Canadian industries.

After a gap of 22 years the Conservative party took over the federal government under John Diefenbaker (1957–63), and were then supplanted by the Liberals again led first by Lester Pearson (1963–68) and thereafter by the lively French Canadian lawyer, Pierre Elliott Trudeau. The problem of French Canadian rights did not seem to improve with either party. Trudeau wished to follow a more independent national course for Canada, though he maintained the strong defensive alliance with the United States. He proclaimed the pursuit of a 'Just Society', with greater steps towards bilingualism (more official use of French), more freedom of action for the provinces and clear independence from Britain. He did not however, agree to repudiate the Queen and to turn Canada into a republic.

Canada, despite its rural and 'great-outdoors' self-image, was now a modern, industrial, urban society. A century after confederation three-quarters of its population lived in towns and cities, two-thirds in only 2 out of the 10 provinces, Quebec and Ontario. The far western provinces of Alberta and British Columbia were the fastest-growing of the 10, the 4 Atlantic provinces the slowest. Manitoba and Saskatchewan had together less than 10% of the entire population (which numbered 21,568,000 in 1971—a tenth of the size of the US population). Only 10% of Canadians still lived on farms. The over 6,000,000 *Canadiens* of Quebec, and the additional million or so French-speaking Canadians who lived outside that province were too many to be called a 'minority' any more. They were a majority in Quebec and the largest single 'minority' within Canada, unless one groups all the 'British' together, including English, Scots, Irish and Welsh. Even then, the 'British' had been under half of the population for some years; they were about 57% in 1901 but only 43% by 1961. By the 1960s growing demands from the *Canadiens* threatened the very existence of Canada as a nation, according to an influential study made by a *Royal Commission on Bilingualism and Biculturalism* appointed in 1963.

For decades the French had grumbled. What they most resented was their lack of representation in the highest echelons of business and administration, the armed services, the voluntary agencies and elsewhere, even in Quebec where they were the overwhelming majority. Quebec had many rights and privileges, almost as many as a separate state: control over education, economic and social services, a lively French press, radio and television service, and even a French civil code of law. But a new and rising young élite of French Canadians—engineers, management people, technicians—felt they could not advance to the very top and fulfil themselves as Canadians. The French language, they argued was rarely used in federal civil service examinations and was non-existent in the army. The predominantly English-speaking provinces had virtually ruled out the possibility of French schools. Moreover, since the school system in Quebec was more élitist and less extensive than else-where, the mass of French Canadians qualified only for manual and low-prestige positions. In truth the new barrage of complaints and demonstrations against the dominant Anglo-Canadians also covered an *internal* revolution within French Canada, the growing rejection by the young and the technocrats of the old rural French ways, the role of the parish and the Church, and of the old-fashioned humanistic, classical college. French Canada was divided by social class and by the battle between traditional and modern. This 'quiet revolution' of deep self-criticism within Quebec complicated the process of change.

Most so-called English Canadians, especially those remote from Quebec, could see little that was wrong with the political and economic structure of Canada and were baffled and hurt by the increasingly violent and disruptive attitudes of some French Canadians. The English Cana-dians were not strongly anti-French or totally unsympathetic, they simply did not know what was going on in Quebec. Meanwhile, especially since World War I, other nationalities had entered Canada: Germans, Ukrain-ians, Dutch, Poles and Italians for example. Where would they stand? Most of them identified with the English-speaking sections, and some feared they would be crushed in the middle of the struggle between the two 'founding races'. At least 14% of Canadians had a mother tongue that was neither French nor English. Still, the worst problem was that of French-speaking Canadians. Few of the rest realised that in Quebec province fully 75% of the population spoke nothing but French—not a word of English. The old, complacent English-speaking view that the French language and French ways would eventually and inevitably die out was unfounded.

The French were divided themselves. A small minority supported the separatists who wished to see a totally independent state of Quebec. Some English Canadians, embittered by this idea, told the Royal Com-missioners that if this happened there would be little reason why the rest of Canada should not join the United States. Generally however the deep love of Canada felt by all Canadians, and the conviction that their best future lay with a united nation, prevailed. What enlightened and shocked the commissioners however was the discovery that, though the extreme separatists were a minority, *all* French Canadians felt a deep need for some drastic change in the situation. French and English-speaking

Canadians held mutually exclusive views of each other and of past Canadian history, as well as of the future of Canada. The French thought they were the original settlers of Canada and the English were invaders; they regarded the executed Riel as a patriot, and the English saw him as a murderer; they saw Lord Durham as the assimilator who would eliminate French culture, while the English saw him as the great decoloniser. In truth these long-past conflicts had merely scarred over and had not truly healed. The coming of modernisation in the Quebec economy of the 1950s and 60s and the rise of the French technical and professional élite, brought open conflict.

23. *A police guard of honour carrying the coffin of Pierre Laporte, Canadian Labour Minister, into the court-house in Montreal. He was murdered by the FLQ in October 1970 after the government refused to meet their ransom demands.*

Under Trudeau, the French Canadian, came the worst violence so far over the Quebec issue. During the last months of Pearson's administration the president of France, intensely nationalist Charles De Gaulle, had visited Canada. Reversing the usual order, he went first to Quebec instead of to the capital of Ottawa. In one of the most unusual interventions in the domestic affairs of a host nation, General De Gaulle gave a public speech demanding French Canadian separatism and a 'Free Quebec'. Though on a state visit he recommended to the Montreal audience the separation of Quebec from the rest of Canada, and culminated with the cry: 'Vive le Québec! Vive le Québec Libre! Vive le Canada Français! Vive la France!' (24 July 1967). The Canadian government issued a strong rebuke, and the general left the country without conferring with Pearson. He never recanted, and on 31 July the French government reaffirmed its goal of aiding the province of Quebec to win 'the objectives of liberation that they themselves have set'. Prime Minister Pearson stated the opposite view:

> The people of Canada are free. Every province of Canada is free. Canadians do not need to be liberated. ... Canada will remain united and will reject any effort to destroy her unity.

It is not possible to gauge the impact of this extraordinary crisis on the French separatist movement in Quebec, though De Gaulle lived to witness a dramatic act of terrorism in Canada. He died on 9 November 1970; in October the *Front de Libération Québeçois* (FLQ) organised a spectacular kidnapping, first of a British trade official, J. R. Cross, who was eventually released unharmed, and second, of the Quebec Labour Minister, Pierre Laporte (5 October and 10 October, performed by two different cells of the FLQ). Laporte was eventually found murdered—strangled and dumped in a car boot. Cross was released after 59 days. At first Trudeau refused the demand of half a million dollars in gold and safe passage out of Canada for the terrorists. Later, Cross's seven kidnappers were flown to Cuba. Laporte's killers were found. Invoking the War Measures Act, Trudeau had set up a vast manhunt for the FLQ men, a controversial step in peacetime. While this kidnapping was but one of many in the world at large, a world of dramatic gestures and terrorism by countless groups, its foundations lay in three hundred years of Canadian history.

US economic penetration of Canada

The second major issue that De Gaulle pointed to in 1967 was the US influence over Canada. From the 1950s US investments in her northern neighbour had begun to expand markedly. In 1956 one estimate was that almost half of all Canadian manufacturing was foreign-owned, and the

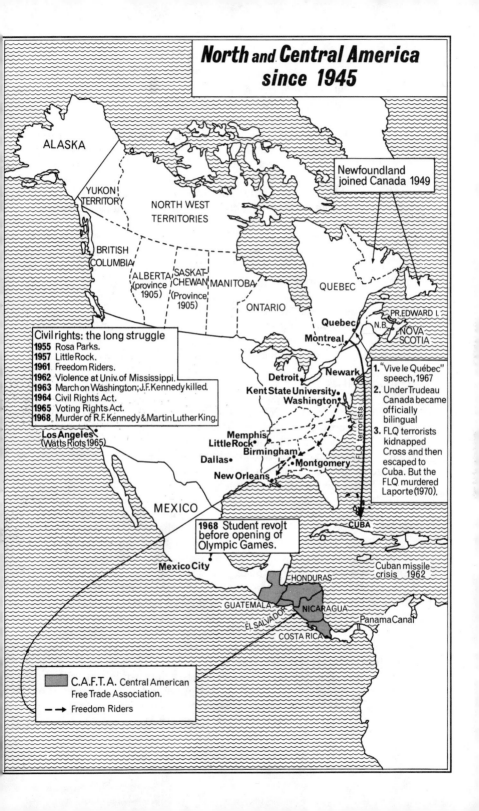

North and Central America since 1945

Newfoundland joined Canada 1949

ALASKA

YUKON TERRITORY

NORTH WEST TERRITORIES

BRITISH COLUMBIA

ALBERTA (province 1905)

SASKAT CHEWAN (Province 1905)

MANITOBA

ONTARIO

QUEBEC

PR. EDWARD I.

N.B.

NOVA SCOTIA

Quebec

Montreal

Civil rights: the long struggle
1955 Rosa Parks.
1957 Little Rock.
1961 Freedom Riders.
1962 Violence at Univ. of Mississippi.
1963 March on Washington; J.F. Kennedy killed.
1964 Civil Rights Act.
1965 Voting Rights Act.
1968 Murder of R.F. Kennedy & Martin Luther King.

Detroit

Newark

Kent State University

Washington

1. "Vive le Québec" speech, 1967
2. Under Trudeau Canada became officially bilingual
3. FLQ terrorists kidnapped Cross and then escaped to Cuba. But the FLQ murdered Laporte (1970).

Los Angeles (Watts Riots 1965)

Memphis
Little Rock
Dallas
Birmingham
Montgomery
New Orleans

MEXICO

1968 Student revolt before opening of Olympic Games.

CUBA

Cuban missile crisis 1962

Mexico City

HONDURAS

GUATEMALA

NICARAGUA

EL SALVADOR

PanamaCanal

COSTA RICA

C.A.F.T.A. Central American Free Trade Association.

- - -> Freedom Riders

other half foreign-controlled. 'Foreign' meant largely US. Thus the important management decisions for large sectors of the economy were made outside Canada, for non-Canadian reasons. Sixty per cent of all dividends paid out in Canada were said to go to non-residents.

On the other hand, US capital had helped the Canadian economy to grow and had been initially welcomed. One problem was that such foreign capital went into selected areas—mainly primary products (metals, timber, petroleum) and some secondary manufactures (auto-mobiles, rubber for example). Because US capitalists quite naturally chose to invest in sectors of Canada complementary to the US economy, their investments could only perpetuate the 'neo-colonial' status of Canada, or so many Canadians believed. Nevertheless the Canadian economy grew. Per capita income in Canada made that nation one of the two richest in the world. How to maintain friendship and creative economic partnership with the United States, and yet survive as an autonomous nation and a free economy was the problem for future decades. As a nation Canada was unique and distinguishable, with a clearly different and remarkable history, despite the encroachments of popular culture from the United States, despite economic penetration, and despite defence commitments and foreign policy constraints.

National values

National values change but slowly. However, in the United States and other nations in the 1960s a 'Youth Movement' of large proportions seemed to presage some sort of social revolution, if not a political or economic upheaval. Lessons learned in civil rights struggles and from black leaders encouraged youth organisations. Violence broke out on college campuses from 1964 (Berkeley), organised by groups with shifting aims, but always united in opposition to the draft and the Vietnam war, and always rising in militancy. The best schools suffered the most damage, especially the most expensive private colleges and universities. Consequently, critics complained of 'rich radicals'. This charge of 'elite radicalism', usually implying as the opposite, 'blue-collar' or 'ethnic' commonsense on the part of the 'mainstream', was kept alive up to 1972 and played a large role in the defeat of Senator George McGovern in the presidential campaign of that year. By then the campus violence had long since vanished. The radicalism of American students was undercut considerably by President Nixon's reform of the draft after 1968 and by his withdrawal, however slowly, of American troops from Vietnam.

As American radical groups began to break up and factionalize, small splinter-organisations, like the 'Weathermen' faction of the Students for a Democratic Society (SDS), turned to urban vandalism and to bombing. They eventually vanished underground and were unheard of by the early 1970s. When President Nixon ordered an invasion of Cambodia in April 1970, student protests did flare up again. At Kent State University in

Ohio national guardsmen shot and killed four students. The revived student movement did not last very long. In truth, the most extreme and violent groups lacked any contact with the grass-roots—either with the growing National Welfare Rights Organisation of the truly poor, or with the black civil rights movement. Black leaders usually rejected the student radicals as 'adventurists' and romantics, self-indulgent kids, wearing the clothes of the poor as a sort of game. Perhaps many in the various youth movements were simply 'ego-tripping' (in the language of the day). Certainly the black liberation movement had more to do with bringing about the subtle changes in national values in the 1960s than did white student groups. Yet together they did produce a noticeable alteration of US public attitudes towards a whole range of topics: minority rights, individual freedoms in matters of dress, sexual habits and deviations, and women's place in society. How profound and permanent such changes in values were, was not certain by the early 1970s.

Politically there is no doubt that youth support for the candidacy of Senator Eugene McCarthy within the Democratic party in 1968 did much to unseat President Lyndon Johnson as leader. The outcome was a victory for Richard Nixon and the Republicans in the election, but the *constituencies* of which all politicians now had to take note, had been greatly multiplied in number. Early in the 1970s political managers became anxious about youth and many pressed for extending the vote to 18-year olds. Only a low percentage of these new voters even bothered to go to the polls in 1972, and when they did, many of them voted for Nixon as president. The youth aura of his opponent, Senator George McGovern, did not carry him very far in terms of votes, even among younger people.

In the commercial consumer culture of the US mass media, the 'revolution' was rapidly assimilated. Youth and black liberation phrases, such as 'Right On!', and later women's liberation slogans, were captured by advertisers and immediately adopted for selling deodorants or other merchandise on television. Consumer pressures in the 1960s and 70s, in that society increasingly obsessed with pleasure, with individual 'liberations' of many kinds, and with sex, eroticism and violence, made that old American bugaboo 'revolution' a saleable commodity.

The continuing contrasts, North and South

To many people in other parts of the Americas outside Canada and the United States, such intense concern for personal freedoms, for ecology, for women's rights, for student responsibilities, for toleration of homosexuals, for individualistic 'life-styles' and 'consciousness-raising', for all these and more, was pure luxury. The rich northern half of the hemisphere went through a subtle change of values but the southern portion continued to struggle for economic survival. In the forests and jungles, in the mountains of the Andes and along the tropical coast-lands, the life-

THE FACTS OF LIFE

	Birth rate (Live-births per 1,000 persons)	Death rate (Deaths per 1,000 persons, excluding stillbirths)	Infant mortality (Deaths of infants under one year old per 1,000 livebirths)
USA (1970)	18.2	9.4	19.8
Canada (1969)	17.5	7.3	19.3
Argentina (1967)	21.7	8.8	58.3
Chile (1968)	26.6	9.0	91.6
Colombia ⎫	44.6	10.6	70.4
Costa Rica ⎬ (1965–70)	45.1	7.6	67.1
Ecuador ⎭	44.9	11.4	91.0
Guatemala (1970)	39.0	15.0	88.4
Mexico (1970)	43.4	9.9	68.5
Peru ⎫ (1965–70)	41.8	11.1	72.5
Venezuela ⎭	40.9	7.8	46.9

Source: US Bureau of Census: *Statistical Abstract of the US, 1972* (Washington, D.C., 1972).

Note: The combined population of Central and South America was about 300 million by 1970 and is projected to exceed 550 million by the year 2000, at its present high rate of growth.

and-death struggle for a material existence continued unabated. In the wealthier nations like Argentina or Mexico, intense hardship and poverty, malnutrition and illiteracy were still being fought; in other nations conditions were far worse. Modern medicine, often supplied through US foundation aid, helped prolong life but did not provide the means for a decent existence. The massive reforms and social legislation of the Kennedy-Johnson years pushed the US towards higher standards of material civilisation, comfort and tolerance, despite the tensions and violence of the day. American public attention was drawn back to conditions in Central and South America only by dramatic events like the sudden fear of 'communism' occasioned by the democratic election of the avowed Marxist Salvador Allende in Chile in 1970, or by the tragic and fearful earthquake which wiped out the city of Managua, Nicaragua at Christmas, 1972.

After the 1972 re-election President Nixon, now totally absorbed in international manoeuvring and the politics of *détente*, cut back most of the reforms of the Great Society years—civil rights, education, welfare and cultural programmes—and paid no attention to South America, except to revive the counter-revolutionary attitudes of the 1950s. Nixon warned nations south of the border not to attempt to emulate Chile, Peru, Ecuador and Bolivia in 'expropriating' the assets of US corporations. If they did so, he threatened, all aid would be cut off and the US would block attempts by such nations to borrow from the Inter-American Development Bank. He continued a measure of military aid to Chile after

INEQUALITY IN THE WESTERN HEMISPHERE

	Year of estimate	Calories per day	Food Availability (Pounds available per year)			Homes with piped water	Public Education spending as % of GNP, 1969	Gross Domestic Product per head, in US $. (Current rates of exchange) 1970
			Cereals	Potatoes	Meats			
USA	(1969)	3,290	145	101	243	94% (1970)	6.3%	$4,734
Argentina	(1967)	3,170	220	199	259	53.1% (1960)	2.0%	974 (1969)
Canada	(1969)	3,150	147	168	204	95.2% (1967)	8.9%	3,676
Uruguay	(1964–6)	3,020	209	140	274	—	2.0% (1968)	816
Mexico	(1964–6)	2,620	305	28	44	49.4% (1970)	—	668
Brazil	(1966–8)	2,540	184	406	73	32.8% (1970)	—	362
Chile	(1964–6)	2,520	286	146	66	62% (1960)	4.6%	681
Venezuela	(1966)	2,490	204	270	65	67.1% (1961)	4.5%	979
Peru	(1967)	2,200	185	455	51	21.1% (1961)	4.2%	398
Bolivia	(1964–6)	1,760	192	339	49	—	—	194 (1969)

Source: US. Bureau of Census: *Statistical Abstract of the US, 1972* (Washington, D.C., 1972).

257

Allende's election because he did not wish to alienate the Chilean military élite. The giant US international conglomerate, ITT (International Telephone and Telegraph) was justly accused by Chileans and others of plotting to prevent Allende's election, and when Allende was brought down by the military in 1973, ITT was undergoing investigation by Congress. So was President Richard Nixon himself, in the gigantic 'Watergate' conspiracy. The White House was accused of involvement in a variety of wild schemes, ranging from tax evasion to an attempt to fix the 1972 election by disrupting opposition meetings and 'bugging' the headquarters of the Democratic Party. As the charges widened and it was revealed in 1973–74 that widespread use of electronic listening devices and extra-legal methods has been adopted by White House employees, credibility in the word of the US government fell to its lowest ebb in history. To some extent the frank public investigations of these misdoings served to show the world that most Americans at least, really believed in the democratic system, whatever the temporary occupants of high office felt. In August 1974 President Nixon partly confessed his involvement in covering up Watergate and in obstructing justice. He resigned in mid-term and was replaced by conservative Vice-President G. Ford who faced the serious challenges of inflation with recession ('stagflation') at home, and approaching communist victories in Cambodia and Vietnam.

For South Americans the Watergate scandal, though it exposed ITT intrigues against Allende, was of less importance than the US policy of placing them too low on the scale in matters of foreign aid. Nixon's absorption in Great Power politics did nothing to alter the balance of US foreign aid programmes, in which nations like S. Korea or S. Vietnam received so much attention. The irony of US fears for its alleged security in far-off SE Asia was compounded when the administration, anxious to pull out of Vietnam, announced a vague plan and promise of billions in aid to reconstruct Vietnam, North and South, once the war was over. For US troops at least, the war was finally over in January 1973. No massive aid followed, but there was no doubt that US policy-makers would continue to favour SE Asia over South America.

Economic retardation—the tragedy of South America

During the consumer boom years of the 1950s and 60s in Canada and the US, Brazil and Argentina suffered economic retardation and paralysis. What happened to the industrialization process in South America? Since the world depression of the 1930s, in which relative prices of agricultural staples and primary products declined, some South American countries began to encourage a degree of industrialisation to make up for imports for which they could no longer pay (not being able to earn as much from exports of their primary products). Often the industrialisation was brought about by foreign, chiefly US, companies building subsidiary

branches in South America and manufacturing there, instead of manufacturing in the US and shipping their manufactures to the south. This
form of 'import-substitution' industrialization had some advantages for
the nations concerned; it did begin to provide necessary goods and jobs.
But it brought grave dangers too and most of the benefits accrued to the
international corporations.

In truth, import-substitution could be a mere *pseudo*-industrialisation
which did not bring modernisation in its wake. If it was not based on a
growing home market, it did not lead to an enlarged middle class and the
spread of wealth and purchasing-power throughout the population. The
modernisation of some sectors of the economy did not spread to other
sectors. Instead, small, highly developed import-substituting industries,
foreign-controlled, stood out like islands in peasant and pre-industrial
societies. American fixed investments in South America (actual subsidiary installations of US firms) increased in value from $780,000,000
to $2,714,000,000 between 1950 and 1965, the heaviest fixed investments
being found in Mexico, Brazil and Argentina—nations not marked by
general economic growth. Even where the total dollar value of US fixed
investment was smaller, the impact was great in small nations like Peru,
Colombia or Venezuela. In a range of products like chemicals and transportation equipment, American companies created direct subsidiaries in
South America and substituted their manufactures there for imports.

This sort of economic evolution separated the particular industries
from the rest of the national economy and exaggerated still further internal social and economic splits within the nation concerned. Worse,
national decision-making was seriously weakened. Giant international
conglomerates could take grave decisions which deeply affected the
future of Venezuela, or Brazil or some other country, and base their
decisions on matters of no importance whatsoever to that nation. An
investment or business decision would necessarily be based on the international affairs of the corporation. Nations which encouraged or permitted this form of pseudo-industrialisation thus lost a measure of independence and national dignity. US and Canadian growth had been
based on the satisfaction of a large home market which grew out of mass
immigration, territorial expansion and the spreading of the benefits of
industrialisation to wider sectors of the population—the consumer
revolution based on purchasing-power and credit. This was lacking in
South America and no genuine industrialisation, which would bring
modernisation in its wake, could come without it. The social structure
and income-distribution patterns of South American nations were too
often little affected by pseudo-industrialisation. In this framework one
can grasp the reasons for the aborted economic take-off of Argentina and
the economic paralysis of Brazil in the 1960s.

By the 1970s many nationalist-minded leaders in South America were
aware of these conditions, though the way out of their economic predica-

ment would not be easy given the structure of world trade. The bulk of international trade in the 1970s took place not between the developed and the less developed nations but among the developed nations themselves. Advanced industrial nations no longer had the growing, elastic demand for primary products they had in the 19th century. Even the advanced technology they could offer to the less developed world was not always useful, being essentially labour-saving and capital-intensive. There was however a growing *global* scarcity of raw materials which could change the relative trading position of South American exporters, as fuel scarcity had transformed the Arab situation after 1973.

While harsh, military, right-wing regimes controlled leading nations in the early 1970s (like Brazil, and Chile after Allende) and Peronism had returned temporarily to Argentina, the long-run tide of change was in favour of a trend towards socialism. For the 'other' Americans south of the Rio Grande some sort of socialist future seemed not unlikely, as the growth of Christian Socialism in several nations illustrated: the *Golconda* movement in Colombia, the *Onis* movement in Peru, the work of the MAS (Movement Towards Socialism) group in Venezuela, Chile's Catholic Marxists and Argentina's 'Third World Priests'. These groups were often badly persecuted, as in Brazil and Chile, but they seemed likely to survive and to combine socialism, nationalism and the Faith in a powerful appeal for national renewal. The much higher level of politicisation in the world at large, the richer examples of Canada and the United States, to say nothing of Western Europe and Japan, the new example of Arab united action, and the infuriating economic policies of the North Americans, could only serve to raise popular expectations and produce boiling resentments in the 1970s. That combination of nationalism, raised expectations, economic underdevelopment, inequality, and population pressure could not be held in check for long.

A Bookshelf of Readings

There are countless textbooks of US history, of which Hofstadter, Miller and Aaron's *The American Republic* (Englewood Cliffs, N. J.: Prentice-Hall, 1959) is excellent for cultural and literary history, and the classic two volumes of *The American Republic* by Morison and Commager, now revised by Leuchtenburg (Oxford: OUP, 1969), remain outstanding in their thoroughness. Shorter introductions include J. M. Blum *et al.*, *The National Experience* (New York: Harcourt, 1973) and my own *The United States* (Homewood, Ill.: Dorsey, 1975). Good on recent history is Walter Nugent's *Modern America* (Boston: Houghton Mifflin, 1973). Economic history is dealt with in short compass in Peter d'A Jones, *The Consumer Society: A History of American Capitalism* (Baltimore and Harmondsworth: Penguin, 1967). Good readings and documents are to be found in Quint, Albertson and Cantor's *Main Problems in American History* (Homewood, Ill.: Dorsey, 1972). My own *The Robber Barons Revisited* (Boston: Heath, 1968) offers edited readings on business leadership in the late 19th century and a brief essay-review of the problem. The best account of the black experience is still John Hope Franklin's classic *From Slavery to Freedom* (New York: Vintage, 1969).

To be introduced to the Canadian story, read the well-known text by J. B. Brebner, *Canada* (Ann Arbor: U. of Michigan Press, 1960). Brebner however is unsympathetic towards French Canada. Donald Creighton's lively and opinionated *Canada's First Century* (Toronto: Macmillan, 1970) is good reading. A varied set of essays is J. M. S. Careless and R. Craig Brown (eds.), *The Canadians, 1867–1967* (Toronto: Macmillan, 1967). The briefest history is *Canada: A Modern Study* by Ramsay Cook with J. T. Saywell and J. C. Ricker (Toronto: Clarke, Irwin, 1963). Among the many suggestive readings try to see Peter Russell (ed.), *Nationalism in Canada* (Toronto: McGraw-Hill, 1966) and John Meisel's *Working Papers on Canadian Politics* (Montreal and London: McGill-Queen's University Press, 1972). Mason Wade's *The International Megalopolis* presents the reports of the 8th University of Windsor Seminar on Canadian-American Relations, which discussed the

Detroit-Windsor area (Toronto: University of Toronto Press, 1969). This problem of transnational urbanisation illustrates clearly the growing impossibility of merely national history in the present century. For economic history a useful survey volume is W. T. Easterbrook and Hugh G. J. Aitken, *Canadian Economic History* (Toronto: Macmillan, 1956). For readers who know little of Canada and for those who know a good deal alike, the essay volume by W. L. Morton, *The Canadian Identity* (Madison: U. of Wisconsin Press, 1961) will be stimulating.

Among the textbook surveys of Central and South America one of the shortest, but by an authority, is Lewis Hanke's *South America* (2 vols., New York: Van Nostrand, 1967). A quick overview of regional problems is Frank Tannenbaum's *Ten Keys To Latin America* (New York: Vintage, 1962). One older textbook still used in the US is the late Hubert Herring's *History of Latin America* (New York: Knopf, 1968) which is better for earlier than for more recent decades. For the arts, of great significance in the region, a short introduction is Leopoldo Castedo's *History of Latin American Art and Architecture* (New York: Praeger, 1969). The fate of Indians is treated in the classic of Las Casas now available in paperback; one version is edited by A. M. Collard: Bartolomé De Las Casas, *History of the Indies* (New York: Harper, 1971). Additional readings to enrich the story include Charles Gibson (ed), *The Black Legend: Anti-Spanish Attitudes in the Old World and the New* (New York: Knopf, 1971). A great Brazilian classic on slavery is Gilberto Freyre's *The Masters and The Slaves* (New York: Knopf, 1964). For the view of Columbus as predator see C. O. Sauer's *Early Spanish Main* (Berkeley: U. of California Press, 1966).

Good paperback histories of individual nations, to which I owe much, include James R. Scobie's *Argentina: A City and A Nation* (New York: Oxford, 1971), R. E. Poppino's *Brazil* (New York: Oxford, 1968), Charles Cumberland's *Mexico: The Struggle for Modernity* (New York: Oxford, 1968) and Howard F. Cline's *Mexico: Revolution to Evolution* (New York: Oxford, 1963). See also a special monograph by Ramón E. Ruiz, *Mexico: The Challenge of Poverty and Illiteracy* (San Marino: Huntington Library, 1963). There are many readings on economic problems, including paperback editions, by Josué de Castro, *Death in the Northeast* (New York: Vintage 1969) on the extremes of poverty in Brazil; Ernest Feder, *The Rape of The Peasantry* (New York: Anchor, 1971) on landholding; and R. Stavenhagen (ed.), *Agrarian Problems and Peasant Movements in Latin America* (New York: Anchor, 1970). Two outstanding economic interpretations whose influence can be seen on my pages are the brilliant short volume by Stanley J. and Barbara Stein, *The Colonial Heritage of Latin America* (New York: Oxford, 1970), which goes far beyond its title in scope, and the work of the Brazilian economist in exile, Celso Furtado, *Economic Development of Latin America* (New York: Cambridge University Press, 1970) and *Obstacles to Development in Latin America* (New

York: Anchor, 1970). These authors develop the concepts of 'neo-colonialism' and 'import-substitution' industrialization. The ideas on the need for expansion of internal national markets (which I use at the end of the volume) link up with the major theme of my interpretation of US economic history, *The Consumer Society*.

Two explosive themes are illustrated in readings by Luis E. Aguilar (ed.), *Marxism in Latin America* (New York: Knopf, 1968) and by S. L. Baily (ed.), *Nationalism in Latin America* (New York: Knopf, 1971). See also I. L. Horowitz *et al.*, (eds.), *Latin American Radicalism* (New York: Vintage, 1969). For the Cuban revolution see Ramón E. Ruiz, *Cuba: The Making of a Revolution* (Amherst: U. of Massachusetts Press, 1968) and the brilliant attack on US policy by the late C. Wright Mills, *Listen, Yankee!* (New York: Ballantine, 1960). For recent revolutionary changes in Chile (overturned in 1973) see Régis Debray, *The Chilean Revolution: Conversations with Allende* (New York: Vintage, 1971). Naturally, those readers who know Spanish and or Portuguese are at a great advantage in understanding South America; I have not tried to list writings in Spanish but have confined the list to publications in English. The serious student will desire to read works by South Americans in the original. Is there a common experience in the Western Hemisphere? Or are the many re-publics of the West too different and varied for common treatment? This classic problem is dealt with in a good collection of readings which centre on the theories of the late Professor Herbert Bolton of California: Lewis Hanke (ed.), *Do The Americans Have A Common History?* (New York: Knopf, 1964). The reader must make up his or her own mind on this question. My own views are explicit enough in the text. Students will no doubt treat my conclusions and predictions with the correct degree of modern scepticism.

INDEX

ABC nations, 144, 148, 151, 188, 197
Aberhart, William, 179
abolitionist movement, 48, 100f; Brazil
    82, 130
Academy of Science, Argentina, 122
Acadia, *see* Nova Scotia
Acción Democrática, 220f
Adams, John, 63f, 65, 68, 94
Adams, Sam, 61f, 64f
advertising, US, 255
Africa, 16f, 48, 111f, 140, 152, 155, 168;
    see also Negroes
Agrarian Reform Act, 1964 (Peru), 213
Agricultural Adjustment Administration
    (AAA), 172
Agriculture, Dept of (US), 105; Ministry
    of (Argentina), 149
Aguinaldo, 141
Aguirre Cerdá, Pres., 198
AID, 240
Alabama, 96, 99
Alamo, 23, 114
Alarcón, Juan Ruiz de, 46
Alaska, 3, 58
Alberdi, Juan Bautista, 121f
Alberta, 145, 178f, 249
alcabalas, 148
alcalde mayores, 19
Aleijadinho, 82
Alem, L. N., 150
Alemán, Pres., 243
Alessandri, Jorge, 197f
Aleutians, 3, 59, 142
alfalfa, 149f

Algeria, 200
Algonquin Indians, 27f
Alien and Seditions Acts (1798), 94
Allende, Pres. Salvador, 198, 200f, 239,
    256, 258, 260; 201 *illn.*
Alliance for Progress, 199, 228, 237, 240f,
    242
Alsace-Lorraine, 161
altiplano, 127, 214
Amazon, 118, 152, 202f, 213
amendments to US Constitution, *14th* 105,
    244; *15th* 105; *18th* 163
American Antislavery Society, 101
American Civil War, *see* Civil War
American Dream, 31, 85f, 135
American Federation of Labor (AFL),
    136, 159, 165, 174
'Americanisation', 43
American Plan, 162
American self-consciousness, 5, 44, 51f,
    67
'American system of manufacture', 96
Anderson, Jack, 200
Andes, 4, 10f, 24, 75f, 90, 118, 122, 125f,
    148, 209f, 213, 218, 255
Andros, Gov., 41
'Anglo-America', 3, 55
Anglo-American mystique, 158
Anglo-conformity, 135
Anglo-French wars, 93
Angola, 16f
Angostura, Congress of (1819), 76
anticlericalism, 47, 80, 118f, 185, 191,
    209f, 218

anti-communism, 162, 224, 232f, 243; *see also* Containment
anti-draft agitation, *US*, 159, 254; *Canada*, 160, 229
Antioquia, 218
Anti-Re-Election Party, 181, 184
anti-Semitism, 204
anti-*Yanqui* feelings, 211
APRA movement, Peru, 212f
Arab-Israeli war, 1967, 195
Arab oil states, 260
Aramburu, Pres. P., 245
Arawak Indians, 10
Araucanian Indians, 10, 46, 148f
Arbenz, Pres. J., 226
architecture, 24f, 44f, 205
Arctic, Canadian, 145
Arévalo, Pres. J. J., 226
Argentina, 3f, 12, 17, 72, 75f, 79, 81, 84, 90, 101f, 111f, 119f, 124, 133, 144, 148f, 149 *map*, 156f, 188f, 195, 197, 202, 205, 217, 226, 228, 241, 243f, 256, 258f; *see also* Plata, Rio de la
Argentine Dream, 111, 189, 191
Arias, Archbishop R., 221
Ariel, 147, 166, 211
Arizona, 102
Armory Show, 166
Army of the Andes, 76
army, role in politics: *Argentina*, 190, 192f, 245; *Brazil*, 202f, 204f, 260; *Chile*, 197f, 260; *Ecuador*, 210; *Uruguay*, 194, 196; *Venezuela*, 220f
Arroyo, Father G. 202
art 24, 46, 82, 166, 184, 211
Articles of Confederation (US) 85
Artigas, José, 124
Ashcan School, 166
Athabascan Indians, 169 *map*
Atitlan, Lake (Guatemala), 225 *illn.*
atomic bomb, 231f
atrocities, Brazil, 208
Attucks, Crispus, 62f
audiencias, 18f, 20 *map*
automobile industry: *US*, 164; *Brazil*, 208; *Venezuela*, 223
Axis powers, 188, 205
Ayacucho, battle of (1824), 75
Aymará Indian language, 4, 83, 127
Aztecs, 10f, 184

Back country, 55f
Bacon's Rebellion (1676), 42, 55f
Bahamas, 32
Bahía, 16, 79f, 82, 152
Bailén, 72
Baldwin, James, 166
Balmaceda, Pres., 150
Baltimore, Maryland, 54
Baltimore, Lord (George Calvert), 39
banana plantations, 116, 125f, 204, 209, 224
'banana republics', 90, 116
Banda Oriental (Uruguay), 120
bandeirantes, 16, 24, 80, 82, 97f
Baranov, A., 59
Barbados, 34f, 35 *map*
baroque style, 43f
Barrientes, Gen., 215, 217
Barrios, J. R., 116f
Baptists, 41
Basque immigrants, 83, 121
Batista, Pres. F., 237
Batlle y Ordóñes, Pres. J., 194f
Battle of Britain, 228
Bay of Pigs, 200, 237
Beecher, Rev. Lyman, 100
Belaúnde Terry, Pres. F., 212f
Bellamy, Edward, 137
Bennett, Prime Minister R. B., 178f
Bering, Capt. V., 57f
Bétancourt, Pres. Rómulo, 220f
bicycle mania, 202
Big Stick policies, 158
bilingualism, Canada, 170, 227, 248f
Bill of Rights, US, 84, 98
bills of exchange, 54f
Birmingham, Alabama, 247
Bishop of Pernambuco, 208
bishoprics, Anglican, 67f
Black abolitionists, 101
Black Boy, 165
Black Americans (US), *see* Negroes
Black Codes, 105f
Black Hawk War, 97
Black Hills, S. Dakota, 57
Black, Justice Hugo, 174
'Black is Beautiful' movement, 166
Black Legend, 22
Black Muslims, 248
blancos, 113, 124

'Bleeding Kansas', 104
bleus, 146
Blue Eagle, 172
Board of Trade, 53
Bogotá, 76, 117, 119, 218f, 219 *illn*.
boleadores, 119
Bolívar, Simón, 68f, 117, 127
Bolivia, 3f, 75f, 78, 90, 120, 127, 156, 191, 214f, 241, 256; 214 *map*
booms, economic: *Argentina*, 152; *Canada*, 80, 146, 168, 245; *Chile*, 151, 197; *Ecuador*, 209; *US*, 134, 163f, 236; 245
Bonaparte, Joseph, 71
Bonus marchers (1931), 171
Bordaberry, Pres. J. M., 196
Borden, R. L., 160
Boston, Massachusetts, 41, 44, 53, 61f
Boston Massacre (1770), 62f
Boston Tea Party (1773), 63
Boulder Dam, 171
Bradford, Gov. W., 37
Bragança, House of, 81, 130
Brattle Street Church, Boston, 41
Bray, T. 67
Brasília, 206f
Brazil, 3f, 16f, 30, 43, 48, 51, 71, 79f, 81, 83 *map*, 84, 98f, 106, 124, 129f, 133, 144, 150f, 156, 191, 194, 202f, 203 *map*, 241f, 258f, 260
bread colonies, 54f
Brewster, William, 36
Bristol, 29, 55
Broom Farm, 100
Brown, George, 146
Brown, John, 101
Brown v. Board of Education of Topeka (1954), 245
British Columbia, 109 *map*, 145, 179, 230f, 249
British interests in Western Hemisphere, 3, 18, 29f, 71f, 78f, 85, 89f, 120, 158f; *Argentina*, 191; *Brazil*, 129, 152, 202; *Canada*, 145, 168; *Chile*, 151; *Ecuador*, 209; *British Guiana*, 83; *Mexico*, 143f, 181, 187; *Peru*, 126f, 210; *Uruguay*, 124, 194f; *Venezuela*, 220, *see also* West Indies
British North America Act (1867), 59, 90, 106, 110, 145, 158
Bryan, William Jennings, 138

Buenos Aires, 20, 72, 76, 112, 119f, 122, 124, 149f, 188, 190f, 192
Bulnes, Pres. Manuel, 125
Bunker's Hill, battle of, 65
bureaucracy, 52, 228f
Burgesses, House of (Virginia), 33, 39, 61
Burke, E., 60
Burnt-Over District (New York), 100
business (US), 31f, 85, 117, 134, 136, 146, 159, 163f, 178, 200, 224, 226, 228f, 232, 258, 261
business, schools of, 134
Bustamente, Pres., 212

cabildos, 19f, 52, 72, 112
Cabot, John, 29
cacao boom, 209
caciques, 9, 11, 17, 21, 185
Cadiz, 13, 52, 72
Caldera, Prof. R., 222
Galgary, Alberta, 179
Calhoun, John C., 95, 102
California, 102f, 117, 230, 236
California Oil Co., 191
callampas, 199
Callao, Peru, 12
Calles, Plutarco, 85f, 243
Calvinism, 100
Camacho, Pres. A., 188
câmaras, 79
Cambodian invasion (1970), 254
campesinos, 215
Campillo, J., 52
campus riots, 254f
Canada, 3, 5, 44, 53, 56f, 60f, 63f, 65, 84f, 90, 92, 95, 106f, 112, 114, 140, 145f, 155f, 158f, 168f, 227f, 229, 248f; *French Canada*, 3, 59, 108f, 145f, 156, 160, 169f, 179, 227, 229, 248f, *see also* Quebec, Ontario, bilingualism
Canada Act (1791), 66
Canadian army, 229
Canadian Pacific Railroad, 109 *map*, 145
Candango Monument, Brasília, 207 *illn*.
Candomblé, 82
Cape Breton Island, 57
Cape Cod, 36
capitalism, 85f, 90, 92f, 105, 134, 163f, 177f; *see also* business, industrialization
Captaincy-General of Chile, 20; of Cuba, 20

Carabobo, battle of (1821), 117
Caracas, 75f, 117f, 220f
Cárdenas, Pres. Lázaro, 185f, 189, 243
Carías, Gen., 224
Carnegie, Andrew, 134, 141
Carranza, Pres. V., 144, 182f
Carrera, Rafael, 116
carro completo, 181
Cartagena, 75, 119
Cartagena Manifesto (1812), 75
Cartier, Jacques, 26, 29
Casa de Contratación, 13f, 18, 48, 53
castas, 47f, 71, 82
caste war, 73
Castile, 5, 13, 19, 68
Castilla, Ramón, 126f
Castillo Armas, Gen., 226
Castro, Fidel, 157, 188, 199, 215, 221, 228, 236f, 242
Castroite agitators: Bolivia, 215f; Mexico, 243; Venezuela, 221
Catholic education, Canada, 146, 248f
Catholic Marxism, 202, 260
Catholics, US, 39f; Canada, 63f, 146, 248f
Catholic social action, 260; Chile, 199f; Venezuela 221f
caucus system, 96
caudillos, 17, 19, 34, 75f, 78, 85, 90, 111f, 114, 118f, 122, 126f, 144, 152, 156, 190, 220f, 224
cattle ranching, 80, 119f, 124, 145f, 149, 188, 193, 195
'Cavalier' South (US), 99
Cedillo, Gen. S., 187
Celman, J., 148f
Census of 1790 (US), 3, 44
Central America, 83 map, 116f, 223f
Central American common market, 241
Central American Federation, 116
Central Intelligence Agency (CIA), 156, 200, 224f, 237, 258
centralists, 112, 120
Ceylon, 204
Chacabuco, battle of (1817), 76
Chaco War, 214f
Champlain, 27f
chattel slavery, 48f, 99
Charles I, 39; II, 40f, 51; III, 20, 24, 52, 80; V, 9, 18
Charleston, S. C., 53, 63

checks and balances, 84
Cherokee Nation, 97
Chesapeake Bay, 31, 65
Chiang Kai-Shek, 233
Chibcha Empire, 10, 83
Chickasaw Indians, 42, 57
Chile, 5, 75f, 79, 84, 90, 113, 122, 125, 127, 143f, 150f, 188, 191, 197f, 210, 214 map, 217, 221, 241, 256, 258, 260
Chilpancingo Congress, 74
Chicago, 112, 135, 139, 161, 163, 170f, 248
Chicago race riot (1919), 161f
child labor (US), 139
children's aid, 101, 175
Children of Sanchez, 242
China, 141f, 155, 233
Chinese Immigration Act, 1923 (Canada), 169
cholos, 127, 209f
'Christ the King' movement, 185
Christian Democrats, 198f, 102, 221, 226
Christian socialism, 202, 260; see also Frei, socialism
Church of England, 30, 34
Church rôle in C. and S. America, 7, 11, 21f, 24f, 46f, 79, 90, 113f, 118f, 123, 130, 156, 200, 260; Argentina, 191f; Brazil, 208; Chile, 199f; Colombia, 218f; Ecuador, 126, 209; Guatemala, 116, 226; Mexico, 148, 185, 242; Peru, 210; Venezuela, 221f
churrigueresque style, 44f
científicos, 148, 181, 188
Cimarron Strip, 103 map
Cisneros, Cardinal, 9
city growth, 44, 53, 90, 106, 163f; Brazil, 202; Canada, 146f, 170; Mexico, 242; US, 133, 139; Venezuela, 223
city-rural tensions, 112f, 119
city reformers, 130f
'City Upon A Hill' (Puritan), 36
Ciudad Juárez, Mexico, 181
civil rights (US) 253 map; 159, 174, 177, 229f, 235, 241, 245f, 256
Civil Rights Act (1964), 247, 248
civil rights cases (1883), 106
Civilian Conservation Corps (CCC), 173
Civil War (England), 30, 39f
Civil War (US), 90, 96, 99, 101f, 104f, 110, 115, 242

INDEX

clear and present danger, legal doctrine,
159
Clear Grits, 146
Clay, Henry, 95, 102
Clayton Act (1914), 139
Clayton-Bulwer Treaty (1850), 116
clergy reserve, 108
Cochabamba, Bolivia, 217
cod fisheries, 26, 39, 55, 76
coffee plantations, 80, 90, 116, 129f, 150f,
202, 204, 218, 220, 224
Colbert, J. B., 28f, 52
Cold War, 156, 227f, 232f
Colt revolver, 96
Collier, John, 175
Colombia, 75f, 78f, 90, 102, 117, 126, 143,
214 map, 217f, 241, 259
Columbus, Christopher, 7f, 48, 143
Columbus, New Mexico, 144
colonialism, 6, 12f, 85, 116, 199, 202; see
also imperialism, neo-colonialism
Colonial Laws Validity Act (1865), 158
Cólonida movement, 211f
Colorado (US), 138
colorados, 113, 124, 194f
combine harvester, 137
committees of correspondence, 63
'Common Man' 95
Common Market, 196; for South America
155, 196; see also LAFTA
Commonwealth, British, 68, 160
communes, Indian, 15f, 186; US 100; see
also Jesuits
communism: Brazil, 204; Bolivia, 215;
Chile, 198f; Mexico, 184; Peru, 212f;
Venezuela, 222; US, 224, 227f
Company of 100 Associates (1627), 28
company unions, 162
Compromise of 1820, 96; of 1850, 102
Concord School, 100
Confederation of Canada (1867), 109 map
Confederación de Trabajadores Mex-
icanos, 186
Congregational church, 41
Congress of Industrial Organizations
(CIO), 174, 180
Connecticut, 25, 32, 35, 39, 53
conquistadores, 7, 37
Conrad, Joseph, 223
Conselheiro, A., 152

consensus (US), 235
conservation-ecology movement, 139, 173,
235, 255
Conservative Party: Canada, 146, 178f,
249; Colombia, 218
conservatives (US), 236
conspiracy fears, 67f, 162, 224
constitutions: 112f, 180; Argentina, (1853)
121, 190; Brazil, (1824) 81, (1891) 151,
202; Chile, (1833) 125, (1925) 197;
Colombia, (1821) 78, (1886) 119; Costa
Rica, (1871) 117; Ecuador, 126, (1906)
209; Mexico, (1824) 183, (1857) 115,
180, 183, (1917) 85, 144f, 182f, 185; US,
(1787) 56, 84f, 95, 101, 115; Uruguay,
(1917) 194f, (1951) 195f
consulados, 13f
consumer booms, 163f, 228, 232
consumer durables, 164, 208
consumer capitalism (US) 161f, 245
containment (creoles), 89f, 111f
containment (of communism), 232f
Continental Congresses, 65, 68
Contract Labor Law, 105
contracts, federal (US), 159, 178, 228f, 232
Coolidge, Pres. C., 162f, 166, 170
Cooperative Commonwealth Federation
(CCF), 179, 229
cooperatives (US), 134, 138, 228
COPEI, 222
copper industry: Chile, 151, 197f; Peru, 210
Cordoba, Argentina, 245
CORE, 247
Cornwallis, Lord, 65
coronéis, 112, 202
corregidores, 19, 21
Cortés, 10, 184
Costa, Lúcio, 205
Costa Rica, 3, 75, 83, 89, 113, 116f, 224
cotton, 80, 85, 95, 98f, 129f, 213
cotton gin, 95
Cotton, John, 41
Council of the Indies, 18f
Counter-Reformation, 21
cowboys, 76, 118f, 220
Crash, Great (1929), 134f
Creek Indians, 95
Creel, George, 159
Creoles, 12f, 19f, 51, 71f, 73f, 79f, 89f,
111f, 131f

Cristeros, 185
Croatoan, 29
Cromwell, Oliver, 26, 40f
Cross, J. R., 252
Cruz, Juana Inés de la, 46
Cuautla, Mexico, 181
Cuba, 16, 48f, 83, 99, 104, 140f, 142, 152,
   156f, 193, 198f, 200, 215, 221, 237f, 239,
   map, 241, 252
Cuban missile crisis (1962), 228, 237f, 238
   illn.
Cuernavaca, Mexico, 184
cubist-realists (US), 166
Cullen, Countee, 166
culture-contact, 97
culture-shock, 10f
Cunha, E. da, 152
Curaçao, 16f
curacas, 11
currency reform, 137f, 139
Custer, S. Dakota, 177
Cuzco, 10

Dakota, South, 137, 176f, 195, North 165
Daniels, Amb. Josephus, 187
Danish colonies, 84
Dare, Virginia, 29
Darío, Rubén, 211
Dawes Act (1887), 175
dealership organisations (US), 134
Debs, Eugene V., 136
debtors, 101
debt-peonage, 15, 106, 111, 139
decena, la, 182
declension, Puritan, 41
Declaration of Independence (US), *see*
   independence
Declaratory Act, 62
deficit spending, 172f, 178; *see also*
   Keynes, New Deal
De Gaulle, Pres. Charles, 252f
Delaware, 32
De Leon, Daniel, 136
De Lôme Letter, 140f
De Mello, Admiral, 151
Democratic national convention (1968),
   248
demographic catastrophe, 9f, 10 *map*
Demuth, Charles, 166
Denmark Vesey plot (1822), 99

Department of Defense (US), 236f, 240
depopulation, 9f
depression: 1890s 146, 1930s 143, 156,
   170f, 178f, 198, 205 (*Brazil*), 218, 258
descamisados, 190
Dessalines, Pres., 69
détente, 256f
Detroit race riot (*1943*) 230; (*1967*) 248
Dewey, Admiral, 141
De Witt, General, 230
Dia, El, 194
diamond strikes, Brazil, 80
Díaz, B., 46
Díaz, Porfirio, 90, 112, 116, 148, 157, 180f,
   188, 220
Dickinson, John, 62
Diefenbaker, Prime Minister John, 249
differentiation in the Americas, 82f, 89f,
   passim
discrimination, racial, 160f, 229f, 245f
Divine Right of kings, 5, 26, 30
dollar diplomacy, 187
Dolores, Mexico, 73
Dominican Republic (Santo Domingo),
   9, 22f, 71, 142f, 199f, 221, 224
Dominion status, British, 68, 110, 160
Doña Barbara, 221
Dongan, Gov. T., 56
Dos Passos, J., 166
Douglas, Major C. H., 179
Douglas, Senator Stephen, 102, 104f
Douglass, Frederick, 101
draft laws (US) 159, (Canada) 160
draft resistance (US) 159, 254, (Canada)
   229
Drake, Sir F., 29
DuBois, W. E. B., 168
Dukhobors, 168
Duquesne, Fort (Pittsburgh), 57
Durham Report, 108f, 251
Duplessis, Maurice, 179
Dutch colonies, 15f, 24f, 29, 79, 82, 84
Dutch Guiana, 83
Dutch West Indies Co., 16

earthquakes: Lisbon (1775) 80, Chile
   (1939) 198, Nicaragua (1972) 256
Eastern Europe, 233
East India Co., 40, 63
East St. Louis race riot (1917), 161

ecology, *see* Conservation
economic growth: *Argentina*, 121, 148f, 188, 191; *Brazil*, 130f, 208; *Canada*, 146f, 168, 248f; *Colombia*, 219; *Ecuador*, 209; *Guatemala*, 116f; *Mexico*, 148, 180f, 188, 241f; *Peru*, 127; *US*, 85, 94f, 115, 158f, 163f, 232; *Uruguay*, 195; *Venezuela*, 118, 220, 222f
economic miracles, Western Europe, 185
Ecuador, 3, 23, 46, 76f, 89f, 113, 117, 125f, 209f, 214 *map*, 241, 256
education, public, 132, 180; *Argentina*, 122f, 192; *Ecuador*, 209; *Mexico*, 184; *US*, 165, 235
Education, Ministry of, Brazil, 205
Eisenhower, Pres. Dwight D., 193, 221, 231, 235, 237, 247
ejidos, 115, 148, 186f
El Cóndor Pasa, 212
elections: *Argentina*, 192, (1868) 121, (1958) 192, (1960) 193, (1962) 193, (1973) 245; *Canada*, (1896) 146, (1957, 1963, 1968) 249; *Chile*, (1932) 197, (1946, 1958) 198, (1964) 199, (1970) 200; *Costa Rica*, (1889, 1948) 224; *Ecuador*, (1895) 209; *Mexico*, (1910) 181, (1916) 188, (1924, 1934) 185; *Peru*, (1956, 1962) 213; *US*, (1800) 92, 104, (1824, 1828) 97, (1840) 95, (1860) 104, (1892, 1896) 138, (1960, 1965) 235f, (1968) 231, 248, 255, (1972) 236, 254f, 258; *Uruguay*, (1972) 196; *Venezuela*, (1958) 221, (1964, 1968) 222
Elgin, Gov. Gen., 109
El Greco, 46
Eliot, T. S., 166
Elizabeth I, 29, 34
El Salvador, *see* Salvador
El Supremo, 124
emancipation of slaves, 83, 100, 105f, 247; *Brazil*, 130; *Ecuador*, 126; *Peru*, 126
Embargo Act, 93
Emerson R. W., 100
encomiendas, 22
energy crisis, 1970s, 222
engenhos, 98
Enlightenment, 47, 52, 80
Erie, Lake, 95
Eskimos, 3, 269
Española, 9, 20, 23, 48, 69

Esquilache, 52, 80
estancias, 15, 17, 152
Estrada Doctrine, 242
expropriation, oil (1938), 186f

Fabian socialists, 140
Facundo, 122
Fair Deal, 232f, 235
Fair Employment Practices Committee (FEPC), 229f
Fair Labor Standards Act (1938), 174
Family Compact, 108
family allowances (Canada), 249
Farmer-Labor Party, 165
farmers: *US*, 18, 137f, 164f, 172; *Canada*, 178f, 249; *Brazil*, 205; *Mexico*, 243
Farmers' Alliances, 137f
fascism, 190, 198, 204. *See* Hitler, Mussolini
favelas, 202
fazendas, 15, 130
federalists: S. America, 89, 112f, 120; *US* 89, 93f
Federal Reserve System, 139
feudalism in New World, 5, 7, 15f, 28f, 40
feminists, 101, 161
Ferdinand and Isabella, 13
Ferdinand VII, 74
Figueres, José, 224
filibuster raids, 117, 140
Finlay, Dr. Carlos, 141
fiscales, 19
Fitzgerald, Scott, 165f
Five Year Plan (Brazil), 205
Florida, 26f, 46, 79, 95, 103, 221
Fonseca, Gen. D. de, 130, 151
Fonseca, Rodriguez de, 9, 13
Food for Peace, 240
Ford, Pres. Gerald, 258
Founding Fathers, 56, 75
Fort Caroline, 27 *map*
Forty Niners, 103
Fourth World, 155
Fox Indians, 42, 57
Francia, Dr. José, 123
Franciscans, 22, 46
Franklin, Benjamin, 65
Freedmen's Bureau, 105
Freedom Riders, 247
Free Negroes, 49

Free Silver, 138
Frei, Pres. E. M., 198f
French and Indian War, 56f
French colonies, 24f, 56f
French Guiana, 83
Frente, 198f, 100
frescoes, Mexican, 184
Freyre, Gilberto, 47
Frondizi, Pres. A., 192f, 245
Front de Libération Québeçois (FLQ), 251f
frontier: US 94f, 139; Canada 146
Fugitive Slave Laws, 101f
fueros, 115
fundos, 199
free trade, 26, 39

Gabriel's Revolt (1801), 99
Gadsden Purchase, 103 *map*
Gage, General, 65
Gaitán, J., 218
galeones, 15, 28, 52
Gallegas, Rómulo, 220f
Galloway, Joseph, 68
Gama, Luiz, 82, 129
Gandhi, 247
Garrison, W. L., 101f
Garvey, Marcus, 166f, 167 *illn.*
Gaspé Peninsula, 56
gauchos, 83, 102, 112, 119f, 122, 204
'Generation of 1910', 210
generation gap: *Mexico*, 243; *US*, 254f
genocide, 37
George III, 63, 65, 67
George, Henry, 137, 164
Georgia, 32, 40, 64
German immigrants to New World, 40, 52, 168f, 205
Germany, 144, 158f, 161, 175, 187, 190f, 196f, 208
ghettoes, US, 139, 161, 166, 248
Gilbert, Sir H., 29
Gilded Age (US), 134, 146
Golconda movement, 260
gold fever, 7f, 18, 37f, 80, 127
Golden Age (Spain), 7, 24, 46
gold standard, 148
Goldwater, Senator Barry, 236
golondrinas, 150
golpistas, 192f
Gómez, Juan V. (Venezuela), 220f

Goméz, L. (Colombia), 218f
Gompers, Samuel, 136
gongorismo, 46
González Prada, M., 210f, 213
González Videla, 198
Good Neighbor policy, 187f, 223
governors, colonial (UK), 53f
Granada, Nicaragua, 117
Gran Chaco dispute, 214 *map*
Gran Colombia, 76, 78, 117, 126
granger movement, 137f, 164
Grant, Gen. U. S., 105
Great Awakening, 100
Great Gatsby, 165
Great Exhibition (1851), 96
Great Society, 173, 235f, 256
Great Western Railroad (Canada), 107f
Greek-Turkish Aid Act (1947), 233
Greenbacks, 105
Greensboro, N. Carolina, 247
Greenwich Village, 166
Grenville, George, 61f
Grey, Lord, 101
gringo imperialism, 223
Grito de Dolores, 73
Grito de Ypiranga, 81
Group of 80, 202
Guadeloupe, 28
Guam, 141f
Guanajuato massacre, 73f
guano, 126
Guaraní Indian language, 4, 22, 83, 124, 215
Guardia, Tomas, 117
Guatemala, 3, 10, 16, 75, 83, 113, 116f, 156, 202, 224f, 225 *illn.*, 233, 241
Guayaquil, Ecuador, 77f, 126, 209
guerillas, urban, *see* terrorists
Guevara, Ché, 215f
Guiana, 16
Guinea, 16f
Gulf Oil Co., 209
Guzmán Blanco, A., 118, 120

habitants, 28
haciendas, 15, 17, 84, 152, 181, 186
Haiti, 4, 9, 20, 28, 69f, 76, 142f, 168, 224
Half-Way Covenant, 41
Hamilton, Alexander, 92f, 102, 113
Hancock, John, 55, 64f
Hapsburgs, 51

Harding, Pres. W. G., 162f
Harlem, New York, 139, 161, 166
Harlem Renaissance, 166
Harper's Ferry, Virginia, 101, 103 map
Harrington, Michael, 235
Harrison, Pres. W. H., 95, 111
Hartford, Treaty of (1650), 25
Hausa Moslems, 82
Havana, 52, 114, 140
Hawaii, 141f, 230
headrights, 31f, 40
Henry, Patrick, 62
Herrera, J., 46
Hidalgo y Costilla, M., 73f, 84, 90
hill-billies, Brazil, 151f
Hillsborough, Lord, 62
Hiroshima, 231f
Hitler, Adolf, 190f, 205, 228
Hobson, J. A., 172
Holmes, O. W., 159
home market, 223, 259
Homestead Act, 105
Honduras, 10, 75, 83, 116, 224, 241
Hooker, Thomas, 41
Hoover, President H., 171
housing (US), 173
Houston, Sam, 114
Huasipungo, 209
Hudson river, 26
Hudson's Bay, 57, 145
Huerta, Victoriano, 143f, 182
Huguenots, 26f, 29, 52
Hughes, Langston, 166
Humphrey, Hubert H., 248
Hutchinson, Anne, 38

Ibarra, Pres. Velasco, 209f
Icaza, J., 209
Ickes, Harold, 173
Idaho, 138
Iguala, Plan of (1821), 75
Illinois, 97, 112
immigration, 3, 6, 21f, 30, 39f, 52, 59, 90,
   106, 114, 117, 121, 139; US, 85, 96, 235;
   Argentina, 122f, 149f, 189; Brazil, 131,
   150f; Canada, 146, 168f, 169 map; Chile,
   197; Peru, 212; Uruguay, 194
Immigrants' Hotel, Buenos Aires, 150
impeachment, 105, 258

imperialism, 139f, 142 map, 147, 158, 184,
   223f
import-substitution, 259
Incas, 10f, 46, 126f, 209, 211f
income tax, 138f, 179, 218
initiative and referendum devices, 138
Inner Light doctrine, 40
indentured labour, 34
independence movements: 44, 51f, 68f, 83
   map, 111; US, 52f, 54, 60f, 65, 83, 85,
   95; Venezuela, 117f
Independence, Declaration of: US, 65, 83;
   Venezuela, 75
independent labour parties, Canada, 179
Indianism, 46, 74f, 184, 210f, 212
Indians: 3f, 9f, 11, 15f, 23f, 28, 42 map,
   44f, 47f, 51, 53, 57, 74f, 80, 83 map, 85,
   89, 106, 111, 116, 120, 125f, 131f, 147f,
   152, 169, 176 map, 184, 201, 209, 214,
   251; communal lands, 111f, 115, 186f,
   212; US, 36, 56, 84, 95f, 175f, 176;
   Bolivia, 215; Brazil and Paraguay, 4;
   Ecuador, 210; Guatemala, 226; Peru,
   213f; and passim.
indigo, 55, 67
industrial capitalism, 134
industrialization: US, 29f, 60, 68, 84, 96,
   106; Canada, 146f; South America, 258f;
   Argentina, 191f; Brazil, 203, 205; Chile,
   198; Mexico, 187f, 242; Peru, 213
infrastructure, 7
Indochina, 233
inequality (Table), 257
inflation: Argentina 193, 245; Bolivia 217;
   Chile 198f, 200; US 236; Uruguay 195
inquilinos, 151, 197, 199
Inquisition, 21, 79
insane asylums, 101
integralistas, 204
intellectuals (US), 165f, 177
intendentes, 52
Inter-American Conference (1954), 226
Inter-American Development Bank, 240,
   258
Interim Committee (atom bomb), 231
International Monetary Fund (IMF), 240
ITT, 200, 258
IWW, 136, 159
ICC, 247
Irigoyen, H., 150, 188

iron industry, 30, 204
Iroquois Indians, 28, 57
irrigation, 11; *Chile*, 198; *Peru*, 213
Isthmus of Panama, 116, 143
Italian immigrants to New World, 122, 131, 150f, 194, 196f
Iturbide, Agustín de, 74f

Jackson, Pres. Andrew, 26f, 95, 97f, 100, 108, 111, 120
Jamaica, 30, 32, 34, 52
James II, 40
James, William, 141
Jamestown, Virginia, 27, 31f
Japan, 156, 169, 187, 205, 208, 228, 230f
Japanese immigrants, 131
Japanese-Americans, 169 *map*, 230f
Japanese-Canadians, 169 *map*, 230
Jay Treaty (1795), 93f
jazz, 161, 165f
jefes politicos, 117
Jefferson, Thomas, 92f, 102
Jesuits, 22f, 79f, 116, 120, 126
jet engine, 231
Jews, 21
Jim Crow laws, 106, 247
Jiquilpan, Mexico, 186
John VI (Portugal), 71, 80f; John XXIII (Pope), 200, 220
John of the Cross, 21
Johnson, Pres. Andrew, 105
Johnson, Gen. Hugh, 172
Johnson, Pres. Lyndon B., 173, 199, 223, 235f, 255f
joint stock companies, 29f, 40, 52
Juarez, B., 48, 114f, 188
judiciary, independent, 68, 84, 204; *see also* Supreme Court
jungles, 152, 203, 213, 221, 255
juntas, 72, 76, 120, 245
justicialism, 190f, 245

Kallen, Horace, 135
Kansas, 101, 104, 137f
Kansas-Nebraska Act (1854), 104
Keith brothers, 117
Kennecott Corporation, 199
Kennedy, Pres. John F., 155, 193, 199, 228, 234 *illn.*, 235, 237f, 240, 247f, 256
Kennedy, Robert F., 234 *illn.*, 237, 247f

Kent State University shootings, 254
Kerner ('white racism') Report (1968), 248
Kew Gardens, 204
Keynes, John M., 134, 172f, 236
Khrushchev, Nikita, 228, 237
King, W. L. Mackenzie, 160, 168, 229, 249
King, Dr. Martin Luther, 247, 248
Korea, 155, 228, 233f, 239 *map*, 240f
Korematsu v. the US (1944), 230
Kubitschek, Pres., 206f
Ku Klux Klan, 162, 168, 247

La Araucana (1568), 46
labour: 157, 188; *Argentina*, 190; *Bolivia*, 215; *Brazil*, 205; *Chile*, 197f; *Colombia*, 218f; *Mexico*, 185f; *US*, 135f, 162f, 174; *Venezuela*, 222
labour shortage, 31f, 51, 55
Labrador, 26
laissez-faire, 85, 93, 119, 236
La Follette, R., 165
land reform: 16, 74, 90, 115, 152, 181; *Argentina*, 149; *Bolivia*, 215; *Chile*, 199; *Colombia*, 218; *Ecuador*, 210; *Guatemala*, 226; *Mexico*, 143, 148, 185f, 242f; *Peru*, 212f; *Venezuela*, 222
Lanusse, Pres. A., 245
La Paz, Bolivia, 127
Laporte, Pierre, 251 *illn.*, 252
La Salle, 27f, 56
Las Casas, B. de, 9, 21f, 46, 48
lasso, 119
latifundia, 15f, 89, 152
LAFTA, 196, 208, 241
Latorre, Pres., 194
Laurier, Sir W., 146
Law of Free Birth (1871), 129
Laws of the Indies (1542), 22
Lawrence, Massachusetts, 136
League of Nations, 159f
Leahy, Admiral W. D., 231
Le Corbusier, 205
Leeward Islands, 34
legalistas, 192
Legal Tender Act, 105
Leguía, Pres. A., 210, 212
Lei Aurea (1881), 130
Leisler's Rebellion (1689), 42, 55
Le May, Gen. Curtis, 231

Leo XIII, Pope, 200
León, Nicaragua, 117
León, Ponce de, 143
Lewis, John L., 174
Lewis, Oscar, 242
Lewis, Sinclair, 165
Lexington, battle of, 64
ley de fuga, 180f
Leyden, Holland, 36
Ley Juárez (1855), 115
Ley Lerdo (1856), 115, 186
liberal freedoms, 180, 204
Liberal Party: *Canada*, 146, 168, 178f, 249; *Colombia*, 218; *Ecuador*, 209; *Mexico*, 114f
libraries, Mexico, 184
Lima, Peru, 13, 18, 20, 23f, 46, 75f, 210f, 212
Limantour, J., 148, 181
Lincoln, Pres. Abraham, 104f, 177
Lisbon, 79f
Little Big Horn, battle of, 176 *map*
Little Rock High School, Alabama, 247
living standards: *Argentina*, 193f; *Bolivia*, 215; *Colombia*, 218; *US*, 134f, 256; *Tables*, 256, 257
llaneros, 76, 118f, 220
Locke, John, 52, 68
López, C. A., 123f
López, F. S., 124
López, Pres. Alfonso, 218
Los Angeles, 229, 236
Lost Colony, 29
Louis XIII, 28; Louis XIV, 26, 28f, 52, 56
Louisbourg, 57
Louisiana, 42, 56, 59, 69, 93, 96, 99, 102, 112; *Purchase*, 93, 96, 102
L'Overture, Toussaint, 20, 69f, 168
Loyalists, 57, 65, 106
loyalty hysteria (US), 232f
loyalty oaths, 162
lumber industry, 30, 146
Lundy, Benjamin, 100
lynching (US), 139, 160, 162, 247

MacArthur, Gen. D., 235
McCarthy, Senator Eugene, 255
McCarthy, Senator Joseph, 224
Macdonald, J. A., 110, 146
McGovern, Senator G., 254

Mackay, Claude, 166
Mackenzie, W. L., 108
McKinley, Pres., 140f
McNary-Haugen scheme, 165
Macumba, 82
Madero, Francisco, 143, 181f
Madison, James, 93
Magdalena river, 118f, 218
Mahan, Capt, A. T., 139f
Maine, 31f, 39
Maine, 140f
majoritarian politics, 97f
mamelucos, 80
Managua, Nicaragua, 256
Manaus, 203f
Manhattan, 26
Manhattan Project, 231
Manifest Destiny, 140
Manila, 52, 141
Manitoba, 109 *map*, 145, 249
man-land ratio, 121
Mann, Mrs. Horace, 122
'Manure Age', 126
Maracaibo, Lake, 220
March on Washington movement (1941), 177, 299f
March on Washington (1963), 246 *illn.*, 247
Marco Polo, 26
Marcia of Portugal, 81
Mariátegui, José C., 212f
Marin, John, 166
maroons, 82
Marshall Plan, 239 *map*, 240f
Martinique, 28
Marx, Karl, 242
Marxism, 221; *Chile*, 197f, 200f; *Peru*, 212; *Catholic*, 202, 260
Maryland, 32f, 39f, 55, 99
Massachusetts Bay Colony, 32
Massachusetts, 5, 29f, 31, 36f, 61f
Massachusetts Circular Letter (1768), 62
mass consumption, 134, 156, 163f, 228
mass media (US), 255
maté, 123
Mater et Magistra, 200
Maurice, Gov. John, 16
Maximilian of Austria, 106, 115
Mayas, 4, 10f
Mayflower, 36

Mazatlán, 183 *illn.*
Mazorca, 120
Medicare, 175
Medellín, Colombia, 218
Meiggs, Henry, 127
Melgarejo, Mariano, 127
melting-pot: *US*, 135, 227; *Canada*, 248f;
 S. America, 131f, *see also* pluralism,
 cultural
Memorial Day Massacre (1937), 174
Memphis, Tennessee, 161
Mendoza, Argentina, 76
mercantilism, 12, 28f, 52f, 66f, 91
merchant navy, 30, 39, 54f, 63f, 67
mercury output, 11
mestizos, 11f, 46f, 51, 71f, 74, 80, 82, 84,
 89f, 108, 111f, 114f, 116, 123f, 127, 131,
 152, 209
Meuse-Argonne offensive (1918), 159
Mexican-American War (1846–48), 24,
 102f, 103 *map*, 114, 147
Mexico, 3, 9, 11, 48, 59, 72f, 74f, 79, 84f,
 90, 99, 106, 111f, 113f, 133, 140, 143f,
 148, 152, 156, 169 *map*, 180f, 194, 200,
 202, 205, 220, 226, 241f, 248, 256, 259
Mexico City, 18, 20, 23, 44, 46, 73, 114f,
 182, 186, 242f
Middle Atlantic colonies, 54f
middle class: *Argentina*, 150, 188; *Chile*,
 151; *Colombia*, 218; *Peru*, 213; *US*, 137,
 165; *Uruguay*, 195; *Venezuela*, 220f
Middle Passage (slave-ships), 54
'Middle Way' (social democracy), 199,
 221
Midway Island, 141f
Migration, Great (Negro), 139, 161, 169,
 229
Miguel, Regent of Portugal, 81
military-industrial complex, 231, 235f
Minas Gerais, 80f
mining fronter, Canada, 146
Ministry of the Indies, 20
Miranda, Francisco de, 75
Mississippi, 90, 99, 247
Missouri Compromise (1820), 96
Mistral, Gabriela, 201
mita, 11
Mitre, B., 121, 123
Mitrione, Dan, 196
mixed economy, Uruguay, 194

mobility, US, 135
Modernists: *Brazil*, 82, *Peru*, 211, *US*, 166
Mohawk Indians, 63
Monagas brothers, 118
Monroe Doctrine (1823), 78f
Monroe, Pres. James, 79, 97
Montevideo, Uruguay, 72f, 83, 113, 120,
 124, 147, 195f
Montezuma, 10
Montgomery, Alabama, 247
Montreal, 26f, 57, 108, 147, 170, 229, 252
Montt, J., 151
moon flights, 231
Moors, 21, 47
Morelia Cathedral, Mexico, 45 *illn.*, 46
Morelos y Pavón, J. M., 74f, 84
movies, 165
Movimiento Nacional Revolucionario
 (MNR), 215f
Muckrakers, 137
mulattos, 34, 47f, 51, 69, 98, 129f, 132, 223
mural art, Mexico, 184
music: *US*, 161, 165; *Brazil*, 205
Mussolini, B., 191, 204, 218
Mutual Security Acts, 240

Nabuco, Joaquim, 129f
Nación, La, 121
Nagasaki, 231
Napoleon I, 69, 71, 80, 112f; Napoleon
 III, 106, 115
Narragansett, 38
Nashville, 143
NAACP, 139, 168
National Bank Act, 105
National Bank of Ejido Credit, 186
national debt, 61
National Front (Colombia), 220
nationalisation: *Bolivia*, 215, *Chile*, 199,
 Mexico, 144f, 186f
nationalism: 29, 52, 180, 259f; *Argentina*,
 121, 190; *Brazil*, 202, 204, 206; *Canada*,
 65f, 95, 110, 145f, 156, 160, 168, 179,
 (*French Canada*, 179); *Chile*, 127, 200;
 Colombia, 220; *Mexico*, 114, 181, 183f;
 Peru, 210f; *US*, 92f, 94f, 139f, (*Black
 American* nationalism, 166f, 248);
 Uruguay, 194
National Recovery Administration (NRA)
 172f

National Welfare Rights Organisation, 255
National Youth Administration, 173f
Native Americans (Indians), 177
natural rights, 52
Navigation Acts, 53, 67
negative income tax, 179
Negroes: 4, 15, 21f, 47f; *Brazil*, 129f;
    Haiti, 69; *Panama*, 223; *US*, 33f, 51, 55,
    62, 82, 84, 85, 95f, 97f, 105, 136, 139,
    160f, 166f, 174, 177, 229f, 245f, 254f;
    See also abolitionism, emancipation,
    Haiti, slavery, Harlem
neo-colonialism, 79, 90f, 146f, 152, 168,
    199, 202
Neruda, Pablo, 201
neutral trading (US), 93f, 158f
Nevada, 102, 138
New Amsterdam, 25f
Newark, New Jersey, race riot (1967), 248
New Brunswick, 145
New Deal, 138, 170f, 186f, 194, 205, 232,
    235
New England Anti-Slavery Society, 39
New Era (1920s), 163f
Newfoundland, 26f, 57, 145, 160, 253 *map*
New France, 5, 19, 26f, 27 *map*, 59
New Frontier, 235
New Granada, Vice-Royalty of, 20 *map*,
    77
new imperialism, 140
New Jersey, 32, 40, 248
New Mexico, 57, 102, 144
New Netherlands, 25f
New Orleans, 27 *map*, 56, 112, 161, 236
Newport, Capt. Christopher, 31
New Spain, Vice-Royalty of, 18f, 20 *map*
New Sweden, 25f
New York, 32, 40, 44, 53f, 57, 61f, 134,
    137, 139, 143, 163, 166, 178
Niagara, 95
Nicaragua, 75, 83, 116f, 126, 143, 211, 224,
    241
Niemeyer, Oscar, 205
Nisei, 230
nitrate industry, 125, 151, 197
Nixon, Pres. Richard M., 236f, 254f, 258
Nobel Prize, 201
Nordicism, 162
North, Lord, 63
North Carolina, 32 *map*, 56, 99, 129

Northwest Passage, 26, 29
Nostromo, 223
'No taxation without representation', 54,
    62
Novanglus Letters, 68
Nova Scotia (Acadia), 26f, 42 *map*, 57,
    109, 145
nuclear terror, 231f
Nuñez, Rafael, 119, 218

Oaxaca, Mexico, 148
Obregón, Gen. Alvaro, 111, 182f, 184
Odría, Gen. M., 213
Oglethorpe, J., 40
O'Higgins, Gen., 76, 125
oil: *Argentina*, 191f; *Canada*, 179; *Colombia*, 218; *Ecuador*, 209; *Mexico*, 143,
    181, 187; *Peru*, 213; *Venezuela*, 118,
    241f
O'Keefe, Georgia, 166
Oklahoma, 176 *map*
old age security, Canada, 249
Old Northwest, 63f, 65
Old Southwest, 96
Olinda, Brazil, 79
Olympic Games (1968), 243
one-crop farming, 106, 218
one-party system, Mexico, 185, 243
Oneida community, New York, 100
Onis movement, Peru, 260
Ontario, 108f, 145f, 168, 179, 249f
Open Door, 141f
open shop, 162
Organisation of American States (OAS),
    241f
Oribe, Manuel, 113
Oriente region, 209, 214 *map*
Orinoco river, 76, 117f
Orozco, José Clemente, 184
Orozco, Pascual, 181
Ortega y Gasset, 189
Os Sertões, 152, 202
Ostend Manifesto, 104
Otis, James, 62
Ottawa, 252
over-production, 134

Pacheco Areca, Pres. J., 196
Pacific Railway Act, 105
pacifists (US), 165

Pae João, 82
Paez, José Antonio, 76, 118
Palestine, 232f
Palmer, A. M., 161f
Palmares, Republic of, 16, 82, 83 *map*
pampas, 12, 111, 119f, 121, 124, 189
pamphleteers, 67f
Panama, 12, 78, 116, 128, 143, 214 *map*, 218, 223
Panama Canal, 142 *map*, 143
Pan-American Federation, 78
Pan-American Union, 241
Panics: *1890* (Argentina), 150, *1929*, 134f, 164, 170
Pan-Indianism, 177
papal encyclicals, 200
paper industry, 178
Papineau, L. J., 108
Paraguay, 3f, 22f, 90, 120, 123f, 191f, 214f, 214 *map*, 241
Paraguayan War (1864–70), 121, 123f, 128, 130
Paris, Peace of (1783), 65
Parker, Theodore, 101
Parkman, Francis, 67
Parks, Mrs. Rosa, 247
participatory democracy, 138
Partido Nacional Revolucionario (PNR), 185f, 243
party organisation: 93f, 96f, 112f
passive resistance, 247
Patagonia, 122, 148
Patrocinio, José de 82, 129f
patronage, political, 19, 54, 186, 243
Paul VI, Pope, 200
Pavlova, 203
Pax Porfiriana, 180
Paxton Boys, 56
Paz de Rio steel plant, 219
Paz Estenssoro, Pres., 215f
Paz, Julio de la, 212
Peace Corps, 213, 239
Pearl Harbor, 169, 178, 205, 228, 230
Pearson, Lester, 249, 252
peasantry, 89f, 199, 209f, 215, 222, 226, 242
Pedro I, 81; Pedro II, 81f, 130f
PEMEX, 187
peninsulares, 12, 51, 73
Penn, William, 40

Pennsylvania, 32, 40, 56
Pennsylvania Dutch, 40
People's Party (Populists), 137f
Pequot Indians, 34f, 37
Pérez Jiménez, Pres., 221
perfectibility, doctrine of, 100
Pernambuco, 16, 81, 129, 208
Perón, Pres. Juan D., 157, 190f, 243f; Mrs. Eva D., 191f
personalismo, 112f, 189f, 194
Peru, 3, 9, 11f, 18, 20, 75f, 79, 89, 90, 111, 113, 126f, 141, 143, 199f, 210f, 212, 214, 220f, 241, 256, 259
Pétion, Pres. A. S., 69
Philadelphia, 40, 44, 53f, 64
Philip V, 51
Philippines, 18, 52, 141f
Phillips, Wendell, 101
Pichincho, battle of (1822), 77f
Pilgrims, 29, 32
Pinkerton men, 136
pirates, 32
Pittsburgh, 57, 136
Pizarro, F., 10, 75
Plains, 105, 137
Plains Farmers Assistance Act (Canada),178
plantations: US, 16f, 30, 85, 98
Plata, Rio de la (later Argentina), 12f, 16, 18, 20, 71f, 79, 120
plateresque style, 46
Platt Ammendment, 141
plebiscites, 69
pluralism, cultural, 3f, 5, 40, 89, 135, 153f, 166f, 169 *map*, 213, 227f, 229f, 245f, 248f and *passim*
Plymouth, New, 29, 37
Poland, 228, 233
Poles in Canada, 168
police brutality, 245, 248
Polk, President J. K., 140
Polyforum, 184
Pombal, Marquis, 80
poncho, 120, 122
Pontiac's Conspiracy (1763), 61
poor whites, 106, 138
Pope, 22, 24, 30, 200, 220
Popham, Sir H., 72
Popular Front, Chile, 198f
popular sovereignty, 104
population: 4 (*hemisphere*), 256 (*Table*),

241 (*mix*); *Canada*, 145, 159, 168, 170, 249; *Argentina*, 133, 190, 193; *Brazil*, 133, 208; *Mexico*, 133, 182; *Bolivia*, 215; *Uruguay*, 195; *US*, 232
Populism, 137
Populorum Progressio, 200
Port Bello, 12f
Portugal, 16f, 24, 30, 48, 71, 79f
Potosí, Bolivia, 127
poverty: 256 (*Table*); *Bolivia*, 215; *Brazil*, 204; *Ecuador*, 209; *Mexico*, 181, 184, 242; *US*, 235
Prado, Manuel, 213
Prats, Gen. Carlos, 201
Prensa, La, 192
Presbyterians, 141
presidency, US, 138, 258
Prince Edward Island, 145
Proclamation of 1763, 60
Progress and Poverty, 137
Progressivism: *US*, 137f, 144; *Canada*, 160
Prohibition, 162f
Providence Island, 34f
proyectistas, 52
proprietary colonies, 39f
protectorates, 143
public works: *US*, 172; *Brazil*, 205
Public Works Administration (PWA), 173
pueblos, 148, 175
Puerto Cabello, 77
Puerto Rico, 83, 141f, 169
Punta del Este Conference, 238, 242
purchasing-power (US), 164, 179
Puritans, 5, 29f, 34f, 38f, 41f
pyragues, 215

Quakers, 40, 100
Quebec, 26f, 28, 57, 63, 67, 108f, 145f, 160, 168, 179, 229, 249f
Quebec Act (1774), 63f
Quechua Indian language, 4, 83, 127
quilombos, 82
Quito, 23f, 46, 126, 209
quota laws, 162

race and race-mixing, 33f, 47f, 81f, 99,116f, 131f, 135, 139, 162, 166, 184, 211, 230
race-riots (US), 161f, 230, 248
radar, 231
radicalism: *Argentina*, 150, 188, 192;

Canada, 92, 108, 179; *Chile*, 197f; *Mexico*, 181, 186f; *Peru*, 210f; *US*, 100f, 136f, 162, 164f
Radical Republicans (US), 105
railroad boom, Canada, 106f
Raleigh, Sir W., 29
Randolph, A. Philip, 168, 229f, 247
Raza Cosmica, La, 184, 211
raw material needs, 178, 260
real estate operations, 161, 163
Rebellion of 1837, Canada, 92, 108
recession (US), *1968*, 236, *1970*, 236, *1974–5*, 258
Recife, Brazil, 17
Reconstruction (US), 105, 160
Reconstruction Finance Corporation (RFC), 171
Red Power, 177
Red Scare, 162
reducciones, 22f
Reform Act, 1912 (Argentina), 188
Reforma, La, 114f, 186
refrigerator ships, 149f
Regina Manifesto (1933), 179
Regulators, The, 56
residencia, 19
representative government, problems of: 30, 33, 36, 43, 52f, 61f, 104f, 121, 146, 151 (*Chile*), 180, 188 (*Argentina*), 194f, 197f (*Chile*), 210 (*Ecuador*), 215 (*Bolivia*)
Republic Steel Co., 174
Republicans, Jeffersonian, 93
repugnance, legal doctrine of, 158, 160
Rerum Novarum (1891), 200
Restoration of Stuarts, 1660, 40f
retardation, economic: *S. America*, 258f; *Argentina*, 189, 228; *Brazil*, 204; *Bolivia*, 215; *Mexico*, 115; *Uruguay*, 196
Revere, Paul, 61
revivalism, religious, 100
revolutions: *S. America*, 6, 113, 180f; *Argentina*, (1945), 156; *Brazil*, (1822), 80f, (1930), 156, 204f; *Bolivia*, (1952), 156, 215; *Cuba*, (1958), 156, 188; *Mexico*, (1910), 116, 143, 148, 156, 180f; *US*, 52f, 57, 59f, 66f, 84, 108, 143, 145; *France*, 48, 52, 60, 65, 68, 145; *Russia*, 156, 161
Rhode Island, 38f, 41, 53

rice plantations, 34, 55, 67, 80 (*Brazil*), 209 (*Ecuador*)
Riel, Louis, 146, 251
'rights of Englishmen', 54
Rio Grande, 147, 156
Rio Grande do Sul, 203 *map*, 204
Rio de Janeiro, 26, 79f, 82, 129, 151
Rivadavia, Pres., 120
Rivera, Diego, 184
Rivera, José F., 113
Robber Barons (US), 134, 136, 146, 261
Robbery Under Law, 187
Roca, Gen. J. A., 4, 111, 148, 150
Rockefeller, J. D., 134
Rockingham, Lord, 61f
rococo style, 46, 121
Rodó, J. E., 147f, 166, 211
Rojas Pinilla, Gen., 218f
Rolfe, John, 33
Romantic movement, 112, 114
Roosevelt, Pres. F. D., 171f, 187f, 205, 223, 229f, 232; Mrs. Eleanor R., 177
Roosevelt, Pres. Theodore, 138f, 140f, 158, 163, 173, 218,
Roosevelt alliance, 177
Rosas, Juan Manuel de, 84, 102, 112f, 119f, 122, 124
rouges, 146
Royal Canadian Air Force, 229
Royal Commission on Bilingualism (1963), 249
Royal Nazy, 48, 57, 67, 75, 79f
rubber plantations, 152, 202f
rum, 54
rurales, 180
Russia, 57f, 155f, 200, 227f, 237

Saar, 161
Sáenz Peña, 188f
St. Augustine, Florida, 27f
St. John's river, Florida, 26f
St. Laurent, Louis, 249
St. Lawrence river, 57, 145
St. Louis, 61, 137
Salamanca University, 46
sales of offices (Spanish colonies), 19
Salem witch trials, 41f
Salgado, Plinio, 204
Salvador, El (San), 75, 83, 116, 224, 241
samba, 82

Samoa, 142
San Antonio, Texas, 114
San Francisco de Asis, 23
San Jacinto, battle of (1836), 114
San Martín, José de, 75f, 120, 125
Santa Anna, Gen., 114f, 117
Santa Cruz, California, 23
Santa Cruz, Andrés, 127
Santa Fé, New Mexico, 23
Santiago, Chile, 202
Santiago, Guatemala, 225
Santiago, Miguel de, 46
São Paulo, Brazil, 80, 129, 131, 151, 204, 206 *illn.*
Sarmiento, D. F., 121f, 125
Saskatchewan, 145f, 168f, 178f, 249
Savannah, Georgia, 95
Schneider, Gen. R., 200
school desegregation (US), 245f
Scotch-Irish settlers, 52
seapower, 59
Seattle, Washington, 229, 236f
Sebastião, 82
secession, 102
sectionalism, 54f, 89, 92, 96, 102, 112
segregation (US), 139, 160f, 245f
seigneurialism, 28f, 63, 85
selvas, 127, 213
Seminole Indians, 95, 103
'separate but equal' dogma, 106, 245
separation of powers, 54
separatism: 168; French Canada, 179, 249f
sertanejos, 152
Sevilla, 12f
Shaker communities, 100
sharecroppers: *Argentina*, 150; *Brazil*, 131; *Peru*, 213; *US*, 165
Shawnee Indians, 65, 95
Sheeler, Charles, 166
sheep farming, 148, 150, 195
Sherman Act (1890), 139f, 163
Sigüenza, 46
Sikhs in Canada, 169
silver mining, 11f, 127
Sioux Indians, 42
Siqueiros, David, 184
sit-down strikes, 174
sit-ins, civil rights, 174, 247
Sitka, Alaska, 59

skyscrapers, 163
slavery: 21f, 33f, 48f, 55, 62, 69, 81f, 83
    map, 85, 95f, 97f, 100f, 126, 152;
    breeding, 99; slavery-extension (US),
    162f; slave revolts, 35, 81f, 99; slave-
    trade, 15, 17 map, 28, 48, 54, 99, 129
smallpox vaccination, 111
Smith, Capt. John, 36
social contract theory, 30
Social Credit, 179
Social Gospel, 137
social-imperialism, 139f
socialism: S. America, 156, 260; Argen-
    tina, 190; Canada, 179; Chile, 198f, 200;
    Guatemala, 226; Mexico, 185; Peru,
    210f, 212; US, 136f, 162, 165, 171
socialism, Christian: US, 137, Chile, 202
Socialist Labor Party, 136
Social Security Act (1935), 175
Somoza, Gen., 224
sonar, 231
Sons of Liberty, 61
South (US), 55, 85, 98f, 103 map, 106,
    139, 229, 247
S. Carolina, 32, 55, 102
Southern Christian Leadership Council
    (SCLC), 247
South Side, Chicago, 139, 161
Spain, 3f, 6f, 12f, 44f, 95, 100, 104, 114,
    127, 140f, 162
Spanish-American War (1898), 84, 128,
    140f
Spanish Civil War (1936), 184
Spanish immigration: Argentina, 150;
    Uruguay, 194
Spanish Main, 7, 9, 14 map, 117f, 217
Spencer, Herbert, 119
spoils system, 243
Stalin, 189
Stamp Act Congress, 61f
Standard Oil Co., 137
'state of siege', 113
state-aided growth (US), 94f
statism, 85
'starving time' (Virginia), 31
Stevens, Thaddeus, 105
Stimson, Sec. H. L., 231
stock market, 163f, 170
Stoddard, Rev. S., 41
Stowe, Harriet B., 101

strikes: Canada, 160; Chile, 198; Honduras,
    224; US, 136, 162, 174
Stroessner, Gen. A., 215
Student Non-Violent Coordinating Com-
    mittee (SNCC), 247
student movements: Mexico, 243, US,
    254f
Students for a Democratic Society (SDS),
    254f
Stuyvesant, Gov. Peter, 26
submarine warfare, 158f
Sucre, Gen., 77f, 127
sugar plantations, 9, 16f, 24, 34, 51, 54f,
    69, 98f, 130, 140, 143, 213
Supreme Court (US), 106, 159, 230, 245
Sweden, 6, 24f, 199
Swift, Gustavus, 134
syndicalists (US), 162

Tacna-Arica dispute, 214 map
Tallmadge Amendment, 96
Tampico incident, 144
tariffs (US): 1828, 102, 1861, 104, 1890,
    1894, 140
Taxco, Mexico, 23, 46
Tea Act (1773), 63
technology (US), 96, 165, 220, 231f
Tecumseh, 95
tenancy, farm, 138
tenentismo, 204f
Teniente, El, 199
TVA, 173
Tenochtitlán, Mexico, 10
Terra, Pres. Gabriel, 195
Terraza family, 84
terrorism, left-wing: Argentina, 243;
    Uruguay, 195f, 222; Bolivia, 215;
    Mexico, 243; Venezuela, 221f
Texaco Co., 209
Texas, 99, 102, 114, 144
theocracy, 41
Theresa of Avila, 21
Third World, 155f, 200, 233, 260
'Third World priests', 156, 260
Thirteen Colonies, 32, 42, 54, 56f, 60f, 109
Thousand Day War (1899–1902), 218
tidewater, 55f, 96
tin mining, 127, 215
Tippecanoe, battle of (1811), 95
Tiradentes (José da Silva Xavier), 81

Titicaca, Lake, 127f, 128 *map*
tobacco, 18, 31, 34f, 35 *map*, 39, 55, 69, 143
Tocqueville, Alexis de, 68
Toledano, L., 186
Toomer, Jean, 166
Tordesillas, Treaty of (1494), 17
Toronto, 95, 108, 146f
Torre, Haya de la, 212f
Tory imperialism, Canada, 108
townships, Puritan, 62f
Townshend, Charles, 62f
tractors, 165
trade unions: *Argentina*, 157, 190f, 192; *Bolivia*, 157; *Canada*, 160, 178; *Chile*, 197f; *Mexico*, 186f; *US*, 136, 138, 159, 162, 168, 174, 178
Trail of Tears, 97f, 98 *illn.*
Transcendentalism, 100
transfer of political power, peaceful, 6, 84, 93f, 121, 190, 192, 243
triangular trade, 54f
Triangulo, 203 *map*
trickle-down theory, 163
triple melting-pot, 135
Trudeau, Prime Minister Pierre E., 249f
Trujillo, Pres., 221
Truman, Pres. Harry S., 231f
Truman Doctrine, 232f
trust-busting, 138f
two-party system: 94, 112f, 188; *Chile*, 151; *Uruguay*, 195
Tudor government, 30
Tupamaros terrorists, 196, 222
Turkey, 232f, 238
Twain, Mark, 141

Ukrainians in Canada, 3, 147, 168f, 250
Uncle Tom, 101, 168
unconditional surrender, 231
under-consumption, 134
Underground Railroad, 101
unemployment insurance (Canada), 249
Union, Act of (1840), 108
Unión Civica, 150
L'Union Nationale, 179
Unitarios, 101f, 120
United Fruit Co., 117, 224, 226
United Mineworkers, 174
United Nations, 240f

United Provinces (C. America), 75
US foreign investments: 140, 143f, 146f, 239, 258, 259 (totals); *Argentina*, 191; *Brazil*, 208; *Bolivia*, 215, 217; *Canada*, 252f; *Chile*, 151, 197; *Colombia*, 218; *Mexico*, 181, 187, 242; *Paraguay*, 215; *Peru*, 210f, 213; *Venezuela*, 220f, 222
US foreign aid: 155, 228, 232f, 238f, 239 *map*, 240 (*Table*)
universities, Brazil, 79
universities, Spanish colonies, 46f
University of San Marcos, Peru, 210
urban guerillas, *see* terrorists
urbanisation, *see* city growth
Urban League (US), 139, 168
urban renewal, 173
Urquiza, J. J. de, 121, 123
Uruguay, 3, 22, 72, 81, 90, 113, 124f, 147, 166, 194f, 222, 241
Utah, 102
utopianism, 34f
Utrecht, Treaty of (1713), 51f, 57

Vancouver, 169, 179
Vanderbilt, W. H., 117
Vargas, Pres. G., 204f, 208
Vasconcelos, José, 184, 211
Vega, Garcilosa de la, 46
Vélasquez, 46
Venezuela, 16, 69, 75f, 77 *map*, 90, 99, 117f, 128, 143, 199, 220f, 241, 259
Venezuela boundary dispute, 128
Vérendrye, P., 57
Verrazano, 26, 29
Veracruz, 13, 114f, 144, 182
Versailles Treaty (1919), 160f
Vietnam, 155, 200, 231, 233, 235, 239 *map*, 240f, 254f, 258
Villa, Pancho, 144, 181f
Villa-Lobos, H., 205
Virgin of Guadelupe, 74
Virginia, 7, 31f, 36, 39, 55, 61, 63, 67, 97, 99, 129
Virginia Dynasty, 97
Virgin Islands, 143
Visible Saints, 41
Volta Redonda steel plant, 203 *map*
voting rights, Black Americans, 105, 248
vulcanisation process, 202

Waco, Texas, 160
Wagner, Senator R. F., 174
Wake Island, 141f
Walker, David, 101
Walker, William, 117
Wall Street, 163f
Walpole, Sir Robert, 52, 54
War of 1812, 94f
War Hawks, 95
War Measures Act, Canada, 252
War, American Civil, *see* Civil War
wars in C. and S. America: 90, 128 *map*;
  214 *map*; 81 (Brazil-Argentina); 117
  (Guatemala-Salvador); 125, 127f, 128,
  210, 214 (War of the Pacific, 1879–83);
  127 (Spain-Peru); 150 (Chile); 151
  (Brazil); 115, 182 (Mexico); 209 (Ecua-
  dor); 214 (Panama-Colombia, Peru-
  Ecuador, Bolivia-Paraguay, Peru-
  Chile); 218 (Colombia); 224 (Costa
  Rica; Nicaragua-Costa Rica); *see also*
  World War
Warren, Chief Justice Earl, 245
Washington, Goerge, 65, 92
Watergate Scandal, 258
Watts riot (1965), 248
Waugh, Evelyn, 187
Weber, Max, 166
welfare state: *Argentina*, 192; *Canada*,
  249; *Chile*, 197f; *Colombia*, 218; *Guate-
  mala*, 226; *US*, 175, 236; *Uruguay*, 220f;
  Venezuela, 220f
Weld, Theodore, 101
Welland Canal (1829), 106
Welles, Sumner, 187
Welsh immigrants, 40, 52
West, *Canadian*, 110, 168f, 179; *US*, 53,
  60f
West Indies, 32 *map*, 43, 49, 53f, 61, 65,
  67, 166
Westminster, Statute of, 160
westward movement, 53, 60f
wheat farming, 54f, 145f, 160, 168, 178, 188
Whig Party, 104

Whig Revolution (1688), 30, 39, 41, 52,
  62, 68
White, Ango-Saxon, Protestant (WASP),
  135, 139
White Citizens' Councils, 247
'white man's burden', 140
white supremacists (US South), 105f, 160,
  248
Whitney, Eli, 95
Williams, Roger, 38, 41
Wilson, Ambassador H. L., 182
Wilson, Pres. Woodrow, 138, 143f, 158f,
  160f, 182f
Winnipeg, 109, 160 (General Strike of
  1919), 169, 179
Winthrop, John, 36f, 40
wiretapping, 162, 258
Wisconsin, 28, 57, 165, 175, 224
World War I, 139, 147, 156, 158f, 165,
  189, 197, 204f, 229
World War II, 155, 159, 161, 187, 190,
  220, 227f
Wolfe, Gen., 57
women's rights: *Chile*, 197; *Uruguay*, 194;
  US, 29, 101, 161, 255
Woodsworth, J. S., 229
Wounded Knee, S. Dakota, 176 *map*, 177
Wright, Richard, 165
Wyoming, 102, 138

Yaqui Indians, 111
yellow fever, Cuba, 141
'Yellow Peril', 169
yellow press, 140
Yorktown, battle of (1781), 65
youth (US), 161, 173f, 254f
Yucatan, 4, 111
yungas, 127

zambos, 47
Zangwill, Israel, 135
Zapata, E., 181f, 186
Zuñiga, Ercilla y, 46
Zurbarán, 46